"This book critically examines traditional principles of IP, such as the incentive theory for justifying exclusivity and IP protection's linkage with trade and investment, from new perspectives for the 21st Century. Professor Dreyfuss and Professor Ng brought together global academic leaders to tackle challenging topics: Whether IP is necessary? How human rights, culture and other significant values are incorporated in the current international IP norms? Both students and professionals will benefit from innovative analysis presented in each chapter."

Toshiko Takenaka, Ph.D., Washington Research Foundation / W. Hunter Simpson Professor of Technology Law, University of Washington

"A fresh and engaging reassessment of first principles that underlie arguments for different levels of IP protection. The book offers an array of disciplinary, doctrinal, and geographic perspectives, with a special focus on Singapore. Blending the global and the local, and high- and low-protectionist perspectives, the contributors thoughtfully reflect on the value of different frames for enriching and extending contemporary debates over IP rights."

Laurence R. Helfer, Harry R. Chadwick, Sr. Professor of Law, Duke University

"In this book, a first-rate group of experts provide a sophisticated and candid analysis of the advantages and limitations of various justifications for intellectual property protection, including incentive-based theory, facilitating trade among nations, and protecting public health, culture, and human rights. The book also contains a valuable discussion of empirical studies and doctrinal and institutional reforms. It is essential reading for anyone interested in improving intellectual property laws in our global marketplace."

Lisa P. Ramsey, Professor of Law, University of San Diego School of Law

FRAMING INTELLECTUAL PROPERTY LAW IN THE 21ST CENTURY

As knowledge production has become a more salient part of the economy, intellectual property laws have expanded. From a backwater of specialists in patent, copyright, and trademark law, intellectual property has become linked to trade through successive international agreements and appreciated as a key to both economic and cultural development. Furthermore, this law has begun to engage the interest of economists, political theorists, and human rights advocates. But because each discipline sees intellectual property in its own way, legal scholarship and practice have diverged and the debate over intellectual property law has become fragmented. This book is aimed at bringing this diverse scholarship and practice together. It examines intellectual property through successive lenses (incentive theory, trade, development, culture, and human rights) and ends with a discussion of whether and how these fragmented views can be reconciled and integrated.

ROCHELLE COOPER DREYFUSS is the Pauline Newman Professor of Law at New York University School of Law and co-Director of its Engelberg Center on Innovation Law and Policy. She is a member of the American Law Institute and was a co-Reporter for its Project on Intellectual Property: Principles Governing Jurisdiction, Choice of Law, and Judgments in Transnational Disputes. She was a consultant to the Federal Courts Study Committee, to the Presidential Commission on Catastrophic Nuclear Accidents, and to the Federal Trade Commission and served on the Secretary of Health and Human Services' Advisory Committee on Genetics, Health, and Society.

ELIZABETH SIEW-KUAN NG was the Vice-Chairwoman and Director of the Intellectual Property Unit of the EW Barker Centre for Law and Business, and Associate Professor of Law at the National University of Singapore. She served as an Intellectual Property Adjudicator at the Intellectual Property Office of Singapore and as amicus curiae for the Supreme Court of Singapore. In her specialized area of patents, she was retained as a consultant by the World Intellectual Property Organization in Geneva to report on the impact of the patent regime on developing countries.

"Framing IP Law in the 21st Century" by Li Jie

The center pentagon emerald gem represents intellectual property fusing the five themes with shine and reflective sheen. Incentive is presented in an intangible form such as the beauty of the sunrise view from the peak of Mount Everest. This expression also depicts efforts like conquering Mount Everest and receiving the ultimate triumph and warmth. Trade is represented by the mysterious turquoise seascape of the Dead Sea in Israel. Salt was considered a valuable commodity in earlier centuries and trade has evolved from there on. Development is seen as a journey on the Silk Road sand-scape. The process may be long with discoveries, experiences and growth. The modernistic metallic cyborg hand represents that the journey of development is filled with more discoveries, experiences and growth waiting to be uncovered. Culture and Human Rights are set on the base as foundation pillars for all the other essential themes. Expressions come in the form of the gliding bird, with freedom to fly and explore in the turquoise sky. Inspirations are drawn from the beauty of several cultural representations such as Australia's Aboriginal art, New Zealand's Maori art and other intricate patterns with Southeast Asian touches.

FRAMING INTELLECTUAL PROPERTY LAW IN THE 21ST CENTURY

Integrating Incentives, Trade, Development, Culture, and Human Rights

Edited by

ROCHELLE COOPER DREYFUSS

New York University

ELIZABETH SIEW-KUAN NG

National University of Singapore

CAMBRIDGE
UNIVERSITY PRESS

CAMBRIDGE
UNIVERSITY PRESS

University Printing House, Cambridge CB2 8BS, United Kingdom

One Liberty Plaza, 20th Floor, New York, NY 10006, USA

477 Williamstown Road, Port Melbourne, VIC 3207, Australia

314–321, 3rd Floor, Plot 3, Splendor Forum, Jasola District Centre, New Delhi – 110025, India

79 Anson Road, #06–04/06, Singapore 079906

Cambridge University Press is part of the University of Cambridge.

It furthers the University's mission by disseminating knowledge in the pursuit of education, learning, and research at the highest international levels of excellence.

www.cambridge.org
Information on this title: www.cambridge.org/9781107135383
DOI: 10.1017/9781316471647

First published 2018

Printed and bound in Great Britain by Clays Ltd, Elcograf S.p.A.

A catalogue record for this publication is available from the British Library.

Library of Congress Cataloging-in-Publication Data
Names: Dreyfuss, Rochelle Cooper, 1947–, editor. | Ng, Elizabeth Siew Kuan, editor.
Title: Framing intellectual property law in the 21st century : integrating incentives, trade, development, culture, and human rights / edited by Rochelle Cooper Dreyfuss, Elizabeth Siew-Kuan Ng.
Description: New York : Cambridge University Press, 2018.
Identifiers: LCCN 2018022369 | ISBN 9781107135383 (hardback)
Subjects: LCSH: Intellectual property. | BISAC: LAW / Intellectual Property / General.
Classification: LCC K1401 .F725 2018 | DDC 346.04/8–dc23
LC record available at https://lccn.loc.gov/2018022369

ISBN 978-1-107-13538-3 Hardback

DEDICATION TO ELIZABETH SIEW-KUAN NG

Elizabeth Siew-Kuan Ng

Elizabeth, a dear friend and respected colleague, left this world on 5 February 2018 after a short illness. Her sudden demise was a shock to many, in particular her colleagues at NUS Law who mourn the loss of a caring teacher and respected colleague.

Elizabeth joined the NUS Faculty of Law in 1986. One of the first subjects she taught was Intellectual Property Law. Although barely older than some of her students, Elizabeth quickly earned their respect as an excellent tutor. Over the years her reputation as a very fine teacher grew. She gave much of herself to her students, spending hours on preparation of materials and classes. Generations of students have much to thank her for.

Since 2013, I have had the privilege and pleasure of working closely with Elizabeth at the EW Barker Centre for Law and Business, first as the Centre's Director of Intellectual Property and later when she concurrently served as Deputy Chairwoman of the Centre. Elizabeth was a great partner in this endeavor. She provided strong academic leadership in our Intellectual Property cluster, and played an instrumental role in developing the Centre's reputation. I could always count on her wise counsel, and valued her views immensely, especially when they ran counter to mine. Our slightly different personalities complemented each other to ensure that decisions taken were more thoughtful and holistic. Hers was a strong and courteous voice that I shall greatly miss. The Centre is the poorer for her loss.

In the last several years, Elizabeth was also coming into her own on the research front. For many years she was highly regarded internationally, as demonstrated by her work with organizations such as the World Intellectual Property Organization, the Intellectual Property Organisation of Singapore, and the State Council of Thailand. In more recent years, she had begun turning this wealth of knowledge and insight into academic articles and chapters, while leading some extremely interesting research projects. This was a very fertile and exciting phase of her development as a scholar that has now ended all too prematurely. Elizabeth leaves behind her loving husband, Adrian, whom she met at university, and their daughter Chantal, whom Elizabeth absolutely doted on.

Professor Tan Cheng Han, SC
Chairperson
EW Barker Centre for Law and Business
National University of Singapore

CONTENTS

FIGURES

TABLES

NOTES ON CONTRIBUTORS

GRAEME W. AUSTIN is a Professor of Law at Melbourne University, and Chair of Private Law at Victoria University of Wellington. Before returning to Australasia, he was the J. Byron McCormick Professor of Law at the University of Arizona. He has been the Yong Shook Lin Visiting Professor in Intellectual Property at the National University of Singapore, and was a Senior Solicitor at Chapman Tripp in Auckland, New Zealand.

GRAEME B. DINWOODIE is Global Professor of Intellectual Property Law at Chicago-Kent College of Law. He returned to Chicago in 2018 after nine years as the Professor of Intellectual Property and Information Technology Law at the University of Oxford, where he was also Director of the Oxford Intellectual Property Research Centre, and a Professorial Fellow of St. Peter's College. Professor Dinwoodie was previously a Professor of Law at Chicago-Kent College of Law from 2000 to 2009, and from 2005 to 2009 he also held a Chair in Intellectual Property Law at Queen Mary College, University of London. Professor Dinwoodie has held a number of visiting or honorary positions, including as the Yong Shook Lin Visiting Professor of Intellectual Property Law at the National University of Singapore, a Global Professor of Law at New York University School of Law, an Honorary Professor of Law at the University of Strasbourg, the George P. Smith II Distinguished Visiting Chair at Indiana University Maurer School of Law, and a Visiting Professor of Law at the University of Pennsylvania School of Law. Professor Dinwoodie holds an LL.B. (Hons) degree from the University of Glasgow, an LL.M. degree from Harvard Law School (where he was a John F. Kennedy Scholar), and a J.S.D. degree from Columbia Law School (where he was a Burton Fellow). He was elected as a member of the American Law Institute in 2003, and served as President of the International Association for the Advancement of Teaching and Research in Intellectual Property (ATRIP) from 2011 to 2013. In 2008, the International Trademark Association awarded Professor Dinwoodie the Pattishall Medal for Teaching Excellence in Trademark Law. Professor Dinwoodie is the author of books, casebooks, and numerous articles. His scholarship has appeared in several leading law reviews and is widely cited by scholars in Europe, the United States and elsewhere. He received the 2008 Ladas Memorial Award from the International Trademark Association for his article *Confusion Over Use: Contextualism in Trademark Law* (with Janis). Professor Dinwoodie has served as a consultant to the World Intellectual Property Organization on matters of private international law, as an Adviser to the American Law Institute (ALI) project on *Principles on Jurisdiction and Recognition of Judgments in Intellectual Property Matters*, and as a consultant to the United Nations Conference on Trade and Development on the Protection of Traditional Knowledge. He currently serves as an Adviser on the ALI's project on *The Restatement of Copyright Law*.

ROCHELLE COOPER DREYFUSS is the Pauline Newman Professor of Law at New York University School of Law and Co-Director of its Engelberg Center on Innovation Law and Policy. Dreyfuss holds B.A. and M.S. degrees in Chemistry. A research chemist before entering Columbia University School of Law, she served as Articles and Book Review Editor of the Law Review. She clerked for U.S. Court of Appeals for the Second Circuit Chief Judge Wilfred Feinberg and for U.S. Supreme Court Chief Justice Warren E. Burger. She is a member of the American Law Institute and was a Co-Reporter for its project on *Intellectual Property: Principles Governing Jurisdiction, Choice of Law, and Judgments in Transnational Disputes*. She was a consultant to the Federal Courts Study Committee, to the Presidential Commission on Catastrophic Nuclear Accidents, and to the Federal Trade Commission and served on the Secretary of Health and Human Services' Advisory Committee on Genetics, Health, and Society. She was also a member of the National Academies Committees on Intellectual Property in Genomic and Protein Research and Innovation, on Intellectual Property Rights in the Knowledge-Based Economy, and on Science, Technology, and Law.

SUSY FRANKEL is Professor of Law, Chair of Intellectual Property and International Trade, and Director of the New Zealand Centre of International Economic Law, at Victoria University of Wellington. She was the President, 2015–2017, of the International Association for the Advancement of Teaching and Research in Intellectual Property (ATRIP). Since 2008 she has been Chair of the Copyright Tribunal (NZ). She is a member of the editorial boards of the *Journal of World Intellectual Property Law* and the *Queen Mary Journal of Intellectual Property* and a member of the board of the New Zealand Pacific Economic Co-operation Council. She teaches copyright, trademarks, patents, international intellectual property, and international trade law. She has been a Visiting Professor at several universities including as Reinhold Cohn Chair at the University of Haifa, University of Iowa, University of Western Ontario, and as a Senior Fulbright Scholar and Senior Hauser Global Research Fellow at New York University School of Law. Susy's scholarship focuses on international intellectual property and particularly treaty interpretation and the protection of indigenous peoples' knowledge and innovation.

ALBERT GUANGZHOU HU is an Associate Professor of Economics at the National University of Singapore. He received a Bachelor's degree in international finance from Nankai University, P.R.C., and a Ph.D. in international economics from Brandeis University, USA. His research interests include technological change, economic growth and development, and the Chinese economy. His research has appeared in academic journals such as *Review of Economics and Statistics, Journal of Development Economics*, and *Research Policy*. He has consulted for the Asian Development Bank, the World Intellectual Property Organization, and the World Bank.

ANNETTE KUR is a senior member of research staff and Head of Unit at the Max Planck Institute (MPI) for Intellectual Property, Competition and Tax Law. She is Associate Professor at the University of Stockholm and Honorary Professor at the University of Munich (LMU). She also teaches at Munich Intellectual Property Law Center (MIPLC), and is a member of foreign faculty, Santa Clara University (CA). In fall 2006 and spring 2009, she was a Visiting Professor (Hauser Global Law School Program) at NYU School of Law, New York. She has served as adviser in the American Law Institute's project *Intellectual Property: Principles Governing Jurisdiction, Choice of Law, and Judgments in Transnational Disputes*. She was President of the International Association for the Advancement of Teaching and Research in Intellectual Property (ATRIP) for the term 2007–2009. Professor Kur is the author of books and numerous articles in the field of national, European, and international trademark, unfair competition and industrial design law as well as international jurisdiction and choice of law.

MARK FUNG-CHIAN LIM heads the Hearings & Mediation Department in the Intellectual Property Office of Singapore (IPOS) where he is the Director/Chief Legal Counsel, Hearings & Mediation Department, IPOS; Senior Faculty, IP Academy. Prior to joining IPOS in 2010, Mark was a lawyer in private practice for fifteen years. His work encompasses all areas of intellectual property (IP) law. Mark is regularly consulted on IP matters by various government agencies and invited to speak at both national and international IP conferences. In addition, he has published extensively in leading local and international journals, and provided insights and/or new perspectives on a broad spectrum of IP issues. At the IP Academy, Mark oversees the development and curation of training programs in the area of IP law for the legal community as well as the public sector in Singapore.

ELIZABETH SIEW-KUAN NG was deputy chairwoman and director (Intellectual Property Unit) at the EW Barker Centre for Law and Business; director of the Graduate Certificate in Intellectual Property program; and an Associate Professor of Law, National University of Singapore's Faculty of Law. She pioneered and taught the Law of Intellectual Property, Biotechnology Law and Global Exploitation of IP. She was appointed amicus curiae by the Singapore Court of Appeal on intellectual property matters in a criminal reference in *Public Prosecutor v. Koh Peng Kiat* [2016] 1 S.L.R. 753. She was an intellectual property adjudicator of the Intellectual Property Office of Singapore (2014–2018). She graduated with an LL.B. (Honors) (Queen Mary College, University of London), where she was awarded the Sweet & Maxwell Law Prize and Faculty of Law Prize. She was a barrister-at-law of Middle Temple (England) and an advocate and solicitor (Supreme Court, Singapore). A Fellow of the Cambridge Commonwealth Society, she was a consultant of the World Intellectual Property Organization. She has held visiting positions at the Max Planck Institute, City University of Hong Kong, and U.S. Court of Appeals for the Federal Circuit. She delivered more than ninety invited papers including in Australia, China, Fiji, Hong Kong SAR, Malaysia, Mongolia, Myanmar, Singapore, South Korea, Sri Lanka, Switzerland, and Thailand, and convened many major public intellectual property conferences. She published extensively in Europe, the United Kingdom, India, South Korea, Switzerland, Thailand, the United States, Australia, and Singapore, and was an author of studies commissioned by the World Intellectual Property Organization. She obtained an LL.M. (First Class) (University of Cambridge) on a Cambridge Commonwealth Trust scholarship and was conferred the Clough Prize. Her latest co-edited book, *International Intellectual Property and the ASEAN Way: Pathways to Interoperability*, was published by Cambridge University Press in October 2017.

WEE LOON NG-LOY is Professor at the Faculty of Law, National University of Singapore. She teaches "Law of Intellectual Property" which focuses on Singapore's IP regime, as well as "International Trademark Law and Policy" and "International Copyright Law and Policy." Amongst her academic publications is the text on *Law of Intellectual Property of Singapore* (2d ed., 2014). Outside of the university, her involvement in the legal landscape of Singapore includes the following: a member of the Board of Directors of the Intellectual Property Office of Singapore (2000–2001); a member of Singapore's Copyright Tribunal (since 2009); a member of the Singapore Domain Name Dispute Resolution Policy Panel (since 2014); IP Adjudicator with the Intellectual Property Office of Singapore (2014–2015). In 2013, she was conferred the "Singapore Law Merit Award" by the Singapore Academy of Law in recognition of her contributions made to the development and advancement of Singapore law. In January 2016, she was appointed "Senior Counsel (honoris causa)" by the Singapore Court of Appeal for her special knowledge in law and her contributions to the development of the law and to the legal profession, in particular her assistance to the Court in her role as amicus curiae.

RUTH L. OKEDIJI is the Jeremiah Smith Jr. Professor of Law at Harvard Law School and a Director of the Berkman Klein Center for Internet and Society at Harvard University. She teaches contracts, international intellectual property (IP), copyright, and other courses on law and development, and Christian Legal Studies. She has written widely on a range of matters related to technology, innovation policy, global knowledge governance, and sustainable development. Her current research focuses on the regulation of publicly funded technologies, the protection of traditional knowledge, and the intersection of Artificial Intelligence and copyright law. Professor Okediji is chair of the expert working group on international intellectual property, traditional knowledge and genetic resources at the International Law Research Program of the Centre for International Innovation Governance (CIGI) in Waterloo, Canada. She is a co-author of the leading casebook, *Copyright Law in a Global Information Economy* (Aspen, 4th ed., 2015), and of *The World Blind Union Guide to the Marrakesh Treaty: Facilitating Access to Books for Print-Disabled Individuals* (Oxford University Press, 2017). Her most recent book, *Copyright Law in an Age of Limitations and Exceptions*, was published by Cambridge University Press in 2017. Professor Okediji is an elected member of the American Law Institute and an Editor of the *Journal of World Intellectual Property Law*.

JEROME H. REICHMAN is the Bunyan S. Womble Professor of Law at Duke University School of Law, Durham, North Carolina. He has written and lectured widely on diverse aspects of intellectual property law, including comparative and international intellectual property and the connection between intellectual property and international trade laws. His articles in this area particularly address problems that developing countries face in implementing the Agreement on Trade-Related Aspects of Intellectual Property Rights (TRIPS Agreement). He is consultant to numerous intergovernmental and nongovernmental organizations, a member of the Board of Editors for the *Journal of International Economic Law*, and of the Scientific Advisory Board of *Il Diritto di Autore* (Rome). He is a graduate of the University of Chicago, where he was a Hutchins Scholar and an early entrant. He is also a graduate of Yale Law School. He worked for the U.N. in Geneva in the 1970s and then taught at Ohio State and at Vanderbilt. He has taught at Duke for the last seventeen years. He recently published two books: *Governing Digitally Integrated Genetic Resources, Data and Literature: Global Intellectual Property Strategies for a Redesigned Microbian Research Commons*, co-authored with Tom Dedeurwaerdere and Paul Uhlir (Cambridge University Press, 2016) and *The World Blind Union Guide to the Marrakesh Treaty*, co-authored with Lawrence Helfer, Molly Land, and Ruth Okediji (Oxford University Press, 2017). In collaboration with Keith Maskus, he published *International Public Goods and Transfer of Technology under a Globalized Intellectual Property Regime* (Cambridge University Press, 2005). His most recent publication in this area is *Why the Nagoya Protocol to the CBD Matters to Science and Industry in Canada and the United States* (Centre for International Governance Innovation [CIGI], Ontario, Canada, 2018). Other relevant publications include *Intellectual Property in the 21st Century: Will Developing Countries Lead or Follow?* (2009); *Compulsory Licensing of Patented Pharmaceutical Inventions: Evaluating the Options* (2009); *Rethinking the Role of Clinical Trial Data in International Intellectual Property Law: The Case for a Public Goods Approach* (2009); *Harmonization Without Consensus: Critical Reflections on Drafting a Substantive Patent Law Treaty* (2007) (co-authored with Professor Rochelle Cooper Dreyfuss); and *The Doha Round's Public Health Legacy: Strategies for the Production and Diffusion of Patented Medicines Under the Amended TRIPS Provisions* (2007) (co-authored with Professor Fred Abbott).

MEGAN RICHARDSON is a Professor of Law, Director of the Intellectual Property Research Institute of Australia and Co-Director of the Centre for Media and Communications Law at the Melbourne Law School, the University of Melbourne. She works across privacy, personality, and intellectual property law. Recent books include *Fashioning Intellectual Property: Exhibition, Advertising and the Press, 1789–1918* (Cambridge University Press, 2012), with Julian Thomas, and *The Right to Privacy: Origins and Influence of a Nineteenth-Century Idea* (Cambridge University Press, 2017).

CHRISTOPHER JON SPRIGMAN teaches intellectual property law, antitrust law, competition policy, and comparative constitutional law at the New York University School of Law. He also serves as Co-Director of NYU's Engelberg Center on Innovation Law and Policy, and as the Reporter for the American Law Institute's *Restatement of Copyright*. Sprigman's research focuses on how legal rules affect innovation and the deployment of new technologies. His widely cited works – which include law review articles, writing in the popular press (including in the *New York Times*, *The New Yorker*, *Slate*, the *Washington Post*, the *Los Angeles Times*, the *Wall Street Journal*, *Forbes*, and *The Atlantic*), and a book, *The Knockoff Economy: How Imitation Sparks Innovation* – have had an influence on important aspects of copyright and trademark law, and often belie the conventional wisdom about intellectual property rights. Sprigman was an appellate counsel from 1999 to 2001 in the Antitrust Division of the U.S. Department of Justice, where *U.S. v. Microsoft* was among his cases, and later was elected partner in the Washington, DC, office of King & Spalding before becoming a residential fellow at Stanford Law School's Center for

Internet and Society. Sprigman received his B.A. in history *magna cum laude* from the University of Pennsylvania in 1988, and a J.D. with honors from the University of Chicago Law School in 1993. He subsequently clerked for Judge Stephen Reinhardt of the U.S. Court of Appeals for the Ninth Circuit and Justice Lourens H. W. Ackermann of the Constitutional Court of South Africa. Sprigman also taught at the University of the Witwatersrand's law school in Johannesburg.

DAVID TAN is Vice Dean (Academic Affairs) at National University of Singapore's Faculty of Law where he oversees the undergraduate and postgraduate teaching curriculum, and is the first to be appointed to the Dean's Chair there. He is concurrently Director (Communications) where he oversees the faculty's branding and strategic communications. He holds Ph.D., LL.B. (First Class Honors) and B.Com. degrees from the University of Melbourne and an LL.M. from Harvard. He has visited at the University of Hong Kong Faculty of Law and Melbourne Law School, teaching courses in intellectual property and popular culture. At NUS Law, Tan pioneered courses in Freedom of Speech and Entertainment Law. His areas of research cover personality rights, copyright, trademarks, freedom of expression, and tort law, and his articles have been cited by Singapore's highest appellate court. His law publications have appeared in a wide range of journals that include *Yale Journal of International Law, Harvard Journal of Sports & Entertainment Law, Cardozo Arts & Entertainment Law Journal, Fordham Intellectual Property, Media & Entertainment Law Journal, Sydney Law Review, Singapore Academy of Law Journal, Media & Arts Law Review*, and *Law Quarterly Review*. His monograph, *The Commercial Appropriation of Fame: A Cultural Analysis of the Right of Publicity and Passing Off*, was published by Cambridge University Press in 2017. Tan is also an accomplished fine art and fashion photographer, having published a coffee-table book *Visions of Beauty* in association with the luxury fashion house of Versace, and *Tainted Perfection* in collaboration with Cartier in Singapore. His photographic works comprising fashion editorials and advertisements have appeared in magazines such as *Time, Vanity Fair, Harper's Bazaar, Elle*, and *The New Yorker*.

YIH-SAN TAN served the Intellectual Property Office of Singapore as the Chief Executive from 2011 to 2015. He brought IP closer to the world of innovation through development, education, and internationalization. As Chair of the ASEAN IP community, he helped build a closer and more interoperable ASEAN IP community so as to engender greater investment flow into the emerging markets of ASEAN. He was selected as among the fifty most influential people in IP in 2015 by the magazine *Managing Intellectual Property*. He continues to cheer the exciting development of IP thought leadership in Singapore and in Asia, in his current role as a general partner in an investment firm.

JULIAN THOMAS is Director of the Social Change research platform at RMIT University, Australia. He works on information law and policy and the histories of new communications technologies. With co-author Megan Richardson, he has also published *Fashioning Intellectual Property: Exhibition, Advertising and the Press, 1789–1918* (Cambridge University Press, 2012). His other recent work includes *Internet on the Outstation: The Digital Divide and Remote Aboriginal Communities* (INC, 2016) and *The Informal Media Economy* (Polity, 2015).

SANDRA YU is Assistant Director for Strategic Planning & Policy Department/Partnership & Programme Department at the Intellectual Property Office of Singapore.

PREFACE

Introduction

With the emergence of the knowledge industries as a salient sector of the economy and the development of new geographically dispersed (and dispersing) business models, methods of production, and technologies of distribution, the demand for intellectual property protection has sharply increased. Responses range from the revision of domestic regimes to new multilateral, bilateral, and regional agreements – all of which tend to harmonize protection at ever higher levels. These changes have engendered considerable controversy. From a backwater of specialists in patent, copyright, and trademark law, developments in intellectual property law have piqued the interest of scholars in such diverse fields as international relations, political theory, business, human rights, medicine, psychology, and economics. It is not surprising that this is so. Intellectual property laws may be intended to promote creative production, but the protection afforded touches on many issues of fundamental importance to human existence, including identity, culture, expressivity, curiosity, education, health, safety, food security, development, and the environment.

It is certainly enriching to welcome new participants into the debate over the proper scope of intellectual property rights and the appropriate balance between the proprietary interests of right holders and the access interests of the public. However, the discussion has become fragmented and heated. Important issues remain unresolved. In our experience, the problem appears, at least in part, to be that those participating in the debate begin with different premises. As a result, they frame the questions involved in balancing interests quite differently. At one end of the spectrum are observers who see intellectual property through a frame of incentives, who believe that strong exclusive rights are necessary to prevent free riders from competing down the price of innovations and undermining the returns available from taking the risks entailed in creative production. Without strong protection, they say, there would be insufficient impetus to develop new medicines, technologies, educational materials, or cultural products for society to enjoy. To a large extent, their voices are joined by groups interested in improving social welfare by reaping comparative advantages and promoting interdependence among nations. They see in harmonization at high levels a way to facilitate international trade in knowledge products. At the other end of the spectrum are cultural theorists, who examine how society is structured through *both* the creation *and* the sharing of information goods (books, symbols, technology), and human rights advocates, who emphasize human flourishing and development goals, which likewise demand access to the fruits of human ingenuity.

We do not expect this volume to resolve the important questions raised in the debates over the proper scope and strength of intellectual property regimes. Rather, we endeavor to clarify the terms of the debate by examining the underlying premises. The contributors to this volume interrogate the frames that influence the ways in which those participating in the debate perceive intellectual property law. Nine of the chapters examine a particular approach to crafting intellectual property law and identify its limits. They are divided into two sections: the first looks at the frames that fall toward the high-protectionist end of the spectrum; the second examines the frames on the other side. Chapter 10 considers whether these frames can be assembled to work effectively together. The book concludes with commentary on how the themes investigated in the book relate to Singaporean interests.

The Book

High Protectionist Frames: Incentives and Trade

In the opening two chapters of FRAMING INTELLECTUAL PROPERTY LAW, Rochelle Cooper Dreyfuss and Christopher Sprigman examine the limits of the Incentives Frame; in the next pair of chapters, Jerome Reichman and Susy Frankel consider the Trade Frame. In her piece, Dreyfuss asks whether intellectual property rights are necessary to promote creative production. After suggesting that they are not always needed, she investigates the question of how creators and inventors would respond in the absence of these regimes. She then compares the social costs of the intellectual property system with these alternatives. While she finds that awarding exclusive rights may sometimes be the preferred approach, she argues that that there is nonetheless considerable room for public-regarding principles that protect access interests.

Sprigman closely examines empirical and experimental studies on the relationship between copyright and creativity to see whether, in fact, there is an evidentiary basis for the claim that increasing protection will motivate more innovation. In most situations, he finds the proof inconclusive. He ends with recommendations for sharpening empirical scholarship and using it to expand our understanding of the incentives frame and the factors that promote creativity.

Jerome Reichman begins with what he calls the Trade Paradigm and suggests that in many ways, the effort to facilitate trade though harmonization has, in fact, harmed innovation and distorted trade. He argues that because harmonization tends to be closely correlated with expanding the reach of intellectual property rights, fundamental science – the wellspring from which both commercial and noncommercial products emerge – has become the subject of exclusive rights. As a result, Reichman says, trade-related rationales can lead to less rather than more inventive activity. In addition, he notes that because developing countries are behind the technological frontier, they are poorly positioned to benefit from stronger protection; indeed, they are hurt by the higher costs associated with intellectual property rights: protection not only makes goods unavailable, it also decreases opportunities for less developed countries to become creative in their own right. Worse, harmonization prevents countries from experimenting with other approaches to incentivizing innovation. Reichman concludes that negotiators must turn their attention to developing trade rules that take better account of the impact of ratcheting up protection in the name of promoting trade.

In her piece, Frankel goes even further and questions the premise that promoting free trade requires high levels of protection. She notes that, at one time, strong rights of exclusivity were regarded as barriers to trade and that even after a contrary view took hold, the main international intellectual property instrument – the Trade-Related Aspects of Intellectual Property (TRIPS) Agreement – imposed minimum standards of protection that left substantial room for national variation. Linkage of intellectual property with trade has, however, created a potent platform for compelling countries to adopt levels of protection that vastly exceed that which is necessary to motivate innovation. Frankel ends with suggestions for countering these effects through interpretations of trade law that keep the object and purpose of the TRIPS Agreement in focus, through the development of stronger access norms, and through a realistic appraisal of how the innovation landscape might change.

Low Protectionist Frames: Health, Culture, and Human Rights

Moving to the other end of the spectrum, Elizabeth Siew-Kuan Ng and her coauthor, Albert Guangzhou Hu, look at IP protection through the Health Frame; Megan Richardson, with her coauthor Julian Thomas, and David Tan consider the Cultural Frame; while Graeme Austin and Ruth Okediji investigate the limits of the Human Rights Frame. Ng and Hu begin the discussion with an empirical piece on how Asian countries have implemented the flexibilities in the TRIPS Agreement to protect public health. Finding significant differences among these countries, they relate a country's reliance on TRIPS flexibilities to its stage of economic and technological development and to its public health needs. They show that the more innovative a country is, the stronger the protective regime it enacts. Importantly, however, demands for healthcare (as measured by the prevalence of HIV infections) drive the adoption of flexibilities.

Richardson and Thomas consider the reach of the Culture Frame. Using three cases, one involving Hugo Zacchini, a circus performer, and the others involving Paul Hogan (Crocodile Dundee) and the singer Rihanna, they show how a commitment to human flourishing can justify increasing (rather than decreasing) protection. Thus, they advocate for the adoption of novel intellectual property rights that enable people to control their self-presentation. The authors counsel, however, that intellectual property rights in images should come with appropriate limits and defenses and take account of the interplay between the creator and the audience.

David Tan explores that public dimension of the move to protect images. He uses the cultural usage of Mickey Mouse, postmodernist sensibilities, and semiotics to demonstrate how extensively the value of images depends on recoding by the audience. He then examines the flexibilities in copyright law to see how well they permit the public – the audience – to enjoy the value it adds to images of cultural significance.

Ostensibly, the harshest critique of strong intellectual property rights derives from the Human Rights Frame, which regards education, health, and human flourishing as fundamental rights. But as Graeme Austin notes, the Universal Declaration of Human Rights also recognizes the rights of an author to the moral and material interests in his or her work. To reconcile these positions, Austin argues for what he calls an author-focused human rights approach that provides a justification for limiting intellectual property while protecting the dignity interests of human (as opposed to corporate) creators.

Focusing on the technological side of intellectual property protection, Ruth Okediji expresses similar skepticism about the ability of human rights to improve social welfare and act as a counterweight to efforts to increase intellectual property protection. Like Austin, Okediji notes that the human rights approach to intellectual property law has come late in the game, after the basic principles of protection were embedded into law and practice. Furthermore, she argues that protecting human rights requires effective institutions for implementation – institutions that are lacking in many of the places where there is a recognized need to moderate the exclusivity of intellectual property rights. Thus, she suggests, progress toward obtaining the highest levels of social justice will require novel approaches to both intellectual property and human rights law.

Integration

In the final chapter, Graeme Dinwoodie and Annette Kur discuss the characteristics of each of the frames set out in the earlier chapters. They consider the functions of frames – to constrain, support, or set up – and ask whether the frames can, or should, be deployed so as to compose a conceptual whole – a "Theory of Everything." The authors conclude that such a theory is neither possible nor desirable. Rather, they see each frame as serving a different purpose in the law – justifying it, calibrating its reach, and managing the influences that are brought to bear upon it.

The Commentary

After the intriguing conclusion contributed by Graeme Dinwoodie and Annette Kur, comments by Yih-San Tan and coauthor Sandra Yu, Mark Fung-Chian Lim and Wee Loon Ng-Loy provide a Singaporean perspective based on their experience as practitioners, regulators, and legal scholars.

Tan and Yu consider how the architecture of the intellectual property system will change as new nations, such as China and Korea, emerge as centers of innovation, and as digital methods of distribution become ever more common. The authors note that Singapore will be required to change its laws if it is to prosper in this new environment. They suggest that its response should be grounded in three principles: providing accessibility for local innovators, promoting connectivity, and ensuring quality. Looking specifically at the Incentives Frame, Lim agrees with Dreyfuss that the overall goal is to provide incentives but to balance them against access and fairness considerations. However, he stresses that for businesses, lawyers, adjudicators, and regulators, predictability and certainty are of prime importance. Thus, Lim argues, the intellectual property system must strive to produce rules that can be readily and reproducibly applied. In a way, Loy's comment illustrates the problem of uncertainty by focusing on how the image rights proposed by Richardson and Thomas should be interpreted in Singapore.

Acknowledgements

The authors wish to thank Nicole Arzt for her administrative assistance in keeping track of the drafts as they evolved into finished chapters. Checking citations and formatting are thankless jobs and we are grateful to Yihang Ng and Claudia Sue-Min Lee for their hard and accurate work, and their admirable perseverance throughout the entire production process. We extend special thanks to the EW Barker Centre for Law and Business and the National University of Singapore Faculty of Law for convening the conference on which this book is based. The opportunity the conference provided to exchange ideas enhanced all of the contributions in the volume. We also thank Li Jie of Pathlight School for furnishing the lively artwork used on the conference program and for permission to reproduce a grayscale version for this book.

Rochelle Cooper Dreyfuss
Elizabeth Siew-Kuan Ng

* * *

As this volume was about to go to press, after all but one chapter were finished and edited, and this Preface completed, my dear coeditor Elizabeth Siew-Kuan passed away. This book, as well as the conference on which it was based, would not have happened without her vision and leadership. She was an earnest scholar, a deeply engaged member of the faculty of the National University of Singapore, and extremely proud of her appointment as Deputy Chairwoman and Director of the Intellectual Property Unit of the EW Barker Centre for Law and Business. She was also my friend and collaborator. We spent many hours together on the Internet organizing the conference, choosing contributors, developing the book proposal, writing the Preface, and choosing the cover image. She was wonderfully easy to work with. She sent greetings for every holiday recognized in our religions – and sometimes for occasions of her own devising. I will miss her.

Rochelle Cooper Dreyfuss

ABBREVIATIONS

ACTA	Anti-Counterfeiting Trade Agreement
AIDS	Acquired Immune Deficiency Syndrome
ASEAN	Association of South East Asian Nations
ATRIP	Association for the Advancement of Teaching and Research in Intellectual Property
BIT	bilateral investment treaty
BRIC	Brazil, Russia, India, and China
BRICS	Brazil, Russia, India, China, and South Africa
CBD	Convention on Biological Diversity
CETA	Comprehensive Economic and Trade Agreement
CGIAR	Consultative Group on International Agricultural Research
CPTPP	Comprehensive and Progressive Agreement for Trans-Pacific Partnership
DSB	dispute settlement body
ECtHR	European Court of Human Rights
EDB	Economic Development Board, Singapore
E.U.	European Union
FAO	United Nations Food and Agriculture Organization
FTA	free trade agreement
GATS	General Agreement on Trade in Services
GATT	General Agreement on Tariffs and Trade
GDP	gross domestic product
GII	Global Innovation Index
GIPC Index	U.S. Chamber International Intellectual Property Index
GIPI	Taylor-Wessing Global Intellectual Property Index
GNP	gross national product
GP Index	Ginarte-Park Index of Patent Rights
HIV	human immunodeficiency virus
ICESCR	International Covenant on Economic, Social and Cultural Rights
IE	International Enterprise, Singapore
IP	intellectual property
IPPFI	Intellectual Property (Patent) Flexibility Index

ITPGRFA	International Treaty on Plant Genetic Resources for Food and Agriculture
MFN	most-favored nation
NGO	nongovernmental organization
OECD	Organisation for Economic Co-operation and Development
SIPO	State Intellectual Property Office of China
SPLT	Substantive Patent Law Treaty
TPP	Trans-Pacific Partnership Agreement
TRIPS	Trade-Related Aspects of Intellectual Property Rights
TTIP	Transatlantic Trade and Investment Partnership Agreement
UAE	United Arab Emirates
UDHR	Universal Declaration of Human Rights
U.K.	United Kingdom
UNCTAD	United Nations Conference on Trade and Development
UNESCO	United Nations Educational, Scientific and Cultural Organization
UNHRC	UN Human Rights Council
UPOV	International Union for the Protection of New Varieties of Plants
USA	United States of America
USTR	United States Trade Representative
VIP	visually impaired person
WDA	Workforce Development Authority, Singapore
WFCC	World Federation for Culture Collections
WHO	World Health Organization
WIPO	World Intellectual Property Organization
WTO	World Trade Organization

1

In Praise of an Incentive-Based Theory of Intellectual Property Protection

ROCHELLE COOPER DREYFUSS*

> The Congress shall have the Power . . . To promote the Progress of Science and useful Arts, by securing for limited Times to Authors and Inventors the exclusive Right to their respective Writings and Discoveries . . . [1]

With knowledge production becoming increasingly significant in the economy, more attention needs to be paid to the impact of intellectual property rights on human rights, culture, and development. As the above quotation from the United States Constitution suggests, intellectual property rights are traditionally justified as a mechanism for generating incentives to innovate.[2] Inherent in this instrumental rationale for creating *private* rights to exclude is the idea that the ultimate goal is the *public* good: promoting progress for the benefit of society. The law, in short, has long been premised on balance, balance among generations of innovators and between creators and those who would benefit from the works they produce.[3] Thus, so long as the creative industries can capture enough return to recoup costs

* The author wishes to thank Susy Frankel and Elizabeth Ng Siew-Kuan for their helpful comments, Eileen Woo, NYU Class of 2016, for her research assistance, and the Filomen D'Agostino and Max E. Greenberg Research Fund of NYU for financial support.

[1] U.S. Const., art. I, § 8, cl. 8.

[2] *See generally*, William M. Landes & Richard A. Posner, *An Economic Analysis of Copyright Law*, 18 J. Legal Stud. 325 (1989). *See also* Robert P. Merges, Justifying Intellectual Property (2011) (discussing the role of utilitarian theory in justifying intellectual property protection); Mark A. Lemley, *Property, Intellectual Property, and Free Riding*, 83 Texas L. Rev. 1031 (2005); Dan L. Burk & Mark A. Lemley, *Policy Levers in Patent Law*, 89 Va. L. Rev. 1575, 1595–615 (2003); Mark A. Lemley, *Taking the Regulatory Nature of IP Seriously*, 92 Tex. L. Rev. 107, 108 (2014).

[3] *See, e.g.*, Mazer v. Stein, 347 U.S. 201, 219 (1954): "The economic philosophy behind the clause empowering Congress to grant patents and copyrights is the conviction that encouragement of individual effort by personal gain is the best way to advance public welfare through the talents of authors and inventors." *See also* Golan v. Holder, 565 U.S. 302, 347–51 (2012) (Breyer, J., dissenting).

and earn a significant profit,[4] the United States has always considered itself free to promote other public goals, such as health, education, and free expression. But in a study of successive international intellectual property instruments, including the World Trade Organization's (WTO) TRIPS Agreement (TRIPS), free trade agreements (FTAs), and bilateral investment treaties (BITs),[5] Susy Frankel and I concluded that the linkage of intellectual property with trade – and even more so, with investment – is triggering a reconceptualization of this fundamental principle at the international level. The *quantitative* approach underlying the incentive theory, which asked how much exclusivity is necessary to promote innovation, has given way to a *qualitative* approach, which treats intellectual property as equivalent to a commodity or an investment asset and considers any impairment of value a taking, with its effect largely calculated from the perspective of the right holder.[6]

Intriguingly, at the same time that commodification (through trade agreements) and assetization (through investment treaties) were eclipsing the incentive-based approach within the international community, the legal academy was beginning to challenge the idea that intellectual property incentives are necessary at all. Pointing, as one example, to the flourishing fashion industry, where intellectual property rights are ineffective and copying is rampant, theorists such as Chris Sprigman and Kal Raustiala argue that in many sectors there are other dynamics that can spur creativity and protect private gains from

[4] To be sure, these profits must be significant because the payoff must compensate for the cost and risk associated with dry holes (innovative activity that does not result in a commercializable product): *see* F. M. Scherer, *The Innovation Lottery: The Empirical Case for Copyright and Patents*, in EXPANDING THE BOUNDARIES OF INTELLECTUAL PROPERTY: INNOVATION POLICY FOR THE KNOWLEDGE SOCIETY 3–21 (Rochelle Cooper Dreyfuss et al. eds., 2001).

[5] Agreement on Trade-Related Aspects of Intellectual Property Rights, Apr. 15, 1994, Marrakesh Agreement Establishing the World Trade Organization, Annex 1C, Legal Instruments—Results of the Uruguay Round, vol. 31, 33 I.L.M. 81 (1994) [hereinafter TRIPS]; for a sample list of free trade agreements (FTAs), see Office of the United States Trade Representative, *Free Trade Agreements*, OUSTR, www.ustr.gov/trade-agreements /free-trade-agreements; for a list of sample bilateral investment treaties (BITs), see Office of the United States Trade Representative, *Bilateral Investment Treaties*, OUSTR, http:// tcc.export.gov/Trade_Agreements/Bilateral_Investment_Treaties/index.asp.

[6] Rochelle Cooper Dreyfuss & Susy Frankel, From Incentive to Commodity to Asset: How International Law is Reconceptualizing Intellectual Property, 36 *Mich. J. Int'l L.* 557 (2015). *See also* Peter K. Yu, *Intellectual Property and Human Rights in the Nonmultilateral Era*, 64 FLA. L. REV. 1045 (2012).

innovation.[7] To these commentators, intellectual property rights can often be unnecessary. Thus strengthening them is largely misguided.

Given these opposing challenges to the incentive-based approach, the time appears ripe to reconsider it. In Section I of this chapter, I examine the evidence on intellectual production outside standard intellectual property regimes. While it is easy to agree that considerable creativity occurs in that realm, I conclude that exclusive intellectual property rights remain important in the modern economy. In Section II I suggest, however, that a return to incentive theory would protect public-regarding values without unduly sacrificing the benefits derived from linking intellectual property with trade and investment in international agreements.

I Are IP Incentives Necessary?

Certainly, there is much to what Sprigman and Raustiala say. It is now clear that there are many fields where significant progress can occur without strong intellectual property rights. As Eric von Hippel showed in a series of articles and books, users (or "lead users") make advances because they need them for their own projects and thus are not typically driven by the profits generated through exclusivity.[8] Von Hippel also demonstrated that there are sectors in which strong norms support a no-copying regime, making exclusive legal rights unnecessary to capture the financial benefits of creative production.[9] Developing on this work, Kathy Strandburg examined innovation in the academic sector, where

[7] Kal Raustiala & Christopher Jon Sprigman, The Knockoff Economy: How Imitation Sparks Innovation (2012). *See also* Michele Boldrin & David K. Levine, Against Intellectual Monopoly (2008); Jonathan M. Barnett, *Shopping for Gucci on Canal Street: Reflections on Status Consumption, Intellectual Property, and the Incentive Thesis*, 91 Va. L. Rev. 1381 (2005).

[8] Eric Von Hippel, Democratizing Innovation (2005), http://web.mit.edu/evhippel/www/democ1.htm; Eric Von Hippel, The Sources Of Innovation (2008), http://web.mit.edu/evhippel/www/sources.htm; Eric von Hippel, Jeroen P. J. de Jong & Stephen Flowers, *Comparing Business and Household Sector Innovation in Consumer Products: Findings from a Representative Study in the UK*, 58 Mgmt. Sci. 1669–81 (2012); Jeroen P. J. de Jong & Eric von Hippel, *Measuring User Innovation in Dutch High Tech SMEs: Frequency, Nature and Transfer to Producers* (MIT Sloan Research Paper No. 4724–09, 2009), http://evhippel.files.wordpress.com/2013/08/jeroeneric-user-to-producer-transfer-mar-2–09.pdf; Dietmar Harhoff, Joachim Henkel & Eric von Hippel, *Profiting from Voluntary Information Spillovers: How Users Benefit by Freely Revealing Their Innovations*, 32 Res. Pol'y 1753 (2003).

[9] *See, e.g.*, Emmanuelle Fauchart & Eric von Hippel, *Norms-Based Intellectual Property Systems: The Case of French Chefs*, 19 Org. Science 187 (2008).

norms, user needs, and curiosity combine to create a strong impetus to advance science.[10] Other spurs to innovation have also been considered. For example, Brian Wright, Joseph Stiglitz, and others have shown that prizes can function effectively.[11] Indeed, even before most of these commentators entered the picture, the need for exclusive rights was questioned. In the mid-1980s, Edwin Mansfield surveyed industry and found that, in most sectors, corporate research managers list secrecy and lead time well ahead of patents as a tool for appropriation.[12] Others showed that sharing can create comparative sectorial advantages that compensate for the lack of exclusivity.[13] To be sure, in his classic work on the patent system, Fritz Machlup suggested that "volunteer" innovators would never be well enough organized to make complicated inventions on an enduring basis.[14] However, Yochai Benkler decisively demonstrated that modern technologies (principally the internet) can structure cumulative research extremely effectively.[15]

This work is more than theoretical: many important advances have been made through novel modes of creative production that do not rely on formal patent or copyright protection. Wikipedia, Apache, Linux, and

[10] Katherine J. Strandburg, *Curiosity-Driven Research and University Technology Transfer*, in UNIVERSITY ENTREPRENEURSHIP AND TECHNOLOGY TRANSFER: PROCESS, DESIGN, AND INTELLECTUAL PROPERTY 93 (Gary D. Libecap ed., 2005). *See also* Katherine J. Strandburg, *User Innovator Community Norms: At the Boundary Between Academic and Industry Research*, 77 FORDHAM L. REV. 2237 (2009); Katherine J. Strandburg, *Legal But Acceptable: Pallin v. Singer and Physician Patenting Norms*, in INTELLECTUAL PROPERTY AT THE EDGE: THE CONTESTED CONTOURS OF IP (R. C. Dreyfuss & J. Ginsburg eds., 2013).

[11] Brian D. Wright, *The Economics of Invention Incentives: Patents, Prizes, and Research Contracts*, 73 AM. ECON. REV. 691 (1983). *See also* Joseph E. Stiglitz, *Economic Foundations of Intellectual Property Rights*, 57 DUKE L.J. 1693 (2008). *See generally*, DAVA SOBEL, LONGITUDE: THE TRUE STORY OF A LONE GENIUS WHO SOLVED THE GREATEST SCIENTIFIC PROBLEM OF HIS TIME (1995).

[12] Edwin Mansfield, *Patents and Innovation: An Empirical Study*, 32 *MGMT. SCI.* 173 (1986). *See also* Wesley M. Cohen, Richard R. Nelson & John P. Walsh, *Protecting Their Intellectual Assets: Appropriability Conditions and Why U.S. Manufacturing Firms Patent (or Not)* 32 tbl.1 (Nat'l Bureau of Econ. Research, Working Paper No. 7552, 2000), www.nber.org/papers/w7552.

[13] *See, e.g.*, Robert C. Allen, *Collective Invention*, 4 J.ECON BEHAV. & ORG. (1983). *See also* Michael J. Madison, Brett M. Frischmann & Katherine J. Strandburg, *Constructing Commons in the Cultural Environment*, 95 CORNELL L. REV. 657 (2010).

[14] STAFF OF SUBCOMM. ON PATENTS, TRADEMARKS, & COPYRIGHTS, S. COMM. ON THE JUDICIARY, 85TH CONG., AN ECONOMIC REVIEW OF THE PATENT SYSTEM 45 (Comm. Print 1958) (prepared by Fritz Machlup).

[15] YOCHAI BENKLER, THE WEALTH OF NETWORKS: HOW SOCIAL PRODUCTION TRANSFORMS MARKETS AND FREEDOM (2006).

Firefox are well-known examples, but there are many others,[16] ranging from open source library and educational systems,[17] to open source attempts to prevent bee colony collapse.[18] As with fashion, the work of chefs, comedians, magicians, and athletes is not directly appropriable through conventional intellectual property rights, yet society continues to enjoy new recipes, jokes, tricks, and sports moves.[19] Commons-based innovation is also growing in importance,[20] as are collaborations between open and proprietary projects;[21] there is similarly renewed interest in

[16] *See, e.g.*, AXEL BRUNS, BLOGS, WIKIPEDIA, SECOND LIFE, AND BEYOND (2008); Black Duck Open Hub, *Discover, Track and Compare Open Source*, BLACK DUCK, www.openhub.net/. For information on Apache, an open-source HTTP server, see https://httpd.apache.org/; for Linux, an operating system, see Ubuntu, www.ubuntu.com/; for Firefox, a free desktop browser, see www.mozilla.org/en-US/firefox/desktop/.

[17] Nicole C. Engard, *Getting Started with Koha, An Open Source Library System*, OPENSOURCE.COM (Mar. 4, 2013), https://opensource.com/education/13/3/koha-library-system; MITOPENCOURSEWARE, http://ocw.mit.edu/index.htm; Robert Terry & Robert Kiley, *Open Access to the Research Literature: A Funder's Perspective*, in OPEN ACCESS: KEY STRATEGIC, TECHNICAL AND ECONOMIC ASPECTS 101 (Neil Jacobs ed., 2006).

[18] Tristan Smith, *The Open Source Solution to the Bee Colony Collapse Problem*, OPENSOURCE.COM (Dec. 11, 2013), http://opensource.com/life/13/12/open-source-beehive.

[19] *See* Dotan Oliar & Christopher Sprigman, *There's No Free Laugh (Anymore): The Emergence of Intellectual Property Norms and the Transformation of Stand-Up Comedy*, 94 VA. L.REV. 1787 (2008); Jacob Loshin, *Secrets Revealed: How Magicians Protect Intellectual Property Without Law*, in LAW AND MAGIC: A COLLECTION OF ESSAYS (Christine A. Corcos ed., 2008), http://ssrn.com/abstract=1005564; Christopher J. Buccafusco, *On the Legal Consequences of Sauces: Should Thomas Keller's Recipes Be Per Se Copyrightable?*, 24 CARDOZO ARTS & ENT. L.J. 1121 (2007); Carl A. Kukkonen, III, *Be a Good Sport and Refrain from Using my Patented Putt: Intellectual Property Protection for Sports Related Movements*, 80 J. PAT. & TRADEMARK OFF. SOC'Y 808 (1998) (reviewing attempts to protect sports moves).

[20] *See, e.g.*, Ryan G. Vacca et al., *Intellectual Property and Public Health – A White Paper*, 7 AKRON INTELL. PROP'Y J. (2013); David E. Winickoff et al., *Opening Stem Cell Research and Development: A Policy Proposal for the Management of Data, Intellectual Property, and Ethics*, 9 YALE J. HEALTH POL'Y, L. & ETHICS 52 (2009); Paul A. David & Paul F. Uhlir, *Creating the Information Commons for e-Science: Toward Institutional Policies and Guidelines for Action*, CODATA Newsletter 91, Int'l Council for Sci., Paris, France (July 2005), www.codata.org/resources/newsletters/newsltr91A4.pdf. *See generally*, BRETT M. FRISCHMANN, INFRASTRUCTURE: THE SOCIAL VALUE OF SHARED RESOURCES (2012).

[21] *See* Yochai Benkler, *Commons and Growth: The Essential Role of Open Commons on Market Economies*, 80 CHI. L. REV. 1499 (2013) (describing various collaborative regimes); Dan Phair, *Orphan Drug Programs, Public-Private Partnerships and Current Efforts to Develop Treatments for Diseases of Poverty*, 4 J. HEALTH & BIOMEDICAL L. 193 (2008). For examples, see Global Alliance for Vaccines and Immunization, www.gavialliance.org; Global Fund to Fight AIDS, Tuberculosis and Malaria, www.theglobalfund.org/en/; Stop TB Partnership, www.stoptb.org/; Roll Back Malaria Partnership, www.rbm.who.int.

prizes and tax incentives.[22] With this ferment have come numerous efforts to study and develop methods for governing the relationships among project participants and between proprietary and sharing regimes.[23]

Because the advances attributable to open innovation span so many intellectual endeavors, it is easy to understand why students of "IP without IP" (intellectual production without intellectual property) have begun to ask whether there is any real need for intellectual property protection. But as I have suggested in earlier work,[24] the intellectual property system is not likely to disappear in the near future. First, these projects are not always as free from intellectual property protection as they may appear. Fashion relies heavily on trademark law;[25] chefs depend, at least in part, on copyright to protect their cookbooks and some even patent methods of food preparation;[26] comedians (along with many chefs) hope to star in copyrighted movies and television shows.[27]

[22] On prizes, see, for example, Michael J. Burstein and Fiona E. Murray, *Governing Innovation Prizes*, abstract available at http://law.scu.edu/wp-content/uploads/Burstein-Governing-Innovation-Prizes-abstract.pdf; Petra Moser & Tom Nicholas, *Prizes Publicity and Patents: Non-Monetary Awards as a Mechanism to Encourage Innovation*, 61 J. Indus. Econ. 763 (2013); Heidi Williams, *Innovation Inducement Prizes: Connecting Research to Policy*, 31 J. Pol'y Analysis & Mgmt. 752, 757 (2012); Liam Brunt, Josh Lerner & Tom Nicholas, *Inducement Prizes and Innovation*, 60 J. Indus. Econ. 657 (2012). On tax incentives, see, for example, Daniel Jacob Hemel & Lisa Larrimore Ouellette, *Beyond the Patents-Prizes Debate*, 92 Tex. L. Rev. 303 (2013).

[23] Governing Knowledge Commons (Brett M. Frischmann, Michael J. Madison & Katherine J. Strandburg eds., 2014); Open Access Policy, *Wellcome Trust*, www.wellcome .ac.uk/About-us/Policy/Policy-and-position-statements/WTD002766.htm;
Siobhan O'Mahony & Fabrizio Ferraro, *Managing the Boundary of an "Open" Project, IESE Business School, WP N* 537 (2004), www.iese.edu/research/pdfs/DI-0537-E.pdf; Siobhan O'Mahoney & Beth A. Bechky, *Boundary Organizations: Enabling Collaboration among Unexpected Allies*, 53 Admin. Sci. Q. 422–59 (2008).

[24] *See* Rochelle Cooper Dreyfuss, *Does IP Need IP? Accommodating Intellectual Production Outside the Intellectual Property Paradigm*, 31 Cardozo L. Rev. 1437 (2010); Rochelle Cooper Dreyfuss, *Fragile Equilibria*, VA. L. Rev. – In Brief (Jan. 22, 2007), http://ssrn .com/abstract=964242.

[25] *See, e.g.*, Louis Vuitton Malletier v. Dooney & Bourke, Inc., 454 F.3d 108 (2d Cir. 2006); Louis Vuitton Malletier v. Dooney & Bourke, Inc., 561 F. Supp. 2d 368 (S.D.N.Y. 2008); Tiffany (NJ) Inc. v. eBay, Inc., 576 F. Supp. 2d 457 (S.D.N.Y. 2007); Calvin Klein Trademark Trust v. Wachner, 129 F. Supp. 2d 254 (S.D.N.Y. 2001).

[26] *See, e.g.*, Bobby Flay: The Official Web Site, www.bobbyflay.com (click "Shop"; then click "Cookbooks"). *See also* U.S. Pat. No. 9, 690, 294 (Cooking and serving system and methods) & U.S. Pat. No. 7,307,249 (System and methods for preparing substitute food items), both held by Homaro Cantu, chef at Moto, a renowned Chicago restaurant.

[27] See, e.g.,Seinfeld, www.imdb.com/title/tt0098904/; Louie, www.imdb.com/title/ tt1492966; Iron Chef America, www.foodnetwork.com/shows/iron-chef-america.html.

At least some participation in developing computer projects such as Linux, Apache, and Firefox is aimed at establishing a reputation that can be cashed out in the for-profit computer sector, where copyrights and patents are of major significance.[28] Some of these efforts are also supported by firms and industries dependent on intellectual property rights. For example, IBM supports Linux because it wants a free operating system on which to run its proprietary software. That way, IBM need not worry about renewing its licenses to the underlying system. And because the operating system is free, it is highly likely to command a significant market share (and thus make IBM's software valuable to more users).[29]

Second, the norms necessary to maintain these communities can be fragile. Many of these projects are heavily dependent on philanthropic motivation. Consider, for example, work in the life sciences that is aimed at curing the diseases of nonmarket economies (dengue fever, malaria, and the like).[30] Since there is little chance of earning a profit in these markets, those who participate likely reap hedonic benefits, in the form of feeling good about volunteering. By the same token, some projects are begun when an industry is immature and it is unclear whether the work will be commercializable; sharing mitigates the risk that the work will never yield profits. However, as soon as profits do become available for this work, cooperation often collapses,[31] especially in cases where some members begin to earn money but others do not.[32] Norms can break down for other reasons as well. Technological change can alter the

[28] *See* RAUSTIALA & SPRIGMAN, *supra* note 7, at 188.

[29] *See e.g.*, Ronald J. Mann, *Commercializing Open Source Software: Do Property Rights Still Matter?*, 20 HARV. J.L. & TECH. 1, 3 (2006).

[30] *See, e.g.*, Lorrae van Kerkhoff & Nicole Szlezák, *Linking Local Knowledge with Global Action: Examining the Global Fund to Fight AIDS, Tuberculosis and Malaria through a Knowledge System Lens*, 84(3) BULLETIN OF THE WORLD HEALTH ORGANIZATION 629 (2006), www.scielosp.org/pdf/bwho/v84n8/v84n8a14.pdf.

[31] Peter B. Meyer, *Episodes of Collective Invention* 12–14 (US Department of Labor, Bureau of Labor Statistics, Working Paper 368, 2003), www.bls.gov/osmr/pdf/ec030050.pdf (describing the home brew computer club).

[32] *See* O'Mahony & Ferraro, *supra* note 23; Paul A. David, *The Economic Logic of "Open Science" and the Balance between Private Property Rights and the Public Domain in Scientific Data and Information: A Primer*, (SIEPR, Discussion Paper No. 02-30, 2003), http://129.3.20.41/eps/dev/papers/0502/0502006.pdf. *Cf.* Wendy J. Gordon, *Render Copyright unto Caesar: On Taking Incentives Seriously*, 71 U. CHI. L. REV. 75 (2004) (noting the problems arising when reciprocity of gifting is not present). But this does not always occur. Linus Torvalds is reported to be a multi-millionaire, see The Richest, www.therichest.com/celebnetworth/celebrity-business/tech-millionaire/linus-torvalds-net-worth/. Yet Linux continues to flourish.

efficacy of the appropriation mechanisms on which the project relied or drastically reduce the benefits of sharing.[33] Legal changes can have unanticipated ramifications. For example, the Bayh Dole Act, which encourages universities to take patent rights in the fruits of federally funded research, has led to greater faculty interest in proprietary research models and created conflicts of interest within universities that can undermine traditional sharing norms.[34]

Third, there are good reasons to be concerned about the kinds and numbers of works that are likely to be produced outside the standard systems. Many of the open projects cited by commentators like Benkler and Sprigman have low upfront costs. Software engineers, for example, are often self-taught and the only real expense they incur at the outset is the cost of buying a computer to program. In contrast, there are socially valuable projects that depend on participants with significant education and the availability of expensive equipment; without intellectual property protection it is doubtful the acquisition costs will be sunk. Pharmaceutical research, for example, requires doctors, pharmacologists, and chemists with advanced degrees, labware, complex instrumentation, and eventually, facilities to conduct clinical trials. While there are many open life sciences projects, they are usually intimately related to the efforts of proprietary firms.[35] Here, the motivation to acquire the

[33] The story behind *International News Service v. Associated Press*, 248 *U.S.* 215 (1918), where the Supreme Court created the tort of misappropriation to protect news stories is instructive. *See, e.g.*, Douglas G. Baird, *The Story of INS v. AP: Property, Natural Monopoly, and the Uneasy Legacy of a Concocted Controversy*, in INTELLECTUAL PROPERTY STORIES 9 (Jane C. Ginsburg & Rochelle Cooper Dreyfuss eds., 2006)(arguing that the norms undergirding sharing broke down when the papers could no longer rely on the exclusivity provided by the high cost of telegraphy) and Richard A. Epstein, *International News Service v. Associated Press: Custom and Law as Sources of Property Rights in News*, 78 VA. L. REV. 85 (1992) (arguing that the norms broke down because of the exigencies of World War I).

[34] 35 U.S.C. §§ 200–212 (2006). *See, e.g.*, Fiona Murray & Scott Stern, *Learning to Live with Patents: Assessing the Dynamic Adaptation to the Law by the Scientific Community* (November 2008), http://fmurray.scripts.mit.edu/docs/Murray.Stern_LearningtoLivewithPatents.pdf; *cf.* Pierre Azoulay et al., *The Determinants of Faculty Patenting Behavior: Demographics or Opportunities?*, 63 J. ECON. BEHAV. & ORG. 599 (2007) (noting that scientists who have collaborated with someone who holds patents are more likely than their peers to depart from the classic norms of science and become patentees themselves).

[35] *See, e.g.*, Katherine Strandburg, Brett Frischmann & Can Cui, *The Rare Diseases Clinical Research Network and the Urea Cycle Disorders Consortium as Nested Knowledge Commons*, in GOVERNING KNOWLEDGE COMMONS, *supra* note 23, at 155, 161–2. For an example of a firm that supports research and education, *see* the Burroughs Wellcome Fund, www.bwfund.org/.

appropriate training may well derive from the prospect of a position in the for-profit sector or the private partnership half of the collaboration – a firm that may be planning to acquire patents.[36] Furthermore, curiosity can take things only so far: in some cases, commercialization is so expensive, it will not always be undertaken without an assurance of exclusivity.[37]

Besides, not all projects are susceptible to the organizational structure that Benkler envisioned in his path-breaking work. His insight is based on the idea that work is granular: the Linux operating system, for example, can be segmented into subroutines that are coded de-centrally and asynchronously.[38] Where work cannot be divided so neatly or where contributors must interact dynamically, a more complex organization may be required. But as soon as hierarchy is introduced, it can produce tension among participants that threaten the operation as a whole.[39] A charismatic leader may be able to hold things together, but it is not always clear that the effort will survive if that leader disappears.[40]

There can also be problems at the back end of the creative process: in some fields, it is relatively easy to appropriate the gains attributable to innovation. New techniques (magic tricks, recipes) can be kept secret. The techniques themselves may be extremely difficult to reproduce (novel sporting maneuvers and cooking methods are examples). In cases where the main market for the work is performance, the ability to control physical access can be sufficient to capture the value of the work.[41] But not all intellectual production can benefit from these factors.

[36] *See, e.g.*, David Blumenthal, *Academic-Industrial Relationships in the Life Sciences*, 349 New Eng. J. Med. 2452 (2003); Anne M. Readel, *Finding A Cure: Incentivizing Partnerships Between Disease Advocacy Groups and Academic and Commercial Researchers*, 26 J.L. & Health 285, 287 (2013).

[37] *See generally* Ted Sichelman, *Commercializing Patents*, 62 Stan. L. Rev. 341 (2010).

[38] Yochai Benkler, *Coase's Penguin, or, Linux and the Nature of the Firm*, 112 Yale L.J. 369, 378–9 (2002).

[39] *See, e.g.*, Aniket Kittur et al., *He Says, She Says: Conflict and Coordination in Wikipedia*, CHI Proceedings 453, 453 (2007), http://dl.acm.org/citation.cfm?id=1240698&bnc=1 ("direct work (on articles) is decreasing, while indirect work such as discussion, procedure, user coordination, and maintenance activity (such as reverts and anti-vandalism) is increasing"). *See also* O'Mahoney & Bechky, *supra* note 23, at 435.

[40] Josh Lerner & Jean Tirole, *The Simple Economics of Open Source* 21–4 (HBS Finance Working Paper No. 00-059, 2000), http://ssrn.com/abstract=224008.

[41] *See, e.g.*, Peter Dicola, *Money from Music: Survey Evidence on Musicians' Revenue and Lessons about Copyright Incentives*, 55 Ariz. L. Rev. 301, 304 (2013) (reporting on a survey finding that musicians earn 12% of their revenue from sources directly related to copyright).

As Justice White put it in a case involving the unauthorized transmission of the act of being shot out of a cannon, intellectual property protection can be necessary to "provide an economic incentive . . . to make the investment required to produce a performance of interest to the public."[42]

While the main concern with eliminating intellectual property protection is likely the fear of underproduction, overproduction is also a significant threat. Fashion is a good example. In Sprigman and Raustiala's telling, fashion benefits from copying because proliferation initially makes certain styles desirable, but ubiquity later makes them obsolescent, thereby inducing people to buy newer outfits. But is it socially desirable to discard clothing that is still wearable? Is it environmentally sustainable?[43] Because style can affect perception,[44] there is an element of social coercion in continuous style changes. Furthermore, the user-generated content that might supplant professional production in a world without intellectual property may be of uneven quantity. Certainly, the upward of 100,000 sleepy kittens available on YouTube suggests that not all knowledge production is equally valuable. And as Steve Maurer has demonstrated, copyright supports not only the production of the initial work, but also important curating and quality-enhancing functions on the part of publishers and editors. In the absence of exclusive rights, those seeking information need to sift through much more material and there is less of a guarantee that the search will yield the best works.[45]

Finally, if intellectual property were eliminated, there would likely be many significant social costs. In the absence of legal protection against free riders, technical information that would otherwise be revealed in a patent might be hoarded. Rather than promote greater

[42] Zacchini v. Scripps-Howard Broad. Co., 433 U.S. 562, 576 (1977) (permitting the "human cannonball" to bring a right of publicity claim when his performance was transmitted in a newscast).

[43] See Pamela Ravasio, *How Can We Stop Water from Becoming a Fashion Victim?*, The Guardian (Mar. 7, 2012), https://www.theguardian.com/sustainable-business/water-scarcity-fashion-industry (noting the industry's heavy use of water and pollution of water resources).

[44] See, e.g., Dorothy U. Behling & Elizabeth A. Williams, *Influence of Dress on Perception of Intelligence and Expectations of Scholastic Achievement*, 9(4) Clothing and Textiles Research Journal 1–7 (1991); Damhorst, M. L., *In Search of a Common Thread: Classification of Information Communicated through Dress*, 8(2) Clothing and Textiles Research Journal 1, 1–12 (1990).

[45] Stephen M. Maurer, From Bards to Search Engines: Finding What Readers Want from Ancient Times to the World Wide Web, 66 S.C. L. Rev. 495 (2014).

openness, the absence of patent or copyright protection could instead distort protection in favor of inventions that can be kept secret.[46] When confidentiality agreements are used to maintain secrecy, knowledge workers may find themselves barred from moving to a new employer where their talents could be better used.[47] Historically, it is often marginalized groups that are denied protection for their work or are cut out from whatever benefits the project generates.[48] Because there are fields where new entrants rely heavily on intellectual property rights, the absence of protection could (perversely) reduce competition.[49] Or as the history of the fashion industry shows, incumbents may organize collusively to prevent competition from copyists – or entry by new firms.[50] Even more objectionable results could obtain. For example, Dan Kevles investigated the activities of breeders during a period when patents were unavailable to protect animals and plants. He found that they exerted considerable control over stocks, leading to severe inbreeding. Sometimes animals were poisoned before being sold to butchers so they could not be used for reproduction.[51]

[46] *See* Petra Moser, *Innovation Without Patents: Evidence from World's Fairs*, 55 J.L. & Econ. 43 (2012) (showing that inventiveness shifts depending on the relative strength of patents and trade secrets); Petra Moser, *How Do Patent Laws Influence Innovation? Evidence from Nineteenth-Century World Fairs*, 94 Am. Econ. Rev. 1214 (2005).

[47] *Cf.* Orly Lobel, Talent Wants to Be Free: Why We Should Learn to Love Leaks, Raids, and Free-Riding (2013) (discussing attempts to protect information at the expense of employee freedom).

[48] *See generally*, Rochelle Cooper Dreyfuss, *Collaborative Research: Conflicts on Authorship, Ownership, and Accountability*, 53 Vand. L. Rev. 1161 (2000); Buccafusco, *supra* note 19, at 1145 ("the lowly status of cuisine was further cemented by the fact that women, either in their capacity as housewives or as domestic servants, performed the cooking in most households. . . . Accordingly, it would have been asking quite a lot of Victorians – or even of twenty-first century copyright law, mired as it is in Romantic notions of originality, creation, and authorship – to recognize the expressive potential of such a dismal affair as food preparation.") (Footnotes omitted). *See generally* The Recipe Reader (Janet Floyd & Laurel Forster eds., 2003).

[49] *See, e.g.*, Ted Sichelman & Stuart J. H. Graham, *Patenting by Entrepreneurs: An Empirical Study*, 17 Mich. Telecomm. & Tech. L. Rev. 111, 115 (2010); Stuart J. H. Graham et al., *High Technology Entrepreneurs and the Patent System: Results of the 2008 Berkeley Patent Survey*, 24 Berkeley Tech L.J. 1255 (2010); Bronwyn H. Hall, *Exploring the Patent Explosion*, 30 J. Tech. Transfer 35 (2004).

[50] *See* Fashion Originators' Guild of America v. Federal Trade Commission, 312 U.S. 457 (1941) (finding agreements among fashion designers per se illegal under U.S. antitrust laws).

[51] Daniel J. Kevles, Patents, Protections, and Privileges: The Establishment of Intellectual Property in Animals and Plants (2007).

II Returning to Incentive-Based Intellectual Property Law

The two phenomena described in the Introduction – the interest in creative production outside the standard intellectual property system, along with the successive commodification and assetization of intellectual property rights – are not entirely disconnected in that the impulse to abolish intellectual property rights can be attributed, at least in part, to the tendency of rising standards of protection to threaten other values. Excessive protection produces high deadweight loss, for those who cannot afford to pay supra-competitive prices must forgo beneficial uses. In cumulative industries and in sectors where interoperability is critical, greater control can also protect incumbents from disruptive market entrants.[52] As the United States Supreme Court put it in a case on patentable subject matter, "We have repeatedly emphasized [the] concern that patent law not inhibit further discovery by tying up the future use of [the] building blocks of human ingenuity."[53]

In our article, Frankel and I provided examples of how continual ratcheting up protection at the international level can affect the public interest. Consider, for example, trade law's emphasis on comparative advantage, which is effectuated, in part, by TRIPS's ban on discrimination based on "whether products are imported or locally produced."[54] The provision gives patent holders discretion to locate manufacturing facilities in the place that maximizes returns. However, it also endangers the power of WTO countries to rely on a carefully crafted provision in the Paris Convention which permits states to compulsorily license patents when patent holders do not work them locally.[55] Some FTAs outright ban

[52] *See, e.g.*, William M. Landes & Richard A. Posner, The Economic Structure of Intellectual Property Law 16–21 (2003).

[53] Alice Corp. Pty. Ltd. v. CLS Bank Int'l, 573 U.S. _ (2014) (internal citation omitted), 134 S. Ct. 2347 (2014).

[54] TRIPS, *supra* note 5, art. 27.1.

[55] Paris Convention for the Protection of Industrial Property, July 14, 1967, 21 U.S.T. 1583, 828 U.N.T.S. 305, art. 5 [hereinafter Paris Convention]. *See* Nuno Pires de Carvalho, The TRIPS Regime of Patent Rights § 27.66 (2010). *But see* Thomas Cottier, Shaheeza Lalani & Michelangelo Temmerman, *Use it or Lose it? Assessing the Compatibility of the Paris Convention & TRIPS with Respect to Local Working Requirements*, at Appendix 4-5 (NCCR Trade Regulation: Swiss National Center of Competence in Research, Working Paper No. 2012/11, 2013), www.wti.org/research/publication/?tx_nccr_pi1%5Bshow%5D=615&cHash=70ccd8fc56eb1a546240ac35c8f25239 (suggesting that working may be permissible for developing countries). A WTO challenge to a compulsory license issued by Brazil was withdrawn: see Notification of Mutually Agreed Solution, *Brazil – Measures Affecting Patent Protection*, WTO

the issuance of compulsory licenses on the grounds of nonworking.[56] And bilateral investment treaties may well treat the implementation of a working requirement as an expropriation.[57] As a result, developing countries may be in the process of losing the power to demand that patent holders create infrastructure, provide training opportunities, or organize their activities in ways that lead them to offer products suitable to local conditions.

Similar observations apply to national regulations intended to protect health and welfare. TRIPS lays down four "general exceptions" tests that impose significant limits on public-regarding actions that limit exclusivity.[58] The drafters took a standard that the Berne Convention had used to protect the most important stick in the copyright bundle (the reproduction right[59]) and applied it with minor adaptation to every intellectual property right, no matter how insignificant. As the WTO resolution of two challenges (one on patents, the other on copyright) shows, interpretation of these provisions centers on the interest of right holders and the protectionist impact of the legislation.[60] Little room remains for adjudicators to consider the public purpose behind, or the public effect of, the intervention. Admittedly, in a later dispute, the trademark exception was interpreted more liberally.[61] However, TRIPS adds another stumbling block in trademark cases: trademarks may not be "unjustifiably" encumbered.[62] Moreover, because investment-backed "expectations" may be interpreted differently from TRIPS standards, an action that

Doc. WT/DS/199/4 (July 19, 2001), www.wto.org/english/tratop_e/dispu_e/cases_e/ds199_e.htm.

56 *See, e.g.*, The Australia–United States Free Trade Agreement, U.S.-Austl., art. 17.9, May 18, 2004, 43 I.L.M. 1248 [hereinafter AUSFTA].

57 *See* Henning Grosse Ruse-Khan, *Protecting Intellectual Property Under BITS, FTAS, and TRIPS: Conflicting Regimes or Mutual Coherence?*, in Evolution in Investment Treaty Law and Arbitration 485, 497(K. Miles & C. Brown eds., 2011) (noting Merck's reaction to a Brazilian decision to require local working).

58 TRIPS, *supra* note 5, arts. 13, 17, 26.2 & 30.

59 Berne Convention for the Protection of Literary and Artistic Works, art. 9(2), July 24, 1971, 1161 U.N.T.S. 31. [hereinafter Berne Convention].

60 *See* Panel Report, *Canada – Patent Protection of Pharmaceutical Products*, WT/DS114/R (Mar. 17, 2000) [hereinafter *Canada – Pharmaceuticals*]; Panel Report, *United States – Section 110(5) of the US Copyright Act*, WT/DS/160/R (June 15, 2000) [hereinafter *U.S.-110(5)*].

61 Panel Report, *European Communities – Geographical Indications for Agricultural Products and Foodstuffs*, WT/DS174/R (Mar. 15, 2005) [hereinafter *EC–GI*].

62 TRIPS, *supra* note 5, art. 20.

the WTO regards as TRIPS-compatible may nonetheless be challenged in arbitration under a BIT.[63]

In our article, Frankel and I argued that protection of the public interest requires that commodification (through TRIPS) and assetization (through investment treaties) should be understood using an incentive-based lens. While we were under no illusion that Rob Merges is correct that there are "computational complexities" inherent in such an approach to intellectual property law,[64] returning to an incentive theory

[63] The difference between the two systems could come to the fore in a series of disputes on the plain packaging of tobacco products: see, for example, Tobacco Plain Packaging Act 2011 (Cth) §§ 18–26 (Austl.) because one set of challenges was lodged in the WTO while another was brought by investors under bilateral investment agreements. For the WTO challenges, see Request for the Establishment of a Panel by Ukraine, *Australia – Certain Measures Concerning Trademarks and Other Plain Packaging Requirements Applicable to Tobacco Products and Packaging*, WT/DS434/11 (Aug. 17, 2012) (panel composed May 5, 2014); Request for the Establishment of a Panel by Honduras, *Australia – Certain Measures Concerning Trademarks, Geographical Indications and Other Plain Packaging Requirements Applicable to Tobacco Products and Packaging*, WT/DS435/16 (Oct. 17, 2012) (panel composed May 5, 2014); Request for the Establishment of a Panel by the Dominican Republic, *Australia – Certain Measures Concerning Trademarks, Geographical Indications and Other Plain Packaging Requirements Applicable to Tobacco Products and Packaging*, WT/DS441/15 (Nov. 14, 2012) (panel composed May 5, 2014); *Australia – Certain Measures Concerning Trademarks, Geographical Indications and Other Plain Packaging Requirements Applicable to Tobacco Products and Packaging*, WT/DS458/1 (May 7, 2013) (panel composed May 5, 2014). There are other agreements that Australia is arguably also violating, in particular the Agreement on Technical Barriers to Trade, Marrakesh Agreement Establishing the World Trade Organization, Annex 1A, Apr. 15, 1994, 1868 U.N.T.S. 120. As to the investment dispute, while Philip Morris's Australian challenge was dismissed on procedural grounds, see *Philip Morris Asia Limited (Hong Kong) v. The Commonwealth of Australia*, Award on Jurisdiction and Admissibility in which it declined jurisdiction, PCA Case No. 2012-12 (Dec. 17, 2015), available at www.italaw.com/sites/default/files/case-documents/italaw7303_0.pdf, its case involving Uruguay was decided in favor of the state's ability to regulate tobacco packaging, see *Philip Morris Brands Sarl v. Uruguay*, ICSID Case No. ARB/10/7 (8 July 2016), available at www.italaw.com/sites/default/files/case-documents/italaw7417.pdf. See generally, Henning Grosse Ruse-Khan, *supra* note 57, at 485, 493–4. But even if investor disputes end in decisions favorable to the regulating countries, defending such cases is extremely expensive. As a result, countries that wish to curb rights to effectuate public purposes may be dissuaded from legislating. Similar problems arise on the patent front, where Eli Lilly had accused Canada of violating the North American Free Trade Agreement (NAFTA) by "expropriating" its patents in respect of the pharmaceutical products, Strattera and Zyprexa. Although Canada prevailed, *Eli Lilly and Co. v. Government of Canada*, Case No. ICSID Case No. UNCT/14/2, Final Award (March 16, 2017), the case leaves a great deal of room for more disputes, see Rochelle Cooper Dreyfuss and Susy Frankel, *Reconceptualizating ISDS: When is IP an Investment and How Much Can States Regulate It?*, _ VAND. J. ENT. & TECH. L. _ (forthcoming, 2018).

[64] MERGES, *supra* note 2, at 3. See also Lemley, *supra* note 2.

does not require *titration* of the rewards made available to encourage innovation. Rough justice would be enough to restore a place for other values. Given the risks outlined above, returning intellectual property to its original justifications is far better than eliminating the possibility of protection.

U.S. Justice Stephen Breyer's dissent in *Golan v. Holder*[65] provides an illustration of how reliance on an incentive-based rationale could work to protect other values. The case was a challenge to a provision of U.S. copyright law enacted in 1994 to comply with an international requirement that all WTO members protect works that remain under copyright in their country of origin.[66] Under the new legislation, copyright could be restored for works protected abroad that had fallen into the public domain in the United States because there was no protection available at the time of publication or because of failure to comply with statutory formalities.[67] The petitioners, orchestra conductors, musicians, publishers, and other users who had formerly enjoyed free access to the works, challenged the restoration as a violation of their right to free speech under the U.S. Constitution.[68]

The majority opinion (penned by Justice Ginsburg) rejected the challenge, principally on the grounds that the petitioners had no vested interest in using these works[69] and that "Congress determined that U.S. interests were best served by our full participation in the dominant system of international copyright protection."[70] In dissent, Justice Breyer took the petitioner's expressive interests in access more seriously. Positing that a "tax on readers for the purpose of giving a bounty to writers" is appropriate only "to encourage new production,"[71] he considered how likely it was that the added protection would, in fact, encourage new production. Finding that the extra motivation would not offset administrative costs or the burden imposed on those in the position of the petitioners,[72] Breyer would have found the new statute a violation of the Constitution. Further, he refuted the notion that international law or global objectives required restoration. He suggested that had negotiators appreciated the incentive function of copyright, they could have secured a reservation permitting the United States to keep the

65 565 U.S. 302 (2012).
66 TRIPS, *supra* note 5, art. 9.1; Berne Convention, *supra* note 59, art. 18.1.
67 17 U.S.C. § 104A (2006). 68 U.S. CONST. amend. I. 69 565 U.S. 302, 331 (2012).
70 *Id.* at 894. 71 *Id.* at 899 (Breyer J., dissenting).
72 *Id.* at 908 ("The statute grants its 'restored copyright[s]' only to works already produced. It provides no monetary incentive to produce anything new").

works in the public domain.[73] Alternatively, the drafters of the Copyright Act could have used the flexibilities in the Berne Convention to craft a better balance.[74] In a dissent in an earlier case, *Eldred v. Ashcroft*,[75] on the constitutionality of extending the term of copyright by twenty years, Justice Breyer made similar points. Calculating the benefit of the extension as worth less than 7 cents, he argued that no author "would be moved by such a sum."[76] Further, he noted that Congress's stated goal of achieving international uniformity would not be fulfilled in any event because of other differences among national copyright laws.[77]

In these decisions, Justice Breyer made three noteworthy observations: local laws should be geared to providing incentives to innovate, not to ensuring maximum return; international flexibilities should similarly be considered in light of an incentive, rather than a profit-maximization, theory; and when negotiating international agreements, negotiators must be alive to this distinction.

A Domestic Law

Golan and *Eldred* considered the duration of protection, but the term of exclusivity is far from the only place where greater attention to incentive theory would protect important social interests. For situations where Sprigman and Raustiala are clearly correct, and there is no need for intellectual property protection to spur creative production, limitations on protectable subject matter provide a useful tool. Patent law furnishes several examples. Thus, many countries do not protect methods of doing business.[78] The theory is that a new method for conducting a business operation is not a technical advance and any cost entailed in developing a business method can be recouped through

[73] *Id.* at 911. Significantly, TRIPS exempted moral rights, which can also inhibit free speech from mandatory protection, TRIPS, *supra* note 5, art. 9., citing Berne Convention, *supra* note 59, art. 6bis.

[74] *Id.* at 911, citing Berne Convention, *supra* note 59, art. 18.3 (providing that "the respective countries shall determine, each in so far as it is concerned, the conditions of application of [the restoration] principle").

[75] Eldred v. Ashcroft, 537 U.S. 186 (2003).

[76] Id. at 254–5 (Breyer, J., dissenting).

[77] Id. at 257–8.

[78] *See, e.g.*, European Patent Convention, art. 52(2)(c), Oct. 7, 1977, 1065 U.N.T.S. 199 [hereinafter EPC]; REPORT ON COMPARATIVE STUDY CARRIED OUT UNDER TRILATERAL PROJECT B3B BUSINESS METHOD RELATED INVENTIONS 13 (2001), http://www.trilateral.net/projects/Comparative/business/Main.pdf (stressing the non-technical nature of business method advances).

lead time advantages, which are often prolonged because of the difficulty that rivals will experience identifying the change in business practice, reverse engineering it, and implementing it themselves.[79] Similarly, basic diagnostic tests tend to be developed by physicians under ethical obligations to treat patients, by academics interested in the etiology of disease, and by pharmaceutical companies interested in selling drugs to those patients who can benefit from them. Accordingly, there have been suggestions that they too should be outside the realm of protection.[80]

In some situations, it may not be that protection is unnecessary, but rather that if intellectual property protection is offered, the return will greatly exceed that which is necessary to induce innovation. Thus, many countries exclude from patentability laws of nature and scientific theories on the ground that they "risk disproportionately tying up the use of the underlying ideas."[81] (What can be protected are individual implementations of these ideas.) In the United States, for example, genomic DNA is excluded, leaving the material free for the use of researchers and patients, but complementary DNA and other human-made alterations of DNA are protectable.[82]

[79] *See, e.g.*, Rochelle Cooper Dreyfuss, *Are Business Method Patents Bad for Business?*, 16 SANTA CLARA COMPUTER & HIGH TECH. L.J. 264 (2000); *cf.* Alice Corp. Pty. Ltd. v. CLS Bank Int'l, 573 U.S. _ (2014), 134 S.Ct. 2347 (2014) (Sotomayor, Ginsburg, and Breyer, concurring in a decision that a computer implemented method for mitigating settlement risk is not patentable subject matter on the ground that business methods are not statutory subject matter).

[80] *See, e.g.*, Mayo Collaborative Services v. Prometheus Laboratories, Inc., 566 U.S. 66 (2012); Sec'y's Advisory Comm. on Genetics, Health, and Soc'y, Report on Gene Patents and Licensing Practices and Their Impact on Patient Access to Genetic Tests,, http://oba.od.nih.gov/oba/SACGHS/SACGHS%20Patents%20Report%20Approved%202-5-20010.pdf. *See also* Rochelle Cooper Dreyfuss, *We Are Symbols and Inhabit Symbols, So Should We Be Paying Rent? Deconstructing the Lanham Act and Rights of Publicity*, 20 COLUM.-VLA J. L. & ARTS 123 (1996) (suggesting that rights of publicity do not serve a motivating purpose and should not be recognized).

[81] Alice Corp. Pty. Ltd. v. CLS Bank Int'l, 573 U.S. _ (2014), 134 S.Ct. 2347 (2014); EPC, *supra* note 78, art. 52(2)(a); Nuffield Council on Bioethics, *The Ethics of Patenting DNA*, at § 5.22 (2002), http://www.nuffieldbioethics.org/patenting-dna/patenting-dna-chapter-downloads ("allowing property rights to be asserted over all uses, or even all diagnostic uses, of DNA sequences for diagnostic tests based on DNA sequences gives inventors too great a monopoly in the light of the contribution and inventiveness of their product [and] may hamper innovation").

[82] *See* Ass'n for Molecular Pathology v. Myriad Genetics, 569 U.S. 576, 589 (2013), 133 S.Ct. 2107, 2116 (2013) (if patents were available on laws of nature, phenomena of nature and abstract ideas, there would "be considerable danger that the grant of patents would 'tie up' the use of such tools and thereby 'inhibit future innovation premised upon them'").

The inventive step requirement in patent law (nonobviousness) can also function as an important policy lever.[83] Starting with the Supreme Court's statement in *Graham v. John Deere* that patents should be awarded only to "those inventions which would not be disclosed or devised but for the inducement of a patent,"[84] Michael Abramowicz and John Duffy have shown that fidelity to what they call the "inducement standard" of patentability can minimize the conflict between public and private interests.[85] A suitably substantial inventive step would eliminate patents on advances that became easy because of exogenous technological developments or because regulatory changes make the advance commercializable; such a standard of inventiveness could also lead to the denial of patents when there are other reasons to invent. As the U.S. Supreme Court put it in *KSR International v. Teleflex, Inc.*:

> [M]arket demand, rather than scientific literature, may often drive design trends. Granting patent protection to advances that would occur in the ordinary course without real innovation retards progress.[86]

Other countries have also used this approach. India, for example, does not award patents on variations of known compounds that do not significantly alter efficacy or on a new use of a known compound unless a new reactant is involved.[87] These marginal improvements are vastly cheaper to make than finding new drugs; improving access to them can substantially lower the price of healthcare.[88] As Diane Zimmerman has argued, similar results could be obtained in copyright law through greater attention to the originality requirement.[89] Several other prerequisites for protection (disclosure, novelty and use in patent law; the idea/expression dichotomy and merger doctrine in copyright law; distinctiveness and continuing use in trademark law) could be leveraged in a similar manner.

[83] *Cf.* Burk & Lemley, *supra* note 2; DAN L. BURK & MARK A. LEMLEY, THE PATENT CRISIS AND HOW COURTS CAN SOLVE IT (2009) (describing how many of the tools mentioned here can be used to tailor the law to the needs of particular industries).

[84] 383 U.S. 1, 11 (1966).

[85] Michael Abramowicz & John F. Duffy, *The Inducement Standard of Patentability*, 120 YALE L.J. 1590 (2011).

[86] 550 U.S. 398, 419 (2007).

[87] The Patents Act, No. 39 of 1970, § 3(d) (Universal 2005) (India); Novartis AG v. Union of India, AIR 2013 SC.

[88] See GRAEME B. DINWOODIE & ROCHELLE COOPER DREYFUSS, A NEOFEDERALIST VISION OF TRIPS: THE RESILIENCE OF THE INTERNATIONAL INTELLECTUAL PROPERTY REGIME 51–3 (2012).

[89] Diane Leenheer Zimmerman, *It's an Original!(?): In Pursuit of Copyright's Elusive Essence*, 28 COLUM. J.L. & ARTS 187 (2005).

Restrictions on protection take an all-or-nothing approach, which may not be suitable in cases where motivating invention requires protection, but protection threatens other values. However, incentive-based approaches to infringement, to defenses to infringement, and to the availability of compulsory licenses also offer avenues for safeguarding human rights, development, and culture. The fair use provision in U.S. copyright law is a perfect example.[90] As Pam Samuelson notes:

> The policies underlying modern fair use law include promoting freedom of speech and of expression, the ongoing progress of authorship, learning, access to information, truth telling or truth seeking, competition, technological innovation, and the privacy and autonomy interests of users.[91]

The statute does not, however, permit unauthorized use – even for important public purposes – if the impact of the use on the market for the copyrighted work is too severe.[92] In patent law, rights to experiment serve essentially the same purposes.[93] As with fair use, experimentation that is "merely for philosophical experiments"[94] does not intrude upon the right holder's profits enough to impair the incentive to produce, yet it facilitates future research and creates opportunities for others to find applications that the right holder is not able or prepared to develop.[95] Trademark fair use is to the same effect: it releases expressive uses to the public while preserving the right holder's ability to distinguish its goods and to send consumers signals about source and quality.[96]

Other infringement doctrines have a similar capacity to mediate between public and private interests. As (now Judge) Kimberly Moore

[90] 17 U.S.C. § 107 (2006).

[91] Pamela Samuelson, *Unbundling Fair Uses*, 99 FORDHAM L. REV. 2537, 2537 (2009).

[92] *See, e.g.*, Harper & Row, Publishers, Inc. v. Nation Enters., 471 U.S. 539, 566 (1985) (the effect of the use on the market for the work is "undoubtedly the single most important element of fair use").

[93] For description of national experimental use provisions, see Heinz Goddar, *The Experimental Use Exception: A European Perspective*, 7 CASRIP SYMP. PUBLICATION SERIES 10 (2001), http://www.law.washington.edu/casrip/Symposium/Number7/1-Goddar.pdf; Jennifer A. Johnson, *The Experimental Use Exception in Japan: A Model for U.S. Patent Law?*, 12 PAC. RIM L. & POL'Y J. 499 (2003).

[94] Whittemore v. Cutter, 29 F. Cas. 1120, 1121 (C.C.D. Mass. 1813) (No. 17,600) (Story, J.).

[95] *See generally*, Janice M. Mueller, *The Evanescent Experimental Use Exemption from United States Patent Infringement Liability: Implications for University and Nonprofit Research and Development*, 56 BAYLOR L. REV. 917 (2004); Katherine J. Strandburg, *What Does the Public Get?: Experimental Use and the Patent Bargain*, WIS. L. REV. 81 (2004).

[96] Rochelle Cooper Dreyfuss, *Expressive Genericity: Trademarks as Language in the Pepsi Generation*, 65 NOTRE DAME L. REV. 397 (1990).

recognized, accurate patent claim construction is an important way to "strike a balance between the need to encourage innovative efforts and the need for competition."[97] On the copyright side, reference to incentives can help determine the limits of the right to control derivative works.[98] For all three intellectual property regimes, the first sale doctrine (exhaustion) reduces deadweight loss. It permits right holders to avail themselves of *a* market for the work, but once an authorized copy is sold, that embodiment can be resold – usually at a lower price.[99] In small and developing countries, the power to import goods previously sold elsewhere ("international exhaustion" or "parallel importation") can be a particularly effective way to secure materials of fundamental importance to education, health, and welfare at reduced cost.[100]

Finally, there is the matter of remedies. Presently, the law generally compensates for the *private* injury sustained,[101] but this is an area in profound need of reconsideration. Calculating the amount of harm has proved complicated in many circumstances. The real cost of premature exposure of a copyrighted work can be difficult to reckon,[102] as can the reputational harm entailed in unauthorized use of a trademark.[103] In patent law, there is no good theory for determining what a right holder

[97] Kimberly A. Moore, *Are District Court Judges Equipped to Resolve Patent Cases?*, 12 FED. CIRCUIT B.J. 1, 33 (2002).

[98] *See, e.g.*, Shyamkrishna Balganesh, *Foreseeability and Copyright Incentives*, 122 HARV. L. REV. 1569 (2009).

[99] *See, e.g.*, Saami Zain, *Quanta Leap or Much Ado about Nothing? An Analysis on the Effect of Quanta vs. LG Electronics*, 20 ALB. L.J. SCI. & TECH. 67 (2010) (discussing Quanta Computer, Inc. v. L.G. Elec., Inc., 553 U.S. 617 (2008)). See also Kirtsaeng v. John Wiley & Sons, Inc., 136 S.Ct. 1979 (2016) ("competition, including freedom to resell, can work to the advantage of the consumer").

[100] *See, e.g.*, CAROLS M. CORREA, INTELLECTUAL PROPERTY RIGHTS, THE WTO AND DEVELOPING COUNTRIES: THE TRIPS AGREEMENT AND POLICY OPTIONS 86–8 (2000). SUSY FRANKEL, TEST TUBES FOR GLOBAL INTELLECTUAL PROPERTY ISSUES: SMALL MARKET ECONOMIES (2015). *See also* Kirtsaeng v. John Wiley & Sons, Inc., 136 S.Ct. 1979 (2016) ("the Constitution's language nowhere suggests that its limited exclusive right should include a right to divide markets or a concomitant right to charge different purchasers different prices for the same book, say to increase or to maximize gain").

[101] *See e.g.* 17 U.S.C. § 504 (a) (2006) ("actual damages") (copyright); 35 U.S.C. § 284 (2006) ("damages adequate to compensate") (patent); 15 U.S.C. § 1117 (2006) ("(1) defendant's profits (2) any damages sustained by the plaintiff") (trademark).

[102] *See, e.g.*, Harper & Row, Publishers, Inc. v. Nation Enters., 471 U.S. 539 (1985); 17 U.S.C. 504(c) (2006) (providing for statutory damages in lieu of actual damages).

[103] *See, e.g.*, Harolds Stores, Inc. v. Dillard Department Stores, Inc., 82 F.3d 1533 (10th Cir. 1996) (admitting survey evidence on what consumers thought about the original when viewing the infringing work).

deserves when its invention is one of thousands necessary to bring the product in which it is found to market.[104] Because of these problems, courts have been prone to overcompensate, but overcompensation has led to windfalls and to the proliferation of opportunistic litigation strategies.[105] To complicate matters, ready access to injunctive relief has historically made it extremely difficult to negotiate settlements with opportunists.[106]

In a path-breaking article on patent law, Ted Sichelman has proposed rethinking what he calls the "private law premise" and substituting an incentive-based approach. To trim excessive awards, he would award only the relief necessary to provide adequate incentives to invest in research and development and to engage in the activity necessary to commercialize the invention.[107] Although Sichelman recognizes that lowering the amount of relief may lead to more infringement, he argues that the cost of sub-maximal enforcement is offset by the reduction in deadweight loss.[108] Reducing the cost of infringement (and occasionally, under-deterring it) would, once again, leave considerable room to further other national objectives. Lowering damages in infringement litigation might also have an impact on the amount of compensation considered appropriate to award in compulsory licensing situations. Bringing the fees closer to the amount necessary to induce innovation would eliminate the concern that these licenses deter innovation and thus would make that a more palatable way to improve access.[109]

104 *See, e.g.*, LaserDynamics Inc. v. Quanta Computers, 694 F.3d 51, 67 (Fed. Cir. 2012); Lucent Techs., Inc. v. Gateway, Inc., 580 F.3d 1301 (Fed. Cir. 2009). *See generally*, Amy L. Landers, *Let the Games Begin: Incentives to Innovation in the New Economy of Intellectual Property Law*, 46 SANTA CLARA L. REV. 307 (2006).

105 *See, e.g.*, James Bessen & Michael J. Meurer, *The Direct Costs from NPE Disputes*, 99 CORNELL L. REV. 387 (2014); J. Cam Barker, *Grossly Excessive Penalties in the Battle Against Illegal File-Sharing: The Troubling Effects of Aggregating Minimum Statutory Damages for Copyright Infringement*, 83 TEX. L. REV. 525 (2004).

106 *See, e.g.*, eBay v. MercExchange, LLC, 547 U.S. 388 (2006). *See also* Mark A. Lemley & Carl Shapiro, *Patent Holdup and Royalty Stacking*, 85 TEX. L. REV. 1991 (2007).

107 Ted Sichelman, *Purging Patent Law of "Private Law" Remedies*, 92 TEX. L. REV. 517 (2014) (noting that, depending on context, the award under an incentives system can be higher or lower than the compensatory award).

108 *See* Ian Ayres & Paul Klemperer, *Limiting Patentees' Market Power Without Reducing Innovation Incentives: The Perverse Benefits of Uncertainty and Non-Injunctive Remedies*, 97 MICH. L. REV. 985 (1999).

109 *See* Colleen Chien, *Cheap Drugs at What Price to Innovation: Does the Compulsory Licensing of Pharmaceuticals Hurt Innovation?*, 18 BERKELEY TECH. L.J. 853 (2003). *But see* Richard A. Epstein & F. Scott Kieff, *Questioning the Frequency and Wisdom of Compulsory Licensing for Pharmaceutical Patents*, 78 U. CHI. L. REV. 71 (2011) (suggesting that compulsory licensing destroys incentives to innovate). See also

Greater attention to incentives would not always mean that the creative community gets less out of intellectual property protection. Sichelman, for example, would increase the award of damages in cases where infringement is difficult to detect.[110] Furthermore, other relief may be appropriate and more valuable. As noted above, innovation without intellectual property rights often occurs because participants are interested in reputational gains. But in many countries attribution is poorly protected. The United States, for example, provides very little protection for moral rights and deems employers the "authors" of works made for hire;[111] other countries provide sparse recognition of inventors.[112] If intellectual property regimes were better designed to ensure that identity of the creator responsible for the work is always publicly available, incentives to innovate could be enhanced without increasing the cost of access.[113]

B *Compatibility with International Obligations*

As Justice Breyer implicitly noted in his discussion of the flexibilities the Berne Convention provides on copyright restoration, countries cannot use the policy levers in domestic law to achieve other goals unless their actions are compatible with international obligations. Although, as Frankel and I found, the scope of these obligations is continually increasing, an incentive-based approach to interpretation would leave considerable leeway to protect important public interests. Furthermore, because international obligations are formulated in terms of standards rather than rules, an incentives-based approach to interpreting the requirements of

James Love, Remuneration Guidelines for Non-Voluntary Use of a Patent on Medical Technologies (2005), http://apps.who.int/iris/bitstream/10665/69199/1/WHO_TCM_2005.1_eng.pdf?ua=1.

110 Sichelman, *supra* note 107, at 525–6.

111 17 U.S.C. §§ 106A (protecting only certain works of visual art) & 201(b) (2006) (works made for hire). The interpretation of the provision on joint authorship, 17 U.S.C. § 201 (a) (2006), collaborators can also be insufficiently rewarded, *see, e.g., Childress v. Taylor,* 945 F.2d 500 (2d Cir. 1991) (requiring each author to make a copyrightable contribution to the overall work). *See also* Dastar Corp. v. Twentieth Century Fox Film Corp., 539 U.S. 23 (2003) (refusing to use trademark law to assure attribution).

112 *See, e.g.,* EPC, Rule 19(2) ("The European Patent Office shall not verify the accuracy of the designation of the inventor."). *Ethicon, Inc. v. U.S. Surgical Corp.,* 135 F.3d 1456 (Fed. Cir. 1998) presents something of the opposite problem: it allocates too much to someone who contributed to only a small number of the claims.

113 *See, e.g.,* Jeanne C. Fromer, *Expressive Incentives in Intellectual Property,* 98 Va. L. Rev. 1745, 1778 & 1789–98 (2012).

international law would not suffer from the computational disadvantages that Merges and others have noted in connection with using incentive theory to calibrate domestic legislation.[114]

For several of the approaches suggested above, TRIPS apparently gives WTO members considerable flexibility. Although the Agreement requires protection of all "inventions . . . in all fields of technology, provided they are new, involve an inventive step and are capable of industrial application," it defines none of the relevant terms.[115] Furthermore, it includes several potential exclusions from patentability, including for diagnostic methods and inventions necessary to protect morality and health.[116] For trademarks, TRIPS mandates certain coverage,[117] but even here, there are apparent flexibilities. Protected marks must be capable of distinguishing the goods and there is no obligation to register foreign marks if they are "devoid of distinctive character" or contrary to morality or public order.[118] As to copyright, international protection has always been more detailed (and author-centric[119]). Nonetheless, there is considerable room for nations to protect public values. Neither Berne nor TRIPS provides a definition of what constitutes authorship, copyright ownership, or originality.[120] There are specific exclusions for ideas, procedures and methods of operation.[121] While Berne includes an obligation to protect moral rights – which some countries see as a major impediment to free speech – TRIPS specifically excludes that

114 *See* Merges, *supra* note 2 (noting computational complexities); Lemley, *supra* note 2, at 112 (noting the difficulty in computing the incentives required to promote innovation and expressing skepticism that the Sichelman model could be implemented in practice).

115 TRIPS, *supra* note 5, art. 27.1. It does say that capable of industrial application" and "inventive step" are synonymous with "useful" and "nonobvious," Art. 27.1 n. 6. but the Agreement does not define these terms either.

116 *Id.* at arts. 27.2 & 27.3.

117 *See, e.g.*, Paris Convention, art. 6 quinquies A (requiring telle quelle registration); art. 6bis (requiring protection of well-known marks); TRIPS Agreement, *supra* note 5, art. 15 (requiring protection for marks that are visually perceptible).

118 TRIPS, art. 15.1; Paris Convention, art. 6 quinquies B.

119 *See, e.g.*, André Lucas & Henri-Jacques Lucas, Traité de la Propriété Littéraire et Artistique (2d ed. 2001); Jean-Luc Piotraut, *An Authors' Rights-Based Copyright Law: The Fairness and Morality of French and American Law Compared*, 24 Cardozo Arts & Ent. L.J. 549 (2006).

120 *See* Jane C. Ginsburg, *The Concept of Authorship in Comparative Copyright Law*, 52 DePaul L. Rev. 1063 (2003).

121 TRIPS, *supra* note 5, art. 9.2. *See generally*, Jane C. Ginsburg, *International Copyright: From A "Bundle" of National Copyright Laws to A Supranational Code?*, 47 J. Copyright Soc'y U.S.A.265, 289 (2000).

obligation.[122] For all the intellectual property regimes, TRIPS also allows members to determine their own rules on international exhaustion.[123] For remedies, the room for national flexibilities is even more pronounced. TRIPS leaves members free to determine implementation methods[124] and the enforcement provisions begin with the proviso that no country is obliged to put in place a judicial system for intellectual property that is distinct from how it enforces the law in general.[125]

Still, the import of these provisions will be a matter of interpretation, for the standards would be meaningless if WTO members were given free rein to define them. For example, even with respect to the relatively deferential standards on remedies, a WTO dispute resolution panel found that "substantive obligations . . . are not simply matters of national discretion."[126] The panel did, however, hold that so long as a country gives its judges the given authority to order monetary and injunctive relief, enforcement obligations have been satisfied, irrespective of whether these authorities are exercised.[127] For many of the other proposed national measures, the three WTO cases that interpreted the general exceptions tests suggest that scrutiny in the WTO may be much more intrusive.[128] And as Frankel and I argued, there may be even less discretion available in the context of FTA and BIT disputes.

Nonetheless, reliance on an incentive-based approach to interpretation at the international level would leave states with considerable flexibility to safeguard human rights as well as cultural and economic development. Take, for example, the working requirement.[129] Working requirements are attractive to developing countries because local exploitation creates jobs and training opportunities. Furthermore, a credible threat to issue a compulsory license can lead patent holders to lower their prices or develop products at price points and with features that are

[122] Berne Convention, *supra* note 59, art. 6 bis; TRIPS, *supra* note 5, art. 9.1.
[123] TRIPS, *supra* note 5, art. 6. [124] *Id.* at art. 1.1. [125] *Id.* at art. 41.5.
[126] Panel Report, *China – Measures Affecting the Protection and Enforcement of Intellectual Property Rights*, WT/DS362/R ¶ 7.507 (Jan. 26, 2009) [hereinafter *China-Enforcement*]. *See also* ¶ 7.513 ("The third sentence of Article 1.1 does not grant Members freedom to implement a lower standard, but rather grants freedom to determine the appropriate method of implementation of the provisions to which they are required to give effect under the first sentence").
[127] *See, e.g., id.* at ¶ 7.240. The China-Enforcement panel did not, however, expressly confront the question whether the remedies provided were sufficient to "constitute a deterrent to further infringements," as required by Art. 41.1.
[128] *See* text at notes 60–62, *supra*. [129] *See* text at notes 54–57, *supra*.

locally attractive. But as described previously, on a commodification approach, such licenses might be ruled impermissible, for they appear to be inconsistent with the theory of comparative advantage, to discriminate by "whether products are imported or locally produced,"[130] and thus to have protectionist dimensions.

On an incentive theory, however, things look very different, at least for developing countries. If Northern markets are sufficiently lucrative to induce invention, compulsory licenses in the global South will not impair incentives to innovate even if the compensation awarded is very low. As Jean Lanjouw explained in connection with pharmaceuticals, "for therapies for global diseases, the profit derived from having a monopoly over sales in poor countries makes only a marginal contribution to the total worldwide profit of pharmaceutical firms and therefore only marginally increases their incentive to invest in research."[131] Given that TRIPS explicitly promises technology transfer to least developed countries,[132] and frames its goals as promoting the dissemination of technology and improving economic welfare,[133] an incentive-based approach to interpretation should leave countries free to impose working requirements. Under an incentive approach, the expectations protected by investment agreements that do not specifically prohibit working could similarly be interpreted as allowing for the possibility that countries will impose these requirements.[134] What counts as an expropriation or due

[130] TRIPS, *supra* note 5, art. 27.1.

[131] *See generally,* Jean O. Lanjouw, *A New Global Patent Regime for Diseases: U.S. and International Legal Issues*, 16 HARV. J.L. & TECH. 85, 90 (2002); *see also id.*, at 89: "about 46% of the world's population is found in countries representing less than 2% of total expenditure on drugs for cardiovascular disease.") *See also* Jean O. Lanjouw & Iain M. Cockburn, *New Pills for Poor People? Empirical Evidence After GATT*, 29 WORLD DEVELOPMENT 265 (2001) (explaining that even with effective patent systems the group of developing country markets may not, by itself, be very attractive given the prices that it can support). *Cf.* Alan O. Skyes, *TRIPS, Pharmaceuticals, Developing Countries, and the Doha "Solution,"* 3 CHI. J. INT'L L. 47, 48 (2002) (suggesting that if developing countries do not contribute to research costs, "relaxing" intellectual property protection would not be a problem). Indeed, if the South had enough wealth to spur innovation, the pharmaceutical sector might be working harder to cure diseases like malaria and dengue fever, which afflict large populations; instead, this is one of the areas where volunteers are actively involved in development.

[132] TRIPS, *supra* note 5, art. 66.2. [133] *Id.* at art. 7.

[134] *See* Dreyfuss & Frankel, *supra* note 6. *See generally* Henning Grosse Ruse-Khan, *The International Law Relation Between TRIPS and Subsequent TRIPS-Plus Free Trade Agreements: Towards Safeguarding TRIPS Flexibilities?*, 18 J. INTELL. PROP. L. 325 (2011).

and equitable treatment within the meaning of these instruments should likewise be determined with an incentives benchmark in mind.

Most significant, however, would be the adoption of an incentive-based approach to the general exceptions tests. As we saw, these tests appear to leave little room for the public interest. They require the adjudicator to consider whether the respondent's legislation is "limited" (for copyright, the TRIPS term is "special"), whether (for patents, trademarks, and designs) the measure conflicts (for patents and design, *unreasonably* conflicts) with normal exploitation of the work, or whether it unreasonably prejudices the legitimate interests of the right holder.[135] In both the patent and copyright disputes, the panels read these provisions as if maximal returns were the benchmark against which to judge the effect of the challenged measure. Thus, although the TRIPS provisions use several modifiers – "limited," "special," "normal," "unreasonable," and "legitimate" – which suggest a more normative approach, the panels determined how much deviation was permissible mainly by looking at whether other countries had enacted similar measures.[136] But a comparative analysis has several drawbacks. It leaves little room for countries that did not have intellectual property protection when TRIPS was adopted to develop their own approaches to balancing interests (or as the copyright panel put it, it tends to freeze exceptions to those that existed when Berne went into force[137]). Analogously, it leaves members with no leeway to deal with problems uniquely posed by post-TRIPS technologies. Moreover, that approach allows (indeed, encourages) countries interested in strong protection to use bilateral or regional agreements to impose higher standards among themselves, knowing that panels will then consider the new standards when determining the norm for the entire WTO.

Better would be to define what is limited, normal, unreasonable, and legitimate by reference to whether the legislation leaves sufficient incentives to induce creative production. In a way, the WTO's trademark report did just that. The trademark exceptions test is different from the others in that it provides an example of a permissible measure – fair use of descriptive terms.[138] When the panel relied on that example to determine that respondents could permit certain unauthorized uses,[139] it was

[135] TRIPS, *supra* note 5, arts. 13 and 30.

[136] *See, e.g., US-110(5)*, *supra* note 60, ¶¶ 6.52 & 6.58; *Canada – Pharmaceuticals*, ¶¶ 7.1–7.42.

[137] *US-110(5)*, *supra* note 60, ¶ 6.59.

[138] TRIPS, *supra* note 5, art. 17.

[139] EC–GI, *supra* note 61, ¶¶ 7.648, 7.654, & 7.683.

essentially invoking an incentives-based standard: as we saw, fair use provisions in national laws are the best example of an incentives approach to protection for they explicitly target socially important uses of the protected work that are not likely to interfere significantly with incentives to innovate.

Starting from an incentives approach, other errors in the panels' analyses of the general exceptions tests become evident. First, the copyright panel was faced with a provision that limited the right to control retransmissions of musical works[140] and it considered only the degree to which that specific right was impaired. Had it instead focused on incentives to innovate, it would have had to ask about the importance of that particular stick in a bundle that also includes the rights to control reproduction, distribution, public performance, initial transmission, and adaptation of the work. From that broader perspective, the measure at issue might have looked significantly less intrusive. Second, both the patent and copyright panels interpreted the parts of the exceptions tests cumulatively. Had the panelists focused on incentives, they might have appreciated the various parts as getting at the problem of determining sufficiency in different ways. If so, they might have used a test akin to the sliding scale that is said to characterize the U.S. fair use test.[141]

Third, and most important, both with the copyright and the patent provisions, the panels managed to read consideration of the public interest out of the tests. The patent panel did it with its cumulativeness analysis: the last part of the provision instructs adjudicators to "[take] account of the legitimate interests of third parties,"[142] but the panel never reached that provision when it held one of the measures at stake insufficiently "limited;" for the provision it approved, it did not need to consider third parties. The copyright panel did the same thing by equating "special" with "limited," thereby excluding the possibility that "special" means that the legislation was animated by special policy objectives, such as protecting human rights or promoting economic or cultural development.[143] To put it another way, the copyright adjudicators did not ask why it was that the copyright provision differed from the

[140] Berne Convention, *supra* note 59, art. 11bis(2).

[141] *But see* Barton Beebe, *An Empirical Study of U.S. Copyright Fair Use Opinions, 1978–2005*, 156 U. Pa. L. Rev. 549 (2008) (suggesting that the test does not work as expected).

[142] TRIPS, *supra* note 5, art. 30.

[143] *Compare* US-110(5), *supra* note 60, ¶¶ 6.103 & 6.106 (US submission), *with* ¶ 6.109 (equating special with limited).

trademark, patent, and design provisions in not mentioning the rights of third parties. Had the panel appreciated intellectual property law as based on a balance between public and private interests, it might have used the fact that only the copyright provision used the term "special" as an indication that it was meant to be the place where countervailing considerations were taken into account.

C Future Negotiations

In some ways, the most significant part of Justice Breyer's dissent in *Golan* was the observation that negotiators could have taken the absence of an incentive rationale for restoration into account when negotiating U.S. entry into the Berne Convention. So far, this article has discussed the compatibility of public-regarding domestic legislation with TRIPS and, to a lesser extent, to existing FTAs and BITs. However, these are not the final word on international intellectual property law. As Frankel and I noted, the newer FTAs and a spate of plurilateral and regional proposals, including the Anti-Counterfeiting Trade Agreement (ACTA),[144] the Trans-Pacific Partnership Agreement (TPP), and the Transatlantic Trade and Investment Partnership Agreement (TTIP), would impose new obligations.[145] For example, some of these agreements require patents on second uses of known products,[146] bar parallel importation,[147] limit the power to award compulsory licenses,[148] measure injuries by the retail price suggested by the right holder (irrespective of whether infringers would have purchased at that price),[149] and constrain decisions on price controls.[150]

144 Anti-Counterfeiting Trade Agreement, Dec. 3, 2010, *opened for signature* May 1, 2011, 50 I.L.M. 243 (2011), http:// trade.ec.europa.eu/doclib/docs/2010/december/tradoc_147079.pdf[hereinafter ACTA].

145 *See, e.g.*, https://wikileaks.org/tpp/, which includes a link to a leaked text of the TPP; for the TTIPS, *see* http://ec.europa.eu/trade/policy/in-focus/ttip/.

146 *Id.*, TPP, art. 18.37(2).

147 AUSFTA, *supra* note 56, art. 17.9(4). *See also* Agreement on Free Trade, U.S.–Morocco, art. 15.9, para. 4, June 15, 2004 [hereinafter U.S.–Morocco FTA], Agreement Between the United States of America and the Hashemite Kingdom of Jordan on the Establishment of a Free Trade Area, U.S.–Jordan, art. 4, para. 11, Oct. 24, 2000; TPP, art. QQ.G.3.

148 *See, e.g.*, AUSFTA, *supra* note 56, art. 17.9(7).

149 ACTA, *supra* note 144, art. 9(1). ACTA also requires party to maintain a system for pre-established damages or presumptions for determining compensatory damages, and for copyright, additional damages, art. 9(3).

150 United States–Korea Free Trade Agreement, U.S.–S. Kor., June 30, 2007, arts. 5.3(1) and (2). In a Confirmation Letter, Korea also agreed to ensure that the body setting prices be independent of the health authorities.

Taken together, the changes rather clearly embed the notion that all of the value generated by a creative work ought to belong to the right holder. Because, on this view, exceptions would be extremely limited, national power to protect other interests would certainly decline. In part, this may be the preference of the developed countries that are demanding adherence to these agreements. For them, strong intellectual property protection is a source of foreign revenue and can balance out the trade deficits caused by losses in the manufacturing sector.[151] Or they may equate intellectual property with jobs, and therefore think of protection as a way to maintain employment in a post-manufacturing economy.[152]

In part, however, the maximalist approach may stem from the failure of negotiators to fully understand the rationale underlying intellectual property and how crucial fidelity to that rationale is in striking the right balance among innovators and between innovators and the public. As many commentators have noted, negotiators tend to hear more from incumbent creative industries than from user groups or potentially disruptive start-ups.[153] While many of these agreements include developing countries that would be inclined to protect their authority to further other purposes, these nations do not often enjoy equivalent bargaining power and may be particularly disadvantaged by having to undertake multiple negotiations, in multiple locations, with multiple

[151] *See, e.g.*, Deborah Mall, *The Inclusion of a Trade Related Intellectual Property Code under the General Agreement on Tariffs and Trade (GATT)*, 30 SANTA CLARA L. REV. 265, 268 (1990) (citing former United States Trade Representative Clayton Yeutter as stating that "[W]e could shrink [the U.S.] $170 billion trade deficit appreciably simply by adding proper protection for our intellectual property rights around the world."); Janet Hamilton, *What's Going on in Intellectual Property Law?*, 84 AM. SOC'Y INT'L L. PROC. 256, 265(1990).

[152] *See, e.g.*, United States Department of Commerce, *U.S. Commerce Department Releases New Report Showing Intellectual Property-Intensive Industries Contribute $5 Trillion, 40 Million Jobs to US Economy*, COMMERCE.GOV (Apr. 2012), http://www.commerce.gov/news/press-releases/2012/04/11/us-commerce-department-releases-new-report-showing-intellectual-prope.

[153] *See, e.g.*, SUSAN K. SELL, PRIVATE POWER, PUBLIC LAW: THE GLOBALIZATION OF INTELLECTUAL PROPERTY RIGHTS (2003); Cynthia M. Ho, *Private Power, Public Law: The Globalization of Intellectual Property Rights*, 18 EMORY INT'L L. REV. 117, 126 (2004); Mohamed Omar Gad, *Impact of Multinational Enterprises on Multilateral Rule Making: The Pharmaceutical Industry and the TRIPS Uruguay Round Negotiations*, 9 *L. & BUS. REV. AM.* 667 (2003). *Cf.* Sean Flynn, *Special 301 and Global Administrative Law*, in BALANCING WEALTH AND HEALTH: THE BATTLE OVER INTELLECTUAL PROPERTY AND ACCESS TO MEDICINES IN LATIN AMERICA 225 (Rochelle Cooper Dreyfuss & Cesar Rodriguez Garavito eds., 2014) (detailing capture in the context of Special 301 Reports).

parties.[154] Furthermore, as Kate Miles has argued, the principal experiences of trade negotiators lie in the world of commercial transactions; to them "IPRs" (intellectual property rights) are simply another commodity.[155] Theoretically difficult problems, such as determining whether stronger protection really does translate into greater creativity and more jobs, and moral questions sounding in distributive justice and human rights, may be lost in their calculus.

Solving this problem will not be easy. Part of the answer may lie in more transparent, participatory, and accountable global governance.[156] Many nongovernmental organizations (NGOs) are poised to contribute information on the impact of stronger intellectual property within their special areas, be it health, education, or development.[157] But even when they are invited to stakeholder meetings, they do not always have access to the draft treaties on which they are asked to comment, which makes it impossible for them to make concrete suggestions.[158] As important,

[154] *See, e.g.*, Susan K. Sell, *TRIPS Was Never Enough: Vertical Forum Shifting, FTAS, ACTA, and TPP*, 18 J. INTELL. PROP. L. 447 (2011); Susy Frankel, *The Legitimacy and Purpose of Intellectual Property Chapters in FTAs*, in CHALLENGES TO MULTILATERAL TRADE: THE IMPACT OF BILATERAL, PREFERENTIAL AND REGIONAL AGREEMENTS (Ross Buckley, Vai Io Lo & Laurence Boulle eds., 2008); Peter Drahos, *When the Weak Bargain with the Strong: Negotiations in the World Trade Organization*, 8 INTER'L NEGOTIATION 79 (2003); Peter Drahos, *BITS and BIPS: Bilateralism in Intellectual Property*, 4 J. WORLD INTELLECTUAL PROP'Y 791 (2001).

[155] Kate Miles, *Reconceptualising International Investment Law: Bringing the Public Interest into Private Business*, in INTERNATIONAL ECONOMIC LAW AND NATIONAL AUTONOMY 295, 296 (Meredith Kolsky Lewis & Susy Frankel eds., 2010).

[156] *See, e.g.*, Benedict Kingsbury, Nico Krisch & Richard B. Stewart, *The Emergence of Global Administrative Law*, 68 L. AND CONTEMP. PROBS. 15, 15–61 (2005). *See also* Rochelle Cooper Dreyfuss & César Rodríguez-Garavito, *The Battle over Intellectual Property Laws and Access to Medicines in Latin America: A Primer on Global Administrative Law, Intellectual Property, and Political Contestation, in* BALANCING WEALTH AND HEALTH: THE BATTLE OVER INTELLECTUAL PROPERTY AND ACCESS TO MEDICINES IN LATIN AMERICA (Rochelle Cooper Dreyfuss & César Rodríguez-Garavito eds., 2014) (with César Rodríguez-Garavito).

[157] *See, e.g.*, Amy Kapczynski, *The Access to Knowledge Mobilization and the New Politics of Intellectual Property*, 117 YALE L.J. 804 (2008).

[158] *See, e.g.*, Tim Cushing, *USTR Claims 1,200 Meetings with Congress Just As Good as Actual Transparency*, TECHDIRT (Apr. 4, 2014), https://www.techdirt.com/articles/20140404/12180926802/ustr-claims-1200-meetings-with-congress-just-as-good-as-actual-transparency.shtml/; Pirate Party Australia's Presentation to Trans-Pacific Partnership Stakeholders Meeting in Melbourne (Mar. 4, 2012), http://pirateparty.org.au/2012/03/04/pirate-party-australias-presentation-to-trans-pacific-partnership-stakeholders-meeting-in-melbourne/. *See also* David S. Levine, *Bring in the Nerds: Secrecy, National Security, and the Creation of International Intellectual Property Law*, 30 CARDOZO ARTS & ENT. L.J. 105 (2012).

greater attention to incentives and balance may require a cultural transformation among negotiators so that they better understand the values at stake when intellectual property law is expanded beyond its customary boundaries. But as Laurence Helfer has argued, it may also be that intervention by supranational courts[159] and regime shifting – engaging multiple international fora in intellectual property lawmaking[160] – will lead to regulatory competition, input from international organizations with expertise in other areas (such as health and development), and ultimately, a better balanced international regime.

III Conclusion

Successive negotiations in a variety of fora have raised the standards for intellectual property protection and reduced the opportunity for countries to protect important local interests, such as human rights, culture, and domestic development. At the same time, however, intellectual property scholars have demonstrated that creators are motivated by many different factors. While the accounts of the phenomenon of IP without IP do not convincingly prove that intellectual property protection is superfluous, they do suggest that the place for protection is more modest than international negotiators assume. An "inducement standard" for protection – that is, a return to the traditional incentive-based rationale for awarding exclusive rights to intellectual products – could go a long way towards restoring flexibilities into the system.

The standard of protection (and the concomitant room for safeguarding public interests) is a function of domestic law, international obligation, and the interpretive approach of international adjudicators. Accordingly, improving the relationship between trade, investment, culture, development, human rights, and intellectual property is a tall order. It requires cultural change, education, and adaptation at all three levels.

159 Laurence R. Helfer, Karen J. Alter & M. Florencia Guerzovich, *Islands of Effective International Adjudication: Constructing an Intellectual Property Rule of Law in the Andean Community*, 103 Am. Soc'y Int'l L. Proc. 483 (2009); Laurence R. Helfer, *The New Innovation Frontier? Intellectual Property and the European Court of Human Rights*, 49 Harv. Int'l L.J. 1 (2008).

160 Laurence R. Helfer, *Regime Shifting: The TRIPS Agreement and New Dynamics of International Intellectual Property Lawmaking*, 29 Yale J. Int'l L. 1 (2004). *See also* Gráinne de Búrca et al., *New Modes of Pluralist Global Governance*, 45 N.Y.U. J. Int'l L. & Pol. 723 (2013).

2

Copyright and Creative Incentives: What Do(n't) We Know?

CHRISTOPHER JON SPRIGMAN*

The grounding justification for copyright law is that the grant of exclusive rights in artistic and literary works will incentivize authors to invest in new creativity. The economic theory undergirding this justification is straightforward. By preventing competition from copyists, copyright law helps to ensure that the rents (if any) generated by a particular act of artistic or literary creativity will flow to the creator, and not to a competitor. The improved prospect of gain will, it is believed, motivate additional creative effort.

This is an entirely sensible story, but is it right? On that most foundational question, we have mostly surmise, and little empirical evidence. We have a small number of *event studies* designed to investigate copyright incentives. We also have a growing number of *qualitative studies* of copyright incentives in the branch of IP scholarship that some refer to as Intellectual Production Without Intellectual Property ("IP Without IP")[1] and others as the "Negative Space" scholarship.[2] And we have a very small number of *lab experiments* investigating copyright incentives.

Together, these scattered bits of empirical evidence suggest that the relationship between copyright and creativity is . . . complicated. There is evidence that copyright incentivizes some sorts of creativity sometimes – although that evidence is thin and contestable. Other evidence suggests that copyright incentives may, in some settings, do little or nothing to encourage creative output – but again, this evidence is far from definitive.

* Thanks to the Filomen D'Agostino and Max E. Greenberg Research Fund for a grant that supported this work.

1 *See* Rochelle Cooper Dreyfuss, *Does IP Need IP? Accommodating Intellectual Production Outside of the Intellectual Property Paradigm*, 31 CARDOZO L. REV. 1437 (2010).

2 *See* Kal Raustiala & Christopher Jon Sprigman, *The Piracy Paradox: Innovation and Intellectual Property in Fashion Design*, 92 VA. L. REV. 1687 (2006).

The partial, hazy picture that has emerged so far calls to mind what Professor Fritz Machlup said about patents in a 1958 report to the United States Congress:

> If we did not have a patent system, it would be irresponsible on the basis of our present knowledge of its economic consequences, to recommend instituting one. But since we have had a patent system for a long time, it would be irresponsible on the basis of our present knowledge, to recommend abolishing it . . . [3]

Some progress has been made since 1958 in understanding the effect of our patent laws on innovation and social welfare, although our understanding remains partial. The state of our knowledge regarding the net social benefits of copyright law is, by comparison, truly rudimentary. Copyright remains a legal regime driven by interest group lobbying and intuition, rather than evidence.

This chapter highlights representative examples of the existing empirical scholarship on the relationship between copyright and creative incentives, and assesses how well the existing scholarship informs us regarding the supposed link between the two. The existing evidence is equivocal, and, most importantly, poorly developed relative to what would be necessary in order to provide better guidance for policymaking – a situation that should be profoundly frustrating for anyone who isn't content to turn over copyright policymaking to a mix of interest group politics and nonutilitarian theories. The problem with relying on interest group politics should be obvious – the political economy of copyright has been, and remains, dominated by producer interests, and there is little reason to believe that producer-dominated policy making will reflect the public interest, or advance social (rather than merely producer) welfare. Reliance on deontic (nonutilitarian) justifications is just as unsatisfying. While the variety of Lockean labor-based arguments and Kantian or Hegelian "personality" theories that have been offered do succeed, at a general level, at explaining why we have some sort of copyright system rather than nothing at all, these nonutilitarian theories are not much use in explaining what the particular rules of the copyright system should be at a level relevant to lawmaking (the task that should matter to lawyers and lawmakers). Should the copyright term be longer or shorter? How close must copying be before we recognize it as "infringement"? Should copyright

[3] Fritz Machlup, *An Economic Review of the Patent System*, U.S. Congress, Senate Subcommittee Patents, Trademarks and Copyright, Study No. 15, 80 (1958).

contain a "fair use" doctrine, and, if so, of what sort? What is the best distribution of rights as between first-stage creators and those who follow them and who use elements of pre-existing work in their own work? On all these questions, deontic theorists have little to say, not least because the moment deontic theories attempt to approach copyright policy questions at the level of particularity required to construct and justify an actual copyright system, they break down immediately into utilitarianism.

In sum, it is difficult, given the parlous state of our knowledge about the effects of copyright rules on creative incentives, to offer helpful input to policymakers regarding the likely effect of many proposed changes to existing law. And in the absence of real evidence, policymakers are left at liberty to heed their biases and the blandishments of lobby groups.

The balance of this chapter reviews some of the recent empirical scholarship investigating the link between copyright rules and creative incentives. We shall begin with a study that is perhaps the most supportive in the recent literature – albeit with substantial caveats – of the link between copyright and creativity. It is a historical study of Napoleonic-era Italy, and of the relationship between the introduction of copyright law and the output of Italian operas.

I Copyright and Creativity – Evidence from Italian Operas[4]

Today opera fans are rich, old, and increasingly rare. But it wasn't always that way. In the eighteenth century, opera was the closest thing to mass entertainment, especially in Italy. And that fact provides a platform for economists Michaela Giorcelli and Petra Moser to say something interesting about the effect of copyright law on creativity. Giorcelli and Moser's *Copyright and Creativity – Evidence from Italian Operas*,[5] is a paper that provides a valuable historical perspective on the relationship between copyright and incentives to create.

Giorcelli and Moser's paper is a natural experiment using historical data surrounding an "external shock" – viz., Napoleon's invasion and

[4] This portion of the chapter is adapted from Christopher Jon Sprigman, *A Lesson from the History of Italian Opera: Some Copyright Good/More Copyright Useless*, Jotwell (Jan. 15, 2016), http://ip.jotwell.com/a-lesson-from-the-history-of-italian-opera-some-copyright-goodmore-copyright-useless/.

[5] Michela Giorcelli & Petra Moser, *Copyrights and Creativity: Evidence from Italian Operas* (2016), http://papers.ssrn.com/sol3/papers.cfm?abstract_id=2505776.

occupation of northern Italy between 1796 and 1802. The northern Italian states of Lombardy and Venetia adopted copyright laws in 1801, as a direct consequence of French rule. Six other Italian states studied by Giorcelli and Moser only began adopting copyright laws during a period that began a quarter-century later. Giorcelli and Moser collect historical data on 2,598 operas that premiered across the eight Italian states in question between 1770 and 1900, the most fertile years of Italian opera production, and a period that both precedes and follows the adoption of copyright by Lombardy and Venetia.

Comparisons across the period reveal a statistically significant increase in new operas produced in the states that adopted copyright in 1801. Giorcelli and Moser estimate that Lombardy and Venetia produced an average of 2.12 additional operas per year after 1801. This increase is relative to a baseline of 1.41 operas per state per year before 1801, thus yielding an apparent increase of approximately 150 percent, versus an increase in production of approximately 54 percent in the states that had not adopted copyright.

The authors then inquire whether the increase in number was accompanied by an increase in overall quality of the operas produced. Using other historical data sets, Giorcelli and Moser estimate a 4.6-fold increase in the production of historically popular operas in response to the adoption of copyright, and a ten-fold increase in the production of durably popular operas (i.e. those for which full-length recordings continue to be available on Amazon in 2014).

The data also shows that after Lombardy and Venetia adopted copyright, opera composers began to immigrate to those states. "Between 1801 and 1821, 43 composers who were born outside of Lombardy premiered an opera in that state. Another 13 composers born outside of Venetia premiered an opera in Venetia," the study states. "By comparison, all other Italian states together only saw premieres by 5 composers who were born outside the state."

In sum, assuming that the production of operas is a reasonable proxy for artistic and literary production generally – and I am not so sure it is, but more on that in a moment – the Giorcelli and Moser study suggests that the adoption of a copyright term that is short by today's standards (average life expectancy in Italy in 1800 was about 30 years, so a life-plus-10 copyright term is perhaps a third as long as today's life-plus-70) provides an incentive that produces more creative output versus an environment in which there is no copyright protection and creative output is consequently more vulnerable to appropriation.

However, the study also suggests that subsequent extension of the copyright terms from life of the author plus 10 years to life plus 40 had no clear effect on either the number or quality of operas produced. This second conclusion is particularly important because our contemporary debate is usually not whether to have copyright at all, but rather whether to extend already very long copyright terms. On that question, Giorcelli and Moser provide evidence that a bit of copyright is enough, and more copyright does not necessarily lead to more creative production.

Of course, longer copyright terms do have a cost. They perpetuate monopolies, with all the social costs that monopolies typically produce, plus extra costs that arise when the spread of knowledge goods like books or even operas is restricted by monopoly's high costs and scarcity. Cheap books help spread literacy. Cheap operas help spread cultural literacy. Both forms of learning enrich society. Copyright terms that are too long limit the spread of knowledge while producing little, if any, additional creative output.

Like any piece of empirical work, the Giorcelli/Moser paper raises methodological and data-quality questions. I want to focus on the latter first.

The paper's conclusions are only as strong as the data on which the researchers rely, and I would have liked to have seen more discussion of why we should trust the completeness of the records listing opera premiers during the period. Giorcelli and Moser consult multiple sources, but these are historical records from an often chaotic time and place in which it is not intuitively obvious that all opera premiers would have been recorded. This is especially worrisome because the difference between post-Napoleonic output in Lombardy/Venetia versus the other Italian states in which copyright had not yet been introduced during the data period is, in absolute numbers, very small – it is essentially one additional opera per year premiering in Lombary/Venetia versus the other states. If the rate at which the premiers failed to be recorded varied across the Italian states – perhaps because the Napoleonic government maintained better law and order in Lombardy and Venetia – that variance could cause a significant perturbation in the data, with corresponding effects on the results.

To be fair, Giorcelli and Moser use more modern sources to account for omissions from the historical records, but it is difficult to judge from the paper the confidence one reasonably can place in the amended records. The paper contains an admirable level of detail regarding

Napoleon's client states in northern Italy, but I cannot help but wonder whether there might have been important disuniformities in Napoleon's administration of the conquered territories that may, if considered in the analysis, blunt or even eliminate the effect.

More important are questions about the generalizability of the Giorcelli/Moser findings from opera (today, not a particularly significant creative enterprise) to other, more modern and commercially important, forms of creativity. I suspect that the answer depends on how closely the economics of a particular form of creativity resembles the economics of opera production. Opera has very high fixed costs; authoring an opera represents a large and sustained creative effort, and the production of an opera is also costly (hiring singers, musicians, and opera halls is expensive, as are the often-lavish sets and costumes). Opera is, in short, a paradigm of the sort of creativity that is unlikely to flourish without some way to prevent copying, because the originator needs an extended period of exclusivity in order to earn back those high fixed costs.

Like opera, some modern forms of creativity feature very high fixed costs. For example, blockbuster movies. But other commercially important forms of creativity – pop music, or poetry, or much visual art – are produced with relatively low fixed costs. Just to focus for a moment on one economically and culturally significant form of creativity, it is cheap these days to write and record pop music. Is the sort of lengthy monopoly created by copyright law necessary to stimulate the production of this lower-cost creativity? On that question, the Giorcelli/Moser paper is silent. There is, however, a branch of IP scholarship that has examined the effect of copyright – and of copyright's absence – on forms of creativity that, unlike opera, are not subject to particularly high fixed costs. I turn to this empirical scholarship now.

II The "Negative Space" Scholarship[6]

The law and economics of intellectual property has long rested on a foundational, if implicit, premise: that intellectual property law is best understood by studying how legal rules operate in markets for

[6] This section has been adapted from Kal Raustiala & Christopher Jon Sprigman, *When Are IP Rights Necessary? Evidence from Innovation in IP's Negative Space*, in RESEARCH HANDBOOK ON THE ECONOMICS OF INTELLECTUAL PROPERTY RIGHTS (VOL. I – THEORY) (Peter Menell & Ben Depoorter eds., forthcoming).

creative work in which intellectual property rights have a role. To understand copyright, for instance, scholars have explored copyright-dependent fields such as music, film, and publishing, seeking to understand how copyright law shapes innovation in these contexts. In other words, IP scholars have generally studied creative fields where IP is present.

The assumption that we best understand a body of legal rules by looking at the fields they directly address is eminently reasonable. Yet this way of analyzing the effect of IP is incomplete. IP rules are purposive; the core goal and rationale of IP is to incentivize creative and innovative production. But looking only at the creative fields in which IP law is present leaves open, or at least incompletely addresses, a host of important and fascinating questions. Can innovation flourish in the absence of IP protection? Can market incentives, psychological factors, social norms, first-mover advantages, or any number of other causes, including path-dependency or even happenstance, serve as substitutes, in whole or in part, for IP rights? And is it possible that, under some conditions and in some industries, IP protection is counterproductive – that is, it inhibits rather than incentivizes innovation?

One way to answer these questions is to look beyond the space affirmatively covered by IP law, to the "negative space" of IP. By "negative space"[7] I mean those creative and innovative fields that, for historical, doctrinal, or other reasons, are not addressed by IP law. In fashion, cuisine, tattoo artistry, professional magic, financial services, sports, and many other areas of creativity, IP rights are absent or highly limited, and yet substantial creativity occurs. The challenge is to describe the factors other than formal IP that support creativity.

A number of commentators have focused on the fashion industry as a large, commercially important creative industry that operates in IP's negative space. Additionally, commentators have observed that other creative fields, such as cuisine, were not protected by copyright.[8] For the most part these facts were simply mentioned; occasionally the

[7] This term was first used in the IP context in Raustiala & Sprigman, *supra* note 2.

[8] *See, e.g.*, Malla Pollack, *Intellectual Property Protection for the Creative Chef, Or How to Copyright a Cake: A Modest Proposal*, 12 Cardozo L. Rev. 1477 (1991); Karolina Jesien, *Don't Sweat It: Copyright Protection for Yoga . . . are Exercise Routines Next?*, 5 Cardozo Pub. L. Poly & Ethics J. 623 (2007); Proloy K. Das, *Offensive Protection: The Potential Application of Intellectual Property Law to Scripted Sports Plays*, 75 Ind. L.J. 1073 (2000).

absence of protection was bemoaned. Apparel design in particular was the subject of several articles in the 1990s and 2000s that decried the lack of protection for clothing designs and generally proposed some doctrinal fix.[9]

What distinguishes the newer "negative space" research is its concern not only with delineating how hitherto un- or under-explored creative fields operate, but also with examining the larger implications of negative space for our understanding of IP theory, doctrine, and practice. By looking at a sufficient number of low-IP creative areas, we can perhaps begin to understand the various ways in which innovation incentives can succeed or fail. And ultimately, it may be possible to say something deeper about the strength and breadth of IP's incentives justification.

Whatever larger insights have emerged from studies of negative space, this literature has undeniably generated a clutch of fascinating case studies. At a minimum, these studies substantially enhance our understanding of the empirics of innovation across a strikingly wide range of human endeavor. Studies of the fashion industry,[10] cuisine,[11] fan fiction,[12] pornography,[13] nineteenth-century U.S. commercial publishing,[14] video games featuring significant user-generated

[9] *See e.g.*, Jennifer Mencken, *A Design for the Copyright of Fashion*, B.C. INTELL. PROP. & TECH. F. (1997); Rebeca Sanchez-Roig, *Putting the Show Together and Taking It on the Road: Copyright, the Appropriate Protection for Theatrical Scenic and Costume Designs*, 40 SYRACUSE L. REV. 1089 (1989).

[10] Jonathan Barnett, *Shopping for Gucci on Canal Street: Reflections on Status Consumption, Intellectual Property, and the Incentive Thesis*, 91 VA. L. REV. 1381 (2005); Raustiala & Sprigman, *supra* note 2; C. Scott Hemphill & Jeannie Suk, *The Law, Culture, and Economics of Fashion*, 61 STAN. L. REV. 1147 (2009); Kal Raustiala & Christopher Jon Sprigman, *The Piracy Paradox Revisited*, 61 STAN. L. REV. 1201 (2009); Jonathan M. Barnett, Gilles Grolleau & Sana El Harbi, *The Fashion Lottery: Cooperative Innovation in Stochastic Markets*, 39 J. LEGAL STUD. 159 (2010); Hemphill, C. Scott & Jeannie C. Suk, *The Fashion Originators' Guild of America: Self-Help at the Edge of IP and Antitrust*, in INTELLECTUAL PROPERTY AT THE EDGE (Rochelle Cooper Dreyfuss & Jane Ginsburg eds., 2014).

[11] Christopher J. Buccafusco, *On the Legal Consequences of Sauces: Should Thomas Keller's Recipes Be per se Copyrightable?*, 24 CARDOZO ARTS & ENT. L. J. 1121 (2007); Emmanuelle Fauchart & Eric von Hippel, *Norms-Based Intellectual Property Systems: The Case of French Chefs*, 19 ORG. SCI. 187 (2008).

[12] Rebecca Tushnet, *Economics of Desire: Fair Use and Marketplace Assumptions*, 51 WM & MARY L. REV. 513 (2009).

[13] Kate Darling, *IP Without IP? A Study of the Online Adult Entertainment Industry*, 17 STAN. TECH. L. REV. 655 (2014).

[14] ROBERT SPOO, WITHOUT COPYRIGHTS: PIRACY, PUBLISHING, AND THE PUBLIC DOMAIN (2013).

content,[15] stand-up comedy,[16] roller derby,[17] software,[18] jam bands,[19] tattoos,[20] magic,[21] and the flu vaccine[22] detail an extraordinary variety of creative and innovative work, and show the ways in which creative production can flourish with relatively little or no IP protection.[23] Related studies of scientific innovation document communal practices that emphasize sharing, and resist the full potential for propertization of research.[24] And as Eric von Hippel and others have shown, a lot of innovation is generated by users, in contexts as varied as extreme sports, surgery, library science, and commercial high-tech manufacturing, who work mostly in the absence of IP incentives, and who often share the fruits of their creativity with others.[25]

[15] Greg Lastowka, *Minecraft as Web 2.0: Amateur Creativity & Digital Games* (Oct. 5, 2014), http://papers.ssrn.com/sol3/papers.cfm?abstract_id=1939241.

[16] Dotan Oliar & Christopher Jon Sprigman, *There's No Free Laugh (Anymore): The Emergence of Intellectual Property Norms and the Transformation of Stand-Up Comedy*, 94 VA. L. REV. 1787 (2008).

[17] David Fagundes, *Talk Derby to Me: Intellectual Property Norms Governing Roller Derby Pseudonyms*, 90 TEX. L. REV. 1093 (2012). *See also* Gerard N. Magliocca, *Patenting the Curve Ball: Business Methods and Industry Norms*, BYU L. REV. 875 (2009) (discussing industry norms against patenting and arguing that business method patents should not be expanded to cover industries where such norms exist).

[18] Yochai Benkler, THE WEALTH OF NETWORKS: HOW SOCIAL PRODUCTION TRANSFORMS MARKETS AND FREEDOM (2007); Jon M. Garon, *Wiki Authorship, Social Media, and the Curatorial Audience*, 1 HARV. J. SPORTS & ENT. L. 95 (2010); Catherine L. Fisk, *Credit Where It's Due: The Law and Norms of Attribution*, 95 GEO. L. J. 49 (2006); Josh Lerner & Jean Tirole, *The Economics of Technology Sharing: Open Source and Beyond*, 19 J. ECON. PERSP. 99 (2005).

[19] Mark F. Schultz, *Fear and Norms and Rock & Roll: What Jambands Can Teach About Persuading People to Comply with Copyright Law*, 21 BERKELEY TECH. L. J. 651 (2006).

[20] Aaron Perzanowski, *Tattoos and IP Norms*, 98 MINN. L. REV. 511 (2013).

[21] Jacob Loshin, *Secrets Revealed: Protecting Magicians' Intellectual Property Without Law*, in LAW AND MAGIC: A COLLECTION OF ESSAYS 123 (Christine Corcos ed., 2010).

[22] Amy Kapczynski, *Order Without Intellectual Property Law: The Flu Network as a Case Study in Open Science* (unpublished working draft on file with author).

[23] *See also* the collection of essays in MAKING AND UNMAKING INTELLECTUAL PROPERTY (Mario Biagioli, Peter Jaszi & Martha Woodmansee eds., 2011).

[24] Katherine J. Strandburg, *Curiosity-Driven Research and University Technology Transfer*, in UNIVERSITY ENTREPRENEURSHIP AND TECHNOLOGY TRANSFER: PROCESS, DESIGN, AND INTELLECTUAL PROPERTY 93 (Advances in the Study of Entrepreneurship, Innovation and Economic Growth Vol. 16, Gary D. Libecap ed. 2005); Fiona Murray et al., *Of Mice and Academics: Examining the Effect of Openness on Innovation* (Nat'l Bureau of Econ. Research, Working Paper No. 14819, 2009), http://www.nber.org/papers/w14819.

[25] ERIC VON HIPPEL, DEMOCRATIZING INNOVATION (2005); Jeroen P. J. de Jong & Eric von Hippel, *Transfers of User Process Innovations to Process Equipment Producers: A Study of Dutch High-Tech Firms*, 38 RES. POL'Y 1181 (2009); Fred Gault & Eric von

Relevant markets, incentives, participants, practices, and norms vary enormously across the negative space literature. In many respects the only shared quality is that creative production occurs in an environment that can be characterized as at least low-IP, and sometimes no-IP. Still, some broad features across cases can be discerned. In what follows, I briefly describe some of this work and highlight its broad themes, commonalities, and contrasts.

A *Social Norms*

Many negative space studies have documented the powerful role social norms play in stimulating innovation and constraining appropriation. In many of these cases IP law is formally relevant but is displaced by the social norms of a particular creative community. These social norms are almost exclusively producer norms, and typically reflect a shared sense of professional or artistic identity that allows such norms to develop and become entrenched.[26] A large body of work has developed over the past decade analyzing creative industries that feature relatively robust social norms.

An early study by the author and Dotan Oliar on copying among stand-up comedians is in this vein. Technically copyright law covers comedy. The issue then, as now, is that copyright protection only adheres to a specific formulation of a joke or routine, and not to the general premise or structure. In practice this means that infringement claims are difficult to bring, and rarely cost-effective. Oliar and Sprigman describe the development of social norms among comics through two eras: the post-vaudeville era of joke slingers like Henny Youngman, Milton Berle, and Phyllis Diller, and the modern age of personalized comedy which started with people like Lenny Bruce and Mort Sahl and is today represented by comedians as diverse as Sarah Silverman, Amy Schumer, Louis C.K., and Trevor Noah.

The post-vaudeville era was marked by two features. The currency of comedy was the joke (understood as a one-liner, or maybe a simple premise + punchline). And comedians of the day freely appropriated whatever jokes they desired. Jokes were part of a commons that comedians

Hippel, *The Prevalence of User Innovation and Free Innovation Transfers: Implications for Statistical Indicators and Innovation Policy* (MIT Sloan Sch. of Mgmt. Research Paper No. 4722–09, 2009), http://papers.ssrn.com/sol3/papers.cfm?abstract_id=1337232.

26 An interesting exception is in the jam-band community associated with acts such as Phish and the Grateful Dead. Schultz, *supra* note 19.

could access. A famed Milton Berle quip summed up this state of affairs: Berle, known as "the Thief of Bad Gags" would come up on stage and say about the previous act, "I laughed so hard I nearly dropped my pencil." In short, post-vaudeville era comics operated on a norm of open access.

By the 1960s, however, comedy was undergoing major change. Whereas the first era was largely about the rapid-fire slinging of jokes, the second era featured longer, individualized narratives that were tied to a particular comedic persona. And as the nature of comedy changed, so too did the social norms. Comedians still do not sue one another over copying. Instead, they operate via a set of well-developed and widely accepted social norms governing appropriation. Oliar and Sprigman describe norms against copying and addressing ownership, coauthorship, and joke transfer. These norms are backed by a surprisingly stiff regime of community-imposed, extralegal sanctions. For the most part, these sanctions are reputational, but they appear to be effective in policing joke-stealing. On rare occasions, norm-breakers are subject to group boycotts (i.e. cooperative refusal by comedians to work with a perceived joke thief) and even the threat of violence or (very rarely) actual violence. The overall result is a fairly robust, but thoroughly private and extralegal, system of rules governing the appropriation of creative work. And comedy remains a highly creative and very productive field, without depending on formal copyright law.

In a similar vein, Aaron Perzanowski has studied tattoo artists and the ownership of tattoo designs.[27] As with comedy, nominally tattoo designs fall within copyright's positive space. But, in practice, they are rarely if ever governed by the laws of IP.[28] Instead, a complex set of social norms operates to govern tattoo artists and their designs. There are, Perzanowski argues, five core norms:

> First, tattooers as a rule recognize the autonomy interests of their clients both in the design of custom tattoos and their subsequent display and use. Second, tattooers collectively refrain from reusing custom designs – that is, a tattooer who designs an image for a client will not apply that

[27] Perzanowski, *supra* note 20.

[28] Litigation is rare but not nonexistent. *See, e.g.*, Whitmill v. Warner Bros. Entertainment, No. 411-cv-752 (E.D. Mo. Sept. 21, 2013). The case, which settled, involved the appearance of a tattoo look-alike, copied from boxer Mike Tyson, on the face of actor Ed Helms *See also* Solid Oak Sketches LLC v. Visual Concepts LLC et al., U.S. District Court Southern District of New York, No. 16–00724 (Aug. 2, 2016) (dismissing claim for copyright statutory damages based on alleged infringement of tattoo designs, but allowing copyright actual damages claims to proceed).

> same image on another client. Third, tattooers discourage the copying of custom designs – that is, a tattooer generally will not apply another tattooer's custom images to a willing client. Fourth, tattooers create and use pre-designed tattoo imagery, or "flash", with the understanding that it will be freely reproduced. Finally, tattooers generally embrace the copying of works that originate outside of the tattoo industry, such as paintings, photos, or illustrations.[29]

As with comedians, tattoo artists around the United States are generally familiar with and subscribe to these norms.[30]

High-end chefs also exhibit substantial adherence to social norms governing appropriation. Whereas tattoo designs and comedy routines are formally covered by copyright, if in practice rarely addressed by it, cuisine is much like fashion: it is almost entirely unprotected in its two core features: the recipe and the finished dish.[31] A creative chef who develops an original and delicious recipe can try to keep it from rivals as a trade secret. But since talented chefs can often reverse-engineer a dish they have eaten, the utility of this strategy is limited. Moreover, for many top chefs cookbooks provide substantial income and are part of a larger brand-building effort. And by definition, cookbooks supply recipes for any reader to recreate. In short, recipes are open to appropriation by others.

In practice, however, chefs – at least at the higher levels – have developed a set of norms and practices to constrain appropriation and reward ingenuity. Both Chris Buccafusco and the team of Emmanuelle Fauchart and Eric von Hippel have documented these practices and the ways they sustain culinary innovation. In particular, they note the strong norm of attribution, in which a given dish may be copied freely as long as the originator is noted (sometimes directly on the menu; even more often in a cookbook recipe's notes.)[32]

In short, social norms have been found to play a powerful, innovation-facilitating role in a host of creative industries, from chefs and comedians to roller derby, magicians, and jambands.[33] To be sure, many of these

29 Perzanowski, *supra* note 20, at 515.

30 An interesting question is whether there is a difference in the power or scope of such norms since comics travel widely and tattoo artists are generally local.

31 Patent law could theoretically cover cooking techniques, and some pioneering molecular gastronomy processes have indeed been patented. But because virtually all cooking techniques have been known to the public for centuries or millennia, patent law is irrelevant.

32 Buccafusco, *supra* note 11; Fauchart & von Hippel, *supra* note 11.

33 Fagundes, *supra* note 17; Schultz, *supra* note 19.

industries are small, though not all are. Modest size appears to help create the sort of community of interest and sense of shared professional identity that can originate and perpetuate robust social norms. Again, in most of these studies these norms develop and are sustained among producers of content. To the degree content producers lack a shared professional identity norms may tend to break down, or perhaps work only in a local or regional context. Or, as with chefs, norms may segment by category. Truly world-class chefs, for example, are loathe to copy because much of their reputation rests on their innovative capacity. And when they do, they tend to attribute creations to originators. But further down the food chain, these norms are less apparent and copying becomes much more prevalent.

In much of the research into social norms in IP's negative space, moreover, the industries involved tend to feature relatively low costs of innovation. Low-cost innovation is important because it is likely to facilitate the effective operation of social norms. If innovation were extremely expensive – as is the case, for example, in pharmaceutical development or blockbuster filmmaking – the power of producer-policed, reputation-based social norms might be wholly insufficient to constrain copying to an appreciable degree. Still, the extant literature suggests, if only by the topics most widely covered, that social norms are more robust and meaningful in creative fields where investment in creation is relatively low.

B Products versus Performances

Sometimes industries preserve creative incentives by shifting away from forms of creativity that are easily copied, refocusing on forms of creativity that are more resistant to appropriation. The online pornography industry is instructive of this dynamic. Adult entertainment is currently protected by copyright, though (under American law at least) prior to the Fifth Circuit's decision in *Mitchell Bros Film Group v. Cinema Adult Theater*,[34] its IP status was unclear. Nonetheless, perhaps because pornography for so long resided in the negative space of IP, the industry is a comparatively light user of IP litigation and lives with very high rates of free and pirated content.

[34] 604 F.2d 852, 854–55, 858 (5th Cir. 1979) (holding that the Copyright Act neither explicitly nor implicitly prohibits protection of "obscene materials," such as the films at issue there, and rejecting the defendant's affirmative defense of "unclean hands").

As Kate Darling has described, ready access to free online content, most notably through the ubiquitous "porntube" sites,[35] has affected the industry's output of new content.[36] Darling argues that production in the industry has shifted away from pornographic feature films and toward cheaper scenes (i.e. shorter bits of recorded pornography, not embedded in any larger story). These are designed to be viewed, for free, on the porntube sites, which have entered into deals with many producers to split ad revenue. Darling also documents the rise of "cam girls" – women (and men) who perform live over the Internet using webcams. Clients pay to watch these performances, and sometimes pay more to essentially direct them. The revenue stream that results is resistant to piracy for much the same reason that live music performances are resistant to piracy – what is valuable is the immediacy of the live (streamed) performance. This is true even when the performance is made over an internet connection, because a feature of these performances is interactivity.

When the performance is a significant element of the total offering, the product can be copied with fewer negative ramifications. As discussed earlier, social norms among producers often play an important role in constraining appropriation, or mitigating its putative negative effects. The emphasis on performance over product attacks the problem of appropriation in a different way: in essence reducing the ability of the consumer to find a true copy, rather than (as with social norms) constraining producers' willingness to copy one another.

The product-performance continuum has been highlighted by work focused on the negative space of IP, but the insights that result are not limited to it. As just noted, the music industry demonstrates the same tendencies. It is undeniable that music sales are down more than 50 percent from their peak in 1999 of approximately $14.5 billion – in fact, adjusted for inflation, sales are almost 67 percent lower. It is also clear that many consumers continue to pirate (or share) music. And yet recorded music continues to thrive. Online music piracy hasn't reduced the quantity of music produced, or indeed its quality, as a series of studies by Joel Waldfogel demonstrates.[37] And, importantly, even as the

[35] Websites, such as pornhub.com, redtube.com, and xvideos.com, that offer clips of pornographic content in a format similar to the way nonpornographic content is offered by YouTube.

[36] *See* Darling, *supra* note 13.

[37] *See* Joel Waldfogel, *Bye, Bye, Miss American Pie? The Supply of New Recorded Music since Napster* (NBER Working Paper No. w16882, Mar. 2011), http://papers.ssrn.com/sol3/papers.cfm?abstract_id=1789463; Joel Waldfogel, *And the Bands Played On: Digital*

recorded music business has withered, revenues from live music have boomed – in 2014, North American revenues from concert ticket sales grew to approximately $6.3 billion, rising from less than $1.5 billion in 1999 – more than a four-fold nominal increase, and still a three-fold increase adjusted for inflation.[38] The music industry is reconfiguring to emphasize performance and experience over product – a shift in the industry's output that is provoked by piracy, but that does not appear to have blunted incentives to create new music. Indeed, recorded music is increasingly seen as advertising for live performance, rather than the other way around.[39] This inversion of the traditional relationship renders copying far less harmful, and, arguably, at least in some instances, even positive.

The centrality of performance and experience helps explain the coexistence of some otherwise-contradictory trends in a number of industries. Consider the willingness of customers to pay high prices for movie tickets in some theaters, even as streaming video in the comfort of one's home grows ever more common. Why pay to go out to a movie theater when you can watch the exact same film on your widescreen high-definition television, thanks to one of the many torrent websites that feature illegal content? One answer is that the experience is quite different, and many smart theater owners have been rapidly moving to accentuate that difference as dramatically as they can.

C *Creativity-enhancing Copying*

Sometimes creative incentives coexist relatively easily with copying, because copying sets trends that accelerate consumption of creative goods and, in turn, their production. The fashion industry, which is rife with copies, is the leading example of this dynamic. Take Forever 21, a multibillion dollar retailer that is growing in the U.S. and now also in Europe. Forever 21's entire business model is based on appropriating others' designs and selling them, perhaps slightly tweaked, for far less.

Disintermediation and the Quality of New Recorded Music (July 2012), http://papers.ssrn.com/sol3/papers.cfm?abstract_id=2117372.

[38] Statista, *Concert ticket sales revenue in North America from 1990 to 2015 (in billion U.S. dollars)*, STATISTA, http://www.statista.com/statistics/306065/concert-ticket-sales-revenue-in-north-america/.

[39] *E.g.*, a recent review of the EP "Big Grams" in *Rolling Stone* argued that even star guest musicians couldn't make it "feel like anything more than an attempt at landing a better festival slot." David Turner, *Review of Big Grams*, ROLLING STONE (Sept. 25, 2015), http://www.rollingstone.com/music/albumreviews/big-grams-big-grams-20150925.

In the U.S., this practice is entirely legal; fashion is a paradigmatic negative space industry. Knockoffs are ubiquitous in the industry and expected if not demanded by consumers. What is striking, however, is how rampant copying fails to drive down the level of creativity and creative production in the apparel industry. Fashion seems to dramatically violate the fundamental premise of IP rights, for the freedom to copy not only does not destroy the creative impulse; it actually incentivizes and accelerates it.[40] Fashion is a status-laden good, whose value, for many, is dependent on its scarcity and novelty. When a design is fresh and new it is desirable. But as it spreads into the marketplace, and becomes more common, the early adopters no longer value it and seek to move on to newer designs. By stimulating demand for new designs, the regime of free appropriation that exists in the apparel world actually spurs innovation in design.

Copying is thus a basic element of the industry's trend-driven business model. This is implicit in the cycle just described; designs are adopted by others once there is some (often very early) evidence of their market appeal. The result, if copying is widespread enough, is a trend, and trends are the centerpiece of the fashion world. Copying first helps to set or identify trends, and then to anchor consumers' expectations about what is in style at a given moment. This benefits the fashion industry by lowering consumers' information costs about what is and is not currently in style and easing the decision about what to wear – which, of course, encourages more apparel purchases by lowering the risk of purchase. And as copying spreads still further the regime of free appropriation helps to kill the trend that it birthed. As a design becomes very widely copied, its cachet typically falls. Copying is, in short, the engine that drives the fashion cycle faster.

Are there other creative industries that sustain incentives to innovate based on trends? Certainly, trends feature in a number of industries. For example, trends have been identified in the design of new typefaces.[41] Likewise, there are trends in the music industry, although it is unclear how much they are connected to either consumers' consumption decisions or incentives to innovate.

As in the case of social norms, and product versus performance, more work remains to be done for the negative space literature to offer

[40] Raustiala & Sprigman, *supra* note 10.

[41] Kal Raustiala & Christopher Sprigman, The Knockoff Economy: How Imitation Sparks Innovation (2012).

a more complete understanding of when trend-driven consumption might be relevant to extra-IP incentives to create. That said, the broad import of the negative space scholarship is clear: There are a number of forms of creativity, most (but not all) involving low fixed costs, in which the incentives of formal copyright law do not appear to play much of a role in maintaining substantial ongoing incentives to create.

So far, then, we have at best a conditional narrative linking copyright incentives to creativity. And that narrative doesn't grow stronger when we examine some recent evidence from lab experiments involving creativity, a topic to which we now turn.

III Lab Experiments and Creative Motivation[42]

People can be motivated to create for a variety of reasons, but psychologists generally distinguish two classes of motivation: extrinsic and intrinsic.[43] Extrinsic motivation is motivation to engage in an activity that comes from a source that is external to the individual, such as payment of money, evaluation from a third party, or surveillance.[44] Intrinsic motivation, by contrast, is motivation that comes purely from a person's intrinsic enjoyment of or interest in the activity at hand.[45]

The effectiveness of IP rules depends in part on the interactions between internal and external motivation. To varying degrees, the kinds of creativity that IP law deals with involve both kinds of motivation. Creators and inventors have manifold internal and external reasons for engaging in their work. To these reasons, IP law adds an additional external motivator: the opportunity to receive formal rights that potentially increase economic returns on creativity.

From a classical economic perspective, the answer is simple: Motivation is motivation, and more of it is better. In order for a person

[42] This section has been adapted from Christopher Buccafusco & Christopher Jon Sprigman, *Experiments in Intellectual Property*, in RESEARCH HANDBOOK ON THE ECONOMICS OF INTELLECTUAL PROPERTY LAW (VOL. II – ANALYTICAL METHODS) (Peter Menell & David Schwartz eds., forthcoming).

[43] Edward L. Deci, *Intrinsic Motivation, Extrinsic Reinforcement, and Inequity*, 22 J. PERSONALITY & SOC. PSYCHOL. 113, 113 (1972).

[44] Teresa M. Amabile, Beth Ann Hennessey & Barbara S. Grossman, *Social Influences on Creativity: The Effects of Contracted-for Reward*, 50 J. PERSONALITY & SOC. PSYCHOL. 14, 15 (1986); Deci, *supra* note 43, at 113.

[45] Deci, *supra* note 43.

to do something, she needs to have sufficient incentives that exceed the costs of engaging in the behavior.[46] As long as the benefit she receives exceeds the cost of performing the task, she can be expected to engage in it. Moreover, the nature of the motivation does not matter, only its level does.[47] On this view, extrinsic and intrinsic motivations are substitutable for one another, and the addition of extrinsic motivation to an already intrinsically motivated person should increase motivation and performance.[48] As Dan Ariely and others explain, "[t]he expectation that increasing performance-contingent incentives will improve performance rests on two subsidiary assumptions: (1) that increasing performance-contingent incentives will lead to greater motivation and effort and (2) that this increase in motivation and effort will result in improved performance."[49]

Over the past several decades, however, experimental social-science research has significantly complicated this otherwise simple story. Despite general findings that extrinsic incentives tend to enhance performance on tasks that are algorithmic (simple or straightforward),[50] many studies suggest otherwise with regard to the effect of incentives to complete tasks that are creative. At least in some cases, these studies suggest that intrinsic and extrinsic incentives for creativity may not be substitutes for one another and that the provision of greater creativity incentives does not necessarily result in more or better performance.[51]

[46] *See* William M. Landes & Richard A. Posner, The Economic Structure of Intellectual Property Law 20 (2003) (discussing investments that yield social benefits in excess of costs as desirable).

[47] *See* Roland Bénabou & Jean Tirole, *Intrinsic and Extrinsic Motivation*, 70 Rev. Econ. Stud. 489, 489 (2003) (implying that economists have neglected psychological research showing that incentives can undermine performance).

[48] *See* Deci, *supra* note 43, at 113–14 (assessing impact of different extrinsic motivations upon intrinsically motivated people).

[49] Dan Ariely, Uri Gneezy, George Loewenstein & Nina Mazar, *Large Stakes and Big Mistakes*, 76 Rev. Econ. Stud. 451, 451 (2009).

[50] *See* Kenneth O. McGraw, *The Detrimental Effects of Reward on Performance: A Literature Review and a Prediction Model*, in The Hidden Costs of Reward: New Perspectives on the Psychology of Human Motivation 33, 55–57 (Mark R. Lepper & David Greene eds., 1978) (summarizing study results and finding that rewards are least disruptive when the task is adversive to the subject and algorithmic).

[51] *See generally* Robert Gibbons & John Roberts, *Economic Theories of Incentives in Organizations*, in The Handbook of Organizational Economics 56 (Robert Gibbons & John Roberts eds., 2013) (discussing the interplay between intrinsic and extrinsic incentives as posited by Bénabou & Tirole). Roland Bénabou & Jean Tirole respond to the psychological results showing that incentives can harm creativity by

To understand the interrelationship between motivation, creativity, and incentives, psychologists examine the effects of intrinsic motivation and extrinsic motivation on creativity. Some psychologists' studies find that intrinsic motivation is more conducive to creativity than extrinsic motivation.[52] These studies typically investigate overjustification: having subjects engage in a task that they already might like to do with the promise of extrinsic reward.[53] Subjects engage in a creative task, such as drawing or collage making or puzzle solving.[54] Some are told that they will receive a reward for performance, while others are not.[55] In these situations, those subjects acting with reward expectation are judged to produce significantly less creative work than those acting without reward expectation.[56]

Despite this line of findings, there are other studies that suggest that extrinsic rewards do not always undermine creativity and can, in fact, enhance it. For one thing, studies by behavioral psychologists tend to find that providing reward– external motivation – increases subjects' creative performance with regard to whatever aspect the subject is being told will be judged (such as originality or fluency).[57]

These two strands of studies may be reconciled. The incentive studies instruct subjects specifically how (or with regard to which aspect) to perform creatively and the extrinsic reward then helps enhance creativity, whereas the overjustification studies do not so instruct and the extrinsic

building an economic model that incorporates these psychological insights and shows why they can be rational. Bénabou & Tirole, *supra* note 47.

52 Amabile et al., *supra* note 44, at 79.

53 Teresa M. Amabile, *Effects of External Evaluation on Artistic Creativity*, 37 J. Personality & Soc. Psychol. 221, 222 (1979).

54 *Id.* 55 *Id.*

56 *E.g.*, Amabile, *supra* note 53, at 222 (discussing experimental results showing that rewarded subjects produced less creative responses than those not rewarded for participation); Regina Conti, Teresa M. Amabile & Sara Pollak, *The Positive Impact of Creative Activity: Effects of Creative Task Engagement and Motivational Focus on College Students' Learning*, 21 Personality & Soc. Psychol. Bull. 1107, 1109 (1995) (noting that "salient extrinsic motives, such as focusing on external evaluation, have been found to undermine . . . creativity"); Beth A. Hennessey, *The Effect of Extrinsic Constraints on Children's Creativity While Using a Computer*, 2 Creativity Res. J. 151 (1989); *cf.* Ariely, Gneezy, Loewenstein & Mazar, *supra* note 49, at 454–67 (showing that "relatively high monetary incentives can have perverse effects on performance" for cognitively intense tasks, like creative ones).

57 *E.g.* John Glover & A. L. Gary, *Procedures To Increase Some Aspects of Creativity*, 9 J. Of Applied Behavior Analysis 79 (1976) (finding this to be the case for a verbal creativity task in which points were awarded for fluency (number of different responses), flexibility (number of verb forms), elaboration (number of words per response), and originality (statistical infrequency of verb forms)).

reward there then decreases creativity.[58] Moreover, studies that control for both whether specific instructions to perform creatively are provided before engaging in a creative task and whether reward is provided confirm that guidance as to performance metrics seems to explain the difference in the effect of reward.[59] The theory is that when subjects are not instructed on how to perform specifically on a creative task, they are risk averse and choose conventional solutions to the task at hand, which is detrimental to creativity.[60] But when subjects are told the metric by which they will be judged on their creativity, they strive to do well on that metric going beyond obvious approaches to the task when there is a reward.[61] Indeed, some studies show an increase in intrinsic motivation rather than a decrease when subjects are offered a reward and are instructed to perform creatively.[62] Ultimately, however, one cannot

[58] Robert Eisenberger & Linda Shanock, *Rewards, Intrinsic Motivation, and Creativity: A Case Study of Conceptual and Methodological Isolation*, 15 CREATIVITY RES. J 121, 121–5 (2003); *see also* Amabile, *supra* note 53, at 223.

[59] Amabile, *supra* note 53, at 223–32 (studying this question with regard to collage making, but finding that those who received both extrinsic motivation and a general instruction to focus specifically on creativity – without more guidance – performed less creatively than those who got the same instruction but no extrinsic motivation). How specific this instruction to be creative need be is a matter of debate among psychologists. *Compare id.* at 223–32 (finding that those who received both extrinsic motivation and a general instruction to focus specifically on creativity – without more guidance – performed less creatively than those who got the same instruction but no extrinsic motivation), *with* Robert Eisenberger, Stephen Armeli & Jean Pretz, *Can the Promise of Reward Increase Creativity?*, 74 J. PERSONALITY & SOC. PSYCHOL. 704, 709–12 (1998) (showing through experiments that simply instructing subjects that they will be rewarded for unusual drawings along with a basic clarification about the task – rather than being given no such instruction – enhances creativity).

[60] Id. at 223. [61] Id. at 230–1.

[62] Eisenberger et al., *supra* note 58. Another aspect for which the studies showing reward's detrimental effect on creativity might be inapplicable is with regard to professionals. The studies discussed above focus on nonprofessionals. Psychologists speculate that the results might look different for professionals: According to Amabile, "While we might expect that some professional scientists or artists could succumb to the overjustification effect, it seems eminently clear that many highly creative people go on being creative in the face of numerous extrinsic constraints." Amabile, *supra* note 53, at 232. She theorizes that professional scientists and artists internalize how their work will be judged, and, as a result, external motivators have less of an effect on them (at least detrimentally). In addition, their intrinsic motivation is strong – likely much stronger than nonprofessional subjects – and overjustification is less likely to affect them than those whose "internal states are ambiguous or nonsalient." In fact, empirical work bears this out. *Id.* In an archival study, Dean Simonton finds no significant relationship between the creative productivity of ten classical composers at various points in their lives and the external motivation – such as honorary degrees – they received during those points. *See* Dean Keith Simonton, *Creative Productivity, Age, and Stress: A Biographical Time-Series*

simply assume that the addition of an incentive to an already motivated person will yield more or better creative production.

Separate from the question of intrinsic and extrinsic motivation are issues about the magnitude and structure of creativity incentives. Just as classical economic theory predicts that adding external motivation to internal motivation increases total motivation, so too does it predict that higher magnitude incentives produce greater motivation and performance than lower magnitude incentives. Recently, Dan Ariely and others have studied the effects of particular magnitudes of performance-contingent rewards on task performance.[63] Ariely and his coinvestigators studied subjects in both the United States and rural India performing a variety of tasks – based on creativity, cognition, memory, or motor skills – for which the magnitude of reward varied from low to moderate to very high.[64] Payment in each condition depended on performance on the task.[65] For example, in one reported experiment, subjects would receive full payment if performance was very good, half payment if performance was merely good, and no payment if performance did not qualify as good.[66] Across the various experiments, Ariely and the others found that subjects offered low to moderate levels of reward outperformed those offered the very high level of reward.[67] They also found that the propensity to choke on a task due to increasing reward was frequently task-specific and not just based on individual characteristics.[68] The authors suggest that these results are consistent with the idea that "beyond an optimal level of arousal for executing tasks, further increases in arousal can lead to a decrement in performance."[69] Importantly and surprisingly, however, in the study in rural India, the authors did not find variation between tasks involving creativity and those that did not. In each case, the highest incentive level undermined performance.

Analysis of 10 Classical Composers, 35 J. PERSONALITY & SOC. PSYCHOL. 791, 801 (1977).

63 Ariely, Gneezy, Loewenstein & Mazar, *supra* note 49.

64 *Id.* at 454–67. For example, the levels of payment in rural India were 4, 40, and 400 Indian Rupees, respectively, in the low, high, and very high conditions. The payment in the high-incentive treatment is close to the monthly per capita consumer expenditure in the region. *Id.* at 454.

65 *Id.* 66 *Id.* at 454.

67 *Id.* at 454–67. One important exception was the only motor-skills task given to subjects in the United States, wherein performance increased the higher the offered reward was. *Id.* at 462.

68 *Id.* at 463. 69 *Id.* at 467.

Relatedly, Katharina Eckhartz and others recently investigated the effect of incentives on creativity using three different incentive schemes: a flat fee, a linear payment, and a tournament.[70] They presented subjects with a set of letters and asked them to construct as many words as they could within five minutes.[71] For each word, participants received a score that was more than proportionally increasing given the number of letters in the word.[72] They also used an IQ task and a number-adding task as control tasks.[73] Contrary to nearly all of the other studies described above, they found that the choice of incentive had no significant effect on performance for any of the three tasks; rather, they found that "performance depends almost entirely on individual characteristics of participants and can, on the aggregate level, hardly be influenced through incentives."[74] More specifically, they found that "[i] ndividual characteristics explain for all tasks more than 60% of the observed variance in the performance. The presence or absence of different incentive schemes explain for all tasks in this experiment less than 1% of the variance."[75]

All in all, we face a murky picture of the relationship between incentives and creativity. A series of studies suggests that rewards – particularly higher ones – can undermine creativity, but other studies indicate that carefully designed rewards and instructions can instead enhance creativity.

IV Incentives and Creativity in IP Research

In recent years, a handful of legal scholars have made reference to the social-science studies, described above, suggesting a nuanced relationship between incentives and creativity. Some scholars have argued that, as a general matter, copyright law's approach to incentives is incorrect. For example, Julie Cohen argues that copyright law plays little or no role in actually motivating creators. She writes,

> Everything we know about creativity and creative processes suggests that copyright plays very little role in motivating creative work. Creative people are much more apt to describe what they do as the product of desire, compulsion, or addiction, and to understand particular results

[70] Katharina Eckartz, Oliver Kirchkamp & Daniel Schunk, *How Do Incentives Affect Creativity?* (Ifo Inst. Ctr. for Econ. Studies, Working Paper No. 4049, 2012), http://papers.ssrn.com/sol3/papers.cfm?abstract_id=2198760.

[71] *Id.* at 4. [72] *Id.* [73] *Id.* at 5–6. [74] *Id.* at 17. [75] *Id.*

> as heavily influenced by cultural, intellectual, and emotional serendipity.[76]

To Cohen and others,[77] most copyright creators have sufficient intrinsic incentives to create, and additional copyright incentives are unnecessary and wasteful.

Other scholars go further and argue that, consistent with the research discussed above, copyright law's incentives may actually undermine creativity. For example, Diane Zimmerman asks legal scholars to wrestle with the legal implications of findings that "the promise of monetary or other extrinsic rewards for creative activities can actually diminish rather than enhance the likelihood that individuals will be induced to produce high-quality new work."[78] Eric Johnson suggests that, although there might be some exceptions, "[i]n general, the kind of creativity and innovation that benefits society as a whole is not in need of externally supplied incentives."[79] In reliance on this body of literature, Johnson speculates that patent and copyright laws might be counterproductive – or at best unnecessary – for individuals.[80] Similarly, Gregory Mandel worries that "law's ability to promote creativity not only may be limited, but could even be detrimental, to the extent it turns an artist's or inventor's internally motivated activity into one conducted for the

[76] Julie E. Cohen, *Copyright as Property in the Post-Industrial Economy: A Research Agenda*, 2011 WIS. L. REV. 141, 143 (2011). Cohen goes on to propose that copyright should instead be used to "enable the provision of capital and organization so that creative work may be exploited," so that it "creates a foundation for predictability in the organization of cultural production, something particularly important in capital-intensive industries like film production."

[77] Relatedly, some scholars suggest that people will readily create in reliance on their intrinsic motivation, without regard to extrinsic motivations, such as IP-related incentives. *E.g.*, Yochai Benkler, *Coase's Penguin, or Linux and the Nature of the Firm*, 112 YALE L.J. 369, 426–34 (2002); Rebecca Tushnet, *Economies of Desire: Fair Use and Marketplace Assumptions*, 51 WM. & MARY L. REV. 513, 513 (2009) (exploring "the ways in which the desire to create can be excessive, beyond rationality, and free from the need for economic incentive," and suggesting as a result that copyright law should not "treat creative activity as a product of economic incentives"); *see also* YOCHAI BENKLER, THE WEALTH OF NETWORKS: HOW SOCIAL PRODUCTION TRANSFORMS MARKETS AND FREEDOM 92–9 (2006) (analyzing different models for motivation, including "intrinsic motivation").

[78] Diane Leenheer Zimmerman, *Copyrights as Incentives: Did We Just Imagine That?*, 12 THEORETICAL INQUIRIES L. 29, 43 (2011).

[79] Eric E. Johnson, *Intellectual Property and the Incentive Fallacy*, 39 FLA. ST. U. L. REV. 623, 625 (2012).

[80] *Id.* at 675–8.

copyright or patent prize."[81] Nonetheless, Mandel leaves open the possibility that IP laws might enhance creativity:

> To the extent intellectual property law is perceived as creating competition, constraint, or providing rewards for task (not creative) performance, the law may produce extrinsically motivated efforts that are less creative. To the extent, however, that intellectual property law is perceived as providing potential creators with a wide degree of autonomy and a reward for creative achievement, the law can produce intrinsic motivation that enhances creativity.[82]

To Zimmerman, Johnson, and Mandel, IP laws may be not only socially wasteful expenditures on creativity that would have been produced anyway; IP laws may actually be inhibiting the very creativity that they exist to promote. But aside from Mandel's work and Johnson's intimation, there has been very little discussion in the legal literature of the possibility of structuring incentives to avoid these detrimental effects.

Recently, Buccafusco, Burns, Fromer and Sprigman have studied in an experimental setting how the structure of IP-style incentives affects creativity.[83] The Buccafusco et al. paper begins with the observation that both copyright and patent law aim to incentivize creativity, but those incentives are structured quite differently from one another. Patent law imposes a high bar of novelty and nonobviousness; under these standards only inventions that are truly new are entitled to protection. In contrast, copyright law employs a standard of minimal "originality," which requires only that a creative work not be copied from another and have some spark of creativity, however slight. Is there a difference between exclusive rights structured with a high-threshold (patent) or a low-threshold (copyright) in terms of the amount of creativity produced (all other elements of the right held equal)?

Buccafusco et al. employ a set of creativity tasks to investigate this question. The first is a convergent thinking task involving a mathematical combinatorial optimization problem inspired by the famous 1990s "Oregon Trail" video game. The problem is designed to be very difficult, and perhaps impossible, to calculate a solution in the

[81] Gregory N. Mandel, *To Promote the Creative Process: Intellectual Property Law and the Psychology of Creativity*, 86 NOTRE DAME L. REV. 1999, 2008 (2011).
[82] *Id.* at 2012.
[83] Christopher Buccafusco, Zachary C. Burns, Jeanne C. Fromer & Christopher Jon Sprigman, *Experimental Tests of Intellectual Property Laws' Creativity Thresholds*, 92 TEX. L. REV. 1921 (2014).

time allotted (90 seconds), so subjects must resort to some sort of heuristic to approach the problem. The creativity is in the choice of heuristic; the goal was to model aspects of information aggregation and convergent thinking that play significant roles in intellectual discovery and invention.

Subjects were recruited online and randomly assigned to one of five experimental conditions. In all conditions, subjects were paid a fee to participate. The conditions differed in the manner in which their performance in the game affected their chance of winning a bonus prize. In the first "no incentive" condition, subjects were told that their participation in the experiment would make them eligible for a prize, to be awarded via a (random) lottery. Task performance in this condition was unrelated to payout, whereas in all other conditions payout increased along with the quality of task performance. In the second "copyright" condition, subjects were paid the same flat participation fee, and all participants who successfully completed the task would also be entered into a lottery to win a prize, with the subject's chance of winning the prize improving proportionally to his or her performance on the creativity task. The third, fourth and fifth conditions were structured to imitate patent law's higher creativity thresholds for protection. Subjects in the three conditions that modeled patent thresholds were told that only a certain percentage of contestants would be eligible to win the lottery prize – the top 50 percent in the "patent low" condition, the top 25 percent in "patent mid", and the top 5 percent in "patent high."

The experiment, which was run with almost 800 subjects recruited online, showed that patent-style incentives – i.e. those made available only to those who had surmounted a higher creativity threshold – caused a modest albeit statistically significant positive effect on overall performance on the creativity task. On the other hand, copyright-style incentives provided no measurable increase in overall performance on the creativity task versus the no-incentive (control) condition.

Buccafusco et al. employed the same protocol with two additional creativity tasks, one measuring linguistic creativity and the other figural or visual creativity. The linguistic creativity task involved rapidly generating a list of words that bear an indirect relationship with some target word, usually in the form of a pun. In Buccafusco et al.'s version of the task, subjects were asked to come up with a list of "keys," and they were rewarded for answers that were judged to be creative. For example, "house key" would not be considered a creative answer, while "Keyshawn Johnson," "monkey," "keynote speech," or "John Maynard Keynes" would be considered creative.[84] As in the first experiment, the sample for the Keys creativity task included approximately 800 subjects recruited online. And the results were broadly consistent with the first experiment – the subjects in the patent conditions, on the whole, performed better on the creativity task. In contrast, performance of subjects in the copyright condition was statistically indistinguishable from those in the no-incentives (control) condition.

A third experiment involved a figural creativity task, where subjects were presented with a series of abstract drawings and asked to state what the figures could be. As in the Keys task, only answers judged to be creative scored points (using a judging methodology similar to that employed in the Keys task). In this experiment, neither the patent nor the copyright conditions produced performance measurably better than the no-incentive (control) group.

These results suggest that incentives that are structured to include a relatively high creativity threshold – i.e. incentives structured like patents, which are (at least in theory) made available only to inventions that represent a substantial departure from the prior art – may have a positive effect on creativity. The incentives structured with a low creativity requirement – i.e. incentives structured like copyright, which is made available to any artistic or literary work that manifests even the slightest creative spark – had no measurable effect on performance in any of the creativity tasks employed. In addition, there was no evidence that the higher threshold in the patent-style conditions undermined creative performance, in contrast to studies suggesting that high-magnitude incentives cause subjects to "choke". While far from definitive, these results suggest that policymakers should consider whether copyright's effectiveness as an incentive system might be improved by raising the creativity threshold that authors are required to surmount before gaining rights.

[84] In order to assess the creativity of responses, the subjects' responses were standardized and then rated by online judges. First, every entry was standardized by two independent raters and ties were broken by a third, so that spelling, plurals, and word forms were consistent. Next, raters were recruited online, and then were instructed to evaluate a subset of the unique entries, using their own intuitions to produce the ratings, responding "Creative," "Standard," or "I'm not familiar with this." Any answer receiving more than 50% of total votes as "Creative" was tallied as creative.

Relatedly, Bechtold, Buccafusco, and Sprigman have studied how creators think about cumulative innovation.[85] In particular, they studied how creators decide whether to borrow from existing ideas and pay a license fee or whether to innovate around those ideas. Copyright and patent law are thought to play a role in structuring "follow-on" as well as "pioneering" innovation – by establishing property rights, copyright and patent law make borrowing from pre-existing creativity more expensive. In theory, creators' decisions whether to borrow versus creating anew should be based on their assessments of the relative costs and benefits of each strategy. But does IP actually matter to the borrow/innovate decision?

Bechtold et al. study creators' responses to two factors that should influence this cost-benefit calculus: how costly the license is and how easy it is to innovate around the existing IP. Comparing the costs and benefits of innovating versus borrowing is complex, however, and the authors hypothesized that creators may use "innovation heuristics" – mental shortcuts about innovation decisions – to determine what to do.

The experiments employ two separate creativity tasks. In one, subjects play a version of a knapsack task that requires them to select items to add to a wagon in order to maximize the wagon's value without exceeding its weight limit. They are told that another subject has begun playing the game, and that if they innovate around the other subject's solution, they can obtain more bonus points. The second task involves a Scrabble game in which subjects must create a list of six words using a series of letters provided. Again, another person has submitted a word list, and subjects gain more points by innovating around the other subject's list (defined as using two or fewer of his words). In both tasks, although choosing to innovate results in a bonus, it also constricts the subject's options. Because innovating can be a good or a bad decision, subjects need to weigh the costs and benefits of their choices.

In the first set of experiments, the researchers test whether subjects are sensitive to the cost of borrowing the other subject's solution. Subjects are randomly assigned to conditions that differ in terms of the value of the bonus offered for innovating. In some conditions, the bonus should be too small to induce rational subjects into restricting their options to play the games. In other conditions, the bonus should be far greater than is

[85] Stefan Bechtold, Christopher Buccafusco & Christopher Jon Sprigman, *Innovation Heuristics: Experiments on Sequential Creativity in Intellectual Property*, 92 Indiana L. J. 1251 (2016).

necessary to induce innovation. Despite these differences, subjects tended to innovate at almost identical rates (about 70%) in each condition in both the wagon and the scrabble games. This leads to welfare losses in both the low and high bonus conditions, because many subjects are choosing to innovate when they should be borrowing (and vice versa). The researchers find that although subjects are insensitive to objective changes in the innovation environment, their decisions are largely driven by their own subjective assessments of how easy it is to innovate.

In the second set of experiments, Bechtold, Buccafusco, and Sprigman test whether subjects are sensitive to how easy it is to innovate around the existing solutions. The better the given solution, the more likely it is that people should borrow rather than innovate. In separate studies using each of the creativity tasks, subjects were randomly assigned to conditions in which the strength of the given solution was 60%, 80%, or 100% of the best solution. They were offered a single innovation bonus that remained constant. In the Wagon version of this study, unlike in the first set of studies, subjects demonstrated some sensitivity to how good the given solution was. Subjects were more likely to borrow rather than innovate as the solution strength increased (19.2%, 30.7%, and 39.8%, respectively). This was particularly surprising because they were not told how strong the given solution was.

Yet the truly striking results appeared in the Scrabble version of the study. Between the 60% condition and the 80%, subjects chose to innovate less in the latter (46.8% vs. 40.9%), as standard theory would predict given the smaller innovation space. But subjects in the 100% condition innovated at a substantially higher rate (85.7%) than did those in the other conditions, even though innovating was an overwhelmingly bad option. The authors suggest that subjects in the 100% condition were influenced by an "innovation heuristic." Instead of comparing the ease of finding an innovating solution with the value of that solution relative to the value of borrowing, subjects simply asked themselves how easy it was to generate a list of non-borrowing words. Here, the given solution in the 100% condition had very challenging words, so subjects found it easy to create a non-borrowing list of words. They ignored, however, the low value associated with those words. Rather than assess the full problem, subjects seem to have focused only on a portion of it.

The results of these studies suggest that creators' responses to sequential innovation decisions are not necessarily as rational as copyright (or indeed patent) law predicts. Creators are often insensitive to key aspects of the innovation environment, and their decisions may be motivated more by internal preferences from innovating versus borrowing than by objective factors. Moreover, features of the innovation environment may affect the success of creators' decisions depending on whether heuristics do a good job of proxying for the best decision.

V Conclusion

In short, the results from the lab experiments further complicate the simple theoretical account of how copyright incentivizes creativity. The picture that emerges from the lab experiments, from the negative space studies, and from event studies like Moser/Giorcelli, suggests that copyright may contribute to creative incentives in some contexts and under some conditions, but not in others. And usually not in the manner or to the extent that orthodox economic theory would predict.

The question is what to make of this glimpse into copyright's reality? There are two things to say. First, it is only a glimpse. For the empirical study of copyright incentives to provide a clearer picture of how, and when, copyright motivates creativity, we need a lot more, and more varied, studies in all of the categories this chapter covers. We also need better access to data, often closely held by content producers and distributors, that could help us check empirical findings against real-world facts. And those of us who do empirical research on the link between copyright and creativity need to do more to attract talent into the field. The question of what spurs creativity is of surpassing importance in human life. It is a scandal that we know as little about it as we do.

Relatedly, what good is empirical work if it gives us such a hazy picture of the link between copyright and creativity? It is true that the existing literature tells a complicated and to some extent conflicting story. And it is also true that policymakers want simplicity and consistency. And so the literature as it stands does not provide a particularly attractive foundation upon which to justify, or to reform, existing copyright law.

That said, the existing empirical literature is nonetheless useful, not least because it may, in certain narrow instances, save us from making bad changes to existing law. So, for example, various recent attempts to extend copyright to cover fashion designs have failed, in some small part because the empirical work on fashion provides a counter-narrative where copying and innovation are not inimical, but rather work together.

The most interesting question will be what happens if, in the coming decades, the empirical scholarship on copyright and creative incentives matures, and yet continues to tell the same story that, at a general level, it tells now: viz., that copyright incentives are relevant to some forms of creativity, and in some circumstances, and not in others. Will we see a realignment of policy to tailor copyright's domain to the areas where it is likely to do some good? I'm skeptical. Noninstrumentalist (i.e. deontic) theories of copyright – theories based not in the goal of providing incentives, but instead, in some fairness or justice concern – are the framework in which many, and perhaps most, people approach copyright questions. As I have suggested (but must content myself with explaining in greater detail elsewhere), those theories are very useful for understanding why we have some sort of property rights in literary and artistic expression. But noninstrumentalist theories, I suspect, can accomplish very little in terms of specifying and justifying a copyright system at the level of detail relevant to policymaking. And yet until the important albeit limited utility of noninstrumentalist copyright theories is fully understood, they will continue to influence policy beyond their proper domain.

As a consequence, for the empirical scholarship to achieve its potential, two things must happen. First, empirical scholars need to expand and refine our understanding of the relationship between copyright and creativity. And second, legal theorists must work out the proper relationship between instrumentalist and deontic copyright justifications. Until these tasks are advanced much further, we can expect copyright lawmaking to hew to narrow private interests, forcefully articulated and relatively well understood, often at the expense of the faintly articulated and relatively hazily appreciated public interest.

3

Reframing Intellectual Property Rights with Fewer Distortions of the Trade Paradigm

JEROME H. REICHMAN

I Introduction

The editors of this book have focused attention on the need to "reframe" intellectual property law. To accomplish such a task, would-be protagonists must necessarily take into account the new empirical realities that have characterized the evolution of intellectual property rights since the 1990s.[1] At least three of these developments cannot easily be reconciled with the standard economic justifications for the classical regimes that have protected inventors' and authors' rights since the 1880s:[2]

- First, global intellectual property law has expanded beyond protecting downstream products of human creativity and ingenuity to encompass upstream inputs into the processes of basic and applied research, from

[1] *Compare* Convention on Biological Diversity, June 5, 1992, 1760 U.N.T.S. 79 [hereinafter CBD], *with* Agreement on Trade-Related Aspects of Intellectual Property Rights, Apr. 15, 1994, Marrakesh Agreement Establishing the World Trade Organization, Annex 1C, Legal Instruments – Results of the Uruguay Round, vol. 31, 33 I.L.M. 81 (1994) [hereinafter TRIPS].

[2] Paris Convention for the Protection of Industrial Property, Mar. 20, 1883, as last revised at Stockholm, July 14, 1967, 21 U.S.T. 1583, 828 U.N.T.S. 305 [hereinafter Paris Convention]; Berne Convention for the Protection of Literary and Artistic Works, Sept. 9, 1886, 1161 U.N.T.S. 31 [hereinafter Berne Convention]. *See generally* Giovanni Dosi & Joseph E. Stiglitz, *The Role of Intellectual Property Rights in the Development Process, with Some Lessons From Developed Countries: An Introduction*, in INTELLECTUAL PROPERTY RIGHTS: LEGAL AND ECONOMIC CHALLENGES FOR DEVELOPMENT 1–56 (M. Cimoli et al. eds., 2014); Keith E. Maskus & Jerome H. Reichman, *The Globalization of Private Knowledge Goods and the Privatization of Global Public Goods*, in INTERNATIONAL PUBLIC GOODS AND TRANSFER OF TECHNOLOGY UNDER A GLOBALIZED INTELLECTUAL PROPERTY REGIME 3–45 (K. E. Maskus & J. H. Reichman eds., 2005).

which both commercial and noncommercial end products eventually emerge.[3]

- Second, all over the world, and especially in the developing countries, efforts are under way to elaborate and codify further exceptions and limitations to the exclusive rights that intellectual property laws otherwise mandate.[4]
- Third, scholarly attention in both developed and developing countries has focused increasingly on the benefits of bargaining around exclusive intellectual property rights, in order to maximize the benefits of sharing research results and of open-access objectives in general.[5]

All these phenomena are discussed in the rest of this chapter, with particular reference to their implications for efforts to reframe global intellectual property rights in general.

II From Bundles of Exclusive Rights to Tools of Inclusion

Early in the 1990s, at the very time when negotiations to revise the Paris Convention for the Protection of Industrial Property were breaking down at the World Intellectual Property Organization (WIPO),[6] two novel forms of intellectual property suddenly emerged from diverse

[3] *See generally* Jerome H. Reichman, Paul F. Uhlir & Tom Dedeurwaerdere, Governing Digitally Integrated Genetic Resources, Data and Literature: Global Intellectual Property Strategies for a Redesigned Microbial Research Commons 1–34 (2016) [hereinafter Governing Digitally Integrated Genetic Resources (2016)]. *See also* J. H. Reichman & David Lange, *Bargaining Around the TRIPS Agreement: The Case for Ongoing Public-Private Initiatives to Facilitate Worldwide Intellectual Property Transactions*, 9 Duke J. Comp. & Int'l L. 11 (1998), http://scholarship.law.duke.edu/djcil/vol19/iss 1/2.

[4] *See, e.g.*, Pamela Samuelson, *Justification for Copyright Limitations and Exceptions*, in Copyright Law in an Age of Limitations and Exceptions 12–59 (Ruth L. Okediji ed., 2017); Niva Elkin-Koren, *Copyright in a Digital Ecosystem: A User-Rights Approach*, in Copyright in an Age of Limitations and Exceptions, *supra*, 132–68. *See* further *infra* Sections III., A.1 & 2.

[5] *See generally*, Section III, A.3.

[6] *See, e.g.*, Frederick M. Abbott, *Protecting First World Assets in the Third World: Intellectual Property Negotiations in the GATT Multilateral Framework*, 22 Vand. J. Transnat'l L. 689 (1989); Jerome H. Reichman, *Intellectual Property in International Trade: Opportunities and Risks of a GATT Connection*, 22 Vand. J. Transnat'l L. 747 (1989); Peter Drahos, *Negotiating Intellectual Property Rights: Between Coercion and Dialogue*, in Global Intellectual Property Rights: Knowledge, Access and Development (P. Drahos & R. Mayner eds., 2002).

legislative initiatives. One was the Convention on Biological Diversity of 1992,[7] which expressly recognized the developing countries' sovereign rights over genetic resources and traditional knowledge emanating from their territories.[8] The other was the European Commission's Directive on the Legal Protection of Databases, adopted in 1996.[9] Both of these initiatives created exclusive property rights in upstream inputs to downstream end products that had hitherto been treated as the "Common Heritage of Mankind."[10]

A The Propertization of Plant and Microbial Genetic Resources

Consider, for example, that plant and microbial genetic resources, together with traditional knowledge concerning their uses by indigenous communities, had long been treated as freely available inputs into scientific research.[11] Both pharmaceutical products to cure diseases and plant varieties to improve food security still remain heavily dependent on unrestricted access to these genetic resources.[12] Obviously, the notion of a vast public domain served the interests of the Great Powers, when they presided over biodiversity rich colonies. Nevertheless, it also led to the formation of public seed banks and microbial culture collections, whose ongoing efforts to validate and preserve *ex situ* genetic

[7] CBD, *supra* note 1, art. 15. *See also* Report of the Tenth Meeting of the Conference of the Parties to the Convention on Biological Diversity, Oct. 18–29, 2010, UNEP/CBD/COP/10/27, *Nagoya Protocol on Access to Genetic Resources and the Fair and Equitable Sharing of Benefits Arising from their Utilization (ABS) to the Convention on Biological Diversity* [hereinafter Nagoya Protocol] (entered into force after the deposit of the fiftieth instrument of ratification, acceptance, approval, or accession in 2014), http://www.cbd.int/abs/doc/protocol/nagoya-protocol-en.pdf.

[8] *See, e.g.*, Graham Dutfield, *Intellectual Property, Biological Resources, and Traditional Knowledge*, in Intellectual Property and Information Wealth: Issues and Practices in the Digital Age 319–44 (Peter K. Yu ed., 2007)

[9] Directive 96/9/EC of the European Parliament and of the Council of 11 March 1996 on the Legal Protection of Databases, 1996 O.J. (L 77) 20, 21 [hereinafter EC Database Directive]. *See, e.g.*, Jerome H. Reichman & Pamela Samuelson, *Intellectual Property Rights in Data?* 50 Vand. L. Rev. 52, 113–24 (1997).

[10] *See, e.g.*, Governing Digitally Integrated Genetic Resources, Data and Literature (2016), *supra* note 3, at 50–2 ("Short-Lived Recognition of Plant Genetic Resources as the Common Heritage of Mankind").

[11] *See, e.g.*, *id.* at 37–52 ("Historical Importance of Genetic Resources as Global Public Goods" (citing authorities)).

[12] *See*, e.g., *id.* at 10–19 ("Cutting Edge Applications of Microbiology in Response to Major Global Challenges"); *see also id.* at 46–52 ("Early Efforts to Form an Agricultural Research Commons for Plant Genetic Resources").

resources[13] constitute an integral part of the global scientific research infrastructure, with benefits to humanity at large.[14]

In the last quarter of the twentieth century, however, developed countries in the Global North pressed their former colonies – now sovereign and independent nations – to expand and respect patents on both plant and microbial genetic resources under the Agreement on Trade Related Aspects of Intellectual Property Rights of 1994,[15] or at least to recognize plant breeders' rights under the International Convention for the Protection of New Varieties of Plants of 1991(UPOV).[16] In response, developing countries in the Global South demanded and obtained exclusive rights to plant, microbial, and animal genetic resources and related data originating from their national territories under the Convention on Biological Diversity of 1992 (CBD), as reinforced by the Nagoya Protocol to the CBD of 2010.[17] This tug-of-war between developed and developing countries threatened the very existence of public seed banks and microbial culture collections on which both agricultural research and the life sciences had long depended.[18]

13 *See, e.g., id.* at 173–7 ("Servicing the Broad Microbiological Research Community"); *see also id.* at 179–86 ("From Culture Collections to Biological Resource Centers"). For plants, see *id.* at 46–52 ("Early Efforts to Form an Agricultural Research Commons for Plant Genetic Resources"); Michael Blakeney, *Agricultural Research, Intellectual Property and the CGIAR System*, in GLOBAL INTELLECTUAL PROPERTY RIGHTS, *supra* note 6, at 108–24. For recent developments, *see* Diversity Seek, *Harnessing the Power of Crop Diversity to Feed the Future: White Paper*, DIVSEEK (2016), www.divseek.org.

14 *See, e.g.,* Cletus Kurtzman, *The Agricultural Research Service Culture Collections: Germplasm Accessions and Research Programs*, in DESIGNING THE MICROBIAL RESEARCH COMMONS: PROCEEDINGS OF AN INTERNATIONAL SYMPOSIUM 55 (Paul F. Uhlir ed., 2011); World Federation for Culture Collections (WFCC), *Guidelines for the Establishment and Operation of Collections of Cultures of Microorganisms*, 3d ed. (Feb. 2010), www.wfcc.info/guidelines.

15 *See* TRIPS, *supra* note 1, art. 27.3(b).

16 *See* International Convention for the Protection of New Varieties of Plants (UPOV), Dec. 2, 1961, 815 U.N.T.S. 89 as last amended 1991. Technically, a country that provides effective *sui generis* protection of plant varieties under the TRIPS Agreement is not obligated to join UPOV. *See* TRIPS, *supra* note 1, art. 27.3(b).

17 *See* CBD, *supra* note 1; Nagoya Protocol, *supra* note 7. The Nagoya Protocol to the CBD authorizes seizure of imported end products derived from genetic resources or related traditional knowledge without access and benefit-sharing agreements with provider countries. *See further* GOVERNING DIGITALLY INTEGRATED GENETIC RESOURCES (2016), *supra* note 3, at 142–60 ("New Constraints and Opportunities for Scientific Research under the Nagoya Protocol").

18 *See* GOVERNING DIGITALLY INTEGRATED GENETIC RESOURCES (2016), *supra* note 3, at 111–18 ("Destabilizing the Exchange of Plant and Microbial Genetic Resources as Global Public Goods").

Strenuous efforts were subsequently undertaken to rescue the public seed banks administered by the Consultative Group on International Agricultural Research (CGIAR).[19] Under the aegis of the United Nations Food and Agricultural Organization (FAO), the CGIAR's public seed banks were entrusted to a global Crop Commons that the International Treaty on Plant Genetic Resources for Food and Agriculture (ITPGRFA) established for this purpose in 2001.[20] Now that the Nagoya Protocol to the CBD has expressly validated this multilateral regime of facilitated access to plant genetic resources for breeding and research purposes,[21] as I have elsewhere explained,[22] similar efforts are underway to devise a multilateral regime of facilitated access to the public microbial culture collections governed by the World Federation for Culture Collections (WFCC).[23]

B The Propertization of Noncopyrightable Research Data

Still another major example of the trend to protect inputs, as well as outputs, of the creative process was the European Union's Directive on the Legal

[19] These efforts were led by the United Nations Food and Agricultural Organization (FAO). *See id.* at 115–18 ("The CGIAR's Agricultural Research Infrastructure on the Verge of Collapse").

[20] International Treaty on Plant Genetic Resources for Food and Agriculture, June 29, 2004, 2400 U.N.T.S. 303 [hereinafter ITPGRFA], http://treaties.un.org/doc/publication/UNTS/Volume%202400/v2400.pdf. *See further* GOVERNING DIGITALLY INTEGRATED GENETIC RESOURCES (2016), *supra* note 3, at 118–42 ("An International Treaty to Rescue and Expand the Global Crop Commons"). For theoretical and empirical evaluations of knowledge commons and related issues, see BRETT M. FRISCHMANN, INFRASTRUCTURE, THE SOCIAL VALUE OF SHARED RESOURCES (2012); BRETT M. FRISCHMANN, KATHERINE J. STRANDBURG & MICHAEL J. MADISON, GOVERNING KNOWLEDGE COMMONS (2015); *see also* James Boyle, *Mertonianism Unbound: Imagining Free, Decentralized Access to Most Cultural and Scientific Material*, in UNDERSTANDING KNOWLEDGE AS A COMMONS: FROM THEORY TO PRACTICE 123, 123–40 (Charlotte Hess & Elinor Ostrom eds., 2007).

[21] *See* Nagoya Protocol, *supra* note 7, art. 4.

[22] *See* GOVERNING DIGITALLY INTEGRATED GENETIC RESOURCES (2016), *supra* note 3, at 150–3 ("Recognizing the Link between Public Science and Commercial Benefits").

[23] For the WFCC, see *supra* note 14. *See further* GOVERNING DIGITALLY INTEGRATED GENETIC RESOURCES (2016), *supra* note 3, at 528–538 ("The Global Biological Resource Center Network (GBRCN) Demonstration Project"), 541–544 ("The Next Step: The Microbial Resource Infrastructure (MIRRI) as a European Stepping Stone to the GBRCN"). *See generally id.* at 568–651 ("Governing Digitally Integrated Genetic Resources, Data, and Literature"). *See also* G. PASCUZZI ET AL., COMPARATIVE ISSUES IN THE GOVERNANCE OF RESEARCH BIOBANKS: PROPERTY, PRIVACY, INTELLECTUAL PROPERTY AND THE ROLE OF TECHNOLOGY (2013).

Protection of Databases in 1996.[24] This Directive provided exclusive intellectual property rights to compilers of noncopyrightable collections of data under a *sui generis* regime that had no historical precedents.[25]

International copyright law, as enshrined in both the Berne Convention for the Protection of Literary and Artistic Works of 1886 and the TRIPS Agreement of 1994, had previously mandated the protection of literary compilations whose original selection and arrangement of contents constituted "intellectual creations."[26] However, copyright protection did not extend to the underlying facts and data in any given compilation, which continued to serve as basic inputs to scientific investigation.[27] Notwithstanding this established normative framework, the protection afforded noncopyrightable collections of data under the EC's *sui generis* Database Directive was stronger in certain key aspects than the scope of protection that copyright laws confer on authors of literary and artistic works in general.[28] Although this controversial data protection regime has failed to enhance the share of European publishers in the global market for compilations, which was its legislative justification,[29] the Commission has endeavored to export it to other countries by means of bilateral and regional free trade agreements as well as by a reciprocity provision in the Directive itself.[30]

[24] Directive 96/9/EC of the European Parliament and of the Council of 11 March 1996 on the Legal Protection of Databases, 1996 O.J. (L 77) 20, 21 [hereinafter EC Database Directive].

[25] *See, e.g.*, Reichman & Samuelson, *supra* note 9, at 113–24.

[26] *See* Berne Convention, *supra* note 2, art. 2(5); TRIPS, *supra* note 1, art. 10(2).

[27] This distinction was expressly clarified in TRIPS, *supra* note 1, art. 10(2) (stating that "such protection shall not extend to the data or material itself . . ."); *see also* WIPO Copyright Treaty, art. 5, Dec. 20, 1996, 112 Stat. 2860, 2186 U.N.T.S. 182 [hereinafter WIPO Copyright Treaty] to the same effect. *See further* Jerome H. Reichman & Ruth L. Okediji, *When Copyright Law and Science Collide: Empowering Digitally Integrated Research Methods on a Global Scale*, 96 U. MINN. L. REV. 1362, 1365–8 (2012) (citing authorities).

[28] *See* EC Database Directive, *supra* note 24, arts. 1–11; Daniel J. Gervais, *The Protection of Databases*, 82 CHI.-KENT L. REV. 1109 (2007); Reichman & Samuelson, *supra* note 9, at 113–24; Reichman & Okediji, *supra* note 27, at 1418–25 (citing authorities).

[29] *See, e.g., DG Internal Market and Services Working Paper of the Commission of the European Communities – First Evaluation of Directive 96/9/EC on the Legal Protection of Databases* (Dec. 12, 2005), http://ec.europa.eu/internal_market/copyright/docs/databases/evaluation_report_en.pdf. The U.S. continues to dominate the market for databases. *See further* Reichman & Okediji, *supra* note 27, at 1419, n. 280 (citing authority).

[30] *See, e.g.*, Denise Rosemary Nicholson, *Intellectual Property: Benefit or Burden for Africa*, 32 INT'L FED. LIBRARIES J. 310, 316 (2006); Pedro Roffe et al., *Intellectual Property Rights in Free Trade Agreements: Moving Beyond TRIPS Minimum Standards*, in

Meanwhile, the global research community has increasingly resolved these and other impediments to its internal "Big Data" objectives[31] by pooling data in ever more comprehensive commons and semicommons arrangements that facilitate sharing and access among collaborators on major projects.[32] A growing number of scientific publications have likewise adopted open-access policies that encourage the sharing of both research results and research data, while science funding agencies often mandate this approach.[33]

C *Implications for Legal Theory*

Looking more closely at the foregoing examples, we see mounting evidence that intellectual property legislation has deviated from, and sometimes contradicted, its traditional roles. From an economic perspective, intellectual property rights supposedly operate as tools of exclusion, in order to incentivize authors, artists, and inventors to produce intangible creations that might otherwise remain freely available to second comers who did not incur similar front-end costs. Yet, increasingly, we see intellectual property rights covering selected inputs to the creative process as such, while also supporting open-access policies and methods of distribution that include the pooling of genetic resources, data, and literature in an array of knowledge commons supporting today's global scientific infrastructure.[34]

In so doing, intellectual property rights have also become major tools of inclusion, even as they continue to address market failures as more traditional tools of exclusion. As tools of inclusion, they may also

RESEARCH HANDBOOK ON THE PROTECTION OF INTELLECTUAL PROPERTY UNDER WTO RULES 266–318 (C. M. Correa ed., 2010).

[31] Office of Strategic Coordination, *Big Data to Knowledge*, NAT'L INST. HEALTH (NIH) (Jul. 22, 2013), https://commonfund.nih.gov/bd2k/index.aspx.

[32] *See, e.g.*, GOVERNING DIGITALLY INTEGRATED GENETIC RESOURCES (2016), *supra* note 3, at 406–73 ("Fully Exploiting Data-Intensive Research Opportunities in the Networked Environment"). *See also* Jorge L. Contreras & Jerome H. Reichman, *Sharing by Design: Data and Decentralized Commons*, 350 SCIENCE 1312 (2015).

[33] *See, e.g.*, GOVERNING DIGITALLY INTEGRATED GENETIC RESOURCES (2016), *supra* note 3, at 375–93 ("Surveying the Practices of the Microbiology Journals"); *see also id.* at 441–73 ("Building Transnational Open Knowledge Environments").

[34] *Cf. generally* GOVERNING DIGITALLY INTEGRATED GENETIC RESOURCES (2016), *supra* note 3, at 82–167 ("Tightening the Regulatory Grip: From the Convention on Biological Diversity in 1992 to the Nagoya Protocol in 2010"), 373–406 ("Enabling the Microbiological Research Community to Control Its Own Scholarly Publications"), 406–73 ("Fully Exploiting Data-Intensive Research Opportunities in the Networked Environment") (citing authorities).

logically attract liability rules, rather than exclusive property rights, in appropriate circumstances.[35] For example, a "take and pay" approach was codified in the International Treaty on Plant Genetic Resources for Food and Agriculture, which thus applies a liability rule to *ex situ* plant cultivars made available to science and industry from the Crop Commons established in 2001.[36]

These phenomena alone should persuade scholars of the need to reframe intellectual property rights in keeping with the theme of this book. A different and more perplexing question, however, is whether the merger of intellectual property law with international trade law, which occurred in the Agreement Establishing the World Trade Organization of 1994,[37] requires an even more fundamental reframing of traditional intellectual property law from the bottom up, so to speak.

III Continuing Importance of "Laboratory Effects" in the Domestic Laws

We should not be surprised that intellectual property law has continued to evolve in unpredictable ways. The advent of this regime was itself a comparatively recent phenomenon, without precedents in Roman law to provide a solid historical foundation.[38] Even the nomenclature – "intellectual property" – arose almost by accident, when certain Continental scholars realized that copyrights, patents, and trademarks had more in common with each other than with older, more established subcategories of property law.[39]

For this very reason, Stephen Ladas described the evolution of intellectual property law under the aegis of the Great Conventions of the late nineteenth century[40] as contingent upon a process of national experimentation in implementing then existing international minimum standards of protection.[41] Domestic laws would provide empirical evidence of the

[35] *See generally* Jerome H. Reichman, *Of Green Tulips and Legal Kudzu: Repackaging Rights in Subpatentable Innovations*, 53 VAND. L. REV. 1743 (2000).

[36] *See* ITPGRFA, *supra* note 20; *see further supra* notes 19–23 and accompanying text. For details, see GOVERNING DIGITALLY INTEGRATED GENETIC RESOURCES (2016), *supra* note 3, at 121–30 ("Establishing the Multilateral Regime for Access and Benefit-Sharing").

[37] Marrakesh Agreement Establishing the World Trade Organization, Apr. 15, 1994, 1867 U.N.T.S. 154 [hereinafter Marrakesh Agreement Establishing the WTO]. The TRIPS Agreement, *supra* note 1, is technically Annex 1C of this same WTO Agreement.

[38] STEPHEN LADAS, PATENTS, TRADEMARKS, AND RELATED RIGHTS: NATIONAL AND INTERNATIONAL PROTECTION (1975), at 17–56.

[39] *See id.* at 19–59. [40] Paris Convention, *supra* note 2; Berne Convention, *supra* note 2.

[41] LADAS, *supra* note 38, at 19–94.

impact of different national rules and practices. Armed with this empirical evidence, governments could compare and evaluate proposals for further harmonizing international minimum standards in the light of diverse national experiments and their own economic development needs. On this view, the process of national implementation of international standards of protection was a natural experiment whose "laboratory effects" were then open to objective comparative analysis and horse trading over time.

A Clarifying the Connection between Intellectual Property and International Trade Law

The "marriage of convenience" between intellectual property and international trade law that occurred with the establishment of the WTO in 1994[42] did nothing to change the fundamental paradigm that Ladas had outlined in 1975. The General Agreement on Tariffs and Trade provided a forum in which international minimum standards of intellectual property protection could be traded for concessions in other economic sectors.[43] This trade law framework made it possible to break out of a narrow negotiating platform in which only intellectual property concessions could be exchanged; it also enabled a broader, more comprehensive harmonization of minimum standards than had ever previously been attempted; and it provided a serious enforcement mechanism to support these standards for the first time ever.[44]

[42] R. Michael Gadbaw, *Intellectual Property and International Trade: Merger or Marriage of Convenience?* 22 VAND. J. TRANSNAT'L L. 223 (1989).

[43] General Agreement on Tariffs and Trade, Oct. 30, 1947, 61 Stat. A-11, 55 U.N.T.S. 194 [hereinafter GATT (1947)]; Multilateral Agreements on Trade in Goods, Apr. 15, 1994, Marrakesh Agreement Establishing the WTO, *supra* note 37, Annex 1A, 1867 U.N.T.S. 190 [GATT (1994)].

[44] Jerome H. Reichman, *Universal Minimum Standards of Intellectual Property Protection under the TRIPS Component of the WTO Agreement*, in INTELLECTUAL PROPERTY AND INTERNATIONAL TRADE: THE TRIPS AGREEMENT 27–82 (C. M. Correa & A. Yusuf eds., 3d ed., 2016); Andres Moncayo von Hase, *The Application and Interpretation of the Agreement on Trade-Related Aspects of Intellectual Property Rights*, in INTELLECTUAL PROPERTY AND INTERNATIONAL TRADE, *supra*, 83–134; Denis Borges Barbosa, *Minimum Standards Versus Harmonization in the TRIPS Context: The Nature of Obligations under TRIPS and Modes of Interpretation at the National Level in Monist and Dualist Systems*, in RESEARCH HANDBOOK, *supra* note 30, at 52–109. *See also* Jerome H. Reichman, *From Free Riders to Fair Followers: Global Competition under the TRIPS Agreement*, 29 N.Y.U. J. INT'L L. & POL. 11 (1997).

Nevertheless, this "marriage of convenience" was not a merger of intellectual property and international trade law in any important substantive respects. It did not infuse the basic tenets of intellectual property law with those of trade law, except for the outer boundary imposed by the Most Favored Nation principle.[45] Instead, it provided the impetus for a major upward sweep of stronger international minimum standards, which immediately reopened all the old questions about how such standards should be implemented in national laws and what would be the costs and benefits of different national approaches to this undertaking.[46]

In other words, the TRIPS Agreement of 1994, although a product of the international trade system's indispensable negotiating process,[47] provided no new or deeper understanding of the evolving nature of intellectual property law itself. On the contrary, as others have observed, the intellectual property standards embodied in the TRIPS Agreement were truly broad, open-ended, minimum standards of protection that left all WTO Members considerable freedom with which to implement them in ways that would promote their own innovative or adaptive capacities,[48] while otherwise competing fairly on the global market for knowledge goods.[49] To put it in terms recently expounded by Rochelle Dreyfuss and Graeme Dinwoodie, countries that properly crafted a "federalist" view of TRIPS could legitimately exploit its flexibilities and ambiguities so as to advance their own creative and innovative

[45] *See* TRIPS, supra note 1, art. 4 ("Most Favored Nation Treatment").

[46] *See* Reichman, *Universal Minimum Standards, supra* note 44; Barbosa, *supra* note 44; Graeme B. Dinwoodie & Rochelle Cooper Dreyfuss, *Enhancing Global Innovation Policy: The Role of WIPO and its Conventions in Interpreting the TRIPS Agreement*, in RESEARCH HANDBOOK, *supra* note 30, at 110–45. *See also* Reichman, *From Free Riders to Fair Followers, supra* note 44; Roffe et al., *supra* note 30, at 1–21.

[47] *See, e.g.*, Charles Cliff, *Why IPR Issues Were Brought to the GATT: A Historical Perspective on the Origin of TRIPS*, in RESEARCH HANDBOOK, *supra* note 30, at 266–318.

[48] *See e.g.*, U.N. CONFERENCE ON TRADE AND DEVELOPMENT (UNCTAD), USING INTELLECTUAL PROPERTY RIGHTS TO STIMULATE PHARMACEUTICAL PRODUCTION IN DEVELOPING COUNTRIES: A REFERENCE GUIDE, UNCTAD/DIAE/PCB/2009/19 (2011) (by Christoph Spennemann & Jerome H. Reichman) [hereinafter UNCTAD REFERENCE GUIDE]; Carlos Correa, *Multilateral Agreements and Policy Opportunities*, in INTELLECTUAL PROPERTY RIGHTS: LEGAL AND ECONOMIC CHALLENGES FOR DEVELOPMENT, *supra* note 2, at 417–38. *See also* Jerome H. Reichman, *The TRIPS Agreement Comes of Age: Conflict or Cooperation with the Developing Countries?* 32 CASE W. RES. J. INT'L L. 441 (2000); Peter K. Yu, *The Objectives and Principles of the TRIPS Agreement*, 46 HOUS. L. REV. 979 (2009); Daniel Gervais, *TRIPS and Development*, in INTELLECTUAL PROPERTY, TRADE AND DEVELOPMENT 3 (Daniel J. Gervais ed., 2007).

[49] *See, e.g.*, Maskus & Reichman, *supra* note 2, at 3–45.

interests,[50] within the new international order that combined trade and intellectual property laws to form "an incipient transnational system of innovation."[51]

As was the case after major negotiating rounds under the Great Conventions in the past,[52] the upward harmonizing thrust of the TRIPS Agreement left all WTO Members more in need of Ladas' "laboratory effects" at the national level than ever. Reduced to its simplest terms, the overriding question it posed was how countries at different levels of economic development would implement these higher international minimum standards of intellectual property protection and still successfully advance their own national economic development agendas.[53]

The answer to this question was not to be found in international trade law, nor could it be supplied by ill-conceived pressures for still higher levels of intellectual property protection to be imposed by bilateral and regional free trade agreements.[54] On the contrary, the future role of international minimum standards of intellectual property protection depends largely on the successes and failures arising from diverse national implementation strategies in the post-TRIPS environment. That is why, before we start ratcheting up another batch of untested normative proposals, whose ultimate impact even on *demandeur* countries remains controversial, we need a period of experimentation at the national level so that, by dint of new "laboratory effects," we can properly evaluate the consequences of our last major round of global harmonization.[55]

[50] Graeme B. Dinwoodie & Rochelle Cooper Dreyfuss, A NeoFederalist Vision of TRIPS: The Resilience of the International Intellectual Property Regime 19 (2012). However, many developing countries were persuaded – by one means or another – to adopt relatively high standards of intellectual property protection that made little economic sense in terms of their own economic capabilities. *See, e.g.*, Carolyn Deere, The Implementation Game: The TRIPS Agreement and Global Policies of Intellectual Property Reform in Developing Countries (2009); Drahos, *supra* note 6, at 161–82.

[51] For this term, *see further* Maskus & Reichman, *supra* note 2.

[52] Paris Convention, *supra* note 2; Berne Convention, *supra* note 2.

[53] *See generally* Carlos M. Correa, Intellectual Property Rights, The WTO and Developing Countries: The TRIPS Agreement and Policy Options (2001).

[54] Margot E. Kaminski, *The Capture of International Intellectual Property Law Through the U.S. Trade Regime*, 87 S. Cal. L. Rev. 977 (2014).

[55] *See, e.g.*, Jerome H. Reichman & Rochelle Cooper Dreyfuss, *Harmonization without Consensus: Critical Reflections on Drafting a Substantive Patent Law Treaty*, 57 Duke L.J. 85 (2007).

In this context, the developing countries in general, and the emerging economies in particular, are striving to become "fair followers" rather than "free riders."[56] That task, in turn, has required developing-country governments to master the subtleties of intellectual property law in order to exploit the "wiggle room" still available to them under international minimum standards of protection.[57] Already we can see the pre-existing balance of power in some areas of intellectual property law shifting under our feet, as more countries find new ways to profit from flexibilities afforded by the TRIPS Agreement, or at least to reduce losses that might otherwise have ensued from higher international minimum standards of protection.[58]

1 The WIPO Development Agenda

From this perspective, a turning point occurred in 2007 when Brazil, with the support of other BRICs countries, successfully campaigned for the adoption of a Development Agenda at the World Intellectual Property Organization (WIPO) that would be consistent with overall United Nations development goals and strategies.[59] Brazil's primary objective in proposing the Development Agenda was to block adoption of the pending Substantive Patent Law Treaty (SPLT),[60] which

[56] *See, e.g.*, Reichman, *From Free Riders to Fair Followers, supra* note 44.

[57] *See* Reichman, *The TRIPS Agreement Comes of Age, supra* note 48. *See generally* DEERE, *supra* note 50; Barbosa, *supra* note 44.

[58] *See, e.g.*, Keith Maskus, *TRIPS* at *20: Evidence on Innovation, Use, and International Technology Flows*, WTO Public Forum, Geneva, Oct. 1, 2015; *cf.* Reto M. Hilty, *Ways Out of the Trap of Article 1(1) TRIPS*, in TRIPS PLUS-20: FROM TRADE RULES TO MARKET PRINCIPLES 186–201 (H. Ullrich et al. eds., 2016).

[59] WIPO Development Agenda, www.wipo.int/ip-development/en/agenda; WIPO, *Decision of the 2007 WIPO General Assembly*, WO/GA/34/16 (Nov. 12, 2007), www.wipo.int/meetings/en/doc_details.jsp?doc_id=88957. *See also* Rami Olwan & Brian Fitzgerald, *IP and Development: A Roadmap for Developing Countries in the Twenty-First Century*, in COPYRIGHTS PERSPECTIVES: PAST, PRESENT AND PROSPECT 85 (B. Fitzgerald & J. Gilchrist eds., 2015). The emerging economies – Brazil, Russia, India, China, and South Africa – are also known as the BRICS countries.

[60] *See* WIPO, Standing Comm. on the Law of Patents, Report, at 1–2, WIPO Doc. SCP/10/11 (June 1, 2005); WIPO, Standing Comm. on the Law of Patents, Information on Certain Recent Developments in Relation to the Draft Substantive Patent Law Treaty (SPLT), at 2–3, WIPO Doc. SCP/10/8 (Mar. 17, 2004); WIPO, Standing Comm. on the Law of Patents, Draft Substantive Patent Law Treaty (SPLT), at 2, WIPO Doc. SCP/10/2 (Sept. 30, 2003). *See generally* WIPO Open Forum on the Draft Substantive Patent Law Treaty (SPLT), Geneva, Mar. 1–3, 2006 [hereinafter WIPO Open Forum], http://www.wipo.int/meetings/en/2006/scp _of_ge_06 intl.html (hosting the presentation of papers, lectures, and speeches on the international harmonization of patent law). For the role of Brazil, see

Rochelle Dreyfuss and I criticized in 2007 as both premature and misguided.[61]

The extent to which WIPO's Development Agenda has influenced, or may yet influence, the evolution of intellectual property law in the developing countries remains open to question. In general, these countries do not need declarations in Geneva so much as "facts on the ground" that implement and amplify the TRIPS flexibilities in their domestic intellectual property laws,[62] a process that Amy Kapczynski has characterized as "counter harmonization."[63]

Nevertheless, Brazil's Development Agenda project seems – directly or indirectly – to have generated positive action on intellectual property issues by developing country governments in a number of ways. For example, the task of pinpointing 45 or more basic principles in the Agenda that could elicit developing-country governments' approval at WIPO[64] focused the attention of authorities in those countries on the economic opportunities inherent in the heretofore underutilized flexibilities embodied in the TRIPS Agreement.[65] The Development Agenda also seems to have encouraged or stimulated greater collaboration among these same governments with respect to intellectual property policies and strategies. At the very least, it seems to have made these governments more attentive to the advice of NGOs that criticize maximalist intellectual property agendas and less vulnerable to high protectionist proposals emanating from WIPO's own technical assistance programs.[66]

PEDRO PARANAGUÁ, BRAZIL'S COPYRIGHT REVISION—TROPICALIA 3.0? (2014) (SJD thesis on file at the Goodman Library, Duke Law School).

61 Reichman & Dreyfuss, *supra* note 55. For likely adverse effects of the draft SPLT on both developing and developed countries, see *id.* at 93–122.

62 *See, e.g.*, Hilty, *supra* note 58; *see generally* Jerome H. Reichman, *Intellectual Property in the Twenty-First Century: Will the Developing Countries Lead or Follow?* 46 HOUSTON L. REV. 1116 (Symposium Issue, 2009).

63 Amy Kapczynski, *Harmonization and Its Discontents: A Case Study of TRIPS Implementation in India's Pharmaceutical Sector*, 97 CALIF. L. REV. 1571 (2009).

64 *See* WIPO Development Agenda, *supra* note 59.

65 *Cf.* Rochelle Cooper Dreyfuss, *The Role of India, China, Brazil and Other Emerging Economies in Establishing Access Norms for Intellectual Property Law Making* (Int'l Law & Justice Working Paper 2009/5), http://www.iilj.org/wp-content/uploads/2016/09/Dreyfuss_Role-of-India-China-Brazil-and-other-Emerging-Economies.pdf; *see also* Peter K. Yu, *Access to Medicines, BRICS Alliances, and Collective Action*, 34 AM. J.L. & MED. 345 (2008).

66 *See, e.g.*, CARLOS M. CORREA & SISULE MUSUNGU, THE WIPO PATENT AGENDA: THE RISKS FOR DEVELOPING COUNTRIES (2002), http://www.worldcat.org/title/wipo-patent-agenda-the-risks-for-developing-countries/ocic/52777327Greferer+briefresults. *See also* Catherine Saez, *WIPO Members Flirt with Agreement on WIPO Technica*

2 Mounting Attention to TRIPS Flexibilities in the Developing Countries

Whether for these or other reasons, in the past few years we have seen the BRICS countries take major steps towards exploiting the flexibilities that were always inherent in the TRIPS Agreement, with a view to reforming domestic intellectual property laws initially inherited from the colonial period. In so doing, they seem implicitly to endorse the "federalist" view of TRIPS that Dinwoodie and Dreyfuss have eloquently expounded.[67]

For example, India's efforts to preserve legal and policy space for affordable medicines, and for its highly developed generic pharmaceutical industries, are well known.[68] Section 3(d) of India's Patent law of 2005 denies patents on derivative drugs as well as on new uses of known substances that fail to demonstrate a credible increase in therapeutic efficacy.[69] The Indian Supreme Court upheld this provision in 2013.[70] Meanwhile, in 2012, the Controller of the Indian Patent Office issued a compulsory license on a costly cancer drug, in part by invoking India's own codified misuse doctrine.[71] This medicine had been priced well beyond the reach of all but the most affluent patients in that country. Looking to the future, one would like to see the Indian government begin to fund more basic scientific research at universities and in the private sector, especially with regard to medicines.

Elsewhere, a formidable policy statement calling for "facts on the ground" was published by the Brazilian House of Representatives, in

Assistance, IP-WATCH (Apr. 15, 2016), http://www.ip-watch.org/2016/04/15/wipo-members-flirt-with-agreement-on-wipo-technical-assistance/.

67 DINWOODIE & DREYFUSS, *supra* note 50.

68 *See, e.g.*, Kapczynski, *supra* note 63.

69 The Patents (Amendment) Act, 2005, No. 15 [India], §3(d), Acts of Parliament, 2005 which declares:

> The following are not inventions within the meaning of this Act: The mere discovery of a new form of a known substance which does not result in the enhancement of the known efficacy of that substance or the mere discovery of any new property or new use for a known substance or of the mere use of a known process, machine or apparatus unless such known process results in a new product or employs at least one new reactant.

See also UNCTAD REFERENCE GUIDE, *supra* note 48, at 77–84.

70 Novartis AG v. Union of India, 6 S.C.C. 1 (2013) [India].

71 *In re* Natco Pharm. v. Bayer, Compulsory License Application No. 1/2011 (Indian Controller of Patents, 2012), www.ipub.tn.nic.in/045-2013htm.

a 2013 Report, entitled *Brazil's Patent Reform: Innovation towards National Competitiveness.*[72] Some of the key initiatives that this lengthy document proposed to enact into law, under Bill No. H.R. 5402 (2013) as it stood at that time, are summarized below:

- It would clarify subject matter to be excluded from patentable inventions, for example, second uses of a known substance and new forms of known substances, which are treated as mere discoveries unless they result in improvements of demonstrable therapeutic efficacy (following the Indian example of §3(d), discussed above).
- It would adopt a rigorous standard of nonobviousness in order to leave more incremental innovation open to free competition.
- It would adopt a "best mode" requirement in order to penalize patent applicants who withhold information needed by third parties to practice a given invention.
- It would adopt a pre-grant opposition procedure in order to avoid the necessity of litigation to invalidate poor quality patents and to improve the quality of issued patents, in addition to a post-grant opposition procedure (following India's example).
- It would adopt legislation enabling the government to issue compulsory licenses under TRIPS article 31, including noncommercial government use licenses similar to those under §1498 of the U.S. Code.[73]
- It argues that undisclosed clinical trial data should be protected only against unfair competition under TRIPS article 39.3, without any data exclusivity whatsoever.[74]
- It seeks to establish a fund for research on neglected diseases and other public health measures of particular national interest, with results to be made available under a mandatory open-access framework.

[72] Center for Strategic Studies and Debate, Brazil's Patent Reform – Innovation Towards National Competitiveness (Chamber of Deputies [Brazil], 2013).

[73] TRIPS, *supra* note 1, art. 31; 28 U.S.C. §1498 (2012). *See also* Jerome H. Reichman, *Compulsory Licensing of Patented Pharmaceutical Inventions: Evaluating the Options*, 37 J.L. Med. & Ethics 247, 247–64 (2009) (Symposium Issue). *See also* Frederick M. Abbott & Jerome H. Reichman, *The Doha Round's Public Health Legacy: Strategies for the Production and Diffusion of Patented Medicines under the Amended TRIPS Provisions*, 10 J. Int'l Econ. L. 921, 921–87 (2007); Amy Kapczynski & Aaron Kesselheim, *Government Patent Use: A Legal Approach to Reducing Drug Spending*, 35 Health Aff. 791 (2016).

[74] *See* TRIPS, *supra* note 1, art. 39.3; Cynthia Ho, Access to Medicines in the Global Economy: International Agreements on Patents and Related Rights (2011).

- It also envisions the creation of prize funds for public health purposes, with results to be made available under a nonexclusivity regime.[75]

Brazil's ruling party had also introduced bills that could induce sweeping reforms of the domestic copyright law, with emphasis on a regime of "user's rights" to complement and balance the existing regime of authors' rights.[76] The drafters proposed to strengthen the idea-expression dichotomy; to adopt a first-sale doctrine based on the principle of international exhaustion (except for computer programs and audiovisual works); to impose important limitations and exceptions for research, teaching, libraries and disabled persons; to adopt modified fair use provisions, including a transformative use provision for new technological uses; to adopt a liability rule for orphan works; and to make Technical Protection Measures subject to a misuse provision that would deny content providers the right to obstruct uses permitted by law (including limitations and exceptions).[77] These proposals would also expressly require courts to take human rights, especially free speech, into account when applying copyright law.[78]

Although Brazil's pending reforms had not been enacted into law at the time of writing, they have nonetheless influenced reform proposals in other countries. Perhaps the most important was a planned wholesale revision of South Africa's intellectual property laws that could add significantly more balance to its existing regime.[79] Considerable efforts are also underway to promote local production of pharmaceuticals in South Africa and several other African countries.[80]

China has also begun to consider adding more balance to its robust intellectual property regime. Of course, China already allows utility model protection for small-scale innovations that would not otherwise qualify as patented inventions.[81] This regime stimulates Chinese

[75] Brazil's Patent Reform, *supra* note 72. *See further* Paranaguá, *supra* note 60, at Ch. 4.

[76] *See* Paranaguá, *supra* note 60, at Ch. 4. [77] *Id. See also id.* at Ch. 2.

[78] *See generally, id.* at Ch. 4.

[79] Draft National Policy on Intellectual Property 2013, Government Gazette No. 36816 (Sept. 4, 2013) (South Africa), http://www.gov.za/documents/national-policy-intellectual-property-draft. In practice, however, the pending revision of this country's copyright law codifies only a general fair use regime, without adding to or expanding most existing limitations. *See* Copyright Amendment Bill, 2017, arts. 10–13B, Bill 13–2017 (South Africa).

[80] *See* Abbott & Reichman, *supra* note 73; *see also* UNCTAD Reference Guide, *supra* note 48.

[81] *See, e.g.*, Maskus, *TRIPS at 20*, *supra* note 58.

companies to adapt foreign inventions to local conditions, a strategy that was successfully pursued by Japan in the past.[82] China's success in this regard demonstrates how developing countries could benefit from certain tailor-made, *sui generis* regimes that may be better suited to their own adaptive skills than traditional regimes of exclusive rights.[83] This lesson, if imitated by other developing countries, could also help them to adapt green technologies emanating from OECD countries to their own needs and conditions.[84]

More recently, China has announced its intention to invoke competition law against the abuse of a dominant position by firms otherwise protected by intellectual property rights.[85] China appears to envision the use of remedial compulsory licenses in such cases, particularly with regard to pharmaceutical products. If so, China's example could further encourage other developing countries to make full use of the flexibilities under TRIPS that remain available for such purposes.[86]

Finally, there is new evidence that more African countries have awakened to the need to reform rigid copyright laws inherited from former colonial governments.[87] To this end, efforts to expand and codify more permissive limitations and exceptions to copyright law's exclusive rights are under way in a number of African countries, including the adoption of a fair use regime in South Africa's pending revision of copyright law.[88]

[82] *See, e.g.*, Reichman, *From Free Riders to Fair Followers, supra* note 44.

[83] *See, e.g.*, Jerome H. Reichman & Tracy Lewis, *Using Liability Rules to Stimulate Local Innovation in Developing Countries: Application to Traditional Knowledge*, in INTERNATIONAL PUBLIC GOODS AND TRANSFER OF TECHNOLOGY UNDER A GLOBALIZED INTELLECTUAL PROPERTY REGIME, *supra* note 2, at 337–66; *see also* Reichman, *Of Green Tulips and Legal Kudzu, supra* note 35.

[84] *See, e.g.*, Jerome H. Reichman, Arti K. Rai, Richard Newell & Jonathan B. Weiner, *Intellectual Property and Alternative Strategies for Green Innovation*, in INTELLECTUAL PROPERTY RIGHTS: LEGAL AND ECONOMIC CHALLENGES FOR DEVELOPMENT, *supra* note 2, at 356–91. *See also* Ahmed Latif, Keith Maskus, Ruth Okediji, Jerome Reichman & Pedro Roffe, *Overcoming the Impasse on Intellectual Property and Climate Change at UNFCCC: A Way Forward*, ICTSD Policy Brief No. 11 (Nov. 2011), http://www.ictsd.org/sites/default/files/research/2012/02/overcoming-the-impasse-on-intellectual-property-and-climate-change-at-the-unfccc-a-way-forward.pdf.

[85] *See, e.g.*, Frederick M. Abbott, *Excessive Pharmaceutical Prices and Competition Law: Doctrinal Development to Protect Public Health*, 6 U.C. IRVINE L. REV. 281 (2016).

[86] *See* TRIPS, *supra* note 1, arts. 8 and 40; Abbott, *supra* note 85. *See further* Reichman, *Will the Developing Countries Lead or Follow? supra* note 62.

[87] *See, e.g.*, Olufunmilayo B. Arewa, Technology Disruption and Legal Institutions in Nigeria, paper presented at the Symposium on IP and Global Development, Texas A&M School of Law, Fort Worth, Texas (Apr. 1, 2017).

[88] *See id.; see also supra* note 79.

3 Scholarly Attention to the Limits of Intellectual Property Protection

Efforts to manage the TRIPS flexibilities in both developing and developed countries have elicited renewed scrutiny of the proper limits of intellectual property protection. In the European Union, for example, the Max Planck Institute for Innovation and Competition recently promulgated two major Declarations that advocate an expansive reading of the "flexibilities" available under TRIPS.[89] With inputs from some fifty distinguished law professors, the Institute's objective was to influence courts and legislators in both developed and developing countries to more carefully weigh the exclusive rights of authors and inventors against the larger public interest in accessing, using and building upon their creative and technological outputs.

As regards literary and artistic works, the Institute reexamined provisions in both the TRIPS Agreement of 1994 and the WIPO Copyright Treaty of 1996 that oblige signatory states to subject all limitations and exceptions in their domestic copyright laws to the three-step test[90] initially devised for the exclusive reproduction right under a 1967 revision of the Berne Convention.[91] In its Declaration on a Balanced Interpretation of the Three Step Test, the Institute challenged conventional judicial notions that limitations and exceptions permissible in domestic copyright laws must be narrowly interpreted in order to safeguard authors' exclusive rights. Instead, the Declaration advocates a more nuanced and cumulative approach that in some respects evokes the spirit and practice of the fair use exceptions in the United States and now Canada.[92] This Declaration profoundly influenced the drafters of the pending Copyright Reform Bill in Brazil, which combined a set of

[89] *See* Max Planck Institute for Innovation and Competition, Declaration on a Balanced Interpretation of the Three Step Test in Copyright Law (2008); Max Planck Inst. for Innovation and Competition, Declaration on Patent Protection and Regulatory Sovereignty under TRIPS (2014).

[90] *See* TRIPS, *supra* note 1, art. 13; WIPO Copyright Treaty, *supra* note 27, art. 10; Berne Convention, *supra* note 2, art. 9. *See generally* Martin Senftleben, Copyright Limitations and the Three Step Test: An Analysis of the Three Step Test in International and EC Law (2014).

[91] *See, e.g.*, Senftleben, *supra* note 90, at 48–52.

[92] Max Planck Inst., Declaration on the Three Step Test, *supra* note 89. *See also* Reichman & Okediji, *When Copyright Law and Science Collide*, *supra* note 27, at 1399–404 (criticizing Directive of the European Parliament and the Council of Europe on the Harmonization of Certain Aspects of Copyright and Related Rights in the Information Society, Council Directive 2001/29, 2001 O.J. (L 167) 10 (EC)). For Canada, see *infra* notes 107–110 and accompanying text.

designated exceptions with fair use provisions under a flexible interpretation of the three-step test.[93]

The later Max Planck Declaration on Patent Law and Regulatory Sovereignty under TRIPS (2014) is still more ambitious in scope. It attempts to provide a cogent and authoritative interpretation of all the major flexibilities pertaining to the domestic patent laws that the TRIPS Agreement made available, with a view to exploring the policy space still existing for free competition when domestic patent laws are appropriately calibrated to balance private and public interests.[94] This Declaration has already begun to influence reform initiatives underway in Brazil and South Africa,[95] and it could help future panels in WTO Dispute Settlement cases avoid questionable opinions and biases found in some of the early decisions concerning implementation of the TRIPS Agreement.[96] One may also hope that this Declaration will further inspire courts and legislators in developing countries to make bolder use of the TRIPS flexibilities than in the past, with a view to better tailoring their domestic intellectual property regimes to their own economic strengths and weaknesses.[97]

At the multilateral level, meanwhile, the influence of developing countries on the process of global intellectual property lawmaking seems to be growing. In 2010, for example, the Conference of the Parties finally adopted the Nagoya Protocol to the Convention on Biological Diversity of 1992.[98] As previously noted, the Protocol obliges signatory states to open their courts to direct action against those who use genetic resources and related traditional knowledge from provider-country territories without prior informed consent and mutually agreed terms on access and benefit-sharing otherwise required by the CBD.[99] At the same time,

[93] *See* PARANAGUÁ, *supra* note 60, at Ch. 4; *see also supra* notes 76–78 and accompanying text. For similar developments in South Africa, *see supra* note 79.

[94] *See* MAX PLANCK INST., DECLARATION ON PATENT LAW AND REGULATORY SOVEREIGNTY UNDER TRIPS, *supra* note 89.

[95] *See supra* notes 72–80 and accompanying text.

[96] *See, e.g.,* WTO Panel Report, *Canada – Patent Protection of Pharmaceutical Products,* WT/DS114/13 (Aug. 18, 2000); WTO Panel Report, *United States – Section 110(5) of US Copyright Act*, WT/DS160/R (June 15, 2000).

[97] *See, e.g.*, DEERE, *supra* note 50; *see also* GUSTAVO GUIDINI, RUDOLPH J. R. PERITZ & MARCO RICOLFI, TRIPS AND DEVELOPING COUNTRIES: TOWARDS A NEW WORLD ORDER? (2014).

[98] Nagoya Protocol, *supra* note 7; CBD, *supra* note 1.

[99] *See generally* THOMAS GREIBER ET AL., AN EXPLANATORY GUIDE TO THE NAGOYA PROTOCOL ON ACCESS AND BENEFIT-SHARING (IUCN Environmental Policy and Law Paper No. 83, 2012); *see further supra* notes 11–23 and accompanying text.

this Protocol expressly enables scientific entities that pool genetic resources for facilitated access in research and applications to avoid burdensome, case-by-case benefit-sharing negotiations under the bilateral approach of the CBD as initially drafted in 1992.[100] How the global scientific community can maximize these opportunities by reorganizing their existing *ex situ* collections of microbial genetic resources into a legally recognized knowledge commons is the topic of my recent book.[101]

More recently, in 2013, a Diplomatic Conference at Marrakesh adopted a new treaty mandating limitations and exceptions to the domestic copyright laws that facilitate access to published literary works for the blind and visually impaired.[102] This treaty is the first international instrument to cut back on authors' rights without offsetting new constraints on access to and use of literary works that primarily benefit publishing intermediaries.[103] It also represents the first treaty on literary and artistic works in which a coalition of developing countries (in this case ably led by Professor Ruth Okediji) largely controlled both the design and final configuration of the end product.[104]

B *Countervailing Distortions under Bilateral and Regional Free Trade Agreements*

At the domestic level, the extent to which the Max Planck Institute's Declaration on Patent Law and Regulatory Sovereignty under the TRIPS Agreement could influence legislatures and judicial authorities

[100] *See* Nagoya Protocol, *supra* note 7, art. 4; *see generally supra* Section II. A; *see most recently* Jerome H. Reichman, *Why the Nagoya Protocol to the CBD Matters to Science and Industry in Canada and the United States* (Center for International Governance Innovation (CIGI), 2018).

[101] *See* GOVERNING DIGITALLY INTEGRATED GENETIC RESOURCES (2016), *supra* note 3; *see also* COMMON POOLS OF GENETIC RESOURCES – EQUITY AND INNOVATION IN INTERNATIONAL BIODIVERSITY LAW (E. C. Kamau & G. Winter eds., 2013).

[102] Marrakesh Treaty to Facilitate Access to Published Works for Persons Who Are Blind Visually Impaired or Otherwise Print Disabled, June 27, 2013, WIPO Doc. VIP/DC/8 Rev., 52 I.L.M. 1312.

[103] *See generally* LAURENCE HELFER ET AL., GUIDE TO THE MARRAKESH TREATY TO FACILITATE ACCESS TO PUBLISHED WORKS FOR PERSONS WHO ARE BLIND, VISUALLY IMPAIRED OR OTHERWISE PRINT DISABLED (2016).

[104] *See also* U.N. Secretary General, *Patent Policy and the Right to Science and Culture: Special Rapporteur in the Field of Cultural Rights*, Farida Shaheed, U.N. Doc. A/HRC 70/279 (Aug. 4, 2015); U.N. Secretary General, *Copyright Policy and the Right to Science and Culture, Special Rapporteur in the Field of Cultural Rights*, Farida Shaheed, U.N. Doc. A/HRC/28/57 (Dec. 24, 2014).

in developed countries, as distinct from developing countries, remains to be seen. So far, the one developed country to overtly defend this regulatory space for both copyrights and patents with some vigor has been Canada.

For example, the Canadian Supreme Court has introduced a "users' rights" perspective into that country's copyright laws.[105] In a series of cases, the courts have expanded Canada's "fair dealing" provision into a hybrid fair use regime,[106] more like that of the United States.[107] In so doing, the highest Canadian judicial authorities – following Professor David Vaver – expressly deemed limitations and exceptions in copyright law to be "users' rights" that courts must respect, along with the exclusive rights of authors under copyright law.[108] Canada's example profoundly influenced the drafters of Brazil's pending copyright reforms, who openly advocate a regime of users' rights.[109]

On the patent side of the ledger, Canada had asserted its "promise of the patent" doctrine of utility to invalidate certain derivative pharmaceutical products that were protected in the United States.[110] This approach was, however, challenged under the investment provisions of the North American Free Trade Agreement,[111] a dangerous precedent that demonstrates the potential ability of Free Trade Agreements to narrow or eliminate flexibilities allowed under TRIPS.[112] Despite a positive outcome under the NAFTA arbitration, the Canadian Supreme Court has apparently abandoned this doctrinal approach to utility.[113]

[105] *See, e.g.*, CCH Canadian Ltd. v. Law Society of Upper Canada [2004] 1 S.C.R. 339 (Canada).

[106] *See* David Vaver, Intellectual Property Law: Copyright, Patents, Trademarks (2011) (citing authorities).

[107] *See* 17 U.S.C. 107 (2012).

[108] CCH Canadian Ltd., *supra* note 105; Vaver, *supra* note 106.

[109] *See* Paranaguá, *supra* note 60 (citing and explaining relevant Bills).

[110] Eli Lilly Canada, Inc. v. Mylan Pharmaceuticals ULC, [2015] F.C. 17 (Canada).

[111] North American Free Trade Agreement, Dec. 17, 1992, 32 I.L.M. 289 (1993); Eli Lilly & Co. v. Government of Canada, ICSID Case No. UNCT/14/2, Arbitration Under Chapter Eleven of the North American Free Trade Agreement (NAFTA) and the UNCITRAL Arbitration Rules (Mar. 16, 2017).

[112] *See* Richard Gold & Michael Short, *The Promise of the Patent in Canada and Around the World*, 30 Can. Intell. Prop. Rev. 35 (2014); Jerome H. Reichman, *Compliance of Canada's Utility Doctrine with International Minimum Standards of Patent Protection*, in Proceedings of the 108th Annual Meeting of the ASIL (American Society of International Law ed., 2014).

[113] AstraZenica Canada Inc. v. Apotex Inc., 2017 S.C.C. 36 (Can. Sup. Ct.).

Apart from some intriguing examples in the Canadian courts, however, the developed countries on the whole have moved in the opposite direction. Far from expanding the TRIPS flexibilities in their own territorial laws, they have increasingly adhered to bilateral and regional Free Trade Agreements that tend to narrow the regulatory space otherwise available to all WTO members under that Agreement.[114] This trend, which has particularly serious implications for access to medicines in poor countries, could eventually be capped by the Trans-Pacific Partnership Treaty (TPP), another trade deal negotiated in secret by twelve countries that together account for 40 percent of global GDP.[115]

To understand why a maximalist agenda that has been rejected in multilateral negotiations since the 1990s steadily advances in these bilateral and regional Free Trade Agreements, one must focus on the critical differences between the two types of negotiating forums. Special interest lobbying is no less visible or influential at the multilateral level than it is in FTA negotiations. In multilateral forums, nevertheless, the range of economic interests and stakeholders is usually so broad and varied among countries at different levels of development that no single cohort of special interests can readily impose its will on the assembly as a whole without deep and significant compromises on all sides. At the multilateral level, moreover, representatives of adversely affected interests may be harder to exclude from negotiations that are relatively transparent and open to public scrutiny; while the shared economic interests of many developing-country protagonists may also coincide

114 *See, e.g.*, Pedro Roffe & Christoph Spennemann, *Preferential Trade Agreements and Intellectual Property Rights*, in INTELLECTUAL PROPERTY RIGHTS – LEGAL AND ECONOMIC CHALLENGES FOR DEVELOPMENT, *supra* note 2, at 439–76; Brian Mercurio, *TRIPS-Plus Provisions in FTAs: Recent Trends*, in REGIONAL TRADE AGREEMENTS AND THE WTO LEGAL SYSTEM 215–38 (L. Bartels & F. Ortino eds., 2006).

115 *See, e.g.*, MOHAMMED K. EL SAID, PUBLIC HEALTH RELATED TRIPS-PLUS PROVISIONS IN BILATERAL TRADE AGREEMENTS: A POLICY GUIDE FOR NEGOTIATORS AND IMPLEMENTERS IN THE WHO EASTERN MEDITERRANEAN REGION 125–263 (2010); Reichman, *Intellectual Property in the Twenty-First Century*, *supra* note 62; *Secret TPP Treaty: Advanced Intellectual Property Chapter for All 12 Nations with Negotiating Positions*, WikiLeaks release (Nov. 13, 2013); *see generally* Michael Geist, *The Trouble with the TPP, Day 50 – The Case Against Ratifying the Trans Pacific Partnership*, MICHAEL GEIST (May 14, 2016), http://www.michaelgeist.ca/2016/03/the-trouble-with-the-tpp-day-50-the-case-against-ratifying-the-trans-pacific-partnership/. *See further* Office of the U.S. Trade Rep., TPP Full Text, May 17, 2016, https://ustr.gov/trade-agreements/free-trade-agreements/trans-pacific-partnership/tpp-full-text. However, the U.S. has now pulled out of the TPP by order of the President.

more readily with those of public-interest stakeholders in the developed countries than with the interests of transnational corporations. This diversity of interests necessarily to be taken into account in order to reach a consensus at the multilateral level thus tends to temper extreme demands and to set limits on the bargaining power of even the strongest stakeholders.[116]

The opposite is true in most of the negotiating forums that produce bilateral and regional FTAs, although in the megaregionals there is arguably somewhat less room for the big countries to divide and conquer.[117] Here the economic opportunities sought by special interests based in the major economic powers are typically directed at a narrow range of special interests in the other, much smaller and often poorer country or countries seated at the table. It thus becomes relatively easier for any given set of special interests from both sides to cut their own deals at the expense of the larger public interest, especially when those stakeholders whose interests could suffer the most are not seated at the table or otherwise represented.[118]

Moreover, according to a study by Margot Kaminski at Yale Law School, the legislative mandate that obliges the United States Trade Representative (USTR) to seek to export the substantive intellectual property laws of the United States in these free trade negotiations has been perverted because of the "institutional capture of USTR" by special interests.[119] In particular, these negotiators try to reconfigure unfavorable domestic laws or precedents into more pliable international standards; codify favorable domestic judicial interpretations as international rules; and omit aspects of existing domestic laws that balance intellectual property protection against other values. In short, even when U.S. negotiators are formally tasked with exporting domestic law,

[116] *Cf.* Carlos M. Correa, *Multilateral Agreements and Policy Opportunities*, in Intellectual Property Rights – Legal and Economic Challenges for Development, *supra* note 2, at 417–38.

[117] *See, e.g.*, Rochelle Cooper Dreyfuss, *Harmonization – Top Down, Bottom Up, and Now Sideways: Impact of the IP Provisions of Megaregional Agreements on Third Party States*, in Megaregulation Contested: Global Economic Ordering After TPP (Benedict Kingsbury et al. eds., forthcoming 2018).

[118] *Cf.* Max Planck Institute for Innovation and Competition, Statement of Principles on Intellectual Property Obligations in Free Trade Agreements (2013). For the view that megaregionals – as distinct from regional FTAs – provide more negotiating space for more diverse interests, see Dreyfuss *Harmonization, supra* note 117.

[119] Kaminski, *supra* note 54.

distortions arise because they actually deliver the law in versions favorable to vested interests.[120]

Because the larger public interest in intellectual property issues is thus inadequately represented (or deliberately ignored) in most of these FTA negotiating forums, the end result tends to promote short-term gains from existing but sometimes outdated technical and legislative solutions. Fundamental long-term challenges of reconciling old laws and obsolete business models with the impact of new technologies are largely ignored.

IV Reframing Intellectual Property Rights without the Distortions of a Maximalist Trade Agenda

Arguably, in the 1990s, efforts to attain higher levels of global economic integration could not have succeeded without the "marriage of convenience" between intellectual property law and international trade law.[121] In retrospect, we may posit that the TRIPS Agreement of 1994 was partly a voluntary response to an array of new trade concessions in favor of the developing countries and partly the product of serious threats that continued exports of traditional manufactured goods from developing to developed countries would otherwise be compromised.[122]

At that time, most developing countries had few, if any, international patent obligations of major importance; efforts to impose higher patent and trademark standards of protection under the Paris Convention of 1883 had failed;[123] and the newly industrialized countries freely copied the high-tech innovations generated in more developed countries under a regime of unbridled free-competition that did not violate existing international trade law.[124] Many of these same developing countries

[120] *Id.* Nevertheless, the TPP did evolve away from some of the most extreme intellectual property proposals over time. *See* Dreyfuss, *Harmonization*, *supra* note 117.

[121] *See, e.g.*, Drahos, *Negotiating Intellectual Property Rights*, *supra* note 6; Gadbaw, *supra* note 42; Carlos Alberto Primo Braga, *The Economics of Intellectual Property Rights and the GATT: A View from the South*, 22 VAND. J. TRANSNAT'L L. 243 (1989); Reichman, *Intellectual Property in International Trade*, *supra* note 6.

[122] *See, e.g.*, Hanns Ullrich, *The Political Foundations of TRIPS Revisited*, in TRIPS PLUS-20: FROM TRADE RULES TO MARKET PRINCIPLES, *supra* note 58, at 85, 104–5; Carlos M. Correa, *Pro-competitive Measures under TRIPS to Promote Technology Diffusion in Developing Countries*, in GLOBAL INTELLECTUAL PROPERTY RIGHTS, *supra* note 6, at 40–61.

[123] *Cf.* Paris Convention, *supra* note 2; GATT (1947), *supra* note 43, Art. XX.

[124] Reichman, *Free Riders to Fair Followers*, *supra* note 44; Reichman, *Intellectual Property in International Trade*, *supra* note 6.

were also flooding developed countries with traditional manufacturing goods at low prices that drove local producers to relocate outside their own domestic markets. On paper, at least, the multilateral trade negotiations under the Uruguay Round aimed to produce a win-win outcome for all members of the newly created World Trade Organization.[125]

As a deal-making tool, however, the free trade paradigm added little or nothing to our understanding of intellectual property law. Since then, growing reliance on bilateral and regional Free Trade Agreements has tended to freeze intellectual property norms at the expense of a more comprehensive response to the challenges of new technologies and the emergence of new business models.[126] These challenges still elicit more questions than answers.

As posited earlier in this chapter, for example, we have seen intellectual property laws evolving away from the protection of creative innovations as embedded in end products towards ever more protection for upstream inputs into the creative process itself.[127] This deviation from historical precedent was not just the result of the developing countries' benefit-sharing demands for research uses of genetic resources under the Convention on Biological Diversity of 1992.[128] It was also partly the result of the European Union's decision to protect noncopyrightable collections of data under a *sui generis* regime of rights related to copyright law.[129] This shift of the protectionist scope from outputs to inputs would alone require a major rethinking of both the legal theory and economic rationale underlying traditional intellectual property law.[130]

Meanwhile, the large-scale harmonization of intellectual property rights mandated by the TRIPS Agreement of 1994 has led to a major reexamination of the appropriate balance between intellectual

[125] TRIPS, *supra* note 1. *See, e.g.*, Hanns Ullrich, *The Political Foundations of TRIPS Revisited, supra* note 122, at 85–7. *But see* Annette Kur, *From Minimum Standards to Maximum Rules*, in TRIPS PLUS-20: FROM TRADE RULES TO MARKET PRINCIPLES, *supra* note 58, at 133–59.

[126] *See, e.g.*, Jerome H. Reichman, *The Limits of the "Limitations and Exceptions" in Copyright Law*, in COPYRIGHT LAW IN AN AGE OF EXCEPTIONS AND LIMITATIONS 292–314 (Ruth Okediji ed., 2017); *see also* Mercurio, *supra* note 114; Kaminski, *supra* note 54.

[127] *See generally supra* Section II, *From Bundles of Exclusive Rights to Tools of Inclusion*.

[128] *See* CBD, *supra* note 1, arts. 8, 15 and Nagoya Protocol, *supra* note 7.

[129] *See supra* notes 24–30 and accompanying text.

[130] *See further* GOVERNING DIGITALLY INTEGRATED GENETIC RESOURCES (2016), *supra* note 3, at Part III.

property and free competition in the developing countries[131] and in some developed countries as well.[132] Here again, even good faith advocates of reform have more questions than answers, partly because the long-term legal and economic consequences of deep harmonization have yet to be worked out – or properly evaluated – at the domestic level.[133]

That is why, in 2007, Rochelle Dreyfuss and I strongly opposed WIPO's attempt at premature harmonization under a Substantive Patent Law Treaty in the following terms:

> The evidence shows ... that the worldwide intellectual property system has entered a brave new scientific epoch, in which experts have only tentative, divergent ideas about how best to treat a daunting array of emerging new technologies. The existing system has become increasingly dysfunctional because it operates with a set of rudimentary working hypotheses that have not kept pace with technical change. As different countries put these hypotheses to the test, the focus of international lawmakers – whether at WIPO, the WTO, or in a trilateral coalition – should be on gaining experience and data from living within the parameters set out by the TRIPS Agreement during a prolonged period of open-minded experimentation.[134]

What good faith reformers need, in other words, is a period of empirical investigation and experimentation under the "federalist approach" that Dinwoodie and Dreyfuss recommend,[135] in which different countries seek and test different solutions to the puzzles that new technologies continue to pose for the "incipient transnational system of innovation" that the TRIPS Agreement established in 1994.[136]

If, instead, we continue to succumb to special-interest deals hammered out behind closed doors in so-called Free Trade Agreements, we risk ending up with more artificially constructed barriers to real innovation and creativity that primarily benefit intermediaries and gate keepers. Once such barriers are frozen into domestic laws by treaties along the

131 *See, e.g.*, Correa, Intellectual Property Rights, the WTO and Developing Countries, *supra* note 53; Deere, *supra* note 50. *See generally* TRIPS Plus 20, *supra* note 58.

132 *See, e.g., supra* notes 105–112 and accompanying text (case of Canada). *See also* Henning Grosse Ruse-Kahn, *IP and Trade in a Post-TRIPS Environment, in* TRIPS Plus 20, *supra* note 58, at 114–207.

133 *Cf.* Paranaguá, *supra* note 60.

134 Reichman & Dreyfuss, *Harmonization without Consensus, supra* note 55, at 129.

135 Dinwoodie & Dreyfuss, *supra* note 50.

136 *See* Maskus & Reichman, *supra* note 2.

lines of the TPP,[137] national authorities everywhere will be less able to chart independent policies and strategies based on the real-world empirical impact of elevated intellectual property standards of protection. The likely result could then be less innovation and less global welfare over time, especially if funds needed for investment in new technical and legal strategies were siphoned off by crony capitalists committed to obsolete business models.

It may well be that "the marriage of convenience" between intellectual property law and international trade law[138] has begun to outlive its usefulness. If so, the time has come for a trial separation, not a divorce,[139] in which both partners go their own ways, in search of new solutions to new technological developments based on verifiable empirical evidence. Such a respite does, however, presuppose a halt to secret intellectual property negotiations that prematurely freeze domestic laws while generating mistrust of the international trade system built around the WTO. It responds, instead, to a much greater need to encourage and support the experimentation now gathering strength in the BRICS countries and elsewhere,[140] with a view to reaching a more enlightened, long-term consensus at the multilateral level that truly advances the interests of authors and inventors operating within a more mature transnational system of innovation.

137 *See supra* note 115. 138 *See* Gadbaw, *supra* note 42.

139 *Accord* Matthias Lamping, *Intellectual Property Harmonization in the Name of Trade*, in TRIPS Plus 20, *supra* note 58, at 313, 344–51.

140 *See supra* notes 72–88 and accompanying text. *See also* Donald P. Harris, *The Power of Ideas: The Declaration of Patent Protection and New Approaches to International Intellectual Property Lawmaking*, 6 U.C. Irvine L. Rev. 343 (2016).

4

The Fusion of Intellectual Property and Trade

SUSY FRANKEL

Trade and intellectual property are in a close but not always positive relationship. The link between trade and intellectual property is longstanding. The 1623 Statute of Monopolies which outlawed monopolies except in some circumstances, such as where they were granted by letters patent for "any new manner of manufacture", provided such exceptions should not be made if they were "mischievous to the state by raising prices of commodities at home, or *hurt of trade* or generally inconvenient".[1] Implicit in that Statute was that patents can both assist and "hurt" trade. As Sherman and Bently note, the phenomenon of describing the Statute of Monopolies as the basis of patent law today emerged some centuries later. They point to developments in the nineteenth century as being the basis of modern patent law.[2] That said, much of the Statute of Monopolies and its concepts, including promoting trade, are incorporated into today's patent law in many jurisdictions and the concepts found in it have developed through both statutory reform and the common law.[3]

Put in today's language the relationship between "hurt of trade" and patents (and intellectual property more generally) means that while patents are merited they should not become unacceptable trade barriers.

[1] Statute of Monopolies 1623, § 6.

[2] Brad Sherman & Lionel Bently, The Making of Modern Intellectual Property Law 206–10 (1999).

[3] In the United States, for example, the term "manufacture" is found in 35 U.S.C. §101, which provides, "Whoever invents or discovers any new and useful process, machine, manufacture, or composition of matter, or any new and useful improvement thereof, may obtain a patent therefor, subject to the conditions and requirements of this title."; in New Zealand *Pfizer Inc. v. Commissioner of Patents* [2005] 1 NZLR 362, where the Court of Appeal discusses the Statute of Monopolies and its proviso as part of New Zealand law; in Australia *National Research Development Corp. v. Commissioner of Patents* (1959) 102 CLR 252, discussing the scope of the concept of invention as a result of the Statute of Monopolies.

Intellectual property rights are inherently trade barriers because they prevent the free flow of intellectual property and related goods and services both within territories and across borders.[4] Trade barriers are mostly problematic when they are protectionist. A certain level of intellectual property protection (that which supports innovation and creativity, for example) might be characterized as acceptable or agreed barriers to trade. This acceptability comes from the incentive-based rationales for intellectual property protection,[5] such as the social contract underlying patents. That social contract is premised on the rationale that provided the subject of a patent is new, involves an inventive step and is capable of industrial application,[6] the grant of exclusive rights for a limited term is worthwhile in exchange for the overall benefit to society of the invention.[7] Protection beyond incentive-related goals, however, is likely to be problematic because it provides additional rights which do not either incentivize newcomers or even necessarily incumbents to further innovate.[8] If incumbents lose the incentive to innovate because they receive excess protection then this can become the equivalent of protectionism.

[4] "Intellectual property can always be characterized as a barrier to trade because the very existence of an intellectual property right can be used to prevent the import or export of a product. The status of the TRIPS Agreement as a covered agreement in the WTO has the effect of recognizing intellectual property, within certain agreed limits, as an 'acceptable barrier'. The significance of the trade barriers that intellectual property can create is that over-protecting intellectual property can be an inhibitor to the free flow of technology and the progress of science globally. If in practice real barriers were created, then neither the objectives of intellectual property law nor international trade would be met. Over-protecting intellectual property does not achieve the barrier-lowering objectives of international trade, but in fact inhibits it. The TRIPS Agreement in its preamble makes it clear that it should be read in a way that is consistent with free trade. In fact, any other interpretation would be at odds with the WTO context." (Citations omitted), see S. Frankel, *The WTO's Application of "the Customary Rules of Interpretation of Public International Law" to Intellectual Property*, 46 VA. J. INT'L L. 365, 374–375 (2005).

[5] It is widely accepted that utilitarianism is a key rationale behind intellectual property. *See generally* ROBERT P. MERGES, JUSTIFYING INTELLECTUAL PROPERTY (2011).

[6] Agreement on Trade-Related Aspects of Intellectual Property Rights, art. 27(1), Apr. 15, 1994, Marrakesh Agreement Establishing the World Trade Organization, Annex 1C, Legal Instruments – Results of the Uruguay Round, vol. 31, 33 I.L.M. 81 (1994) [hereinafter TRIPS].

[7] For a discussion of the social contract see PETER DRAHOS, THE GLOBAL GOVERNANCE OF KNOWLEDGE: PATENT OFFICES AND THEIR CLIENTS 27–32 (2010).

[8] Because of this one might question whether therefore, in the trade context, property rules or subsidies are preferable as a way to incentivise research, see SUSY FRANKEL, TEST TUBES FOR GLOBAL INTELLECTUAL PROPERTY ISSUES: SMALL MARKET ECONOMIES, Ch. 4 (2015).

That patents (and other intellectual property rights such as copyright) can both enhance and inhibit trade (and innovation) remains true today, but there are also differences from the seventeenth century. The scope of legal protection of intellectual property has changed both domestically and internationally. Today's global patent standards reflect the model where inventors, manufacturers and initial distributors are in one territory. In the twenty-first century, production of inventive activity is not only territorial. Global value chains[9] and global value networks[10] have emerged as integral to international trade and intellectual property, but patent law does not reflect either global value chains or networks.[11] Copyright law is also territorial and does not reflect the reality of copyright-related global value chains. Copyright law may well be more intrinsically elastic than patent law; however, globalization has also challenged how international copyright operates. While many call for worldwide licensing, this is hard to achieve because of territorial interests and laws that support those interests.[12]

Simultaneously with the expansion of intellectual property protection, barriers to global trade have liberalized (though some protection remains steadfast). Liberalization of trade is the foundation of the World Trade Organization (WTO).[13] Since the formation of the WTO there have been

[9] A global value chain includes all of the activities that begin with the conception of a product to consumers and includes research and development, innovation, design, raw materials and intermediate inputs, marketing, and distribution. *See generally* G. Gereffi, *The Organisation of Buyer-Driven Global Commodity Chains: How US Retailers Shape Overseas Production Networks*, in COMMODITY CHAINS AND GLOBAL CAPITALISM (G. Gereffi & M. Korzeniewicz eds., 1994).

[10] Global value networks differ from global value chains. "In high technology businesses and knowledge intensive services, the value creating system is better understood as a network than as a chain. Value networks differ from value chains in that there are more actors carrying out a broader variety of functions in a value network than in a value chain, where producer-distributor-consumer relationships predominate": see New Zealand Institute of Economic Research (NZIER), *Global Value Networks: How to succeed in business without worrying about scale, distance or thin networks* (Sept. 2015), https://nzier.org.nz/static/media/filer_public/0e/0b/0e0bb50e-afa0-42d1-977b-2d4b7ef4f622/nzier-report-to-nzpecc-global-value-networks.pdf.

[11] *See* FRANKEL, *supra* note 8, Ch. 6.

[12] In essence the rights may be owned by different entities in different jurisdictions. For a proposal to have fair trade music licensing, including across territories, see Eddie Schwartz, *Coda Fair Trade Music: Letting the Light Shine In*, in THE EVOLUTION AND EQUILIBRIUM OF COPYRIGHT IN THE DIGITAL AGE, Ch. 14 (Susy Frankel & Daniel Gervais eds., 2014).

[13] *See generally* John H. Jackson, *Regional Trade Blocs and GATT*, https://deepblue.lib.umich.edu/bitstream/handle/2027.42/75224/j.1467-9701.1993.tb00158.x.pdf?sequence=1/.

a large number of free trade agreements (FTAs) that incorporate intellectual property chapters. There is a longstanding debate about whether FTAs enhance liberalization of trade or impede it through preferences and trade diversion.[14] In relation to intellectual property, FTAs all too frequently strengthen intellectual property rights. The strengthening of rights, which include commodifying intellectual property and protecting it as investment assets, are not in and of themselves necessarily trade enhancing. As Rochelle Dreyfuss and I have concluded these moves reconceptualize intellectual property away from quantitative measures, such as how much do we need to incentivize innovation and creativity, to a qualitatively different sort of protection.[15]

While the link between intellectual property and trade is longstanding, how that link has played out has not been static. We are now in a period where there is more than linkage, rather there is something moving closer to fusion. The TRIPS Agreement (TRIPS) provided a platform for trading in intellectual property to develop. It did not necessarily determine how that would occur. From the platform of TRIPS the last twenty plus years have seen a variety of ways in which trade and intellectual property have interacted. This has included countries implementing the agreement (not uniformly) and countries struggling with implementation.[16] Many countries have found ways to implement their international intellectual property obligations within the trade framework (some of these may be more "within" than others). Some countries have become skillful at calibrating their intellectual property law to meet domestic or regional needs while also complying with TRIPS (and sometimes other relevant international obligations).[17] Compliance with intellectual property obligations, however, has not just been about implementing TRIPS requirements, but also additional obligations found in other instruments. The most conspicuous and also the most detrimental of these other obligations have been the

[14] *See* Jagdish Bhagwati, Like Termites in the Trading System: How Preferential Agreements Undermine Free Trade 37 (2008).

[15] Rochelle Cooper Dreyfuss & Susy Frankel, *From Incentive to Commodity to Asset: How International law is Reconceptualizing Intellectual Property*, 36(4) Mich. J. Int'l L. 557 (2015).

[16] Implementation can take place in different ways because minimum standards are minimums rather than prescription. *See also* TRIPS, art. 1.1.

[17] For a discussion of calibration see Daniel Gervais, *IP Calibration*, in Intellectual Property Trade and Development (Daniel Gervais ed., 2d ed. 2014). *See also*, Ruth Okediji, *Legal Innovation in International Intellectual Property Relations: Revisiting Twenty Years of the TRIPS Agreement*, 36(1) U. Pa. J. Int'l L. 191 (2014)

unencumbered expansion of intellectual property standards through FTAs.[18] This expansion has been coupled with a comparative lack of implementation of flexibilities in some countries. Also, there has been some regime-shifting to new multilateral fora by those seeking to ameliorate the effects of TRIPS and FTAs (such as health, the environment and the protection of traditional knowledge).[19]

TRIPS is a minimum standards framework that is not tight (it never required harmonization or truly amounted to a prescriptive supranational code) and it gives discretion to members as they are "free to determine" how they comply with it and whether or not they include exceptions in their national laws.[20] This framework has allowed for, and in some countries even incentivized, experiments with implementing the minimum standards in ways that amount to compliance and at the same time address some local policy drivers. This has given rise to regimes that protect intellectual property and are different from those found in the United States and Europe, in particular.[21] Despite this flexibility the international regime is not entirely a positive picture as every time a party moves to utilize the flexibilities there is a countermove to limit the flexibilities,[22] but equally so the picture is not all grim. What happened after the formation of TRIPS was not the only possible path, nor are we at the end of the path. There are several ways in which intellectual property and trade can and should better coexist. Section I of this chapter discusses what TRIPS created. Section II discusses developments within that framework. Section III looks at ways in which TRIPS can and in some spheres is being reoriented to harness its positives. Put differently, the trade and intellectual property linkage is not a bad one but (as Professor Joad is quoted as saying in relation to ideas[23]) it all depends on what you mean by trade.

[18] *See* Susy Frankel, *The Legitimacy and Purpose of Intellectual Property Chapters in FTAs*, in CHALLENGES TO MULTILATERAL TRADE: THE IMPACT OF BILATERAL, PREFERENTIAL AND REGIONAL AGREEMENTS 185–99 (Ross Buckley, Vai Io Lo & Laurence Boulle eds. 2008).

[19] *See generally*, Laurence R. Helfer, *Regime Shifting: The TRIPS Agreement and New Dynamics of International Intellectual Property Lawmaking*, 29 YALE J. INT'L L. 1 (2004).

[20] TRIPS, art 1.1.

[21] *See* discussion of Brazil and India in Okediji, *supra* note 17 and see discussion of Israel, New Zealand and Singapore in FRANKEL, *supra* note 8.

[22] Dreyfuss & Frankel, *supra* note 15.

[23] LB (Plastics) Ltd. v. Swiss Products Ltd. [1979] RPC 551, 629 (Lord Hailsham).

I The Creation and Life of TRIPS

A GATT and Intellectual Property

The WTO was formed out of the Uruguay Round negotiation of the GATT Agreement.[24] The history of how TRIPS came to be part of that negotiation and how it was completed is well documented.[25] The scope of intellectual property as part of the GATT system, however, pre-dates TRIPS. Importantly, GATT acknowledges that intellectual property could function as a trade barrier. It provides:[26]

> Subject to the requirement that such measures are not applied in a manner which would constitute a means of arbitrary or unjustifiable discrimination between countries where the same conditions prevail, or a **disguised restriction on international trade**, nothing in this Agreement shall be construed to prevent the adoption or enforcement by any contracting party of measures:
>
> ...
>
> (d) necessary to secure compliance with laws or regulations which are not inconsistent with the provisions of this Agreement, including those relating to ... the protection of patents, trade marks and copyrights, and the prevention of deceptive practices; ...

Two GATT dispute panels (before the WTO was formed) considered this exception.[27] In one of those reports the panel concluded that because of the exception, GATT could not be used to challenge the substantive patent law of a contracting party, but members had an obligation to enforce their patent law in ways that were consistent with GATT.[28] GATT also obliged members to prevent the misuse of trade names.[29]

[24] General Agreement on Tariffs and Trade, Oct. 30, 1947, 55 U.N.T.S. 194 [hereinafter GATT].

[25] *See, e.g.*, Susan K. Sell, Private Power, Public Law: The Globalization of Intellectual Property Rights (2003).

[26] GATT, *supra* note 24, art. XX(d) (emphasis added).

[27] GATT Panel Report, *United States – Imports of Certain Automotive Spring Assemblies*, adopted on 26 May 1983, L/5333 – 30S/107; GATT Panel Report, *United States – Section 337 of the Tariff Act of 1930*, adopted on 7 November 1989, L/6439 – 36S/345.

[28] The GATT panel concluded that contracting parties could take measures to protect patents which otherwise would not be in conformity with their GATT obligations. *United States – Section 337 of the Tariff Act of 1930*, *supra* note 27.

[29] GATT, *supra* note 24, art. IX:6 states that:

> The contracting parties shall co-operate with each other with a view to preventing the use of trade names in such manner as to misrepresent the true origin of a product, to the detriment of such distinctive regional or geographical names of products of the territory of a contracting party as are protected by its legislation. Each contracting party shall accord full and

In one dispute that obligation was interpreted to not require protection of "riesling" or "chateau." [30] TRIPS requires protection of certain geographical indications and thus addresses what some may have seen as a gap in GATT.[31] The advent of TRIPS also means that intellectual property related disputes at the WTO are brought in relation to TRIPS, not GATT. TRIPS in effect modifies the application of the GATT intellectual property overlap.

GATT's allowance for countries to make intellectual property law and the existing international intellectual property rules were not regarded as an adequate international regime for those who wanted better intellectual property protection around the globe. That led to a push to protect intellectual property in the trade regime. Even so, the link between intellectual property and trade is longstanding. It was an uneasy relationship in the pre-WTO regime and continues to raise conflict. Whether it needs to always do so, or the extent to which it has done so, is a further question that is discussed below.

There is a collision of high-level principle between GATT and intellectual property protection. The principle of free (or in reality liberalized) movement of goods and the territorial uses of intellectual property law to prevent free movement of intellectual property related goods, particularly where they are parallel imports, are arguably contradictory.[32] It is

> sympathetic consideration to such requests or representations as may be made by any other contracting party regarding the application of the undertaking set forth in the preceding sentence to names of products which have been communicated to it by the other contracting party.

[30] *Japan – Customs Duties, Taxes and Labelling Practices on Imported Wines and Alcoholic Beverage*, GATT document L/6216. This report was adopted on November 10, 1987, BISD 34S/83. The panel found that the use of marks such as "Riesling" or "chateau" by Japanese manufacturers was not established to be to the detriment of distinctive regional or geographical names of products. As Gervais explains, the ITO Preparatory Committee agreed that "deceptive practices" in GATT, art. XX(d) included the false marking of geographical origin. A contracting party could therefore protect indications of geographical origin under GATT: see DANIEL J. GERVAIS, THE TRIPS AGREEMENT: DRAFTING HISTORY AND ANALYSIS 1.06–1.07 (4th ed. 2012).

[31] TRIPS, arts. 22–24.

[32] *See* discussion in Susy Frankel, *The Applicability of GATT Jurisprudence to the Interpretation of the TRIPS Agreement*, in RESEARCH HANDBOOK ON THE INTERPRETATION AND ENFORCEMENT OF INTELLECTUAL PROPERTY UNDER WTO RULES (Carlos M. Correa ed., 2010). *See also* Paul J. Heald, *Trademarks and Geographical Indications Exploring the Contours of the TRIPS Agreement*, 29 VAND. J. TRANSNAT'L L. 638, 658 (1996), where he suggests that "protecting the profit margin of certain producers by stopping goods at the border is precisely the sort of activity that the GATT was meant to discourage". *See also*, Susy Frankel & Daniel Gervais,

a matter of dispute whether countries preventing parallel imports can justify the interference with the free movement of goods as a means of encouraging local innovation.[33] An issue that remains unresolved is whether the prevention of parallel importation can meet the test of "necessary" found in the GATT exception. Necessary in GATT, article XX(d) refers to securing compliance with patent law. Preventing parallel importation may be desirable but arguably not always necessary to secure such compliance. There is no simple or single answer to what is necessary in regard to the relationship between patent law and parallel importation. In some economies prevention may be necessary and in others the necessity may point to allowing parallel imports.[34] Putting that to one side, as the passage of time has done, under present international intellectual property law, and in particular TRIPS, countries can prevent or permit parallel imports.[35]

Furthermore, the inclusion of TRIPS in the WTO framework was recognition that, at least under the WTO trade model, some intellectual property protection is trade enhancing. At its simplest this is because some intellectual property owners are more willing to trade across borders if they will receive legal protection for their intellectual property in foreign markets. As commentators have explained, the trade and intellectual property linkage is justified because without international intellectual property protection unfair imitations and problem spillovers will prevail.[36] The ever-increasing levels of intellectual property protection and related rent-seeking behavior of some rights owners, however, means that there are questions about whether the WTO style trade and intellectual property linkage was ever a good thing.[37]

International Intellectual Property Rules and Parallel Imports, in INTELLECTUAL PROPERTY EXHAUSTION AND PARALLEL IMPORTS (Irene Calboli & Edward Lee eds., 2016).

[33] Indeed, it may do so if parallel imports would make goods too cheap for local producers to compete in economies where consumers can afford higher process.

[34] *See* CARLOS M. CORREA, INTELLECTUAL PROPERTY RIGHTS, THE WTO AND DEVELOPING COUNTRIES: THE TRIPS AGREEMENT AND POLICY OPTIONS 86–8 (2000) and FRANKEL, *supra* note 8, Ch. 8.

[35] TRIPS, art. 6 provides that exhaustion of intellectual property rights shall not be subject to dispute resolution, effectively allowing countries to adopt national, regional or international exhaustion policies and consequently allow or prohibit parallel importing as they see fit.

[36] K. MASKUS, PRIVATE RIGHTS AND PUBLIC PROBLEMS: THE GLOBAL ECONOMICS OF INTELLECTUAL PROPERTY IN THE 21ST CENTURY, Ch. 2 (2012).

[37] *See generally*, Jerome H. Reichman, *Intellectual Property in International Trade: Opportunities and Risks of a GATT Connection*, 22(4) VAND. J. TRANSNAT'L L. 747, 747–891 (1989).

B TRIPS Platform and More Extensive Protection

TRIPS created a set of minimum standards of intellectual property rights that countries must implement in their domestic laws.[38] As Graeme Dinwoodie and Rochelle Dreyfuss have said, some hoped TRIPS was a kind of supranational code, but this "makes little sense from a normative, prescriptive or pragmatic perspective."[39] It never was such a code although its effects are indeed felt internationally. TRIPS adopted the existing and well-established international intellectual property framework of minimum standards coupled with national treatment.[40] It incorporated large parts of existing intellectual property agreements (the Berne and Paris Conventions[41]); extended protection in copyright[42] and trademarks;[43] added new protection in areas such as geographical indications[44] and undisclosed information;[45] and made significant changes to patent law as it was the first multilateral instrument to provide for substantive patent law standards that require countries to provide both product and process patents in all fields of technology.[46] While members must comply with the Agreement they are "free to determine the appropriate method of implementing the provisions of this Agreement within their own legal system and practice."[47] TRIPS also framed how exceptions and limitations in all areas of intellectual property would develop. The Agreement subjected most exceptions to the three-step test (or varieties thereof).[48]

In addition to requiring protection of substantive protection of intellectual property rights, TRIPS provided minimum standards of civil and criminal enforcement of those rights at domestic law.[49] These obligations

[38] TRIPS, art. 1.1.
[39] G. B. Dinwoodie & R. C. Dreyfuss, A Neofederalist Vision of TRIPS: The Resilience of the International Intellectual Property Regime 14 (2012).
[40] TRIPS, art. 4.
[41] Berne Convention for the Protection of Literary and Artistic Works, Jul. 24, 1971, 1161 U.N.T.S. 31 [hereinafter Berne Convention]; Paris Convention for the Protection of Industrial Property, Jul. 14, 1967, 828 U.N.T.S. 305 [hereinafter Paris Convention].
[42] Computer programs and databases must be protected, TRIPS, art. 10.
[43] Well-known trademarks receive greater protection, *see id.*, art. 16. [44] *Id.* [45] *Id.*
[46] *Id.* art. 27.1.
[47] *Id.* art. 1.1. The importance of the principle was affirmed in WTO Panel Report, China – Measures Affecting the Protection and Enforcement of Intellectual Property Rights, WT/DS362/R ¶ 7.507 (Jan. 16, 2009) [hereinafter China – Enforcement], ¶ 7.513.
[48] The three-step test is found in TRIPS, arts. 13 (copyright), 17 (trademarks), 26.2 (industrial designs), 30 (patents).
[49] TRIPS, Part III.

do not "create any obligation to put in place a judicial system for the enforcement of intellectual property rights distinct from that for the enforcement of law in general."[50]

The "General Provisions and Basic Principles" part of TRIPS, applicable to all of the obligations and the exceptions,[51] include objectives and principles, which were a significant part of what developing countries negotiated. These include key purpose provisions that reference public interests other than rights ownership, such as that intellectual property protection "should contribute to the promotion of technological innovation and to the transfer and dissemination of technology . . . in a manner conducive to social and economic welfare . . . "[52] Unfortunately these public-regarding provisions have struggled for practical and appropriate recognition.[53] The objectives and principles are now recognized as integral not only to TRIPS's interpretation but also in its implementation.[54]

Disputes that can be brought to the WTO dispute settlement system are about whether a WTO member's law complies with TRIPS standards. In WTO terminology such disputes are violation disputes.[55] In some areas the WTO allows for nonviolation disputes.[56] Such complaints involve the allegation that even though the letter of the agreement is not violated a legitimate expectation arising from it is. TRIPS has always excluded nonviolation disputes.[57] The possible inclusion of nonviolation disputes was supposed to be a matter for ongoing discussion.[58] Their

[50] *Id.* art. 41.5.

[51] In addition to the three-step test exceptions to patents are found in *id.*, arts. 27.2, 27.3, 31 and 31bis.

[52] *Id.* art. 7. [53] *See e.g.*, Frankel, *supra* note 4; Dinwoodie & Dreyfuss, *supra* note 39.

[54] The need for the application of interpretative principles to give full weight to TRIPS's objectives and principles contained in Articles 7 and 8 in dispute settlement was underscored in the Doha Declaration. *See* World Trade Organization, Ministerial Declaration of 20 November 2001, ¶ 5.a, WT/MIN(01)/DEC/2, ("[E]ach provision of the TRIPS Agreement shall be read in the light of the object and purpose of the Agreement . . ."); *see also* James T. Gathii, *The Legal Status of the Doha Declaration on TRIPS and Public Health Under the Vienna Convention on the Law of Treaties*, 15 Harv. J.L. & Tech. 291, 292–3 (2002) ("[T]he Doha Declaration should now be regarded as an interpretive element in the interpretation of the TRIPS Agreement under customary international law.")

[55] Understanding on Rules and Procedures Governing the Settlement of Disputes, Apr. 15, 1994, Marrakesh Agreement Establishing the World Trade Organization, Annex 2, Legal Instruments – Results of the Uruguay Round, 1869 U.N.T.S. 401, 33 I.L.M. 1225 (1994) [hereinafter DSU].

[56] *Id.* art. 26 and GATT, *supra* note 24, Art. XXIII 1(b). [57] TRIPS, art. 64.2.

[58] WTO, *TRIPS: 'Non-Violation' Complaints (article 64.2): Background and the current situation* http://www.wto.org/english/tratop_e/trips_e/nonviolation_background_e.htm.

inclusion has been steadfastly opposed by developing and least-developed countries as nonviolation disputes are seen as a potential way to increase TRIPS standards (this is not, however inevitable, as discussed below).[59]

TRIPS also makes the whole agreement subject to national treatment, as is the norm for international intellectual property agreements.[60] The explicit WTO trade linkage introduced most-favored nation (MFN) to international intellectual property law.[61] Not only is MFN now widely recognized as an awkward fit with intellectual property, but it has contributed to the spread of more extensive protection.[62] This partly arises because parties to an intellectual property chapter in an FTA cannot agree to limit their more extensive protection between them. In other areas of trade (GATT and GATS) the effects of preferential bargains can be isolated to the parties (although not all view that as a good thing).[63] Although MFN helps to keep high levels of intellectual property protection in place, it is not the sole or even main mechanism by which increased standards are permitted and maintained. In a manner that is found throughout international intellectual property law treaties, TRIPS allows countries to provide for more extensive protection.[64] Some countries, particularly the United States, have embraced this freedom with vigor and set about creating multiple FTAs that in combination with other FTAs progressively raise the level of intellectual property protection required around the world. These FTAs and their provisions, which are beyond the TRIPS minimums, have been widely criticized because of their effects on access to technology and products (such as pharmaceuticals) and on development generally and developing countries in particular.

As FTAs grew in number it became clear that the structure of TRIPS was a problem because it enabled increases in intellectual property protection to proceed apace with no real opportunity either for international legal challenge or for flexibilities and exceptions to act as an effective counterbalance.[65]

[59] *Id.* [60] TRIPS, art. 3. [61] *Id.* art. 4.

[62] *See* Peter Drahos, *When the Weak Bargain with the Strong: Negotiations in the World Trade Organization*, 8 Inter'l Negotiation 79 (2003); Peter Drahos, *BITS and BIPS: Bilateralism in Intellectual Property*, 4 J. World Intellect. Prop. 791 (2001); Susy Frankel, *The Legitimacy and Purpose of Intellectual Property Chapters in FTAs*, in Challenges to Multilateral Trade: The Impact of Bilateral, Preferential and Regional Agreements, *supra* note 18, at 185.

[63] Bhagwati, *supra* note 14. [64] TRIPS, art. 1.1.

[65] TRIPS, art. 1.1 allows parties to provide more extensive protection. Such protection is supposed to be in accordance with the Agreement. I have suggested elsewhere that means in accordance with TRIPS's objectives and purposes: *see* Frankel, *supra* note 4 and *see* Susy Frankel, *Challenging TRIPS-Plus Agreements: The Potential Utility of Non-Violation Disputes*, 12 J. Int'l Econ. L. 1023 (2009).

In addition, flexibilities became subject to international challenge even though they were based on a test designed to allow a degree of national autonomy. Discretion in implementing exceptions (and other flexibilities) does not mean that obligations need not be complied with. The obligations must be implemented in national law, but equally so the types of exceptions and method of their implementation is, from the perspective of the international framework, a matter of national autonomy.[66]

The two main disputes that tested the three-step framework interpreted the provisions of TRIPS both formalistically and in a way that provided little positive guidance to policymakers.[67] After those disputes questions arose (and still remain) over whether exceptions that some countries had in their laws at the time of TRIPS are three-step test legitimate.[68] While such issues are aired (even if the best answer is that such exceptions are legitimate), exceptions and flexibilities may nevertheless remain elusive for some WTO members. This seems particularly

66 *Id.*

67 *See* WTO Panel Report, Canada – Patent Protection of Pharmaceutical Products, WT/DS114/R (Mar. 17, 2000) [hereinafter Canada – Pharmaceuticals]; WTO Panel Report, United States – Section 110(5) of the U.S. Copyright Act, WT/DS/160/R (Jun. 15, 2000) [hereinafter U.S.-110(5)]. *See* discussion in Jane C. Ginsburg, *Toward Supranational Copyright Law? The WTO Panel Decision and the "Three Step Test" for Copyright Exemptions*, 187 REVUE INTERNATIONALE DU DROIT D'AUTEUR 3, 17 (2001), noting that the U.S.-110(5) panel did not interpret "normal exploitation" in the three-step test as including the possibility for copyright to develop norms on what copyright holders have the power to exploit.

68 For example, some have suggested after the U.S.-110(5) report, *supra* note 67, that the United States' fair use doctrine might not comply with the three-step test. That is not likely to be correct, not least of all because it was never suggested in negotiations that it would not be. *See* The Patry Copyright Blog, *Fair Use, the Three-Step Test, and the Counter-Reformation* (Apr. 2, 2008), http://williampatry.blogspot.co.nz/2008/04/fair-use-three-step-test-and-european.html stating,

> The biggest of the three-step scare tactics is that Section 107 of the U.S. Copyright Act is incompatible with the test. Baloney. WIPO and European copyright experts testified before the U.S. Congress during the hearings on U.S. adherence to Berne . . . Congress even went to Geneva and convened a round table discussion there on November 25 and 26, 1987 with WIPO and European copyright experts, the sole purpose of which was to determine which parts of U.S. law needed to be amended to permit Berne adherence. Not once at this round table or during four years of hearings were the words "fair use" ever raised by a foreign expert who appeared before Congress nor did any domestic witness (of whom there were many dozens) consider there to be a potential problem . . . I can say from direct experience of having been involved in these efforts at the Copyright Office that I never heard a single European expert claim there was a compatibility issue with fair use.

likely both because in some instances legal exceptions cannot alone create enough of a counterweight to protection and those newer to the practice of creating exceptions domestically might understandably hesitate to do so if an international legal challenge looked probable or even possible. The effect of the WTO three-step test decisions was that they suggested exceptions were hard, if not impossible, to defend internationally unless they somehow had universal support.[69] To the extent that countries had difficulty implementing flexibilities the WTO panel reports have served to compound that difficulty.

Unlike other parts of FTAs, which at least in theory liberalize trade (although some argue they enhance protectionism[70]), more extensive intellectual property protections frequently do not support some of the stated rationales for the WTO trade and intellectual property linkage. Increased protections are not about improving intellectual property incentives such as enhancing innovation and technology transfer, but have become mechanisms to extract greater worldwide rents. They in effect protect an investment in intellectual property by rewarding more than what is needed to incentivize the related creativity and innovation.[71]

The reasons that countries would enter agreements which are apparently against their interests were largely because of perceived benefits of trade-offs, particularly in other areas of trade.[72] The wisdom of such trade-offs has been questioned and now is very much in the spotlight. Countries with intellectual property laws which are out of kilter with their stage of development, both because of TRIPS and FTA implementation, are now much more wary of doing deals.

See also Martin Senftleben, *The International Three-Step Test: A Model Provision for EC Fair Use Legislation*, 2(1) Journal of Intellectual Property, Information Technology and E-Commerce Law 67, 67–82 (2010).

[69] In Canada – Pharmaceuticals, *supra* note 67, the contested regulatory review exception in part found support because several countries (particularly the United States) had the equivalent in their laws.

[70] *See* Bhagwati, *supra* note 14.

[71] In addition, investment chapters in bilateral investment treaties (BITs) and FTAs protect intellectual property as an investment. Consequently, as Rochelle Dreyfuss and I have said, intellectual property is progressively being reconceptualized: see Dreyfuss & Frankel, *supra* note 15.

[72] Susy Frankel, *Trade-Offs and Transparency*, 44(8) Int. Rev. Intellect. Prop. Competition. L. 913 (2013).

II Developments within TRIPS Framework

A Ongoing Negotiations

TRIPS did not harmonize and, as its negotiating history shows, could not have harmonized many intellectual property standards. Where FTAs have stepped in to harmonize some norms, such a process is both incomplete and faces greater challenges than any other time in the period post-TRIPS. This may be particularly so where intellectual property is seen to have an impact on regimes which have goals other than protecting intellectual property. Those seeking higher intellectual property standards have a fulsome international agenda,[73] including bilateral[74] and plurilateral[75] negotiations between states and private parties bringing investment disputes. These tactics extend well beyond intellectual property law and can be found, for instance, in the demands of pharmaceutical chapters of FTAs. But even in these spheres the activities of protectionists seeking to control pharmaceutical pricing and squeeze public health care systems, for example, is widely known. What was once dressed up as necessary in the name of innovation and creativity incentives is increasingly questioned and the overstatement of required incentives has become hollow rhetoric. This does not mean that there should not be global intellectual property rules, but rather that intellectual property should be based on innovation and creativity incentives. Even if within an incentives-based regime there are sometimes degrees of both over- and under-protection, a regime underpinned with incentive goals is more justifiable than intellectual property which is predominantly protectionist and rent-seeking.

[73] *See generally*, Susan K. Sell, *TRIPS Was Never Enough: Vertical Forum Shifting, FTAS, ACTA, and TPP*, 18 J. Intell. Prop. L. 447 (2011).

[74] Examples include the United States and E.U. negotiation known as the Trans-Atlantic Trade and Investment Partnership (TTIP) and the Canada E.U. Trade Agreement (CETA), http://trade.ec.europa.eu/doclib/docs/2014/september/tradoc_152806.pdf.

[75] The main example is the Trans-Pacific Partnership (TPP). Parties to the concluded agreement are New Zealand, Australia, Chile, Peru, Brunei, Singapore, Vietnam, Malaysia, Japan, Canada, Mexico and the United States. The United States has subsequently withdrawn from the TPP. The remaining other eleven parties have concluded the agreement, which is now known as the Comprehensive and Progressive Agreement for Trans-Pacific Partnership. The CPTPP makes a considerable number of changes to the intellectual property chapter of the TPP: see Ministry of Foreign Affairs and Trade, *TPP and CPTPP – the differences*, www.mfat.govt.nz/en/trade/free-trade-agreements/free-trade-agreements-concluded-but-not-in-force/cptpp/tpp-and-cptpp-the-differences-explained/.

B *Implementation of International Intellectual Property Norms*

Many WTO members have learned to live with TRIPS and have found new and creative ways to implement intellectual property norms in order to calibrate those norms to meet local objectives and policy goals.[76] Although many details of implementation could not have been predicted it was highly probable, as is the case with all rules and regulations, that some of those who are required to implement the laws will be incentivized to work around the rules and possibly to interpret them differently from how others do.[77] Some FTA standards of protection, even though they are framed as minimum standards, are more prescriptive and allow for less flexibility in implementation than the minimum standards required under TRIPS. In the Canadian European Union Agreement (CETA), for example, parties are required to provide for extended protection for patents[78] and there are provisions in the copyright part relating to internet service provider liability.[79] FTAs with these sorts of provisions are a step closer to harmonized norms. As more detailed protection through FTAs has emerged globalized intellectual property rules have become increasingly difficult for some to calibrate appropriately at national level. The kind of bargain that Canada and the E.U. can work out is not as easily achieved by countries with lesser resources. Although the link between intellectual property and trade provided the platform for moves toward greater harmonization, it was not and even now should not be the inevitable consequence of the trade and intellectual property linkage.

As stronger intellectual property norms proliferate the incentive for domestic calibration becomes ever greater. This effect of modification of stronger intellectual property rights has long since been demonstrated in countries with strong domestic intellectual property laws. In copyright, for instance, it is well recognized that the United States' fair use (even with its difficulties) is one of the most flexible approaches to copyright. The European Union continues to explore expanding copyright flexibilities,[80] as do

[76] *See* Okediji, *supra* note 17 and FRANKEL, *supra* note 8.

[77] Of course one country's interpretation can be challenged through the WTO dispute settlement system.

[78] CETA, *supra* note 74, at 20.7. [79] CETA, *supra* note 74, at 20.11.

[80] E.U. Commission Directorate General Internal Market and Services, *Report on the Responses to the Public Consultation on the Review of the EU Copyright Rules* (July 2014), http://ec.europa.eu/internal_market/consultations/2013/copyright-rules/docs/contributions/consultation-report_en.pdf.

Australia,[81] Canada,[82] Israel[83] and New Zealand.[84] And court decisions from these jurisdictions, including the Supreme Court of the United States[85] and the Federal and Supreme Courts of Canada,[86] have pushed patent law away from restrictive interpretations, which might stifle rather than support innovation. In Australia the standard for patenting has been raised.[87] These changes in the law are for the most part TRIPS compliant. In some instances they are explicitly stated as being so and in others are treated as TRIPS compliant. Often it is not in any state's interest to challenge such changes as they may also utilize analogous flexibilities. The objectors, if any, are private rights holders who have no direct standing in state-to-state dispute settlement, such as at the WTO or under some FTAs. That is why some private rights owners are now challenging intellectual property law and asserting TRIPS and nontrade agreement compliance before investment tribunals.[88]

1 WTO Dispute Settlement

Dispute settlement at the WTO has had mixed results. The panel reports of two disputes about compliance of certain laws with the three-step test (one relating to copyright and the other patents[89]) paid scant regard to the objectives and principles of TRIPS. Particularly, in neither report did the panel's path of analysis fully consider both the objectives and purposes of TRIPS and the domestic policy goals behind the exceptions at issue. This was a failing in at least two ways. First, there was a conspicuous lack of appreciation that the objectives and principles that are expressly part of the TRIPS text are more relevant to the

81 Australian Law Reform Commission, *Copyright and the Digital Economy Report* (May 30, 2012), http://www.alrc.gov.au/inquiries/copyright-and-digital-economy.

82 *See* The Copyright Pentalogy: How the Supreme Court of Canada Shook the Foundations of Canadian Copyright Law (Michael Geist ed., 2013).

83 *See Interlego A/S v. Exin-Line Bros. S.A.*, Civil Appeal 513/89 48 PD (4), 133 where the Supreme Court of Israel adopts United States principles as guidance to Israel's law. For a discussion of goals and the education context in Israel, see Niva Elkin-Koren, Orit Fischman Afori, Ronit Haramati-Alpern & Amira Dotan, *Fair Use Best Practices for Higher Education Institutions: The Israeli Experience*, 57 J. Copyright Soc'y U.S.A. 447, 447–72 (2010).

84 *See* discussion in Frankel, *supra* note 8, Ch. 6.

85 *See, e.g.*, Association for Molecular Pathology v. Myriad Genetics, 569 U.S. 12-398 (2013); Alice Corp. Pty. Ltd. v. CLS Bank Int'l, 573 U.S. _ (2014).

86 *See, e.g.*, Harvard College v. Canada (Commissioner of Patents) [2002] 4 SCR 45.

87 IP Laws Amendment (Raising the Bar) Act 2012.

88 *See also* Dreyfuss & Frankel, *supra* note 15.

89 U.S.-110(5) and Canada – Pharmaceuticals, *supra* note 67.

interpretation of the flexibilities of the Agreement than any other part. They were negotiated to support public-regarding exceptions. Second, there was a general failing to fully use the established principles of treaty interpretation. The process of assessing compliance with TRIPS should have used the full requirements of the Vienna Convention on the Law of Treaties.[90] That is that the ordinary meaning of the terms of a treaty are interpreted in light of their context and of the treaty's object and purpose.[91] A purpose of TRIPS is to allow countries to calibrate their laws to local needs. Where the agreement, as is the case with TRIPS, does not prescribe how that may be done (i.e. mandatory exceptions are not delineated but a broad framework for exceptions is provided) then discretion is part of the agreement and directly relevant to its interpretation. So if an exception is created in order to incentivize innovation (a goal that is consistent with the purposes of intellectual property) that goal ought to feature in interpretation of the exception's compliance with the agreement. It may be that if this process of interpretation was followed the result in the particular disputes would not have been different. Whether that is true or not is not possible to prove, nor the main point. An analysis of the three-step test, however, using the full scope of the Vienna Convention rules should have produced much better guidance about the scope of the three-step test.

The panel reports do not provide effective guidance about the scope of national policy drivers and how they should be interpreted in an analysis of international treaty compliance. In other international agreements one might find that domestic goals are not appropriate in the interpretation process because there has been an obligation agreed to which explicitly negates those domestic goals. In the case of intellectual property related flexibilities the obligation to allow domestic discretion is not negated but is core to the agreement.

In two other WTO disputes, domestic and regional goals seem to have played a greater role in the panel's analysis. In the *European Union – Geographical Indications* dispute the panel when interpreting the trademarks-related three-step test recognized that the test's purpose was to allow flexibility.[92] In the *China – Enforcement* report the panel noted that although TRIPS "does not grant Members freedom to implement a lower

[90] Vienna Convention on the Law of Treaties, May 23, 1969, 1115 U.N.T.S. 331 (entered into force Jan. 27, 1980) [hereinafter VCLT].

[91] *Id.* art. 31.

[92] WTO Panel Report, *European Communities – Geographical Indications for Agricultural Products and Foodstuffs*, WT/DS174/R (Mar. 15, 2005).

standard . . . [it] grants freedom to determine the appropriate method of implementation of the provisions to which they are required to give effect . . . "[93]

2 Cross-Retaliation at the WTO

Just as domestic legal changes can have unexpected effects so too can international legal changes. An example is the use of TRIPS in cross-retaliation. The purpose of retaliation, as part of the WTO dispute settlement rules, is for the losing party to comply with or to reach a mutually agreed solution to the dispute settlement body's (DSB) recommendations following a dispute.[94] Permission to retaliate must be granted through the WTO arbitration process.[95] Retaliation should preferably be under the same agreement that has been violated, but where that is not practical then retaliation under other WTO agreements (cross-retaliation) may be permitted.[96] The often-stated reason for including the possibility for cross-retaliation in the DSU was that the United States thought it would need such an enforcement option when developing countries, in particular, did not comply with DSB recommendations relating to violations of TRIPS. The rationale was that those countries would not have significant intellectual property related assets to enable any effective retaliation and therefore cross-retaliation under other WTO agreements would be needed for enforcement of TRIPS violations.[97] However, that story has not proved true and something different has occurred. There has been no instance of a developing country failing to comply with DSB recommendations following a TRIPS dispute and consequently of cross-retaliation being sought in that context. Instead, cross-retaliation under TRIPS has been used when some large developed countries have not complied with the DSB's recommendations made against them, in relation to violations of WTO agreements other than TRIPS.

[93] China – Enforcement, *supra* note 47, ¶ 7.513 referring to TRIPS, art. 1.1.

[94] For a discussion of the several purposes of dispute settlement see Michelle Limenta, Non-Compliance in WTO Dispute Settlement: Assessing the Effectiveness of WTO Retaliation from its Purpose(s) (2012) (unpublished Ph.D. thesis, Victoria University of Wellington) http://researcharchive.vuw.ac.nz/bitstream/handle/10063/2071/thesis.pdf?sequence=2.

[95] DSU, *supra* note 55, art. 21. [96] *Id.* art. 22.

[97] *See generally* Shamnad Basheer, *Turning TRIPS on Its Head: An "IP Cross Retaliation" Model for Developing Countries*, 3(2) The Law and Development Rev. 197 (2010); Susy Frankel, *The TRIPS Agreement and Cross-Retaliation*, in Trade Agreements at the Crossroads 208–25 (Susy Frankel & Meredith Kolsky Lewis eds., 2013).

WTO arbitration panels have on three occasions allowed the successful complaining party to cross-retaliate under TRIPS against the noncomplying losing party. These disputes have related to Ecuador's success under GATT against the then European Communities banana importing regime;[98] Antigua's successful claim that the United States breached GATS[99] obligations relating to online gambling services;[100] and Brazil's success against the United States' prohibited and actionable cotton subsidies.[101] Ecuador never exercised the cross-retaliation that the arbitration panel had in principle authorized. It appeared to use the potential of cross-retaliation as a lever to negotiate a settlement. In the cotton dispute Brazil came very close to exercising cross-retaliation. That threat of cross-retaliation was most probably effective in leading to a settlement because of Brazil's economic capacity to cross-retaliate. This economic capacity included its pharmaceutical industry and the possibility that cross-retaliation could be directed towards U.S.-owned pharmaceutical patents. Perhaps for that reason, soon after the WTO authorized cross-retaliation, the United States speedily settled the dispute. Antigua, although authorized to cross-retaliate against the United States, was not as successful as Brazil. The United States has taken the position that compliance is optional.[102] The reason may be that the United States had chosen not to respond in order to discourage TRIPS cross-retaliation. When compared with Brazil, Antigua is not likely to be able to have a significant impact on the United States economy.

As noted, the purpose of including cross-retaliation provisions was to back-up the potential "threats" if there was noncompliance with TRIPS. Instead cross-retaliation has been used to potentially suspend TRIPS

[98] Arbitrators Report, *EC-Regime for the Importation, Sale and Distribution of Bananas – Recourse to Arbitration by the EC under article 22.6 of the DSU*, WT/DS27/ARB/ECU (Mar. 24, 2000).

[99] General Agreement on Trade in Services, Apr. 15, 1994, Marrakesh Agreement Establishing the World Trade Organization (WTO Agreement), Annex 1B, 1869 U.N.T.S. 183 [hereinafter GATS].

[100] Arbitrators Report, *US-Measures Affecting the Cross-Border Supply of Gambling and Betting Services Recourse to Arbitration by the United States under article 22.6 of the DSU*, WT/DS285/ARB (Dec. 21, 2007).

[101] Arbitrators Report, *US-Subsidies on Upland Cotton Recourse to Arbitration by the United States under article 22.6 of the DSU*, WT/DS267/ARB/1 and 2 (Aug. 31, 2009).

[102] *See* Intellectual Property Watch, *Bark But No Bite? Antigua Talks Tough on WTO Gambling Case, But No TRIPS Remedy* (Jun. 18, 2014), http://www.ip-watch.org/2014/06/18/bark-but-no-bite-antigua-talks-tough-on-wto-gambling-case-but-no-trips-remedy/.

obligations and lessen their effectiveness (even if sanctioned by the DSB). Overall, cross-retaliation has taken a course different from that which was anticipated when it was negotiated in the Uruguay Round leading to the formation of the WTO.

III What Could Lie Ahead

Better approaches to interpretation should assist with the improved implementation of TRIPS. Ensuring connections between the innovation incentive basis of intellectual property and development of international intellectual property law is necessary in order to prevent the detachment of incentives from intellectual property in a way that reconceptualizes it.[103] As Dreyfuss notes, using incentives to inform norm-making is also critical.[104] Other suggestions might include halting the flow of FTAs or, perhaps more practically, providing principles by which they might less-destructively progress.[105] The development of cross-retaliation may point to other ways to counterbalance the ferocity of increasing intellectual property norms, even within the WTO framework.

When the WTO chose property rules over other methods of protecting intellectual property it did several things. It created an agreement that is structurally different from other WTO agreements. TRIPS, unlike GATT and GATS, is not a market access agreement. The rhetoric that intellectual property protection increases availability of goods in other markets is true only up to a point. It has taken some time for those with a trade-related background to appreciate some of the differences that intellectual property brings to the trade regime. By linking intellectual property into a framework of the WTO's version of economic liberalism, intellectual property has not only found a platform to expand, but it has been shown to be not always compatible with trade-enhancing rationales. From this arise several ways in which TRIPS and related WTO rules could develop.

First, legitimate subsidization of research and development may for some countries be a better way to increase domestic innovation than the

[103] Dreyfuss & Frankel, *supra* note 15.

[104] Rochelle Cooper Dreyfuss, Speech at the National University of Singapore: In Praise of an Incentive-Based Theory of Intellectual Property Protection (Aug. 14, 2014).

[105] *See* Max Planck Institute, *Principles for Intellectual Property Provisions in Bilateral and Regional Trade Agreements*, 44 INT. REV. INTELLECT. PROP. COMPET. L. 878 (2013) and commentaries in the same issue.

imposition of property rules designed in other jurisdictions for other economic circumstances.[106] While research and development subsidies are no longer permitted without question (a "green light") in the WTO framework, they remain permissible provided they are not in violation of the terms of the WTO's Subsidies and Countervailing Measures Agreement.[107]

Second, "be careful what you wish for" is an apt maxim for the outcome of cross-retaliation because those who created those rules have found that they have backfired.[108] The same risk exists for those who insist on pushing for stronger and stronger intellectual property and investment rights and enforcement in the name of trade.[109] Such an approach assumes that the leaders in innovation and creativity will remain in first place. There is already much evidence that this is not so.[110] In the future, those currently in the lead may find themselves ending up having to pay to reduce standards so as to enable them to use the intellectual property of others to innovate.

Third, there are few issues that remain on the TRIPS Council agenda. One example is the nonviolation complaint, a mechanism that those trying to retain TRIPS standards and not extend them have to date eschewed. It is to the nonviolation complaint that this chapter now turns.

A *Nonviolation Complaints*

A nonviolation complaint is one where the letter of the treaty has not been violated (there is no infringed treaty article, i.e. no violation) but a "benefit accruing to [a complainant] . . . is being nullified or impaired or the attainment of any objective of that Agreement is being impeded as a result of the application by a Member of any measure".[111] Nonviolation, as noted above, has been opposed because it is feared as a mechanism that could be used to fill in the gaps and curb the

[106] *See* FRANKEL, *supra* note 8, Ch. 4.

[107] WTO, Agreement on Subsidies and Countervailing Measures, art. 8, 1869 UNTS 183; 33 ILM 1167, (signed 15 April 1994, entered into force January 1, 1995).

[108] Frankel, *supra* note 97.

[109] For a discussion of how investment rights disputes might backfire, *see* Dreyfuss & Frankel, *supra* note 15.

[110] *See, e.g.*, Daniel Gervais, *Adjusting Patentability Criteria to Optimize Innovation: A Look at China and India*, in PATENT LAW IN GLOBAL PERSPECTIVE (Ruth Okediji & Margot Bagley eds., 2014).

[111] DSU, *supra* note 55, art. 26.1.

flexibilities that TRIPS has left. This view is understandable[112] but may be short-sighted.

TRIPS violation disputes are illustrative of both the potential and limitations of nonviolation disputes. The issue of TRIPS and the non-availability of nonviolation disputes arose in *India Patents*.[113] There the Appellate Body underscored that the GATT-developed concept of legitimate expectations should not be read into TRIPS disputes because of the connection between the jurisprudence on legitimate expectations under GATT and nonviolation disputes. As nonviolation disputes are not available under TRIPS,[114] the Appellate Body held that the GATT jurisprudence was not very relevant to TRIPS interpretation. It noted that the "TRIPS Agreement, the entire text of which was newly negotiated in the Uruguay Round[,] . . . occupies a relatively self-contained, *sui generis* status in the WTO Agreement."[115]

Despite the nonavailability of nonviolation disputes some violation disputes have looked a little like nonviolation claims. To the extent that the United States claim in the *US – China Enforcement* dispute, for

[112] This opposition is understandable as the main advocate for nonviolation disputes has been the United States which also "leads" the more extensive protection campaign through FTAs. *See* WTO, Non-Violation Complaints Under the TRIPS Agreement Communication from the United States, IP/C/W/599, Jun. 10, 2014 and see Knowledge Ecology International, *WTO TRIPS Council (June 2014): USTR submission on Non-Violation Complaints Under the TRIPS Agreement* [hereinafter U.S. Non-Violation Note], http://keionline.org/node/2016 discussing the United States' position. Stating at 4.15:

> In this regard, the United States also notes the following considerations conveyed by Switzerland at the February 2014, meeting of the TRIPS Council: A number of delegations in their interventions today referred to their concern as to the potential impact of the application of non-violation complaints on their rights and obligations under TRIPS and more particularly the flexibilities contained in the Agreement. Let me be clear on this important point: It is our firm view that a non-violation complaint cannot be brought against another Member for utilizing a flexibility foreseen in the TRIPS Agreement. One of the necessary conditions that the complaining party must demonstrate is that the offending measure could not have been foreseen. That a Member may make use of a flexibility provided in the TRIPS Agreement is, just as any other right under the TRIPS Agreement, foreseeable by other Members. After all, they were written into the Agreement, agreed by all Members and, as far as pertaining to public health, also confirmed in the Doha Ministerial Declaration on the TRIPS Agreement and Public Health of 14/11/2001.

[113] WTO Panel Report, *India – Patent Protection for Pharmaceutical and Agricultural Chemical Products*, WT/DS50/R (Sep. 5, 1997).

[114] TRIPS, art. 64.2. [115] India Pharmaceutical Panel Report, *supra* note 113, at ¶ 7.19.

example, was a nonviolation argument posed as a violation argument, it lost.[116] Broadly, the United States alleged that China's enforcement system was not "effective" by the United States' standards. If the United States had been allowed to bring a nonviolation complaint on that point the result would not change. This is because the standard, in nonviolation disputes, to measure whether a nullification or impairment of a "benefit or the attainment of any objective ... is being impeded", is not subjective, but rather is an objective analysis in light of the object and purpose of the agreement.[117] Put differently, what makes an expectation legitimate is an objective assessment of that expectation not a subjective assertion of expectation based on something other than the final text.

In the United States' note, to the TRIPS Council, about nonviolation complaints it stated:[118]

> The United States is of the view that the availability of non-violation complaints will protect Members from intentional evasions of obligations under the TRIPS Agreement while preserving the ability of any Member to implement legitimate social, economic development, health, environmental and cultural policies. Non-violation complaints will only be successful if they could not have been foreseen when the Uruguay Round negotiations were underway. Because there are a number of ways to implement social and cultural policy goals, a Member may take this element of non-violation complaints into consideration when crafting measures to protect these goals.

The above quoted note seems to suggest all flexibilities must have been foreseen at the time of the Uruguay round. That cannot be correct. The interpretation of intellectual property agreements is not static; intellectual property is by its nature a dynamic area. It cannot be a requirement of TRIPS that the exact flexibility or exception need be foreseen. First, after TRIPS new international agreements with both obligations to provide certain rights and allowing flexibilities have been agreed to, such as the WIPO Copyright Treaty[119] and the Marrakesh Treaty to Facilitate Access to Published Works for Persons Who Are

[116] This point is fully discussed in Frankel, *supra* note 62. *See also* Robert Howse & Michael J. Trebilcock, *The Fair Trade Debate: Trade, Labor and the Environment*, 16 INT. REV. L. & ECON. 61 (1996). Discussing the problems with nonviolation complaint, see Sungjoon Cho, *GATT Non-Violation Issues in the WTO Framework: Are they the Achilles' Heel of the Dispute Settlement Process?* 39(2) HARV. INT'L L.J. 311 (1998).

[117] *See* Howse & Trebilcock, *id.* [118] U.S. Non-Violation Note, *supra* note 112, at 4.14.

[119] WIPO Copyright Treaty, art. 10(1), Dec. 20, 1996, S. Treaty Doc. No. 105-17, 36 I.L.M. 65 (1997).

Blind, Visually Impaired or Otherwise Print Disabled.[120] Second, given that the three-step test is a framework for future exceptions, a static view of exceptions is not logical.[121] What can be foreseen is that members will make exceptions in accordance with TRIPS.

Because a nonviolation dispute requires assessment of whether a legitimate expectation has not been met it requires that the objectives and principles of the agreement at issue (TRIPS) be examined. In violation disputes those objectives are predominantly interpretative guidance or a policy statement.[122] In nonviolation disputes those statements have the potential to be the center of analysis. In order to make nonviolation disputes effective and to avoid them becoming a problem, like FTAs have become, modalities around their use would be needed.

B Nonviolation Dispute Modalities

The modalities for nonviolation complaints should reflect that they are comparatively rare compared to violation complaints. These modalities should include that nonviolation is not a method by which TRIPS obligations can be extended or its gaps filled. The primary role of dispute settlement remains interpretation of the agreement, not adding to it without negotiation.[123] A nonviolation dispute is designed to meet the

[120] Marrakesh Treaty to Facilitate Access to Published Works for Persons who are Blind, Visually Impaired, or Otherwise Print Disabled, art. 11, Jun. 28, 2013, http://www.wipo.int/treaties/en/ip/marrakesh.

[121] Although as Jane Ginsburg has said the U.S.-110(5) panel did not approach the issue (and particularly the meaning of "normal exploitation") in this way, see *supra* note 67. *See also* Christophe Geiger, Daniel J. Gervais, & Martin Senftleben, *The Three-Step-Test Revisited: How to Use the Test's Flexibility in National Copyright Law*, 29(3) AMER. UNI. INT'L L. REV. 581 (2013).

[122] For discussion of the role of Article 8 of TRIPS and its strength as a policy statement applicable to the whole agreement, see Susy Frankel & Daniel Gervais, *Plain Packaging and Interpretation of the TRIPS Agreement*, 46 VAND. J. TRANSNAT'L L. 1149, 1202–6 (2013).

[123] This is an important principle of treaty interpretation. The rule is also found in the DSU, *supra* note 55, art. 3.2, which states:

> The dispute settlement system of the WTO is a central element in providing security and predictability to the multilateral trading system. The Members recognize that it serves to preserve the rights and obligations of Members under the covered agreements, and to clarify the existing provisions of those agreements in accordance with customary rules of interpretation of public international law. Recommendations and rulings of the DSB cannot add to or diminish the rights and obligations provided in the covered agreements.

legitimate expectations that arise from the text of the agreement based on interpretation of the text.

One party's negotiating position cannot represent a legitimate expectation of the agreements. This is because by definition an agreement reflects multiple negotiating positions and compromise on individual positions. This is precisely why the negotiating position is a secondary means of interpretation under the Vienna Convention.[124] Modalities about nonviolation should state that the negotiating history is not a primary source for interpretation of nonviolation just as it is not the leading source for interpretation of violation.

Nonviolation disputes by their nature are difficult to predict, but that does not mean that they are a means of expanding the wording of TRIPS.[125] Rather because the balancing provisions in TRIPS are general principles akin to policy statements nonviolation analysis is a way of giving full force to those policies. The objectives and principles of TRIPS, particularly those found in Articles 7 and 8, and the incentive rationales that underlie copyright and patent law, have the potential to take center stage in the nonviolation arena.

IV Conclusion

Within the WTO framework TRIPS at best provides various ways in which interpretation can be used to address public-regarding concerns; at worst the Agreement is a blockade to such concerns and FTAs have caused greater problems. As noted above, some of the later WTO dispute settlement reports seem to have been more able to take into account interests other than obligations. Ultimately the ability of countries to access medicines, gain more literary resources for education and create domestic innovation needs more than change at the WTO. Changes in FTAs may help. The TPP, as an example of the twenty-first-century FTA ambitions, while requiring more extensive protection than TRIPS in many areas also contains more balancing provisions than TRIPS. An example of such an additional balancing provision, in relation to copyright, is:[126]

See also art. 19, "[I]n their findings and recommendations, the panel and Appellate Body cannot add to or diminish the rights and obligations provided in the covered agreements.

124 VCLT, *supra* note 90, art. 32. 125 Treaty interpretation rules still apply.

126 TPP, *supra* note 75, art. 18.66a.

> Each Party shall endeavour to achieve an appropriate balance in its copyright and related rights system, among other things by means of limitations or exceptions . . . including those for the digital environment, giving due consideration to legitimate purposes such as, but not limited to: criticism; comment; news reporting; teaching, scholarship, research, and other similar purposes; and facilitating access to published works for persons who are blind, visually impaired or otherwise print disabled.

Also, TRIPS should not be misinterpreted as an inevitable roadblock to public–regarding goals. The interpretation process ought to actively consider that the ability for countries to calibrate laws to their local development needs is an integral part and structural feature of the Agreement (in Vienna Convention language part of the object and purpose of TRIPS).[127] Such an approach to interpretation of the three-step test (in both implementation and dispute settlement) should ensure that when members create flexibilities, which allow for matters such as access to intellectual property or even the creation of local innovation incentives, these flexibilities are assessed taking into account the goals of domestic calibration.

Interpretation involving discussion of object and purpose, as the Vienna Convention mandates, is one mechanism to improve the effectiveness of the intellectual property and trade fusion. In this chapter I have also discussed how nonviolation disputes might give greater life and force to the public-regarding provisions in TRIPS. Counter-norm building is another mechanism. TRIPS cannot solve all issues where there is a collision with intellectual property and to expand its counter-norm building role may ask the WTO and TRIPS regime to do too much. However, interpretation that embodies a version of trade that gives weight to intellectual property incentives, and in addition the appropriate use of nonviolation disputes, could provide effective ways to counterbalance the chilling effects of overprotection that FTAs have created. The trade and intellectual property link is here to stay, but understanding trade as having nonprotectionist goals can help restore and rebalance the functioning and interpretation of TRIPS to enable it to not only protect intellectual property, but to allow for appropriate flexibility within the international framework.

[127] VCLT, *supra* note 90, art. 31.1.

5

Flexibilities in the Implementation of TRIPS: An Analysis of Their Impact on Technological Innovation and Public Health in Asia

ELIZABETH SIEW-KUAN NG* AND ALBERT GUANGZHOU HU

More than twenty years ago, the World Trade Organization's (WTO) Agreement on Trade-Related Aspects of Intellectual Property Rights (TRIPS) was born.[1] A progeny of what Professor Jerry Reichman described as a "marriage of convenience" between intellectual property and international trade law,[2] this multilateral intellectual property agreement profoundly altered the international intellectual property landscape.[3] Yet this offspring was not a true merger of the substantive precepts of international intellectual property and international trade

* The authors would like to thank all the speakers, panelists and participants at the "Framing Intellectual Property Law in the 21st Century: Integrating Incentives, Trade, Development, Culture and Human Rights" Conference held at Orchard Hotel, Singapore, August 14–15, 2014 for their invaluable comments. Special thanks to Rochelle Dreyfuss for insightful comments on earlier drafts. Thanks also to Chiong Song Ning, Victor Lim, Zachary Tay, and Vincent Ooi for research and/or editorial assistance. The views expressed and any errors are solely those of the authors.

1 Agreement on Trade-Related Aspects of Intellectual Property Rights, Apr. 15, 1994, Marrakesh Agreement Establishing the World Trade Organization, Annex 1C, 1869 U.N.T.S. 183, 33 I.L.M. 1197 (1994), https://www.wto.org/english/tratop_e/trips_e/t_agm0_e.htm [hereinafter TRIPS].

2 Jerome H. Reichman, *supra* Chapter 3, *Reframing Intellectual Property Rights with Fewer Distortions of the Trade Paradigm*, citing (at p. 70) R. Michael Gadbaw, *Intellectual Property and International Trade: Merger or Marriage of Convenience?*, 22 Vanderbilt J. Trans. L. 223 (1989).

3 *See, e.g.*, Jerome H. Reichman, *Universal Minimum Standards of Intellectual Property Protection Under the TRIPS Component of the WTO Agreement*, 29 Int'l L. 345 (1995); Ruth L. Okediji, *Legal Innovation in International Intellectual Property Relations: Revisiting Twenty-One Years of the TRIPS Agreement*, 36 U. Pa. J. Int'l L. 191, 199; Peter Drahos, *Developing Countries and International Intellectual Property Standard-setting* (Commission on Intellectual Property Rights Study Paper No. 8, 2002), www.iprcommission.org/papers/pdfs/study_papers/sp8_drahos_study.pdf.

law.[4] Rather, it was a product of a compromise. The developed countries agreed to open up their markets and export technology to less developed countries[5] and they, in return, were required to protect intellectual property rights to certain minimum standards generally observed in the developed world. Yet, as Professors Rochelle Dreyfuss and Graeme Dinwoodie astutely highlighted, these so-called "minimum standards" in actual fact raised intellectual property protection in even the most developed countries such as the United States.[6] Significantly, they were imposed on developed, developing and least-developed countries alike – even those that were neither previously aware, nor accepting, of intellectual property protection within their jurisdiction.

Nonetheless, the Agreement recognized that the implementation of the TRIPS standards may, *inter alia*, raise the barriers to technology diffusion and access, particularly for public health. It therefore left considerable policy space/flexibilities for WTO members to honor their intellectual property commitments. Examples include differentiated timeframes for TRIPS compliance, as well as exceptions and limitations to intellectual property rights. Such flexibilities were negotiated as part of a deal to offset the trade-offs from enhanced intellectual property protection which would necessarily entail some loss of an optimal level of competition and access especially to public health. These TRIPS flexibilities are critical policy enablers which permit countries, particularly the developing and least-developed, to make the right trade-offs when customizing their domestic intellectual property rules in ways that will best serve their national and public interests. In the authoritative words of Professors Graeme Dinwoodie and Rochelle Dreyfuss, TRIPS reflects a "neo-federalist regime" in which "member states retain considerable discretion under TRIPS, but agree to operate within an international framework."[7]

Even so, it is undeniable that the implementation of the TRIPS flexibilities can erode the returns to innovation and prevent creators from capturing their investments in research and development. This brings us back to the age-old question: How can competing tensions be best

[4] See Reichman, *supra* note 2.

[5] Francis Gurry, Director General, WIPO, Lecture delivered at the Melbourne Law School, University of Melbourne, Australia: Rethinking the Role of Intellectual Property (Aug. 22, 2013), www.youtube.com/watch?v=Z5PIJ-mAtpY.

[6] Graeme B. Dinwoodie & Rochelle Cooper Dreyfuss, A Neofederalist Vision of TRIPS 21 (2012).

[7] *Id.* at 5. (Chapter 1 "The Challenges of the TRIPS Agreement").

managed in a country's framing of its intellectual property law so as to achieve the optimal balance between stronger intellectual property protection to incentivize invention and innovation on the one hand, and greater access to knowledge and technology for the promotion of further innovation, development, and public health on the other? Unsurprisingly, the answer continues to elude us today. What seems clear is that some countries have responded directly and explicitly to these TRIPS pressures by properly utilizing the flexibilities in the framing of their intellectual property legislation so as to skillfully limit the effects of the policy costs that a "maximalist global IP regime" can exact on its people and governments.[8] We should understand that the realization of intellectual property rights is not an end in itself. Instead, as Professor Graeme Austin compellingly argues, intellectual property rights should be "regarded as vehicles that, ideally, help us to realize broader social policy outcomes: that people 'get fed, enjoy the benefits of literacy, are healthy, have viable agricultural bases, and can participate in technological and cultural development.'"[9]

In this chapter, we seek to contribute to this discourse on how the WTO countries in Asia have expressly framed their responses to TRIPS by investigating the extent to which these countries have effectively implemented the flexibilities in their national intellectual property legislation. In particular, we focus attention on patent rights, as these posed the greatest challenge during the TRIPS negotiation. The impact of these policy choices on domestic innovative capabilities and access to public health will be evaluated. We hope that this work will help to bridge a gap in the patent law and economics scholarship in this area, and contribute to the broader policy debate on the role that TRIPS flexibilities can play in the framing of intellectual property law in order to balance the diverse interests of the stakeholders in the global patent system.

In Section I, we provide a brief background on the WTO-TRIPS bargain. We highlight the currently polarized multilateral intellectual property regime and the ratcheting of intellectual property standard in the post-TRIPS era *via* international trade and investment instruments. In Section II, we introduce the background economic literature on intellectual property and development. A brief mention will be made of

[8] Okediji, *supra* note 3.

[9] Graeme W. Austin, *Valuing Domestic Self-Determination in International Intellectual Property Jurisprudence*, 77 CHI.-KENT L. REV. 1155, 1191 (2002) and Graeme W. Austin, *Authors' Human Rights in the Intellectual Property Framework*, *supra* Chapter 8.

the contrasting studies of Professors Josh Lerner and Keith Maskus in respect of the relationship between the strength of intellectual property protection and economic development. We point out that the research of Professors Petra Moser and Alessandra Voena provides some evidence in support of TRIP flexibilities. For Sections III and IV, we each focus on different points. In Section III, Elizabeth Siew-Kuan Ng (Ng) constructs an *Intellectual Property (Patent) Flexibility Index* to rank thirty Asian countries according to the degree to which they have implemented TRIPS patent flexibilities using five main indicators: namely, compulsory licensing, parallel importation, experimental/private noncommercial use, regulatory review exception, and TRIPS-specific exclusions.[10] She then uses the Index to investigate whether there is any correlation between a country's flexibility implementation and its innovation capability as measured by the *Global Innovation Index* (GII). In Section IV, Albert Guangzhou Hu (Hu) uses the Index in an empirical analysis to explore the determinants of a country's choice of flexibilities implementation. In Section V, we ultimately suggest that the effective utilization of TRIPS patent flexibilities in the framing of national intellectual property legislation can make a consequential impact on the welfare of developing countries.

I The WTO-TRIPS Bargain

As Professor Ruth Okediji perceptively opined, the "presumptive goal of the Uruguay Round negotiations, and its specific manifestation in the TRIPS Agreement was to secure export markets for a wide variety of knowledge goods in which industrialized countries had long held a competitive advantage."[11] What started as a push by the United States government (later supported by the Europeans and Japanese) to link intellectual property protection to international trade at the Uruguay Round of multilateral trade negotiations culminated in a WTO-TRIPS bargain.[12] There were multiple interests at play in the negotiation of the

[10] Ng's idea of the IP (Patent Flexibility) index will be further developed in her forthcoming work Elizabeth Siew-Kuan Ng, *Understanding Patents for Innovation and Public Health: Making Sense of the Use of TRIPS Flexibilities in Asia.*

[11] Okediji, *supra* note 3.

[12] Daniel Gervais, *Introduction*, in INTELLECTUAL PROPERTY, TRADE AND DEVELOPMENT – STRATEGIES TO OPTIMIZE ECONOMIC DEVELOPMENT IN A TRIPS-PLUS ERA XV (Daniel Gervais ed., 2007). *See also* DANIEL GERVAIS, THE TRIPS AGREEMENT: DRAFTING HISTORY AND ANALYSIS (4th ed. 2012).

TRIPS Agreement. From one standpoint, developing/least-developed countries agreed to protect intellectual property rights, and, in return, developed countries would, *inter alia*, incentivize their intellectual property rights holders to transfer technology to the lesser developed countries to jump-start their domestic innovative capabilities and economic development.[13] Another explanation advanced by Professor Daniel Gervais is that TRIPS demonstrates that "intellectual property rules and their enforcement could be 'traded' for reductions of tariffs or increases in import quotas on textiles, tropical fruit or other mostly low tech goods. In other words, intellectual property can be negotiated and traded against anything else with dollars as a common denominator."[14] An added perspective proffered by Professors Rochelle Dreyfuss and Graeme Dinwoodie is to "view TRIPS as an effort to create an efficient marketplace and to treat its minimum substantive requirements as safeguards against one country using its patent law to undermine the industrial policy of another."[15]

Post-TRIPS, many developing countries and least-developed countries felt that the developed world did not deliver on the promises that the protection of intellectual property rights would bring them. Faced with these unsatisfied assurances, intellectual property protection came to be viewed as a means by which the developed world sought to extract rent from developing and least-developed countries.[16] TRIPS was perceived as having reshaped "the conditions of *future* global competition, particularly

[13] Article 7 of the *TRIPS Agreement* provides that the objectives are that: "The protection and enforcement of intellectual property rights should contribute to the promotion of technological innovation and to the transfer and dissemination of technology, to the mutual advantage of producers and users of technological knowledge and in a manner conducive to social and economic welfare, and to a balance of rights and obligations." *See also*, WTO, *TRIPS Issues: Technology transfer*, www.wto.org/english/tratop_e/trips_e/techtransfer_e.htm.

[14] *See* Daniel Gervais, *TRIPS and Development*, in THE SAGE HANDBOOK OF INTELLECTUAL PROPERTY 95 (Matthew David and Debora Halbert eds., 2014). For an excellent discussion on the emergence and evolution of TRIPS, *see* the authoritative work of Professor Gervais in GERVAIS, THE TRIPS AGREEMENT, *supra* note 12.

[15] Graeme B. Dinwoodie and Rochelle Cooper Dreyfuss, *Diversifying Without Discriminating: Complying with the Mandates of the TRIPS Agreement*, 13 MICH. TELECOMM. & TECH. L. REV. 445 (2007), repository.law.umich.edu/cgi/viewcontent.cgi?article=1091&context=mttlr.

[16] *See* Okediji, *supra* note 3. For excellent discussions on "transfer of rents" and intellectual property enforcement, *see* KEITH MASKUS, *The Global Policy Framework: Intellectual Property Rights and Wrongs?*, in INTELLECTUAL PROPERTY RIGHTS IN THE GLOBAL ECONOMY (2000), www.colorado.edu/economics/courses/maskus/4999/ch6finalrev.doc and GERVAIS, THE TRIPS AGREEMENT, *supra* note 12.

the extent to which developing countries could use intellectual property as a form of industrial policy in pursuit of strategic development objectives."[17] This major source of tension between the North and South has largely contributed to the currently polarized multilateral intellectual property framework.[18] In this new paradigm, consensus on new intellectual property commitments was more easily achieved in the context of trade agreements, where intellectual property is often relegated to one part of a "wider negotiating package" which promises economic growth and development that will lead to more jobs.[19] Successive international free trade and investment instruments have sought to ratchet intellectual property standards way beyond that originally contemplated by the TRIPS Agreement.[20] As Professors Dinwoodie and Dreyfuss wisely surmised: "The current propensity towards unilateral, bilateral, and plurilateral negotiation is producing fragmentation and destroying the predictability necessary in a legal regime aimed at encouraging creative production."[21]

Amidst this turmoil, as the developing and least-developed countries compete for the knowledge and knowledge-intensive goods in a highly competitive global marketplace,[22] the intuitive response may suggest that these countries would make better use of the discretionary policy space in the framing of their intellectual property legislation so as to, *inter alia*, boost their fledgling domestic innovative capabilities and access for

[17] Okediji, *supra* note 3 at 192. [18] Gurry, *supra* note 5.

[19] *See* Pedro Roffe & Xavier Seuba, *Introduction: ACTA and the international debate on intellectual property enforcement*, in THE ACTA AND THE PLURILATERAL ENFORCEMENT AGENDA: GENESIS AND AFTERMATH 11 (Pedro Roffe & Xavier Seuba eds., 2015). *See also*, Kamperman Sander, *The EU and its IP policies: ACTA and third countries*, in THE ACTA AND THE PLURILATERAL ENFORCEMENT AGENDA: GENESIS AND AFTERMATH (Pedro Roffe & Xavier Seuba eds., 2015).

[20] *See* Rochelle Cooper Dreyfuss, *In Praise of an Incentive-Based Theory of Intellectual Property Protection*, Jerome H. Reichman, *Reframing Intellectual Property Rights with Fewer Distortions of the Trade Paradigm*, and Susy Frankel, *The Fusion of Intellectual Property and Trade*, supra Chapters 1, 3 and 4 respectively. Drahos' study is available at www.anu.edu.au/fellows/pdrahos/reports/pdfs/UKCommIPRS.pdf.

[21] DINWOODIE & DREYFUSS, *supra* note 6, at 42 (Chapter 2 "The History and Character of TRIPS").

[22] For an excellent discussion on trade in knowledge goods, see Keith Maskus & Jerome Reichman, *The Globalization of Private Knowledge Goods and the Privatization of Global Public Goods*, 7(2) J. INT'L ECON. L. 279–320 (2004). See also the OECD's measurement of globalization and trade in knowledge-intensive goods: OECD, *Trade in knowledge-intensive goods*, in MEASURING GLOBALISATION: OECD ECONOMIC GLOBALISATION INDICATORS 2010 (2010), www.oecd-ilibrary.org/industry-and-services/measuring-globalisation-oecd-economic-globalisation-indicators-2010/trade-in-knowledge-intensive-goods_9789264084360–54-en.

public health. Yet, in a recent World Intellectual Property Organization (WIPO) commissioned study conducted by one of the authors (Ng) on the effective use of patent-related flexibilities in twenty-three Asian countries, it was revealed that not all of the Asian countries that were eligible to utilize these flexibilities have done so; and those that have, have experienced different impacts.[23]

The question of what are the determinants that influence a country's choice of flexibilities implementation and the impact of such policy choices on domestic innovative capabilities and public health needs are examined below. Before proceeding, a short review of the economic literature on intellectual property and development may serve as a useful backdrop for this discourse.

II Economic Literature on Intellectual Property and Development

The welfare calculus of optimal intellectual property protection centers on the trade-off between promoting innovation (dynamic efficiency) and reducing barriers to technology diffusion (static inefficiency).[24] Efforts to extend such single country, closed economy analysis to a global setting, as the case of TRIPS calls for, have entailed new analytical challenges and produced insights that were not available at the time TRIPS was negotiated. A consensus that has emerged from this literature is that a one-size-fits-all intellectual property regime is unlikely to be in the best interests of either developed or developing countries.

In one of the first thorough and careful conceptualizations and deliberations on this issue, Professors Gene Grossman and Edwin Lai showed that in a globalized world where countries engage in international trade with each other, harmonizing intellectual property protection across countries is neither necessary nor sufficient to maximize world welfare.[25]

[23] Elizabeth Siew-Kuan Ng, *Effective Use of Patent Related Flexibilities and Their Implementation at the National or Regional Level in Selected Asian Countries* 16 (A study commissioned by and presented to the World Intellectual Property Organization (WIPO) 2011, revised 2013) (Executive Summary).

[24] William D. Nordhaus, Invention, Growth and Welfare: A Theoretical Treatment of Technological Change (1969).

[25] Gene M. Grossman & Edwin Lai, *International Protection of Intellectual Property*, 94(5) Am. Econ. Rev. 1635–53(2004). *See also*, Elhanan Helpman, *Innovation, Imitation, and Intellectual Property Rights*, 61(6) Econometrica 1247–80(1993), where the learned author also found that the welfare implication of global IPR harmonization for developed countries can be nuanced, instead of straightforward gains.

Meanwhile, cooperation between countries in intellectual property protection cannot be presumed, as countries can benefit from higher intellectual property protection standards in their trade partners even if they do not increase those of their own. Thus intellectual property cooperation has to be negotiated among countries, particularly between developed and developing countries, and harmonization is not the only or necessary way to achieve the optimal level of global welfare.

Given the unequal distribution of intellectual property among countries in the world, strengthening intellectual property rights in developing countries will necessarily cause developed countries to benefit at the expense of developing ones. While such shifts in the global intellectual property protection may raise the overall welfare of the world as a whole, it is not surprising that developing countries will need to be incentivized to move towards a more efficient global intellectual property regime.

Before the study by Professors Grossman and Lai, a number of empirical studies had shown that the strength of intellectual protection was dependent on the stage of a country's economic development. Professor Josh Lerner had investigated how the strength of patent protection had evolved in sixty countries that had the highest GDP in 1997 over a 150-year period.[26] He found that wealthier countries were more likely to offer stronger patent protection.

Instead of the linear relationship between intellectual property rights and economic development that Professor Lerner's analysis implied, Professor Keith Maskus found a U-shaped relationship between the two.[27] He used a cross-section of seventy-seven developed and developing countries for 1984 and regressed a modified version of the *Rapp and Rozek Patent Index* on the logarithm of per capita income and the square of it.[28] The strength of intellectual property right bottomed out at a per capita GNP of US$523 (1984 dollar value) and the income variables explained half of the cross-country variation in the patent index. Using the *Ginarte and Park Index* for patent protection,[29] Professor Maskus confirmed that the relationship between the strength

[26] Josh Lerner, *The Economics of Technology and Innovation: 150 Years of Patent Protection*, 92(5) American Economic Review 221–5 (2002).

[27] Keith Maskus, Intellectual Property Rights in the Global Economy (2000).

[28] Richard Rapp & Richard Rozek, *Benefits and Costs of Intellectual Property Rights in Developing Countries* (National Economic Research Associates (White Plains, NY), Working Paper No. 3, 1990).

[29] Juan C. Ginarte & Walter G. Park, *Determinants of Patent Rights: A cross-national study*, 26(3) Research Policy 283–301 (1997).

of intellectual property protection and economic development is non-linear, it is U-shaped.[30] Maskus explains the shape as follows. As a developing country progresses toward middle-income development status, it relies on technology diffusion to achieve technological change, the rate of which may be accelerated by adopting laxer intellectual property protection. Beyond the middle-income stage, as a country gradually acquires the technological capacity to innovate, the impetus for technological change becomes driven primarily by technological innovation whereupon a country may benefit from strengthening its intellectual property protection.

The economic analysis shows that the pre-TRIPS world of intellectual property protection was less than optimal and that there was a need for change, including the strengthening of intellectual property protection in developing countries. But this reconfiguration of the global intellectual property regime does not necessarily have to take the form of a one-size-fits-all substantive harmonization of intellectual property laws. More importantly, the gains from such reconfiguration need to be shared between the North and South. Indeed, developing countries signed on to TRIPS as a bargain so that stronger protection of intellectual property would give them better technology transfer from developed countries and greater access to the latter's market. As Professor Maskus pointed out, that bargain never materialized. Furthermore, escalating intellectual property standards have figured prominently in recent free trade agreements.[31]

One issue that has escaped close scrutiny by economists is the effect of TRIPS flexibilities. They are embedded in TRIPS and part of the bargain that developing countries negotiated for. By imposing limits on the rights of intellectual property owners, these flexibilities were meant to mitigate the welfare loss to developing countries as they adopt the higher intellectual property standards of TRIPS.

One such flexibility concerns product patents for drugs, which countries such as India had agreed to adopt by an extended deadline of 2005. In a significant study, Professors Shubham Chaudhuri, Penny Goldberg and Panle Jia (2006) estimated the counter-factual impact of imposing

[30] MASKUS, *supra* note 27. Using a different dataset that comprises sixty-four developing countries, Chen Yongmin & Thitima Puttitanun also found a U-shaped relationship between strength of IPR protection (Ginarte and Park index) and economic development (GDP per capita): see Chen Yongmin & Thitima Puttitanun, *Intellectual Property Rights and Innovation in Developing Countries*, 78(2) J. DEV. ECON. 474–93 (2005).

[31] Keith Maskus, PRIVATE RIGHTS AND PUBLIC PROBLEMS: THE GLOBAL ECONOMICS OF INTELLECTUAL PROPERTY IN THE 21ST CENTURY (2012).

patents on an antibiotics segment of the Indian pharmaceutical market using product level data.[32] The then-status quo was that pharmaceuticals had no product patent, with the market served by both originator drug companies and Indian generics makers. Against this backdrop, a hypothetical enforcement of patented pharmaceutical products would result in a large welfare loss for the Indian consumers (approximately US$255 million), a small profit loss for domestic producers (US$50 million) and an even smaller profit gain for foreign producers (US$19.6 million) per year. The counter-factual exercise assumes the exit of domestic generics makers as a result of patent enforcement.

Another TRIPS flexibility relates to compulsory licensing. In 1917, the U.S. Congress passed the Trading with the Enemy Act, which, along with its amendment two years later, allowed the United States to confiscate all enemy-owned patents. As a result, German-owned patents were freely licensed to American firms. Professors Moser and Voena took advantage of this exogenous event of compulsory licensing and examined how it had affected American firms' innovation.[33] Using patents as an indicator of technology innovation and focusing on chemical inventions, they found that domestic inventions went up by 20 percent after the implementation of the Act. Notwithstanding issues concerning the extent to which this historical episode spoke to the contemporary struggle over this issue, as exemplified by the Doha Declaration, Professors Moser and Voena produced an important piece of evidence for advocates of TRIPS flexibilities.

Despite the paucity of economic research in this area, the limited evidence available seems to suggest that effective TRIPS flexibility utilization can make a consequential impact on the welfare of developing countries. Yet, not all countries that are eligible to utilize them have done so. We decided to embark on this research to examine what determines a country's choice of flexibilities utilization in the Asian context. Toward that end, we constructed an *Intellectual Property (Patent) Flexibility Index* (IPPFI) which was then used to evaluate the impact that such flexibility adoption can have on the domestic innovation and public health needs in the Asian context, and then ran a statistical analysis on this which contributed to our conclusion.

[32] Shubham Chaudhuri, Penny Goldberg & Panle Jia, *Estimating the Effects of Global Patent Protection in Pharmaceuticals: A Case Study of Quinolones in India*, 96(5) AM. ECON. REV. 1477–514 (2006).

[33] Petra Moser &Alessandra Voena, *Compulsory Licensing: Evidence from the Trading with the Enemy Act*, 102(1) AM. ECON. REV. 396–427 (2012).

III Intellectual Property Flexibility Index: A Barometer of TRIPS Flexibilities Implementation in Asia[34]

Many studies and indices have sought to provide a comparative assessment of the relative strength of intellectual property protection in various jurisdictions and expound upon the benefits associated with such strength. Examples include the oft-cited *Ginarte-Park Index of Patent Rights* (GP Index),[35] *U.S. Chamber International Intellectual Property Index* (GIPC Index)[36] and the *Taylor-Wessing Global Intellectual Property Index* (GIPI).[37] Others such as the *Global Innovation Index* (GII) rank the world economies' innovation capabilities with the aim to capture the facets of innovation and "provide the tools that can assist in tailoring policies to promote long-term output growth, improved productivity and job growth."[38]

Yet, none of these indices appraises the relative strength of flexibility utilization nor demonstrates the impact associated with it. Faced with the dearth of any meaningful yardstick, we construct a new Intellectual Property Flexibility Index to rank countries according to the extent to which they have implemented the TRIPS flexibilities in framing their intellectual property legislation. Due to time and resource constraints, we focus on the intellectual property right that gave rise to the most difficult challenge during the TRIPS negotiation, namely patents. Subsequently we intend to construct other flexibility indices centered on copyright, designs, trademark among others with a view to creating an overall composite Intellectual Property Flexibility Index comprising an amalgamation of the various indices.

[34] The idea of an intellectual property flexibility index was developed by Ng while writing this chapter and can be explored in greater detail in her forthcoming work (see Ng, *supra* note 10).

[35] Ginarte & Park, *supra* note 29.

[36] U.S. Chamber International IP Index, www.theglobalipcenter.com/gipcindex/.

[37] For more information about the GIPI, see united-kingdom.taylorwessing.com/en/gipi/about-gipi.

[38] Global Innovation Index (GII) is copublished by Cornell University, INSEAD, and the WIPO, an agency of the United Nations and is available at www.globalinnovationindex.org/. The GII is based mainly on two sub-indices: the Innovation Input Sub-Index and the Innovation Output Sub-Index. The Input Sub-Index captures the elements of the national economy that enable innovative activities, namely: (1) Institutions, (2) Human capital and research, (3) Infrastructure, (4) Market sophistication, and (5) Business sophistication. The Output Sub-Index captures actual evidence of innovation outputs, namely: (6) Knowledge and technology outputs, and (7) Creative outputs.

The *IPPFI* aims to facilitate a comparative assessment of the extent to which countries have effectively utilized the TRIPS patent flexibilities in framing their domestic intellectual property laws. It is hoped that the Index will enable countries to compare their level of flexibility utilization with those of their geographical and/or developmental neighbors so as to inform industry and policymakers on reforms (where needed). It is also envisaged that the Index may be a useful tool in empirical analysis. Two illustrations are provided in the latter part of this work.

Before delving into the details of the *IPPFI*, a few parameters are worth highlighting:First, the Index is focused on a nonexhaustive analysis of five main categories of TRIPS patent flexibilities generally utilized by WTO countries.[39] These are (1) compulsory licensing, (2) exhaustion of rights (parallel importation), (3) research exemption, (4) regulatory review exception, and (5) exclusions from patentability as specifically provided under Article 27 of TRIPS. Other flexibilities, such as those relating to transition period, security exceptions, criminal sanctions, disclosure requirement, etc., whilst no doubt important, are beyond the scope of this chapter. Each category of flexibility is assessed based on three main components. This coverage can be expanded in subsequent studies.

Second, the Index is analyzed from a *de jure* rather than *de facto* perspective. In other words, it examines the statute law based on our interpretation of the patent legislation of the thirty Asian countries and does not look outside of the patent statutory context.[40]

Third, the *IPPFI* is based on a sample size of thirty Asian countries, namely (in alphabetical order): Bahrain, Bangladesh, Bhutan, Brunei, Cambodia, China, Hong Kong (SAR, China), India, Indonesia, Iran, Japan, Jordan, Kazakhstan, Lao PDR, Macau (SAR, China), Malaysia, Mongolia, Nepal, Oman, Pakistan, Philippines, Saudi Arabia, Singapore, South Korea, Sri Lanka, Taiwan (Chinese Taipei, China), Thailand, Turkey, United Arab Emirates (UAE), and Vietnam. This range of countries may be expanded in subsequent studies.

Fourth, there are choices about the way in which the Index can be created; we present one option in this work.

[39] See, e.g., WIPO Secretariat, *Patent Related Flexibilities in the Multilateral Legal Framework and Their Legislative Implementation at the National and Regional Levels*, CDIP/5/4 (Mar. 1, 2010), www.wipo.int/edocs/mdocs/mdocs/en/cdip_5/cdip_5_4-main 1.pdf.

[40] It is based on the patent laws where the English version is available on the WIPO Intellectual Property Laws and Treaties Database (WIPO Lex) as at June 2016.

A Measurement of Patent Flexibilities Utilization

Using a simple point allocation structure, like that used in the *GP Index*, a value ranging from "0" to "1" may be allocated to each of the sub-index for the five categories of flexibilities (per country) depending on the number of variables that are fulfilled. The variables comprise components and/or sub-components (if any), each of which is measured based on a simple binary structure of "yes" (if the condition is satisfied) or "no" (if it is not). Each component within a category is weighted equally with a score of "1/x" where x is the number of components within each category. For example: if there are three components within a category, each component is allocated a value of "⅓" (if the condition is met) or "0" (if it is not). Where a component consists of several sub-components, each sub-component is similarly weighted. For example: if there are two sub-components within a component in the abovementioned category with three components, then each sub-component is given a value of "⅙" (if it is fulfilled) or "0" (if it is not). If there are three sub-components within a component, then each sub-component is allocated a value of "1/9" (if it is

Table 5.1 *Examples of flexibility scoring*

Example 1	Yes: condition is satisfied	No: condition is not satisfied
Component 1	⅓	0
Component 2	–	–
Sub-component 1	⅙	0
Sub-component 2	⅙	0
Component 3	–	–
Sub-component 1	1/9	0
Sub-component 2	1/9	0
Sub-component 3	1/9	0
Sub-total:		
Example 2	**Yes**	**No**
Component 1	⅓	0
Component 2	⅓	0
Component 3	⅓	0
Sub-total:		
***IPPFI* Overall score = Sum of the sub-total for the five categories**		

satisfied) and so forth. The overall composite score for each country in the *IPPFI* Index ranges from "0 to 5" comprising the unweighted sum of the values of all the components in the five categories. A higher score indicates that a country has made greater use of the TRIPS flexibilities. A few examples are provided in Table 5.1.

With this in mind, each of the five categories of patent flexibilities are explored in turn.

B Patent Flexibilities Indicators: Categories and Components

1 Compulsory Licensing[41]

Perhaps one of the most controversial TRIPS patent flexibilities is that of compulsory licensing, which is permissible by virtue of TRIPS Article 31 and which generally occurs when a patent owner is compelled by the State to license the patent to another. This involuntary license between a "willing buyer" and an "unwilling seller" takes place where the "public interest in broader access to the invention is considered more important than the private interest of the right holder to fully exploit his exclusive rights."[42] Although one of the main justifications for compulsory licensing lies in the prevention of "abuse" of patent rights, in some countries it has also been resorted to whenever it is deemed necessary "to safeguard the public interest."[43] Compulsory licensing acts as a form of insurance protection for developing and least-developed countries to overcome market outcomes. Its critical role in safeguarding access to medicine for public health was brought to the fore during the South African AIDS controversy.[44]

[41] This section is based on parts of an earlier work by one of the authors (Ng). *See* Ng, *supra* note 23.

[42] *See* Jerome H. Reichman & Catherine Hasenzahl, *Non-voluntary Licensing of Patented Inventions Part I – Historical Perspective, Legal Framework Under TRIPS and an Overview of the Practice in Canada and the United States of America, Part II – The Canadian Experience*, UNCTA/ICSTD Capacity Building Project on Intellectual Property and Sustainable Development, Geneva, Switz. (2003), www.iprsonline.org/ictsd/docs/ReichmanBridgesYear6N7Oct2002.pdf & www.iprsonline.org/resources/docs/Reichman%20-%20Non-voluntary%20Licensing%20-%20Blue%205.pdf).

[43] *See* FRITZ MACHLUP, AN ECONOMIC REVIEW OF THE PATENT SYSTEM: STUDY OF THE SUBCOMMITTEE ON PATENTS, TRADEMARKS AND COPYRIGHT OF THE COMMITTEE ON THE JUDICIARY OF THE US SENATE 13 (1958). *See, e.g.*, on account of "abuse" in England, or "in the public interest" in Germany where a German decision held that it was intolerable that "two parties should be permitted to prevent each other and the public from using a valuable invention."

[44] *See* William W. Fisher III & Cyrill P. Rigamonti, *The South Africa AIDS Controversy – A Case Study in Patent Law and Policy* (2005), https://cyber.law.harvard.edu/people/

Today, the right of WTO members to protect access for public health has been reaffirmed and entrenched in the Doha Declaration on TRIPS and Public Health (Doha Declaration).[45] Article 4 of the said Declaration explicitly reiterates that WTO members can take measures to protect public health and promote access to medicine for all. Additionally, the Doha Declaration also made available a "Paragraph 6" system to ameliorate concerns that WTO countries that lack the ability to produce pharmaceutical products would not be able to effectively utilize compulsory licensing due to the constraints placed by Article 31(f) of TRIPS, which necessitates that compulsory licenses be "authorized predominantly for the supply of the domestic market" of the Member state authorizing it.[46] The "Paragraph 6" system imposes a temporary waiver on Article 31(f) of TRIPS; it transformed into a permanent TRIPS amendment when Article 31bis was formally introduced into TRIPS on January 23, 2017 after the two-thirds threshold requirement for amending the Agreement was met. This has made permanent a mechanism that permits WTO members that lack production capacity to import pharmaceutical products made under compulsory licensing and is applicable to all WTO members who have ratified the change. Those countries that did not accept the amendment had until December 31, 2017 to do so; in the interim, the "waiver" continued to apply to them until the revision was accepted. This significant event marks the first time that a WTO agreement has been amended since the creation of the organization in 1995.[47]

tfisher/South%20Africa.pdf. The authors provide a detailed discussion of the South African AIDS saga and also highlight that reduction in drug prices can often attract strong criticisms from the pharmaceutical industry and lead to media battle between the government and the Pharmaceutical Manufacturers Association.

45 WTO, *Declaration on the TRIPS Agreement and Public Health,* WT/MIN(01)/DEC/2 (Nov. 20, 2001), www.wto.org/english/thewto_e/minist_e/min01_e/mindecl_trips_e.pdf. For an important discussion on the Doha Agenda, *see* GERVAIS, THE TRIPS AGREEMENT, *supra* note 12.

46 The "Paragraph 6" system denotes the implementation of paragraph 6 of the Doha Declaration on TRIPS and Public Health which provides that "WTO members with insufficient or no manufacturing capacities in the pharmaceutical sector could face difficulties in making effective use of compulsory licensing under the TRIPS Agreement. We instruct the Council for TRIPS to find an expeditious solution to this problem and to report to the General Council before the end of 2002." For further details on this, see, for example, Ng, *supra* note 23, at 20–31; GERVAIS, THE TRIPS AGREEMENT, *supra* note 12, at 54–75; WTO, *Extract From The WHO-WIPO-WTO Trilateral Study: The Paragraph 6 System – Special Export Licences for Medicines*, www.wto.org/english/tratop_e/trips_e/who-wipo-wto2013_par6_extract_e.pdf.

47 See WTO, *Amendment to the Agreement on Trade-Related Aspects of Intellectual Property Rights* (TRIPS) (TRIPS: Factsheet), www.wto.org/english/tratop_e/trips_e/tripsfac

Be that as it may, the ability to grant compulsory licenses "does not necessarily mean such licenses should actually be granted, at least not without taking stock of the social costs that may, in the end, outweigh the benefits of this action."[48] Indeed, the threat of a non-voluntary license may obviate the need to issue one in practice as it may induce the patent owner to consider voluntary licensing instead.[49] Even in countries that have implemented this patent flexibility, compulsory licenses are rarely issued except in circumstances where the public health is at stake. The paucity of its use was noted by the Nuffield Council on Bioethics.[50] Nevertheless, the implementation of compulsory licensing in the national patent legislation of developing and least-developed countries may enhance their bargaining power and exert a downward pressure on prices.[51]

Equally imperative is the need to ensure that the grant of compulsory license is not misused to further vested interests. Take, for example, generic pharmaceutical drugs. If generics (which are generally sold at lower prices) are permitted to constantly override patent rights through grants of compulsory licensing, it may prevent the originator companies from recouping their investments in research and development, which may in turn impact on investments in new and innovative products, with greater long-term costs to all. Fearing a domino effect, pharmaceutical patent owners have strongly opposed compulsory licensing, arguing that the only beneficiary of such erosion of patent rights is the generic drug industry.[52]

Nonetheless, whilst the importance of compulsory licensing in promoting access to medicine is well-known, its role in stimulating domestic innovation seems to have received scant attention. Still, two important studies seem to lend support to this postulation. The first is a study by Professors Moser and Voena[53] which revealed that compulsory licensing may have a positive impact in driving up innovation. The second is that of Professor Scherer which

sheet_e.htm. See also WTO, *WTO IP rules amended to ease poor countries' access to affordable medicines* (January 23, 2017), www.wto.org/english/news_e/news17_e/trip_23jan17_e.htm; WTO, *Amendment of the TRIPS Agreement* (WT/L/641, December 8, 2005), www.wto.org/english/tratop_e/trips_e/wtl641_e.htm.

[48] *See* Reichman & Hasenzahl, *supra* note 42. [49] *Id.*

[50] *See* Nuffield Council on Bioethics, *The Ethics of Patenting DNA: A Discussion Paper* 54–5 (2002) where it was noted that "in practice . . . compulsory licensing is rarely imposed."

[51] *See* F. M. Scherer & Jayashree Watal, *Post-TRIPS Options for Access to Patented Medicines in Developing Countries*, 5 J. Int'l Econ. L. 913 (2002).

[52] Fisher & Rigamonti, *supra* note 44, at 5. [53] Moser & Voena, *supra* note 33.

discovered that "variably many years after compulsory patent licensing decrees had been imposed, the subject companies on average spent *more* on R&D relative to their sales than rival companies not operating under such decrees."[54] This area can undoubtedly benefit from further scholarly research; we have attempted to conduct one below.

a Conditions for Measuring Compulsory Licensing Implementation The *IPPFI* measured the implementation of compulsory licensing based on three components:

- Component 1: Is compulsory licensing available to private parties?
- Component 2: Is it permissible for government use or public non-commercial use?
- Component 3: Has the WTO paragraph 6 (art. 31bis) system been implemented? This evaluation is divided into two sub-components:
  - Sub-component 1: Will the implementing country act as exporter of the pharmaceutical drugs to eligible countries or regions as specified in the relevant treaties?
  - Sub-component 2: Will the implementing country act as an importing member in situations of national emergency or other circumstances of extreme urgency?

The value allocated to each component is either "⅓" (if the response is "Yes") or "0" (if it is "No"). Where a component is divided into two sub-components then the value given to each sub-component is either "⅙" (if the response is "Yes") or "0" (if it is "No").[55]

b *IPPFI* (Compulsory Licensing) Score The Index reveals that around one-third of the countries surveyed have made significant use of this flexibility. A more detailed examination of the countries ranked in the top two positions reveals some interesting data: more than 60 percent of them are "High Income" countries and only around 18 percent are

[54] *See* F. M. Scherer, *The Economic Effects of Compulsory Patent Licensing*, New York University Graduate School of Business Administration Monograph 73 (1977), cited in Scherer & Watal, *Competition Policy and Intellectual Property: Insights from Developed Country Experience* (Harvard Kennedy School Working Paper Series RWP14-013, 2014), web.hks.harvard.edu/publications.

[55] Intuitively, this scoring may seem odd since it may be difficult for countries to implement both sub-components of component 3. Yet, based on our study some Asian countries have in fact done so.

Table 5.2 *Compulsory licensing score*

Country	Income[1]	Ranking
(1) China	UM	1
(2) Hong Kong (SAR, China)	H	1
(3) Philippines	LM	1
(4) South Korea	H	1
(5) Brunei	H	2
(6) India	LM	2
(7) Japan	H	2
(8) Jordan	UM	2
(9) Oman	H	2
(10) Singapore	H	2
(11) Taiwan (Chinese Taipei, China)	H	2

[1] Based on the World Bank List of Economies (July 2016). The World Bank uses the "World Bank Atlas" method to group countries into various categories: Higher Income (H), Upper-Middle Income (UM), Lower-Middle Income (LM), and Lower Income (L). For more details on the World Bank country classification and income group, see https://datahelpdesk.worldbank.org/knowledgebase/articles/906519-world-bank-country-and-lending-groups.

"Lower-Middle Income" countries. This appears counter-intuitive to the rationale that compulsory licensing seeks *inter alia* to promote access to medicine particularly for the poor. Furthermore, the data suggest that Asian developing countries have not sufficiently implemented this flexibility in the framing of their national patent legislation. Whether this finding lends support to the oft-neglected argument that compulsory licensing may also have the unintended consequence of promoting domestic innovation and hence economic development is beyond the scope of this work.

The countries ranked in the top two positions are listed in Table 5.2 (in alphabetical order where the countries are tied).[56]

2 Exhaustion of Rights/Parallel Importation

The doctrine of exhaustion of rights is closely connected to the issue of parallel importation of patented products. Under this doctrine, the

[56] Space constraints limit the listing of all the data. For further details, *see* Ng, *supra* note 10.

patent rights in respect of a patented product are generally exhausted once the patented subject matter has been put on the market by the patent holder or his licensee and sold. Parallel importing deals with the importation of genuine products which have been marketed by the patent owner or its licensees in one country and imported into another country without the consent of the patent owner or its licensees in the country of importation. Parallel importation is sometimes used when products on the market in one country are unavailable in another. However, the major reason for parallel importation is that the price in the country of exportation is lower than in the country of importation. In such instances, the practice can be viewed as a "form of arbitrage" which may lower the product price differences across different markets.[57] Conversely, it may also adversely impact product distribution channels and the businesses of local licensees.

Under Article 6 of the TRIPS Agreement, WTO members have the flexibility to establish their own regime on the exhaustion of patent rights, subject to TRIPS's most favored nation and national treatment provisions.[58] This has led to a proliferation of diverse national policies on parallel import, such as the adoption of "national exhaustion" to prevent parallel importation, "international exhaustion" to permit parallel importation, and "regional exhaustion" to permit parallel importation within a particular geographical region or economic market only. By adopting international exhaustion of rights to permit parallel importation, a country is able to import, into its borders, a product that is sold at a lower price in another country.

An earlier study by Ng revealed that more than 83 percent of Asian countries surveyed have implemented some form of patent exhaustion doctrine in their domestic legislation.[59] Of these, only around half provided for international exhaustion of patent rights. In this section, we will evaluate the implementation of this flexibility in respect of pharmaceutical and nonpharmaceutical products based on the criteria set out below.

[57] Scherer & Watal, *supra* note 51.

[58] *TRIPS Agreement, supra* note 1, art. 3 (most favored nation) and art. 4 (national treatment) respectively.

[59] Ng, *supra* note 23.

a Conditions for evaluating the implementation of exhaustion of rights/parallel importation The implementation of this flexibility is assessed based on the following conditions:

- Component 1: Is parallel importation permitted for nonpharmaceutical products?
- Component 2: Is parallel importation allowed for pharmaceutical products?
- Component 3: Is the permitted parallel importation unconditional? This component is divided into two sub-components:
  - Sub-component 1: Is parallel importation unconditional for non-pharmaceutical products?
  - Sub-component 2: Is the parallel importation unconditional for pharmaceutical products?

The value of each component is either "⅓" (if the response is "Yes") or "0" (if it is "No"). Where a component is divided into two sub-components then the value of each sub-component is either "⅙" (if the response is "Yes") or "0" (if it is "No").

b *IPPFI* (Parallel Importation) Score The Index shows that not many of the countries surveyed (only around one-third) have substantially fulfilled the conditions evaluated above. A glance at the countries ranked in the top two positions shows that they comprise mainly "middle income" countries, as set out in Table 5.3 (in alphabetical order where the countries are tied).

3 Research Exemption/Experimental Use Defense/Private Noncommercial Use

The research exemption (also known as the "experimental use defense") is a safe harbor provision which exempts, from patent infringement, acts done without the consent of the patent holder for the purpose of research, or scientific experimentation.[60] The rationale for this exception is based on:

[60] It has been defined by the WTO panel in the case of *Canada – Patent Protection of Pharmaceutical Product* as the "exception under which use of the patented product for scientific experimentation, during the term of the patent and without consent, is not an infringement." *See* WTO panel in *Canada – Patent Protection of Pharmaceutical Product* case at p 165 quoted in WIPO Secretariat, *Patent related flexibilities in the multilateral legal framework and their legislative implementation at the national and regional levels*, at 20, CDIP/5/4 Rev (Aug. 18, 2010).

Table 5.3 *Parallel importation score*

Country	Income	Ranking
(1) Cambodia	LM	1
(2) China	UM	1
(3) India	LM	1
(4) Malaysia	UM	1
(5) Pakistan	LM	1
(6) Sri Lanka	LM	1
(7) Taiwan (Chinese Taipei, China)	H	1
(8) Thailand	UM	1
(9) Vietnam	LM	1
(10) Brunei	H	2
(11) Singapore	H	2

> [T]he notion that a key public policy purpose underlying patent laws is to facilitate the dissemination and advancement of technical knowledge and that allowing the patent owner to prevent experimental use during the term of the patent would frustrate part of the purpose of the requirement that the nature of the invention be disclosed to the public. To the contrary . . . both society and the scientist have a "legitimate interest" in using the patent disclosure to support the advance of science and technology.[61]

This flexibility plays an important role in optimizing the innovative capability of a country through the use and dissemination of scientific and technological information. If properly calibrated, it may advance the broader goals of patent law by mitigating the blocking effect of patents on researchers during the life of a patent, thereby stimulating innovation (particularly follow-on innovation).[62] Furthermore, some countries have also exempted from patent infringement acts that are done for private noncommercial uses.

a Conditions for Evaluating Research Exemption etc. The Index uses the following indicators to measure this category of flexibility implementation:

[61] *Id.*

[62] *See* Shamnad Basheer & Prashant Reddy, *The Experimental Use Exception through a Developmental Lens*, 50(4) IDEA 831, 835 (2010).

- Component 1: Is an act done for research and/or scientific experiment exempted from patent infringement?
- Component 2: If yes, is the scope of exemption of a broad nature? Examples of exemption with broad scope include permitting commercial research; and acts that extend beyond the usual research "on" the subject matter of the patented invention to encompass research "with" the patented subject matter, such as those found in some European countries.
- Component 3: Is private non-commercial use exempted from patent infringement?
- Each component will be allocated a value of either "⅓" (if the response is "Yes") or "0" (if it is "No").

b *IPPFI* (Research Exemption) Score The data reveal that a majority of the countries surveyed (more than 65 percent) have made substantial use of this TRIPS flexibility in framing their patent statutes. Taking a quick look at the income level of these countries, we did not discern any notable correlation between a country's implementation of this flexibility and its income level. There seems to be a good mix of countries at all income levels.

The countries ranked in the top two positions are listed in Table 5.4 (in alphabetical order where the countries are tied).

4 Regulatory Review Exception/"*Bolar*" Exception

The regulatory review exception (commonly known as the "*Bolar*" exception[63]) permits the early working of a patent by a potential competitor of the patent owner without the patent owner's authorization for the purpose of obtaining regulatory approval. It exempts from patent infringement acts done to support an application for marketing approval of generic versions of a product, while the patent is still in force. This ensures that competitors (particularly manufacturers of generic pharmaceutical products) can compete in the marketplace promptly upon expiry of the patent, thus facilitating the timely access of affordable generic products. The acts permitted under this exception comprise clinical trial activities and may extend to scientific experimentation at preclinical development. This exception was determined by the WTO

[63] Named after a case in the United States which prompted the enactment of this exception: Roche Products Inc. v. Bolar Pharmaceuticals Co., 733 F. 2d 858 (Fed. Cir. 1984).

Table 5.4 *Research exemption score*

Country	Income	Ranking
(1) Macau (SAR, China)	H	1
(2) Taiwan (Chinese Taipei, China)	H	1
(3) Turkey	UM	1
(4) Vietnam	LM	1
(5) Brunei	H	2
(6) China	UM	2
(7) Hong Kong (SAR, China)	H	2
(8) India	LM	2
(9) Indonesia	LM	2
(10) Japan	H	2
(11) Jordan	UM	2
(12) Kazakhstan	UM	2
(13) Malaysia	UM	2
(14) Mongolia	LM	2
(15) Oman	H	2
(16) Philippines	LM	2
(17) Thailand	UM	2
(18) Singapore	H	2
(19) South Korea	H	2
(20) Sri Lanka	LM	2

panel in *Canada – Patent Protection of Pharmaceutical Products* to be compatible with the TRIPS obligations.[64]

A 2010 report by WIPO disclosed that more than half of the countries worldwide and in excess of 90 percent in high-income countries had implemented the "*Bolar*" exception in their national laws.[65] But a slightly

[64] Canada – Patent Protection of Pharmaceutical Products, WT/DS114/R (Mar. 17, 2000). The European Communities alleged that certain provisions of Canada's Patent Act including its regulatory review exception were incompatible with the TRIPS Agreement. The WTO panel's report, which concluded that this exception was not inconsistent with obligations under the TRIPS Agreement, was adopted by the WTO Dispute Settlement Body on April 7, 2000. *See* WTO, *Dispute Settlement: Dispute DS114 Canada – Patent Protection of Pharmaceutical Products*, www.wto.org/english/tratop_e/dispu_e/cases_e/ds114_e.htm. *See also* Gervais, The TRIPS Agreement, *supra* note 12, at paras 2.364–2.369, 2.397–2.399.

[65] *See* WIPO Secretariat, *WIPO Patent-related Flexibilities in the Multilateral Legal Framework and their Legislative Implementation at the National and Regional Levels*, Geneva, CDIP/5/4 (2010), www.wipo.int/meetings/en/details.jsp?meeting_id=19686 quoted in UNDP, *Good*

different picture for Asia emerged in an earlier 2013 study by Ng[66] which showed that less than half of the Asian countries surveyed seemed to have implemented this flexibility either by specifically providing for a "*Bolar*" exception or by way of a broad experimental use exemption in their national patent laws. With this in mind, we will proceed to evaluate the current Asian landscape.

a Conditions for Determining Implementation of the Regulatory Review Exception Three criteria were used to gauge the implementation of this flexibility:

- Component 1: Does the country provide for a regulatory review exception ("*Bolar*" exception)?
- Component 2: Does the exception cover acts done to support an application for foreign regulatory approval?
- Component 3: Does the exception permit the importation of a patented product for use in support of an application for regulatory review approval?

Each component will be assigned a value of either "⅓" (if the response is "Yes") or "0" (if it is "No").

b *IPPFI* (Regulatory Review (*Bolar*) Exception) Score The Index indicates that around 40 percent of the countries analyzed have substantially satisfied the criteria used in this examination. In contrast to the results of the 2010 WIPO report, this study reveals that only around 73 percent of high-income Asian countries have implemented the *Bolar*/regulatory review exemption.[67] A cursory glance at the countries ranked in the top two positions shows little correlation between the income of

Practice Guide: Improving access to treatment by utilizing public health flexibilities in the WTO TRIPS Agreement (2010), http://www.undp.org/content/undp/en/home/librarypage/poverty-reduction/good-practice-guide-improving-access-to-treatment-by-utilizing-public-health-flexibilities-in-the-wto-trips-agreement/.

66 Ng, *supra* note 23.

67 The data includes implementation via a specific "Bolar" exception or by way of a broad experimental use exemption in the national patent laws. However, it should be noted that where the experimental use provisions appear ambiguous as to whether they would encompass a "Bolar" exception, they have not been included in the data. Also, the data does not take into account instances where a "Bolar" exception is not needed: for example, where the country does not require generic producers to obtain regulatory approval or conduct testing of the generic product; or where the country is willing to rely on tests conducted in a different country.

Table 5.5 *Regulatory review exception score*

Country	Income	Ranking
(1) India	LM	1
(2) Taiwan (Chinese Taipei, China)	H	1
(3) Thailand	UM	1
(4) Brunei	H	2
(5) China	UM	2
(6) Jordan	UM	2
(7) Macau (SAR, China)	H	2
(8) Oman	H	2
(9) Pakistan	LM	2
(10) Philippines	LM	2
(11) Singapore	H	2
(12) Turkey	UM	2
(13) Vietnam	LM	2

the country and the use of this exception. There seems to be an even mix of countries in all income levels.

The countries ranked in the top two positions are listed in Table 5.5 (in alphabetical order where the countries are tied).

5 Specific TRIPS-Permitted Exclusions under Article 27

Other than exceptions from patent rights, Article 27 of TRIPS provides four explicit categories of patent exclusions that WTO countries may implement in their domestic laws in order to delimit the scope of patentable subject matter. These are:

1. inventions that are contrary to *ordre public* or morality;[68]
2. diagnostic, therapeutic and surgical methods for the treatment of humans or animals;[69]
3. plants and animals other than micro-organisms;[70]

[68] Article 27.2 permits members to exclude from patentability "inventions, the prevention within their territory of the commercial exploitation of which is necessary to protect *ordre public* or morality, including to protect human, animal or plant life or health or to avoid serious prejudice to the environment, provided that such exclusion is not made merely because the exploitation is prohibited by their law."

[69] TRIPS Agreement, *supra* note 1, art. 27.3(a).

[70] TRIPS Agreement, *supra* note 1, art. 27.3(b).

4. essentially biological processes for the production of plants or animals, other than nonbiological and microbiological processes.[71]

Besides these TRIPS-specific exclusions, some WTO member states have interpreted the reference in Article 27 to "fields of technology" as permitting them to exclude other subject matter from their statutory law.[72] Take, for example, the United Kingdom (U.K.) Patents Act and European Patent Convention, which provide a nonexhaustive list of patent excluded subject matter, such as discoveries; scientific theories; mathematical methods; aesthetic creations; schemes, rules or methods for performing mental acts, playing games or doing business; or a program for a computer; presentation of information; as such.[73] However, these sorts of exclusions were not included in the Index.

a Specific TRIPS-Permitted Exclusions under Article 27 The Index quantifies the implementation of TRIPS-specific patent exclusions based on the following criteria:

- Component 1: Are inventions contrary to *ordre public* or morality excluded from patentability?
- Component 2: Are diagnostic, therapeutic and surgical methods for the treatment of humans or animals excluded from patentability?
- Component 3: Are plants and animals other than micro-organisms, and essentially biological processes for the production of plants or animals other than nonbiological and microbiological processes excluded from patentability?

Each component will be awarded either a score of "⅓" (if the response is "Yes") or "0" (if it is "No").

b *IPPFI* (Article 27 TRIPS Exclusion) Score The Index reveals that many of the countries surveyed (more than 65 percent) recorded positive responses for all three criteria evaluated. These comprise (listed in alphabetical order):

[71] *Id.*

[72] Article 27.1 of the TRIPS Agreement, which provides that " . . . patents shall be available for any inventions, whether products or processes, in all fields of technology, provided that they are new, involve an inventive step and are capable of industrial application . . . "

[73] *See*, U.K. Patents Act (1977), and § 1(2) and art. 52 of the Convention on the Grant of European Patents (15th ed., Sept. 2013) respectively.

Cambodia, China, Hong Kong (SAR, China), India, Indonesia, Iran, Jordan, Lao PDR, Macau (SAR, China), Malaysia, Mongolia, Pakistan, Philippines, Saudi Arabia, Sri Lanka, Taiwan (Chinese Taipei, China), Thailand, Turkey, United Arab Emirates, and Vietnam.

c *IPPFI*: **Some Concluding Remarks** Whilst the score for the different flexibility sub-indices may vary for a particular country resulting in shifts to its ranking from one sub-index to another, a certain pattern/repetition in the position ranking of a particular group of countries can nonetheless be discerned. These groups of countries are consistently ranked either at the top- or bottom-end of the Index across a broad spectrum of sub-indices. For example, across at least three of the sub-indices China, India, Taiwan (Chinese Taipei, China), Thailand and Vietnam are consistently ranked first, whereas Lao PDR, Bangladesh and Nepal are placed last. When viewed holistically based on the overall composite score for all the five sub-indices, another interesting outcome emerged: by and large there is a correlation between a country's implementation of flexibilities and its income level. There are almost twice as many "High Income" countries ranked in the bottom half of the *IPPFI* than in the top half of the Index. This observation lends support to the hypothesis that as a country becomes more developed, it tends to adopt fewer flexibilities in its patent regime. Interestingly, this hypothesis was also borne out in the empirical analysis in Section IV.

What seems less clear is how a country's choice of flexibility implementation impacts on its innovation capabilities and public health needs. We turn to evaluate these issues by examining whether there is a correlation between a country's flexibility implementation and its innovation capabilities based on the data evinced in the *IPPFI* and GII respectively.

C *Using the* IPPFI *to Explore the Impact of Flexibility Implementation on the Innovation Capabilities of an Economy*

We now use the *IPPFI* to correlate the flexibility implementation data of a particular country to that corresponding to its innovation efficiency under the GII. The goal is to determine whether there is any relationship between them.

The GII assesses countries based on the effectiveness of their innovation system and policy by identifying countries/economies that "over- or underperform on innovation relative to their level of development."[74] By measuring the countries' innovation efficiency ratios (i.e. the ratio of the Innovation Output Sub-Index score over the Innovation Input Sub-Index score), the GII distinguishes countries which are efficient innovators from those which are not. It considers countries with "Innovation Efficiency" ratios of equal to or more than 0.66 (i.e. ≥ 0.66) as "Efficient Innovators," while those whose "Innovation Efficiency" ratios are less than 0.66 (i.e. < 0.66) are judged as "Inefficient Innovators." It should be borne in mind that there are, of course, limitations to this classification. For example, as cautioned in the GII report, a country/economy can obtain a "relatively high Innovation Efficiency Ratio" as a result of "particularly low input scores."

Despite the limitation, we find that on the whole there seems to be a positive correlation between a country's innovation efficiency and its flexibility implementation, elaborated as follows:

First, the top five countries on the *IPPFI* have "Innovation Efficiency" ratios ≥ 0.66 and are considered "Efficient Innovators" (EI) under the GII 2016 report (with the exception of Taiwan, for which no data was available). In contrast, those ranked in the bottom five of the *IPPFI* are identified as "Inefficient Innovators" (with the exception of Lao PDR, for which there is no data).

Second, notwithstanding the fact that there are equal numbers of "efficient" and "inefficient" innovator countries under the *IPPFI*, we discern a polarization of these two groups of innovators at the top and bottom half of the Index respectively. A large majority of the countries classified as "efficient" innovators (i.e. around 70 percent of all the "efficient" innovators) are found in the top half of the Flexibility Index, whilst most of the "inefficient" innovators (i.e. about 77 percent of all the "inefficient" innovator countries) congregate at the bottom half of the *IPPFI*.

Table 5.6 provides further illumination. Due to space constraints, only the data relating to the top 5 countries and bottom 4 countries on the *IPPFI* are presented.[75]

Despite the limitations of this examination, we submit that by and large this result indicates that countries classified as "efficient" innovators tend to have made greater use of TRIPS patent flexibilities and those considered as "inefficient" innovators seem less inclined to do so.

[74] *See* the Global Innovation Index (GII) 2016 at 30.

[75] Only the data relating to the bottom four countries (i.e. those ranked in position 27 to 30) have been presented; there are four countries that are ranked equal at position 26, namely Bahrain (H/II), Iran (UM/EI), Saudi Arabia (H/II) and United Arab Emirates (H/II). For further details, see Ng, *supra* note 10.

Table 5.6 *Correlation between flexibility score and innovation efficiency*

IPPFI Top 5 countries	Income	Overall ranking (*IPPFI*)	Innovation efficiency ratio (*GII*)	Efficient innovator (EI)/ Inefficient innovator (II) (*GII*)
(1) Taiwan (Chinese Taipei, China)	H	1	NA	NA
(2) India	LM	2	0.66	EI
(3) China	UM	3	0.9	EI
(4) Thailand	UM	3	0.7	EI
(5) Vietnam	LM	3	0.84	EI
IPPFI Bottom 4 countries	Income	Overall ranking (*IPPFI*)	Innovation efficiency ratio (*GII*)	Efficient innovator (EI)/ Inefficient innovator (II) (*GII*)
(1) Bhutan	LM	27	0.28	II
(2) Lao PDR	LM	27	NA	NA
(3) Bangladesh	LM	29	0.52	II
(4) Nepal	L	30	0.58	II

In light of these observations, we decided to use the *IPPFI* to empirically relate to various country-level characteristics to ascertain the determinants of a country's choice of flexibility implementation. With this in mind, we then proceeded to run extensive statistical analyses.

IV What Determines a Country's Adoption of TRIPS Flexibilities?[76]

In this section, we use the *IPPFI* to empirically evaluate the determinants of a country's choice of flexibilities implementation by relating the *IPPFI* to various country-level characteristics. The data on these country characteristics were retrieved from the World Development Indicators 2015. Two important caveats precede our analysis. First, the authors have not

[76] The authors would like to credit Hu for all the extensive statistical analyses in Section IV, which he ran independently.

yet been able to date the adoption of TRIPS flexibilities by countries in the sample. In other words, the flexibility scores are based on the reading of the countries' intellectual property legislations as at July 2016. Hence the flexibilities may have been implemented at a much earlier date, or may even have existed prior to the countries' accession to the WTO and thus to TRIPS. This uncertainty creates complications since an ideal analysis is one which uses the country characteristics dated before the adoption of the TRIPS flexibilities as potential determinants of the adoption in a regression framework.

We thus faced a trade-off in deciding which years of data to use in the empirical analysis. Several considerations were brought to bear: the earlier the date used, the more likely it will approximate to an ideal computation since the data will probably pre-date the adoption of the TRIPS flexibilities. But the drawback is that it will widen the gap between the earlier dating of the country characteristics and actual adoption date of the flexibilities (at least in the case of some countries surveyed). This will render the country characteristics less relevant in explaining the reason for the adoption of the flexibilities. Another shortcoming is that the data for the early years relating to some of the country characteristics, such as R&D and patents, are scarce and this will shrink the already small sample of countries under review. To get around these constraints, we decided to run two sets of regressions, where the country characteristics were dated in 1995 and 2000, while the dependent variable remained the same flexibility score under the *IPPFI*. We decided to use 1995, the year when TRIPS came into force, as our benchmark year. But we also used 2000 as an alternative date since this was the year which marked the end of the transition period for developing countries – the time when they were expected to fulfill their TRIPS commitments save for those that did not provide for product patent protection in their territories in respect of certain technologies, notably for pharmaceutical drugs.

A further limitation imposed on the already meager sample size is that five of the countries which are included in the Flexibility Index are least-developed countries, which are not expected to fulfill their TRIPS obligations in respect of patenting pharmaceutical products at least until 2033. Even then, this grace period may be subject to further extension. This entails excluding these five countries from the empirical analysis.

Table 5.7 *Summary statistics*

Year/variables		GDPPC[1]	GDP[2]	R&D/GDP[3]	Patent applications[4]	HIV/Pop[5]
1995	Mean	16,948	462,917	–	22,611	0.38
	Std.	19,372	722,818	–	78,894	0.69
	Min.	1,490	5,978	–	21	0.10
	Max.	77,663	2,875,254	–	333,770	2.20
	Obs.	24	24	0	18	9
2000	Mean	19,378	626,022	0.80	27,145	0.39
	Std.	21,055	981,434	0.92	90,846	0.58
	Min.	2,020	7,431	0.07	34	0.10
	Max.	85,641	3,612,218	3.00	384,201	1.90
	Obs.	24	24	14	18	9

Source: World Development Indicators 2015

1 GDPPC: GDP per capita in current prices adjusted for purchasing power parity ($).

2 GDP: GDP in current prices adjusted for purchasing power parity ($million).

3 R&D/GDP: R&D to GDP ratio (%).

4 'Patent applications' refers to the number of patent applications filed by residents with the national patent office.

5 HIV/Pop: ratio of HIV population to total population (%).

A final caveat is that the *IPPFI* Index is based on the laws on the statute books, or *de jure* legal protection. This can be quite different from how these laws are actually implemented, i.e. their *de facto* protection. Thus it is subject to the same criticism that may be levied on other indices such as the Ginarte-Park Index.

Before proceeding with the empirical analysis, it may be useful to provide a summary of the country characteristics statistics that are used in the regression framework. It is worth highlighting that the number of observations available varies greatly for various characteristics. For example, there were nine observations for HIV/Pop (i.e. the proportion of population that is HIV infected); twenty-four observations for GDP per capita (GDPPC) and total GDP (GDP), both of which are measured in U.S. dollars adjusted on the basis of purchasing power parity; and no data for total R&D expenditure as a percentage of GDP for the year 1995. Table 5.7 provides further illumination on this.

A TRIPS Flexibility and Economic Development

The relationship between TRIPS flexibility adoption and economic development was evaluated by producing a scatter plot of the two in Figure 5.1. The level of economic development is measured by GDP per capita in current U.S. dollars, adjusted for international price differences. The flexibility score only varies by country as earlier explained. We plotted the flexibility score against the GDP per capita for two years, 1995 and 2000. Both variables appeared in logarithmic form, as we assumed a proportional relationship between the two. In each figure, a line that best fits the data points was also plotted along with its confidence interval.

Figure 5.1 demonstrates prima facie a negative relationship between TRIPS flexibility utilization and economic development. As a country becomes more developed, it tends to adopt fewer flexibilities in its patent protection regime. Singapore is an outlier, adopting greater flexibilities than the similarly rich oil producers of Bahrain and Oman, for example.

In Table 5.8 we present results from an OLS regression where the overall flexibility score in logarithmic form was regressed against GDP per capita also in logarithmic form. This is the regression that generated the fitted line in Figure 5.1. The estimated coefficients of GDP per capita reported in columns (1) and (3), when the data for 1995 and 2000 were

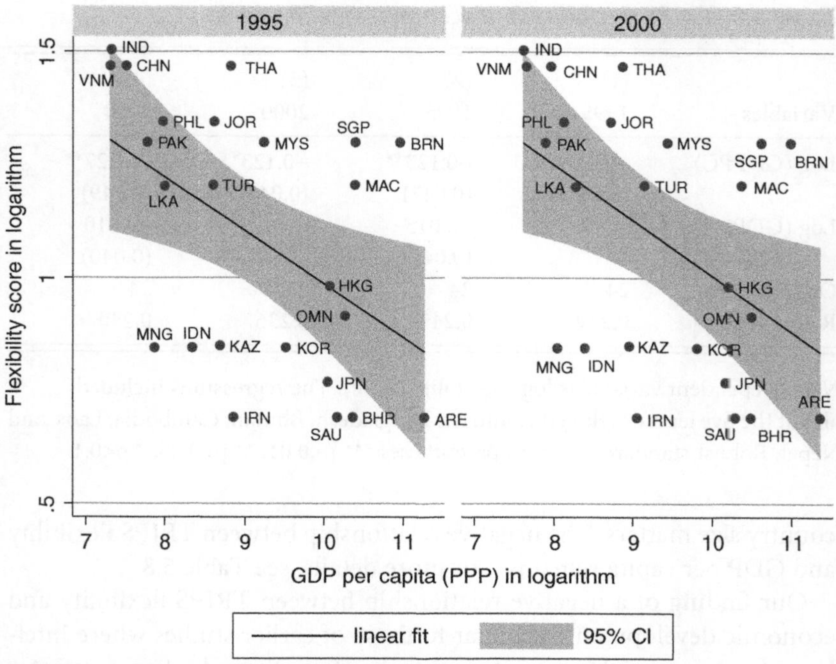

Figure 5.1 Flexibility score and GDP per capita
Note: The fitted line was obtained by regressing log (flexibility score) on log (GDP per capita).

used respectively, were both statistically significant. The estimates suggest that a country that is twice as rich, as measured by GDP per capita, is likely to have 12 to 13 percent fewer TRIPS flexibilities, which is roughly the difference in the flexibility score between the Philippines (3.84) and Vietnam (4.34).

The costs and benefits of adopting TRIPS flexibilities may be proportional to the size of the economy. For example, the welfare gains from issuing a compulsory license for a cancer drug would be greater if there are more cancer patients who would have access to the drug at a lower cost. On the other hand, the cost in the form of lost dynamic efficiency may also be greater, as the reward from developing alternative or newer cancer drugs by either an indigenous pharmaceutical company or a foreign one will also likely be reduced. As indicated by the results reported in columns (2) and (4) of Table 5.8, where we used total GDP to measure country size, there is no statistical evidence to suggest that

Table 5.8 *TRIPS flexibility and economic development*

Variables	(1) 1995	(2) 1995	(3) 2000	(4) 2000
Log (GDPPC)	−0.118** (0.044)	−0.123** (0.047)	−0.123** (0.046)	−0.127** (0.049)
Log (GDP)		−0.015 (0.041)		−0.010 (0.040)
Observations	24	24	24	24
R-squared	0.239	0.245	0.236	0.240

Note: Dependent variable is log (flexibility score). The regressions included all but the five least developed countries: Bangladesh, Bhutan, Cambodia, Laos, and Nepal. Robust standard errors in parentheses *** p<0.01, ** p<0.05, * p<0.1

country size matters. The negative relationship between TRIPS flexibility and GDP per capita remains. For more details, see Table 5.8.

Our finding of a negative relationship between TRIPS flexibility and economic development is similar to those of earlier studies where intellectual property rights were found to be strengthened when a country passes a certain level of economic development, i.e. the upswing part of the U-shaped relationship. All the countries in the sample had a GDP per capita higher than $854 in 1995, the bottom of the U-shaped relationship that Professors Yongmin Chen and Thitima Puttitanun reported, for example.[77]

B TRIPS Flexibility, Innovative Capability and Public Health Needs

We also examined two other potential determinants of a country's choice of TRIPS flexibility implementation, namely innovative capability and public health needs. TRIPS flexibilities, by realigning the interests of intellectual property owners and its users, lower the barriers to technology diffusion and thus reduce the incentives to innovate. The extent of a country's adoption of TRIPS flexibilities thus depends on what is the primary driving force of its technological change. When technological change is primarily driven by technology adoption, greater TRIPS flexibilities are expected; as a country acquires the ability

[77] See Chen & Puttitanun, *supra* note 30.

to innovate, its welfare calculus may shift in favor of rewarding innovation by reducing TRIPS flexibilities. Therefore we hypothesize an inverted U-shaped relationship between TRIPS flexibilities and a country's innovative capability: initially rising as a country acquires the capability to reverse engineer, but eventually falling after the country starts innovating.

Table 5.9 presents the data where a country's innovative capability is measured using two indicators: R&D to GDP ratio and the number of patent applications filed by residents with their home patent office. The first column of the table contains results from regressing the log flexibility score on R&D to GDP ratio and the square of the ratio for 2000. The results corroborate the inverted U-shaped relationship hypothesis: the flexibility score rises in R&D to GDP ratio, but falls once the ratio reaches a certain level, which is imputed from the estimates to be around 1.2 percent. This is somewhat higher than China's ratio of 0.9, but much lower than Singapore's 1.85. R&D data are not available for 1995, thus we could not run the same regression for 1995.

The negative relationship between TRIPS flexibilities and economic development is no longer statistically significant, which seems to suggest that GDP per capita was really a proxy for a country's technology capability, among other characteristics.

We used patent applications instead of R&D to GDP ratio as a measure of a country's technology capability. The results reported in columns (2) and (3) of the table indicate a similar inverted U-shaped relationship between TRIPS flexibilities and technology capability, but it is not statistically significant. See Table 5.9.

Finally, we explored how public health needs may have influenced the country's adoption of TRIPS flexibilities. Since the majority of the flexibility measures that were used to construct the *IPPFI* were related to access to medicine and public health intervention, the intuitive response would be that these public health challenges motivate countries to use the flexibilities as a way to address them. We measured the public health challenges that a country faces by using the proportion of the population that is HIV positive. Data on this measure are only available for nine of the countries in our sample, namely India, Indonesia, Iran, Mongolia, Malaysia, Pakistan, Sri Lanka, Thailand and Vietnam.

The results reported in Table 5.10 show that there is a positive correlation between TRIPS flexibilities utilization and the prevalence of HIV

Table 5.9 *TRIPS flexibility and innovation capability*

Variables	(1) 2000	(2) 1995	(3) 2000
Log (GDP PC)	−0.056	−0.131	−0.171**
	(0.061)	(0.079)	(0.065)
Log (GDP)	0.054	0.056	−0.042
	(0.039)	(0.055)	(0.076)
R&D/GDP	0.564*		
	(0.301)		
$(R\&D/GDP)^2$	−0.229**		
	(0.079)		
Log (patents)		0.063	0.096
		(0.126)	(0.160)
Log $(patents)^2$		−0.006	−0.006
		(0.008)	(0.009)
Observations	14	18	18
R-squared	0.562	0.340	0.369

Note: Log (patents) is the number of resident patent applications.
Regression for column (1) included the following countries/regions: China, Hong Kong (China), India, Indonesia, Japan, Kazakhstan, South Korea, Sri Lanka, Malaysia, Mongolia, Pakistan, Singapore, Thailand, and Turkey. The following countries were included for column (2): China, Hong Kong (China), India, Indonesia, Iran, Japan, Kazakhstan, South Korea, Malaysia, Mongolia, Pakistan, the Philippines, Saudi Arabia, Singapore, Thailand, Turkey, and Vietnam. Column (3) included the following: China, Hong Kong (China), India, Indonesia, Iran, Japan, Jordan, Kazakhstan, South Korea, Sri Lanka, Malaysia, Pakistan, the Philippines, Saudi Arabia, Singapore, Thailand, Turkey, and Vietnam.
Robust standard errors in parentheses
*** p<0.01, ** p<0.05, * p<0.1

infection. But we caution against reading too much into the results given the small sample size and the small effect the estimates imply, even if we can take these estimates at their face value. For example, the estimate for 2000 indicates that a one standard deviation increase (0.58 percent) in the prevalence of HIV infection would only be correlated with an increase of less than one-fifth of one percent in the flexibility score.

Table 5.10 *TRIPS flexibility and public health*

Variables	(1) 1995	(2) 2000
Log (GDP PC)	−0.273	−0.237
	(0.211)	(0.207)
Log (GDP)	0.042	0.038
	(0.053)	(0.053)
HIV/Pop	0.271*	0.316*
	(0.118)	(0.132)
Observations	9	9
R-squared	0.493	0.496

The nine countries included in the regressions are India, Indonesia, Iran, Sri Lanka, Malaysia, Mongolia, Pakistan, Thailand, and Vietnam.
Robust standard errors in parentheses
*** p<0.01, ** p<0.05, * p<0.1

C *Summary of Empirical Analysis*

The analysis in this section is premised on the hypothesis that the extent of a country's TRIPS flexibility adoption is driven by economic considerations including its technology capability and public health needs. As a result, we expected developing countries' adoption of TRIPS flexibilities to reflect the relevant stages of their economic and technological development. It is in this context that we used the newly constructed *IPPFI* to empirically examine this hypothesis.

Despite the limitations of the *IPPFI* and its component indices as earlier highlighted (such as small sample size, inability to date the adoption of the flexibilities for each country and relying on data based on *de jure* flexibilities implementation), our results corroborate the hypothesis of how TRIPS flexibility is related to a developing country's economic and technological development. We found that richer countries tend to adopt fewer TRIPS flexibilities and that countries adopt more flexibilities as imitative activities intensify but reduce their flexibilities utilization as they become more technologically advanced. Finally, as expected, public health needs, which were measured by HIV prevalence, were positively correlated with greater use of TRIPS flexibilities.

V Conclusion

While it is difficult to pinpoint the precise rationale for the framing of each country's patent policies, it would be unrealistic to expect that national support for varying patent standards would be wholly divorced from self-interest. What seems clear is that many of the Asian countries have legal, political, socioeconomic landscapes that differ from many developed countries. Any attempt to harmonize standards or solutions without regard to these differences would undermine the goals of multilateral agreements to the detriment of all nations. We believe that the TRIPS Agreement has appropriately incorporated flexibilities (including exceptions and exclusions) into the international intellectual property (patent) framework. Our study suggests that effective utilization of TRIPS (patent) flexibilities can make a consequential impact on the welfare of developing countries, such as innovation capabilities and public health. This conclusion was also recently echoed in the landmark resolution adopted on June 30, 2016 by the UN Human Rights Council (UNHRC) on access to medicines calling on its members to make "full use" of the TRIPS flexibilities.[78]

At the end of the day, as Professor Jerome Reichman has succinctly summarized in terms recently expounded by Professors Dreyfuss and Dinwoodie:

> Developing countries that properly crafted a 'federalist' view of TRIPS could legally exploit its flexibilities and ambiguities so as to advance their own creative and innovative interests within the new international order

[78] UN Human Rights Council (UNHRC), Resolution on Access to medicines in the context of the right of everyone to the enjoyment of the highest attainable standard of physical and mental health, A/HRC/32/L.23/Rev.1. (Adopted on June 30, 2016 at the Thirty-second Session Agenda item 3 on the Promotion and protection of all human rights, civil, political, economic, social and cultural rights, including the right to development) (UNHRC Resolution on Access to Medicine 2016). See Article 4 of the UNHRC Resolution on Access to Medicine 2016 which:

> Also calls upon States to take steps to implement policies and plans to promote access to comprehensive and cost-effective prevention, treatment and care for the integrated management of non-communicable diseases, including, inter alia, increased access to affordable, safe, efficacious and quality medicines and diagnostics and other technologies, including through the full use of Trade-Related Aspects of Intellectual Property Rights flexibilities.

This resolution, which is calling for an examination of the relationship between IP rights, trade agreements, and access to medicines further underscores the importance of TRIPS flexibilities utilization, particularly in developing and least-developed countries.

that integrated trade and intellectual property within 'an incipient transnational system of innovation.'[79]

Now more than twenty years after TRIPS, the international intellectual property regime is poised at the cusp of another potential wave of intellectual property standard elevation *via* plurilateral trade and investment instruments, such as the Trans-Pacific Partnership and the Regional Comprehensive Economic Partnership. This work aims to take stock of the current landscape on the extent and impact of TRIPS flexibilities implementation in Asia and contribute to the broader policy discourse on how to achieve an appropriate balance between the diverse interests of the various stakeholders of the international intellectual property regime. We submit that the better way is that suggested by the editors of this book: To integrate incentive, trade, development, culture, and human rights in the framing of intellectual property law in the twenty-first century.

[79] *See* Reichman, *supra* note 2 (internal citation omitted). For more details on "an incipient transnational system of innovation", *see* Maskus & Reichman, *supra* note 22.

6

Image Rights and Other Unorthodox Forms of Intellectual Property

MEGAN RICHARDSON AND JULIAN THOMAS

In *Douglas v. Hello! Ltd*,[1] Lord Hoffmann said there was no question of importing image rights or other "unorthodox" forms of intellectual property into English law,[2] despite the case being concerned with the unauthorized magazine publication of celebrity wedding photographs with a remedy granted for breach of confidence.[3] In this chapter we explore the unorthodoxy of image rights. Such rights have been criticized for their repressive effect on the free expression and circulation of public culture. We argue that the public presentation of a person's face or appearance, captured in a photographic or other form, may employ creative processes of cultural fashioning.[4] In Roland Barthes' influential formulation,[5] such representations offer both an "ideology" and a "mirror" through which the audience can identify and relate to the subject's mode of self-presentation. These kinds of creative activities potentially provide a justification – even when barely so – for image

[1] Douglas and Others v. Hello! Ltd. (No. 3) and Others [2006] Q.B. 125, *sub nom* OBG Ltd. v. Allan [2008] 1 A.C. 1.

[2] *Id.* at [124].

[3] Douglas and Others v. Hello! Ltd. and Others (No. 3) [2006] Q.B. 125. *See* TANYA APLIN, LIONEL BENTLY, PHILLIP JOHNSON, & SIMON MALYNICZ, GURRY ON BREACH OF CONFIDENCE 349–50 (2d ed. 2012), concluding that the reasoning of the majority of the House of Lords concerning OK!'s entitlement to bring an action was "rather terse" but that arguably this involved a broad interpretation of the scope of the exclusive right granted to OK! to include "any photographic representation of the wedding". In formal terms, however, the claim was breach of confidence.

[4] Of course, as Richard Dyer points out, "image" might mean more than exclusively visual signs, encompassing a "complex configuration of visual, verbal and aural signs [that] constitute the general image of a person" (talking specifically about "stars" here): RICHARD DYER & PAUL MCDONALD, STARS 34 (2d ed. 1998). But for present purposes we mainly use the term "image" in the narrower more literal sense of a visual photograph or portrait.

[5] Roland Barthes, *Photography and Electoral Appeal*, in MYTHOLOGIES 91, 91–2 (Roland Barthes ed., Annette Lavers & Jonathan Cape trans., 1972).

rights to be legally acknowledged, at the same time underlining the need for clarity around the limits and defenses necessary for communication and cultural production between creators, commentators and their audiences in an increasingly visual culture. Our more immediate goal, however, is to suggest that in some cases there seem to be stronger claims for legal protection and the arguments behind these claims should now be acknowledged and their policy ramifications carefully considered.

I The New Orthodoxy

Lord Hoffmann's statement as to the unorthodoxy of image or other intellectual property rights in personality is a categorical statement of the unavailability of such rights under English law. Several years earlier Baroness Hale had made a similarly categorical statement regarding the prospect of image rights more generally in *Campbell v. MGN Ltd*,[6] noting that "in this country we do not recognize a right to one's own image."[7] On the other hand, in *Campbell*, where the claim was also one of breach of confidence (but with hints already of a tort of misuse of private information, which later courts would treat as law), it was clear that one of the factors that took the decision over the line in Campbell's favor in the House of Lords was the *Mirror*'s use of her photograph in its story about her attending Narcotics Anonymous meetings for treatment of her narcotics addiction. Further, courts in cases since *Campbell* have increasingly acknowledged that the use of a person's image makes a strong case for legal protection under doctrines such as breach of confidence and (now) misuse of private information as well as passing off. So in *Weller v. Associated Newspapers Ltd*, where the claim was for misuse of private information, Dingemans J. referred to the personal character of a person's image in upholding the claim of misuse of private information with respect to publication of photographs of musician Paul Weller's children in the tabloid *Mail Online*[8] – and the claim was upheld on appeal albeit with less discussion of the aspect of image rights.[9] Further, in *Fenty v. Arcadia Group Brands Ltd.*, Birss J. held that the unauthorized use of a photograph of singer Rihanna Fenty taken at a private photo shoot for a music album on t-shirts sold in Topshop stores was passing off liable to confuse Rihanna fans, despite limited evidence of confusion from expert witnesses and none from Rihanna's fans – and again

[6] Campbell v. Mirror Group Newspapers Ltd. [2004] 2 A.C. 247. [7] *Id.* at [154].
[8] Weller & Ors. v. Associated Newspapers Ltd. [2014] EWHC 1163, [152] (Dingemans J.).
[9] Weller & Ors. v. Associated Newspapers Ltd. [2015] EWCA Civ. 1176 (Court of Appeal).

the Court of Appeal upheld Birss J's finding at first instance.[10] In both cases judges expressly disclaimed the existence of image rights as part of English law, citing Lord Hoffmann in *Douglas v. Hello!*.[11] But the fact that they felt the need to make such disclaimers further highlights the incongruity between the legal doctrines being employed and the decisions actually reached on the use of image in these cases.

Arguably, there is a certain Europeanization of English law at work here. Any other position from the English courts on image rights in cases such as *Douglas, Campbell, Weller,* and perhaps *Fenty* as well, would risk contravening the right to private life in Article 8 of the European Convention on Human Rights as interpreted by the European Court of Human Rights in cases including *Von Hannover v. Germany (No. 2)*[12] where it was stated that:

> [A] person's image constitutes one of the chief attributes of his or her personality, as it reveals the person's unique characteristics and distinguishes the person from his or her peers. The right to the protection of one's image is thus one of the essential components of personal development. It mainly presupposes the individual's right to control the use of that image, including the right to refuse publication thereof.[13]

On the other hand, the development need not simply be seen as a matter of human rights. In the U.S., using ostensibly economic reasoning, judges have moved to embrace a "right of publicity" focused on the unauthorized misappropriation in advertising of the commercial value in a person's name or likeness or other personal features. The statement of Frank J. in

[10] Fenty & Ors. v. Arcadia Group Brands Ltd. (T/A Topshop) & Anor. [2013] EWHC 2310 (High Court); Fenty & Ors. v. Arcadia Group Brands Ltd. & Anor. [2015] EWCA Civ. 3 (Court of Appeal).

[11] *Weller* [2014] EWHC 1163, [19] (Dingemans J.); *Fenty* [2013] EWHC 2310, [2] (Birss J.) (High Court); *Fenty* [2015] EWCA Civ. 3, [29]–[32] (Kitchin L.J.) (Underhill and Richards L.JJ. concurring) (Court of Appeal).

[12] Von Hannover v. Germany (No. 2), Eur. Ct. H.R. 228 (2012).

[13] *Id.* at [96]. *Cf.* Axel Springer A.G. v. Germany, Eur. Ct. H.R. 227, at 83 (2012) ("the right to private life includes . . . elements relating to a person's right to their image"). Note, however, the recent case of *Lillo-Stenberg and Sæther v. Norway*, Eur. Ct. H.R. 59 (2014) suggesting that claims around image rights may not always succeed: in that case the European Court held that the Norwegian court had appropriately balanced the article 8 and article 10 interests to conclude that *Se og Hor* was entitled to publish an article which included wedding photographs of the plaintiffs, a popular musician and actress, participating in a private wedding ceremony *inter alia* on the basis that the wedding took place outdoors in a public place and "there was an element of general interest in the article about the applicants' wedding," and bearing in mind the margin of appreciation given to national courts.

Haelan Laboratories v. Topps Chewing Gum, Inc.[14] that "many prominent persons . . . would feel sorely deprived if they no longer received money for authorizing advertisements, popularizing their countenances, displayed in newspapers, magazines, buses, trains and subways"[15] is an example of a judge adapting the law to regulate the market for bubble-gum cards featuring images of well-known sports figures, especially popular among young boys in the 1950s, so as to enable those who contribute creatively and personally to the success of the market to reap a reward.[16] In *Zacchini v. Scripps-Howard Broadcasting Co.*[17] the Supreme Court went further to accept that Ohio's right of publicity extended to a case where a television station showed the plaintiff's cannonball act on the evening news on the basis that the "activity by which the entertainer acquired his reputation in the first place" gives "the strongest case for a 'right of publicity'."[18] In Australia, where courts have been slower to move beyond the language of traditional doctrine, in *Pacific Dunlop Ltd. v. Hogan*,[19] Burchett J. accepted that the unauthorized use of a look-alike in a spoof on actor Paul Hogan aka Mick Dundee's "knife scene" in *Crocodile Dundee* to advertise shoes constituted passing off and misleading or deceptive conduct under the (then) *Trade Practices Act* 1974 (Cth), emphasizing the celebrity's distinctive fame as central to the finding of likely confusion – reasoning rather in the way of the English courts later on in *Fenty*.

These developments in the American and Australian cases were criticized at the time by some legal scholars who could see no good legal or policy reason to develop the law beyond the relatively narrow confines of the traditional intellectual property regimes to more or less embrace publicity rights – albeit less overtly and in a less developed way in the Australian compared to the U.S. cases.[20] But now that English courts are starting to move in the same direction with respect to image rights we can perhaps see a new orthodoxy emerging, and the interesting question is why plaintiffs and courts might be choosing to take this line.

[14] Haelan Laboratories, Inc. v. Topps Chewing Gum, Inc., 202 F.2d 866 (2d. Cir. 1953).
[15] *Id.* at 868.
[16] *See further* J. Gordon Hylton, *Baseball Cards and the Birth of the Right of Publicity: The Curious Case of* Haelan Laboratories v. Topps Chewing Gum, 12 Marq. Sports L. Rev. 273 (2001).
[17] Zacchini v. Scripps-Howard Broadcasting Co., 433 U.S. 562 (1977). [18] *Id.* at 576.
[19] Pacific Dunlop Ltd. v. Hogan (1989) 14 IPR 398 (Austl.).
[20] *See, e.g.*, Sam Ricketson, *Character Merchandising in Australia: Its Benefits and Burdens*, 1 Intell. Prop. J. 191 (1990); Hazel Carty, *Character Merchandising and the Limits of Passing Off*, 13 J. Legal Stud. 289 (1993); Michael Madow, *Private Ownership of Public Image: Popular Culture and Publicity Rights*, 81 Cal. L. Rev. 125 (1993).

II Arguments For and Against

There is a practical logic to treating the desires of plaintiffs to control the commercial use of their likeness or other manifestation of personality as the starting point for legal development. Plaintiffs in the cases we have been discussing often seem determined to go to lengths to protect themselves, even apart from their reliance on law, as for instance with the carefully guarded wedding party in *Douglas v. Hello!*, the secluded photo-shoot in *Fenty v. Arcadia Group Brands*, and the county fair in *Zacchini v. Scripps-Howard* where the plaintiff performed his cannonball act, with entry limited to paying customers only and the defendant's agent explicitly advised not to film the scene. The plaintiffs' arguments in their statement of claim in the *Hogan* case that they "intend[ed] to exploit their merchandising rights in the character"[21] can be seen as another exercise in self-help, marking out a sphere of "authentic" advertising in the use of the character's name and likeness – as the Australian Tourism Commission's "Come and Say G'day" campaign (with Hogan's classic "shrimp on the barbie" line) had already done.[22] These examples suggest that it cannot be assumed that without legal rights the information would simply be allowed to fall into the public domain, free for use by others. Rather, another possible outcome may be that greater efforts will be exerted in keeping the material in private hands.[23] That is, those engaged in crafting celebrity weddings, photo shoots, advertising campaigns, films and cannonball displays may not necessarily concede that the world should be allowed access to the material without their say, including for

[21] *Hogan in Legal Fight over Mick*, THE CANBERRA TIMES, Sept. 6, 1988, at 2.

[22] The success story of the advertisement in which Hogan featured as "spokesperson" for the Australian Tourism Industry is recounted by the director of the "Come and Say G'day" campaign, Bill Baker, together with Peggy Bendel in "*Come and Say G'Day!*", *Travel Marketing Decisions* (Association of Travel Marketing Executives) (2005).

[23] Although behavior can be hard to predict. For instance, in the Australian case of *Victoria Park Racing and Recreation Grounds Co. Ltd. v. Taylor* (1937) 58 CLR 479 (Austl.), where the High Court rejected the plaintiff's claim of an intellectual property right in the spectacle of races conducted on its race ground which could be viewed from a neighboring property used as a vantage point to place a person to report on the races for the defendant radio station, Latham C.J. said that "[i]f the plaintiff desires to prevent [the defendant overlooking the race ground], the plaintiff can erect a higher fence": *Id.* at 494. Instead, racing grounds and radio stations that wished to broadcast details of races negotiated terms: *see* Megan Richardson & Marc Trabsky, *Radio and the Technology of the Common Law in 1930s Australia – Victoria Park Racing v. Taylor Revisited*, 20 GRIFFITH L. REV. 1020 (2011). Our point nevertheless is that one possible outcome may be higher security "fences" – and this may consequently lead to negotiated terms of use in at least some cases.

quite slavishly commercial purposes. Their preference may rather be to employ ever-higher security measures to control unwanted publicity combined with more explicit public statements that the material is theirs and theirs alone (in the way of "beware false labels" advertisements employed at the beginning of the development of trade mark protection in America).[24] More "vulnerable" activities may even be cut back – for instance, large-scale celebrity wedding events, music videos involving outside photographers, live performances in diverse public locations – rather than concede control.

But the deeper and more important question is the value that plaintiffs are asserting and that courts are treating as the basis of intellectual property rights here in a *de facto* or *de jure* sense. As Barthes says, self-presentation "has a power to convert which *must* be analysed."[25] At minimum it may simply be the creative effort that celebrities – even more than the rest of us – exert in developing and projecting a strongly visually focused public persona of themselves. Such interests may be subject, of course, to other interests, especially where those interests involve an element of public commentary on celebrity and its characteristics. Nevertheless, in these cases of creative production of a public persona some minimal protection against commercial appropriation may be warranted. But the difficulty with making generalized responses is that the cases where rights have been successfully invoked seem to be extraordinarily variable, suggesting that more finely grained approaches are needed. In the discussion below we look at three cases that have helped frame intellectual property rights in image to explore their more particular aspects and broader implications.

III Three Cases

Case 1: "The Great Zacchini"[26]

Hugo Zacchini, the plaintiff in *Zacchini v. Scripps-Howard*, said that the act which he performed was "invented by his father and . . . performed

[24] *See* Megan Richardson & Julian Thomas, Fashioning Intellectual Property: Exhibition, Advertising and the Press, ch.11 (2012).

[25] Talking here specifically of the use of photographs by politicians seeking re-election: *see* Barthes, *supra* note 5, at 91 (emphasis added). But the proposition has more general significance.

[26] "[T]he great Zacchini is about the only human cannonball around, these days": trailer to broadcast of Zacchini's cannonball act on the Scripps-Howard television station WEWS-

only by his family for the last fifty years."[27] It was a modest statement of the social and cultural significance of a performance which involved three generations of an extended Italian family brought to America by Ringling Brothers in the late 1920s to display its cannonball techniques,[28] and became an integral part of the American circus tradition – a tradition variously described as "a quintessentially popular performance genre,"[29] "a kind of secular ritual,"[30] and from the turning of the twentieth century in America "an essential component of a burgeoning mass culture" which helped to "bring around [in turn] the development of twentieth-century mass culture forms like radio, television, and Disney's empire that capitalized on middle-class notions of propriety to produce virtuous entertainment for all classes."[31] Human cannonballs can be traced back to the nineteenth century, coming out of its great exhibitions of the arts and sciences, mass-public lectures and demonstrations, theatrical entertainments, and the ever-popular circuses featuring dare-devil human and animal displays.[32] But the Zacchini family members combined the engineering expertise and performance skills to turn their version into a national institution in its own right – fashioning themselves, to use the words of Eric Hobsbawm, as a "tradition" not in the sense of being constructed and formally instituted but rather as one "emerging in a less easily traceable manner within a brief and dateable period."[33] Their acts featured at the New York World Fair in 1939–40, were show-cased in

TV 11.00 evening news program, Aug. 31, 1972, quoted *Zacchini*, 433 U.S. 562, 564 (1977).

[27] *Id.* For an in-depth account of the facts, including that the Hugo Zacchini who featured in the case was the nephew of the more famous Hugo Zacchini who earlier in the century performed in tandem with his brother Edmondo, the younger Hugo Zacchini's father (and part of the second generation of the circus family headed by patriarch Ildebrando Zacchini), who is credited with inventing the canon used in Zacchini performances: see Lee Levine and Stephen Wermiel, *The Court and the Cannonball: An Inside Look*, 65 *Am. U.L. Rev.* 607 (2016).

[28] *See* John Kobler, *The Zacchinis: A Lively Italian-American Family Earns Living Being Shot from Cannons*, LIFE, Apr. 28, 1948, at 111.

[29] Eric Weitz, *Circus, Modern*, in THE OXFORD COMPANION TO THEATRE AND PERFORMANCE 119.2 (Dennis Kennedy ed., 2010).

[30] PAUL BOUISSAC, CIRCUS AS MULTIMODAL DISCOURSE: PERFORMANCE, MEANING AND RITUAL 23 (2012).

[31] JANET DAVIS, CIRCUS AGE: CULTURE AND SOCIETY UNDER THE AMERICAN BIG TOP 34 (2002).

[32] *See* Weitz, *supra* note 29, on the evolution of circuses in the nineteenth century.

[33] Eric Hobsbawm, *Introduction: Inventing Traditions*, in THE INVENTION OF TRADITION 1 (Eric Hobsbawm & Terence Ranger eds., 1983).

Irwin Allen's film *The Big Circus* in 1959,[34] could be seen at the greatest American circuses (including Ringling Brothers and Bertram Mills) as well as numerous lesser varieties tracking the length and breadth of the country for over fifty years around the country before the last of them (Hugo) retired in 1991, not all that long after the case was decided.[35] As historian Byron Rogers puts it, commenting on the dying art form in 2004, " . . . the history of the act is mainly the history of a single Italian family, the Zacchinis."[36]

Given that in this case the actual performance was recorded and shown to the public without Hugo Zacchini's authorization and contrary to his expressed wishes, it seems squarely to fit with the copyright rationale of an unauthorized broadcast of a dramatic work or cinematograph film, only in this instance having the unfixed and ephemeral character of a live performance – albeit a highly scripted one. The analogy with copyright is explicit in the Supreme Court's reasoning on the rationale for a publicity right in this case.[37] In the U.K. and Australia the approach is even more straightforward: the copyright statutes in both jurisdictions provide for a performer's right in a live performance as a protectable commodity and the latter is specifically defined in the Australian Act as including "a performance of a circus act" or "a performance of an expression of folklore."[38] Indeed both seem to apply in this case of a circus act elevated to a cultural tradition, as described above. Of course if this performance were treated as copyright, or analogous to copyright, we might expect that there would be the question of a copyright-style fair use defense (in the U.S.) or fair dealing defense (in the U.K. or Australia).[39] Query

[34] THE BIG CIRCUS (Allied Artists 1959), director: Joseph M. Newman; producer: Irwin Allen; screenplay: Irwin Allen, Charles Bennett and Irving Wallace; cinematography: Winton Hoch.

[35] *See* Bob Garfield, *The Human Cannonball Retires – or Perhaps Refires*, THE INQUIRER, June 8, 1987 (possible retirement already anticipated). In fact his last jump was in 1991: see Paul Guzzo, 'Hugo Zacchini, Who Wowed Crowds as Human Cannonball, Dead at 88', TAMPA BAY TIMES, November 10, 2016.

[36] BYRON ROGERS, THE LAST HUMAN CANNONBALL AND OTHER SMALL JOURNEYS IN SEARCH OF GREAT MEN (2004).

[37] Zacchini v. Scripps-Howard Broadcasting, 433 U.S. 562, 576–7 (1977).

[38] *See* Copyright Act 1968 (Cth.), § 248G (Austl.) (what constitutes unauthorized use) and § 248A (definition of "performance"); Copyright, Designs and Patents Act 1988, § 183 (Eng.) (infringement of performer's rights by use of recording made without consent) and § 180 (rights conferred on performers and persons having recording rights).

[39] Fair dealing defenses are provided for in the performer's rights provisions in the Australian and U.K. Acts: *see* Copyright Act 1968 (Cth.), § 248A (Austl.) ("exempt recording") and especially (f) and (fa) (news and criticism or review); Copyright, Designs and Patents Act 1988, § 189 (Eng.) (acts permitted notwithstanding rights conferred by this chapter) and Schedule 2, cl. 2 (criticism, reviews and news reporting).

however whether the principle of fair use or fair dealing would be available in a case where the entire performance is shown rather than a selected excerpt and little effort is made to engage the audience in any kind of critical or reflective analysis. As one Australian High Court judge said in an early case on fair dealing for news reporting purposes,[40] where publication is "merely a veneer, setting off what is essentially a publication of the plaintiff's document" this will not be privileged.[41] But the difficulty, as Douglas Baird points out, is that in *Zacchini* the analogy with copyright is not carried through to the issue of available defenses.[42] Rather the Supreme Court simply considered the issue as one of the availability or otherwise of the newsworthiness privilege that applies in privacy cases.[43] Moreover, the answer offered on the issue is not entirely clear. At one point the Court notes that "[t]he broadcast of a film of petitioner's entire act poses a substantial threat to the economic value of that performance,"[44] suggesting perhaps that it was the broadcast of the entire act that posed the particular threat. But elsewhere it is said that, because the plaintiff himself was prepared to show his act to any person prepared to pay the entrance fee, "neither the public nor respondent will be deprived of the benefit of the petitioner's performance as long as his commercial stake in his act is appropriately recognised,"[45] suggesting perhaps that a newsworthiness privilege can have no role where the plaintiff is prepared to display his performance to anyone prepared to pay the fee – even if many more people might prefer to view it on television (which offers also the benefit of an archival medium for dying art-forms in the way that live performance does not). If we read

[40] Commonwealth v. John Fairfax & Sons (1980) 147 CLR 39 (Austl.).

[41] *Id.* at 56. *Cf. Harper & Row, Publishers, Inc. v. Nation Enterprises*, 471 U.S. 539 (1984), concerning the Nation's unauthorized pre-publication of excerpts of former President Ford's diaries, where the fair use defense to copyright infringement fails. In particular, the Supreme Court agrees with the first instance judge's assessment that *Nation* "took what was essentially the heart of the book", and notes that, as to the fourth (and as it judged most important) fair use factor, in this case where *Time* magazine which had been planning an authorized pre-publication of excerpts cancelled the serialization, "[r]arely will a case of copyright infringement present such clear-cut evidence of actual damage": *id.* at 564–7.

[42] Douglas Baird, *Human Cannonballs and the First Amendment: Zacchini v. Scripps-Howard Broadcasting Co.*, 30 Stan. L. Rev 1185 (1978).

[43] In particular, the false light privacy case of *Time, Inc. v. Hill*, 385 U.S. 374 (1967), decided ten years earlier. This focus may have been due to the way the case was argued by the parties – the plaintiff having initiated the claim as one in privacy and it was only when the case came to court that it became refashioned as a case about the right of publicity: *see Zacchini v. Scripps-Howard Broadcasting Co*, 1975 Ohio App LEXIS 6700.

[44] Zacchini v. Scripps-Howard Broadcasting, 433 U.S. 562, 575 (1977).

[45] *Id.* at 578.

the decision in the second way the case seems to permit little scope for reformist social commentary or creative refashioning (including some archival uses) – with little credit given also to free speech as not merely an interest but also a right. On the other hand, courts after *Zacchini*, especially in recent years, have read the law in a more liberal way as allowing First Amendment inspired defenses for parody and other forms of commentary that can lead to cultural and social change, rather in the way of fair use.[46]

Case 2: "Paul Hogan is Crocodile Dundee"[47]

In one sense *Crocodile Dundee*[48] and its central character Mick Dundee aka Paul Hogan represent a play on a standard Australian (male) larrikin stereotype of humorously self-deprecating simplicity combined with a high degree of self-reliance and resilience even in unfamiliar environments.[49] But in another sense the character is a more particular stereotype created by Hogan through his television and advertising activities and reinforced as something more palatable than the narrower traditional reading of an Australian (male) larrikin as simply a lout or a hoodlum.[50] Already by the 1980s Hogan had perfected his entertaining

[46] *See* Hart v. Electronic Arts, Inc., 717 F.3d 141 (3d. Cir. 2013). Even the earlier much maligned case of *White v. Samsung Electronics Am*, 971 F.2d 1395 (9th Cir. 1992) does not necessarily preclude a parody defense – rather the court argued in that case that the defendant's advertisement which included a spoof of Vanna White and Wheel of Fortune treated this aspect as "subservient and only tangentially related to the ad's primary message: 'buy Samsung VCRs'" (although the court's suggestion that the distinction between a "knock-off" and parody comes down essentially to a distinction between commercial and noncommercial seems overly simplistic, especially in the light of the fine line that exists between amateur and commercial in the digital environment). And see generally David Tan, THE COMMERCIAL APPROPRIATION OF FAME: A CULTURAL ANALYSIS OF THE RIGHT OF PUBLICITY AND PASSING OFF (2017).

[47] "The publicity for the film opens with the sentence," as Sheppard J. notes in his dissenting judgment in the full Federal Court, adding "I think this is unquestionably correct": *Pacific Dunlop v. Hogan* (1989) 14 IPR 398, 409 (Austl.).

[48] CROCODILE DUNDEE (Paramount Pictures/Twentieth Century Fox 1986), director: Peter Faiman; producer: John Cornell; screenplay: John Cornell, Ken Shady, and Paul Hogan; story: Paul Hogan; cinematography: Russell Boyd.

[49] Or, as some have argued, perhaps this was an American stereotype (the film being directed primarily at American audiences): *see* Ruth Abbey & Jo Crawford, *Crocodile Dundee or Davey Crockett? What Crocodile Dundee Doesn't Say About Australia*, 46(2) MEANJIN 145 (1987).

[50] *See* MELISSA BELLANTA, LARRIKINS: A HISTORY (2012) – and further for a particular example of larrikin understood in the narrower critical sense (a "crafty, bullying black-guard"), Henry Furniss, *Sydney: "The Domain"*, 8 THE WINDSOR MAGAZINE 304 (1898).

persona of "Hoges" through the Australian Tourism Commission's "another shrimp on the barbie" advertisements and his presence in "The Paul Hogan Show."[51] So when it came to the film, as cinema historian Tom O'Regan says, Crocodile Dundee "was a concept extension and transformation which provided a seamless continuation of Hogan's television and advertising persona"[52] – one aspect of that extension being the love story in which he engaged with his costar (and eventual real-life wife) Linda Kowalski. At the same time as furnishing the film's key character, Hogan also featured as a coauthor of the screenplay as well as its star and he was extensively involved in promoting and publicizing the film as a private enterprise in a highly entrepreneurial way (employing a crowd-funding business model which was at the time quite novel in the Australian film environment), along with producer and long-time collaborator John Cornell.[53] So with all this personal creative investment it is not surprising that after the film's remarkable blockbuster success in both Australia and (especially) internationally Hogan would also feature as plaintiff along with Rimfire Films in the case against Pacific Dunlop, after its spoof advertisement of the film's famous "knife scene" featuring a look-alike Mick Dundee fan confronted by a would-be mugger outside the cinema post-film with his admiring girlfriend, displaying his prowess with his Grosby Leatherz shoes began to air on Australian television and in poster form.

The main focus of the evidence in the case, such as it existed, was on the parallels between Hogan's character and persona and those of his almost-avatar leading some "lay witnesses" at least to think the advertisement must have been – or surely should have been – authorized, although actually there were not many witnesses and their evidence was mixed.[54] On its face this was not a personality rights case at all. Rather, the reasoning of the judges was along conventional legal lines as a case about passing off (and more generally misleading or deceptive conduct under the Trade Practices Act 1974 (Cth)) and the minimal remedy of an appropriate disclaimer as to authorization was ordered instead of the usual injunction to stop the advertisement being shown in the future. But the limited evidence of likely confusion coupled with some judicial

[51] As Baker and Bendel note, Hogan was already an established television personality with his own identity at the beginning of the "Come and Say G'Day!" campaign: *see* Baker & Bendel, *supra* note 22.

[52] Tom O'Regan, Australian National Cinema 206 (1996). [53] *See id.*

[54] *See further* Megan Richardson, *Larger than Life in the Australian Cinema*, in Australian Landmarks in Intellectual Property 160 (Andrew Kenyon, Megan Richardson & Sam Ricketson eds., 2009).

language of "inveigl[ing] the emotions" as the key to understanding the confusion in this case,[55] reinforces the sense that the use of Hogan's *Crocodile Dundee* persona had everything to do with the result in the case.[56] In other words, albeit not explicitly, this was a case that responded to what Burchett J. termed "the still relatively new technology of television, and the even newer techniques of the exploitation of personality projected by that medium [at least in Australia in the 1980s]."[57]

Ironically, given that, as O'Regan says, what is on offer in *Crocodile Dundee* is "the image of self-deprecating capacity, both personally and nationally framed by 'our sense of humour',"[58] little credit seems to be given to the argument that the defendant was engaged in a humorous parody of the knife scene.[59] Part of the problem may be that the defendant's spoof was nowhere near as cleverly humorous as the original – as one of the lay witnesses pointed out.[60] Perhaps now there might be a broader understanding of what parody amounts to than when the case was decided. For instance, the knife scene's treatment as a cultural reference point in *The Simpsons* and *The Family Guy* suggests that parody, especially when aligned to pastiche, need not be especially critical (or even necessarily humorous although these ones were), provided there is some cultural referencing. This is an idea that is already starting to be acknowledged in the context of the U.S. fair use defense to copyright infringement,[61] and perhaps will also find its way into fair dealing

[55] Pacific Dunlop v. Hogan (1989) 14 IPR 398, 429 (Burchett J.) (Austl.).

[56] As Burchett J. puts it: "To ask whether the consumer reasons that Mr Hogan authorised the advertisements is . . . to ask a question which is merely a side issue, and far from the full impact of the advertisement. The consumer is moved by a desire to wear something belonging in some sense to Crocodile Dundee (who is perceived as a persona, almost an avatar, of Mr Hogan) . . . [But here] for the product sold by that advertisement really lacks the one feature the advertisement attributes to it" – namely "its association with himself", also identifying this kind of association as both a particular feature of "character merchandising" and of advertising on the particular visual medium of television: *id.*

[57] Id. at 429.

[58] Tom O'Regan, *Fair Dinkum Fillums: The Crocodile Dundee Phenomenon*, in THE IMAGINARY INDUSTRY: AUSTRALIAN FILM IN THE LATE '80S 155 (Elizabeth Jacka & Susan Dermody eds., 1988).

[59] Burchett J. dismisses this argument as "miscalling" the effect of an advertisement better described as a "parasitic copy" of an original performance that is itself a parody: Pacific Dunlop v. Hogan (1989) 14 IPR 398, 430 (Austl.).

[60] *Id.* at 406, Sheppard J. referring to the evidence of Mr. Jedlin as suggesting the advertisement should be viewed as "a travesty" rather than a parody.

[61] *Cf.* David Tan's helpful articulation of the (proper) cultural function of parody in U.S. copyright law: David Tan, *Taking the Mickey out of Disney: A Cultural Approach to the Transformative Use Doctrine in Copyright Law*, supra Chapter 7.

defenses where parody is one of the specified purposes, as in Australia.[62] A difficulty, however, is that as long as the idea is maintained in Australia that the basis of the legal action is misrepresentation rather than misappropriation, there may be little scope to argue for parody and other forms of humorous and/or critical response that might justifiably be grouped under the banner of free speech, except by saying that the audience would not be confused – a hard ask if confusion can so readily be established through "inveigling" the emotions. On the other hand, the possibility of a disclaimer remedy, as was granted in that case, seems to allow some scope for even confusing uses to continue (subject to the making of an appropriate disclaimer), although the possibility has not as yet been developed further in later cases.

Case 3: Rihanna, "style icon"[63]

Music critic Sasha Frere-Jones notes that "Rihanna [is] not a spectacularly gifted singer."[64] Yet she has carved out a career as a world famous pop star, topping charts with multiple hit songs, starring in numerous music videos, conducting an extensive endorsement program with Nike, Clinique, Gucci and River Island, as well as crafting a persona as a Barbadian ambassador, a domestic violence survivor, a role-model for teenage girls, and a sex symbol in fishnet tights. She is a "style leader" in fashion – as Birss J. noted in *Fenty v. Arcadia Brands*.[65] Fashion designer Tom Ford recently observed (rather despairingly) that "customers don't care anymore about reviews or hard-copy publications [of fashion]. They care what picture Rihanna just Instagrammed while she's naked in bed, what new shoes she has on, how she's talking about

[62] *See* Parts 1 and 2 of Condren et al.'s writings for supporting arguments: Conal Condren, Jessica Milner Davis, Sigrid McCausland, & Robert Phiddian, *Defining Parody and Satire: Australian Copyright Law and its New Exception – Part 1: Why US Law and Dictionaries are Unsound Sources*, 13(3) MEDIA & ARTS L. REV. 273 (2008); Conal Condren, Jessica Milner Davis, Sigrid McCausland, & Robert Phiddian, *Defining Parody and Satire: Australian Copyright Law and its New Exception – Part 2: Advancing Ordinary Definitions,* 13(4) MEDIA & ARTS L. REV. 401 (also arguing for a similar approach to the moral right of integrity under the Act).

[63] As Birss J. put it on behalf of Rihanna's fans, "she is their style icon": Fenty v. Arcadia Group Brands [2013] EWHC 2310 (High Court), [74].

[64] Sasha Frere-Jones, *Living on the Radio,* in BEST MUSIC WRITING 51 (Ann Powers ed., 2010).

[65] *Fenty* [2013] EWHC 2310 (High Court), [44].

them."[66] Even then, Ford apparently did not notice the role that Rihanna was already styling for herself as a fashion designer in her own right – designing her own line for River Island, contributing her own t-shirt to H&M's Fashion against AIDS clothing collection, and in her agreement with Gucci insisting that she exercise control over the garments she wore.[67] Rihanna's trajectory from a style icon to a creator of fashion is an intriguing reversal of the trajectory of earlier fashion designer turned Hollywood tastemaker and "it" girl,[68] Lucy Duff-Gordon, whose case involving her former agent left out of her arrangement to become a celebrity designer for the Sears catalogue was an important precursor to the American publicity right.[69]

Yet there was little open recognition of such matters when it came to resolving the legal dispute in the case, centered as it was on passing off, specifically through the sale of "fashion garments bearing [Rihanna's] image,"[70] understood in the fairly conventional sense of the action "[being] likely to deceive [relevant] members of the public into buying the product because they think it is authorised by her; [with the result that there is consequential] damage to her goodwill."[71] There is no reference here even to the possibility of inveigling the emotions, as for instance in the *Hogan* case. "Thinking", as described by Birss J., is presumably a rational activity permitting only certain types of evidence. For instance, one type of evidence not treated as greatly significant was that of Rihanna's creative director Ms. Pardo who said that "Rihanna was working hard to identify her as a serious fashion designer and items such as the t-shirt in issue [did] not support that role."[72] As Birss J. rightly pointed out, logically when it comes to passing off, construed in the way suggested above, the question of how "flattering" the t-shirt was, was not relevant – except perhaps to the point of whether the audience would

[66] *See* Tim Blanks, *It Has to be Renamed the Midlife Achievement Award*, STYLE.COM (May 27, 2014), www.style.com/trendsshopping/stylenotes/052714_CFDA_Tom_Ford/#page-1.

[67] Fenty v. Arcadia Group Brands [2013] EWHC 2310 (High Court), [41] and [42].

[68] JOSEPH ROACH, IT 22 (2007).

[69] As Cardozo J. famously begins his judgment in the case, "[t]he defendant styles herself 'a creator of fashions.' Her favor helps a sale. Manufacturers of dresses, millinery and like articles are glad to pay for a certificate of her approval": *Wood v. Lucy, Lady Duff-Gordon*, 222 N.Y. 88 (1917). The case is cited by Frank C.J. in *Haelan Laboratories*, above note 12, 868 as an early indicator of New York's right of publicity. See also Megan Richardson and David Tan, *Wood v. Duff-Gordon and the Modernist Cult of Personality*, 28 PACE L. REV. 379 (2008).

[70] Fenty v. Arcadia Group Brands [2015] EWCA Civ. 3 (Court of Appeal), [1] (Kitchin L.J.).

[71] Fenty v. Arcadia Group Brands [2013] EWHC 2310 (High Court), [3]. [72] *Id.* at [9].

have thought she had authorized it or not; and in any event he thought it was reasonably flattering even though Rihanna might have disagreed.[73] Yet the reasoning seems to side-step the point that for Rihanna, if styling herself as a fashion creator, the t-shirt's presentation was crucially important. Viewed from this perspective, it is easy to see that a t-shirt carrying a photograph of her disheveled and wearing a bralet from her role of down-at-heel young girl with her mad bad boyfriend in the music video for "We Found Love" would not fit with her ideal of fashion design.[74]

So what was the evidence that was treated as relevant and useful in this case? Interestingly, given that the central question in passing off was posited on the likelihood of public confusion, there was little evidence on this issue, even less than in the *Hogan* case (where at least some "lay" witnesses testified as to confusion). The matters that Birss J. did find legally relevant to the question of whether a relevant audience for the t-shirts would have thought Rihanna had authorized their sale included the fact that Topshop in the past had run a competition with Rihanna fans who could win a style competition, which was very popular,[75] and had also tweeted about her presence in the Oxford Street store, "ridiculously excited . . . Ah, wonder what she'll buy . . . "[76] In addition, reference was made to the fact that the image on the t-shirt was not just any image but rather an apparent publicity shot and "to [Rihanna's] fans who knew her work . . . this particular image might well be thought to be part of the marketing campaign for that project."[77] It is noteworthy that the judge characterized those participating in the Topshop shopping competition as including "a large number of very excited (presumably teenage and female) potential customers."[78] And there is also the

[73] *Id.* at [66].

[74] It is very different from other items designed by Rihanna including her t-shirt for the Clara Lionel Foundation launched at the Hard Rock Café in Paris in June 2014: *see* PR Newswire, *Hard Rock Partners With Rihanna On Limited-Edition Artist Spotlight Merchandise*, The Street (June 6, 2014), www.thestreet.com/story/12734802/2/hard-rock-partners-with-rihanna-on-limited-edition-artist-spotlight-merchandise.html.

[75] Fenty v. Arcadia Group Brands [2013] EWHC 2310 (High Court), [56].

[76] *Id.* at [57].

[77] *Id.* at [69]. Others might disagree with the judge's conclusion. For instance, Robert Furneaux blogged that "few fashion icons produce collections containing pretty basic t-shirts with photos of themselves on. [I]ndeed the River Island collection by Rhianna [sic] contains nothing like it. [I] just don't [sic] think TS customers would be confused in that way": Robert Furneaux, *Passing off – Fenty v. Topshop*, NIPC (Sept. 10, 2013), http://nipclaw.blogspot.com.au/2013/09/passing-off-fenty-v-topshop.html.

[78] *See* Fenty v. Arcadia Group Brands [2013] EWHC 2310 (High Court), [75] (Birss J.'s discussion of those participating in the 2010 Topshop shopping competition at [56]).

"ridiculously excited" language of Topshop itself. Such characterizations suggest that Rihanna's fan base was being imagined as a particularly excitable and youthful (and predominantly female) set of consumers. In the circumstances, it is not surprising that the prominent use of Rihanna's image on the t-shirts was seen as liable to confuse at least some of these fans. Indeed, in the Court of Appeal Underhill L.J. (with Richards L.J. concurring) made the interesting passing comment that of the reasons noted above that influenced Birss J. in finding passing off, "Rihanna's association with Topshop does not seem to me to have been such as to weigh very heavily in the balance."[79] In other words, although still not very weighty (in the view of Underhill L.J.), the decision as to passing off came down more to the "particular features of the image" appropriated by Topshop.

Still, it may be wondered what scope is left for situations where the conduct of the defendant is less one of slavish imitation. Again, the answer might come down to the weight put on the fact that this was a case of simple appropriation of an image created for display on the "We Found Love" video, making it possible for Birss J. to stress that "the relationship between this image and the images of Rihanna for the album and the video shoot would be noticed by her fans."[80] The language hints that had the defendant behaved in a more creative (or critical) way the conclusion in the case would not have been so straightforward. Perhaps the plaintiff as well would have been less likely to take the case to court if Topshop had behaved more creatively (although query if it had behaved critically), bearing in mind that – as Birss J. also noted – "the true relationship between celebrities and stores like Topshop is a symbiotic one."[81] As it was, Rihanna at least seemed prepared to wait until the t-shirts had sold out of stores in the United Kingdom before bringing her action.[82]

IV Concluding Comments

In this chapter our goal has not been to formulate a general argument as to the merits of intellectual property rights in image, although we think

[79] Fenty v. Arcadia Group Brands [2015] EWCA Civ. 3 (Court of Appeal), [63] (Kitchin L. J.).

[80] Fenty v. Arcadia Group Brands [2013] EWHC 2310 (High Court), [69]. [81] *Id.* at 60.

[82] *See* Fenty v. Arcadia Group Brands [2015] EWCA Civ. 3 (Court of Appeal) where the appellants were arguing that costs should not be awarded for this and other reasons – although the application was rejected.

a wider discussion around protecting image rights would be worthwhile, as well as appropriate limits and defenses. Such a discussion should account for the dynamic interplay between creators, commentators, and their audiences that makes "the . . . image the unique phenomenon that it is,"[83] especially as we move towards a more visual internet where this interplay involves a far greater range of activities and far wider group of creators, commentators, and audiences than previously encountered.[84] However, in the particular cases discussed in this chapter, we can see more specific arguments for legal protection as between the plaintiffs and defendants involved. At the same time, we can imagine alternative scenarios of more conciliatory plaintiffs, more creative defendants, and more active audiences engaging in conversations in which all accept that a person who has invested creative energy in developing a performance, character or talent and associating these with their personality should be able to exert some but not complete control over the exploitation of their creative possibilities. These imaginary scenarios help to make more sense of the cases under discussion. So, while sometimes law may seem to strongly protect the plaintiffs in these cases, there are also hints that defendants who creatively engage and adapt will not necessarily lose out entirely – although more still might be done as a matter of law to explicate those possibilities.

[83] Rosemary Coombe, The Cultural Life of Intellectual Properties: Authorship, Appropriation and the Law 94 (1998).

[84] Note already the interesting class action case of *Fraley v. Facebook, Inc.*, 830 F. Supp. 2d 785 (2011), where the publicity right claims brought by ordinary individuals who were nevertheless "local celebrities" to their Facebook friends, objecting to Facebook's use of their "likes" and images for sponsored story advertisements, were allowed to go forward to trial. The case was subsequently settled. And see Graeme Dinwoodie and Megan Richardson, *Publicity Right, Personality Right, or Just Confusion?* in Intellectual Property in Media and Entertainment 425 (Megan Richardson & Sam Ricketson eds., 2017).

7

Taking the Mickey out of Disney: A Cultural Approach to the Transformative Use Doctrine in Copyright Law

DAVID TAN*

This chapter argues that many works protected by copyright law are in fact cultural texts and semiotic signs that also possess significant sets of established meanings and connotations to members of the public who utilize these works in the process of social identity formation and democratic discourse. While copyright owners, especially multinational corporations like Disney, often disapprove of the unauthorized appropriation of their works for the purposes of parody and satire, it is submitted that such secondary uses clearly fall under the protection of the fair use exception. In particular, the Disney characters have become synonymous with a certain conservative, patriarchal, heterosexual ideology which has been associated with American cultural imperialism; many of Disney's texts thus present fertile opportunities for opposite or subversive readings that disrupt the hegemony of a hyperrealist utopian escapism. It is argued that copyright law has become increasingly open to recognizing countercultural recoding as a transformative use of the original work. This chapter examines the current scope of the transformative use doctrine in the first factor of fair use as codified in section 107 of the United States Copyright Act 1976 and postulates that a better understanding of the cultural impact of iconic works, and in particular their semiotic significance, can assist judges in evaluating transformative use in copyright law.

* I would like to acknowledge the invaluable research assistance of Benjamin Foo and Kenneth Wang Ye at NUS Law School.

I Introduction

Copyright law is often premised on the identification of an author of a literary, dramatic, musical or artistic work, and then giving this author exclusive rights for a limited period to control the commercial exploitation of his or her intellectual creation. However, the hegemonic position of the authorial text has been challenged by scholars like Roland Barthes, who argues that "a text's unity lies not in its origin but in its destination" and that "the birth of the reader must be at the cost of the death of the Author."[1] Barthes' work, controversial at the time of publication with its assault on modernity and the primacy of authorial control, has nonetheless laid the groundwork for an important body of scholarship on interpretive communities. Interdisciplinary legal writings, especially in the area of intellectual property and personality rights, have also actively engaged such themes in recent years.[2] For example, Nathaniel Noda contends that copyright law ought to "keep pace with changing times and practices by recognizing that an author implicitly cedes certain interpretive rights to the general public when he or she introduces a work into the stream of public discourse."[3]

While there is much debate over the extent of copyright protection given to fictional literary characters *outside* of the context of the works in which they appear, cartoon characters in meticulously drawn comic books usually have no problem being categorized as pictorial or graphic works[4] that fall within "the core of the copyright's protective purposes."[5] Mickey Mouse, Snow White, Sleeping Beauty and Superman are just some of the iconic characters from the last century that are universally recognized today and are each emblematic of a unique set of character values and semiotic significance, and have become "common points of reference for millions of individuals who may never interact with one another, but who share, by virtue of their participation in a mediated

[1] Roland Barthes, *The Death of the Author*, in IMAGE – MUSIC – TEXT 142, 148 (Roland Barthes ed., Stephen Heath trans., 1977).

[2] *See, e.g.*, David Tan, *Political Recoding of the Contemporary Celebrity and the First Amendment*, 2 HARV. J. SPORTS & ENT. L. 1 (2011); David Tan, *The Fame Monster Reloaded: The Contemporary Celebrity, Cultural Studies and Passing Off*, SING. J.L.S. 151 (2010); Justin Hughes, *"Recoding" Intellectual Property and Overlooked Audience Interests*, 77 TEX. L. REV. 923 (1999); Mark A. Lemley, *Romantic Authorship and the Rhetoric of Property*, 75 TEX. L. REV. 873 (1997).

[3] Nathaniel T. Noda, *Copyright Retold: How Interpretive Rights Foster Creativity and Justify Fan-Based Activities*, 57 J. COPYRIGHT SOC'Y U.S.A. 987, 991 (2010).

[4] U.S. Copyright Act 1976, 17 U.S.C. § 102(a)(5).

[5] Campbell v. Acuff-Rose Music Inc., 510 U.S. 569, 586 (1994) ('*Campbell*').

culture [as the audience], a common experience and a collective memory."[6] Along with the United Kingdom and Japan, China and Russia are now among the largest markets for Disney's movies.[7]

Making its debut on 15 May 1928 at a test screening to a theatre audience in the animated cartoon *Plane Crazy* as a daredevil pilot trying to emulate Charles Lindbergh, Mickey Mouse is perhaps the most successful cartoon character ever created. Within ten years, Disney biographer Bob Thomas notes, "Mickey Mouse was known in every civilized country in the world."[8] Since its creation, the Walt Disney Company has been fiercely protective of its intellectual property rights in Mickey Mouse. As Bob Levin observes in his historical account of the early years of the ascent of Mickey Mouse to global popularity,

> [the Disneys] were not particularly interested in recovering monetary damages, but they wanted to establish their copyright's strength and scope. They possessed a valuable property; they hoped to possess others; and they knew that, all over the world, people would try to steal a piece of their action. They could not stop every thief, but they could make a head-busting, knee-capping defense of their creations a basic part of their company's creed. They especially welcomed cases that would generate publicity and make them look ferocious and cold-hearted, for those cases would scare others off from even thinking about taking them on.[9]

In 1998, with Mickey Mouse on the precipice of falling into the public domain, after intense lobbying and many political donations from Disney, Congress passed the Sonny Bono Copyright Extension Act, stretching the terms of all existing and future copyrights by twenty years.[10]

Leading global brand consulting firm Interbrand positioned Disney at 13th place in its Best Global Brands 2015 rankings ahead of Nike, Louis

[6] JOHN B. THOMPSON, IDEOLOGY AND MODERN CULTURE: CRITICAL SOCIAL THEORY IN THE ERA OF MASS COMMUNICATION 163 (1990).

[7] Interbrand, *Disney – Best Global Brands 2014*, www.bestglobalbrands.com/2014/disney/.

[8] BOB LEVIN, THE PIRATES AND THE MOUSE: DISNEY'S WAR AGAINST THE COUNTERCULTURE 70 (2003).

[9] *Id.* at 71.

[10] For works created by identified natural persons, the term would last from creation until 70 years after the author's death: 17 U.S.C. § 302(a). For anonymous works, pseudonymous works, and works made for hire, the term would be 95 years from publication or 120 years from creation, whichever expires first: 17 U.S.C. § 302(c). This controversial legislative extension of the term of copyright survived a constitutional challenge all the way to the United States Supreme Court: *see* Eldred v. Ashcroft, 537 U.S. 186 (2003).

Vuitton and Facebook,[11] while Forbes ranked Disney at number 8 in The World's Most Valuable Brands List in 2016.[12] In an earlier report, Interbrand was of the view that:

> the [Disney] brand still has a unique ability to take a core idea, develop it through film and television, then extend the property into toys and merchandising, theme parks and resorts, DVD sales, and video games ... As long as Disney can continue to evolve how its core brand delivers against the ideas that have made it relevant for generations, the company will continue to be one of the world's most valuable entertainment and media powerhouses for the foreseeable future.[13]

Indeed the word "Disney" conjures up a fantasy world of cartoons, films, theme parks and toys. Its "appeal to pleasure and the 'child in all of us' is ... rooted in a history that encompasses the lives of many baby boomers" and Disney "invites adults to construct a new sense of agency founded on joy and happiness and to do so by actively participating in their own pleasure."[14]

This chapter argues that copyright law should be more receptive to a postmodern influence that recognizes countercultural recoding as a transformative use of the original work, and that copyright law which looks to the perception of the audience in the fair use analysis is on the right path. Section II briefly examines the current scope of the first factor of fair use as codified in section 107 of the United States Copyright Act 1976, and the prominence of the transformative use doctrine in fair use analysis. Section III explains how an understanding of semiotics and the notion of recoding may be useful to articulating a more nuanced fair use defense. Section IV explores the semiotic and cultural significance of Disney characters, and the recoding potential that they bring to a countercultural discourse that transcends national boundaries. Section V uses the seminal case of *Disney v. Air Pirates*, and a number of artistic works that appropriate Disney characters, to illustrate how the recoding of these characters is highly transformative in nature. Section VI concludes that the recoded use of Disney characters, especially in the

[11] Interbrand, *Best Global Brands 2015*, http://interbrand.com/best-brands/best-global-brands/2015/ranking/.

[12] Forbes, *The World's Most Valuable Brands* (May 2016), www.forbes.com/companies/walt-disney/.

[13] Interbrand, *Best Global Brands 2013*, www.interbrand.com/en/best-global-brands/2013/Disney.

[14] Henry A. Giroux, The Mouse That Roared: Disney and the End of Innocence 5 (1999).

artistic context of critical commentary on social identities, should qualify as fair use in contemporary copyright jurisprudence. These semiotic analyses of works of copyright as "signs" or "myths" that are coded with a set of widely accepted cultural meanings offer a helpful frame to view the transformative use doctrine, especially as articulated by the Second and Ninth Circuit Court of Appeals today: that an original work may be transformed if the audience reasonably perceives new information, new aesthetics, new insights and understandings.

II The "Transformative Use" Doctrine in Fair Use

The ultimate goal of copyright is arguably to benefit society by stimulating creativity through providing economic incentives to create new works.[15] However, without appropriate limitations, the grant of exclusive monopoly rights over exploitation of these works has the potential to impede, not advance, creativity. Hence the fair use/fair dealing doctrine is the primary mechanism that balances the "inherent tension" between copyright protection and creative expression.[16] It creates "breathing space for cultural engagement in the form of reinterpretation and remixing of copyrighted content . . . [and] makes it possible for large commercial entities to build tools such as search engines that make the internet work and to create platforms such as YouTube and Facebook".[17]

Courts and scholars in the United States have long grappled with the fair use doctrine.[18] In the United States, the "fair use" as codified in section 107 of the 1976 Copyright Act provides a legal escape for the defendant when faced with a copyright infringement action, especially if transformative elements may be discerned in the infringing work.[19] Under this provision, "fair use" is decided by balancing four statutory factors: (1) the purpose and character of the use, (2) the nature of the copyrighted work, (3) the amount and substantiality of the use (in relation to the copyrighted work), and (4) the effect of the use on the potential market for or value of the copyrighted work. Nothing in the Act specifies that these four factors should be considered of equal

[15] *E.g.* Sony Corp. of America v. Universal City Studios Inc., 464 U.S. 417, 429 (1984) ('*Sony*'); Twentieth Century Music Corp. v. Aiken, 422 U.S. 151, 156 (1975).

[16] *Campbell*, 510 U.S. at 575.

[17] Matthew Sag, Predicting Fair Use, 73 *Ohio St. L.J.* 47, 85 (2012).

[18] E.g. Barton Beebe, *An Empirical Study of U.S. Copyright Fair Use Opinions, 1978–2005*, 156 U. Pa. L. Rev. 549 (2008).

[19] Copyright Act 1976, 17 U.S.C. § 107. *See also Campbell*, 510 U.S. at 578.

weight, and neither should they be considered individually nor holistically. It appears that the fair use doctrine was designed for maximum flexibility to allow for a case-by-case analysis for the judiciary, and was able to accommodate a panoply of scenarios from literary criticism to parodic entertainment, from contemporary art to uses on digital and technological platforms.

The open-endedness of the fair use defense is both its virtue and vice. In his seminal 1990 article on fair use, Judge Pierre Leval ambitiously outlined a framework upon which fair use cases might be adjudicated.[20] Central to this framework is the notion of transformative use – where factor one is said to be "the soul of fair use" – which served as the philosophical basis for the U.S. Supreme Court's landmark decision on fair use four years later.[21]

In *Campbell v. Acuff-Rose Music*, the Supreme Court drew on Leval's framework, pronouncing that:

> The central purpose of this investigation is to see ... whether the new work merely "supersede[s] the objects" of the original creation, ("supplanting" the original), or instead adds something new, with a further purpose or different character, altering the first with new expression, meaning, or message; it asks, in other words, whether and to what extent the new work is "transformative." Although such transformative use is not absolutely necessary for a finding of fair use, the goal of copyright, to promote science and the arts, is generally furthered by the creation of transformative works. Such works thus lie at the heart of the fair use doctrine's guarantee of breathing space within the confines of copyright.[22]

More importantly, Justice Souter pointed out that "the more transformative the new work, the less will be the significance of other factors, like commercialism, that may weigh against a finding of fair use."[23] This holding has effectively created what is commonly known as the transformative use doctrine in fair use, where post-*Campbell*, a judicial finding of transformative use under the first factor will almost certainly result in a finding fair use. However, it has been observed that *Campbell* "in many ways established the basis for parody claims under fair use, and as a result conceptually tied up issues of transformation with issues of parody."[24] Parodies generally mock well-known and well-regarded people, texts or cultural icons in order to cause audiences to reevaluate

[20] Pierre N. Leval, *Toward a Fair Use Standard*, 103 Harv. L. Rev. 1105 (1990).

[21] *Id.* at 1116. [22] *Campbell*, 510 U.S. at 579. [23] *Id.*

[24] Darren Hudson Hick, *Appropriation and Transformation*, 23 Fordham Intell. Prop. Media & Ent. L.J. 1155, 1168 (2013).

them and reconsider the meanings they propound. By targeting the original literary or artistic work for ridicule or criticism, often accompanied by sarcastic humor, the parodist is seen to have *transformed* the purpose or character of the original work in order to achieve the intended parodic effect.

In respect of the first factor of fair use, the *Campbell* approach requires courts to examine the "purpose and character of the use"; the statute enumerates a nonexhaustive list of purposes "such as criticism, comment, news reporting, teaching (including multiple copies for classroom use), scholarship, or research," but "character" is not defined in the statute.[25] It is evident from the legislative provision that many works that qualify for fair use protection are not parodies, but some change in purpose or character vis-à-vis the original work should be present (i.e. transforming the original work). However, the *Campbell* court did not state that in order for a use to be transformative, it must always comment on the original. Souter J., writing for a unanimous court, explained that "[p]arody needs to mimic an original to make its point, and so has some claim to use the creation of its victim's (or collective victims') imagination, whereas satire can stand on its own two feet and so requires justification for the very act of borrowing."[26] Essentially, parodies need to reproduce the original work in order to poke fun at it, but it is not necessary for satires to reproduce an original work in order to make a humorous comment on society or human foibles. In a footnote, the court clarified that:

> *when there is little or no risk of market substitution*, whether *because of the large extent of transformation of the earlier work*, the new work's minimal distribution in the market, the small extent to which it borrows from an original, or other factors, *taking parodic aim at an original is a less critical factor in the analysis*, and looser forms of parody may be found to be fair use, as may satire with lesser justification for the borrowing than would otherwise be required.[27]

This suggests that the degree or extent of transformation is the salient feature of the first factor of fair use regardless of whether the secondary use is classified as a parody, satire or something else. The second factor is usually relevant only to distinguish between works of fact (compilation works meriting only thin copyright protection) and works that belong to the core of copyright (like literary, musical, dramatic, and artistic

[25] Copyright Act 1976, 17 U.S.C. § 107. [26] *Campbell*, 510 U.S. at 580–1.
[27] *Id.* at 581, footnote 14 (emphasis added).

works),[28] such that the more "creative" the original, the more this factor tends to weigh against a finding of fair use. In cases of parody, however, the original is usually a creative work, and, as such, given the potential cultural value of parody, this factor tends to be disregarded in parody cases. The third factor inquires what, and how much, of the original has been taken in a secondary work. Parodic works, by their very nature, typically require substantial copying in order for the audience to get the joke – thus usually copying the "heart" of the work. Courts, post-*Campbell*, have often given leeway in the amount copied for a parody that would be required to conjure up the original work.[29] For a parody to succeed, the audience must be able to recognize the original work that is the target of what is being mocked, and in the case of a graphical character like Mickey Mouse or Superman, this may nonetheless entail the reproduction of the entire character in order to conjure up the original without fulfilling the demand for the original.[30] For non-parodic works, for instance in the Google Books decisions, the courts are more circumspect on how much of the original had been taken.[31] Finally, the fourth factor examines the effect of the secondary use on the market value of the original. Under the *Campbell* framework, a transformative use is seen to have a different purpose and serve a different market from the original work. In the case of a parody, even if it devalues or suppresses sales of the original, it is nonetheless permissible.

28 *Campbell*, 510 U.S. at 586. *See generally* Feist Publications Inc. v. Rural Telephone Service Company Inc., 499 U.S. 340 (1991); Jane C. Ginsburg, *Creation and Commercial Value: Copyright Protection of Works of Information*, 90 Colum. L. Rev. 1865 (1990).

29 *E.g.* Blanch v. Koons, 467 F. 3d 244 (2nd Cir. 2006) ("*Koons*") (permitting Jeff Koons to use almost the entire photograph that first appeared in a fashion magazine); Suntrust Bank v. Houghton Mifflin Co., 268 F. 3d 1257 (11th Cir. 2001) (permitting Alice Randall to use the characters from the original *Gone with the Wind* novel).

30 *Contra* Walt Disney Productions v. The Air Pirates, 581 F. 2d 751, 757–8 (9th Cir. 1978) ("it is our view that defendants took more than is allowed even under the *Berlin* test as applied to both the conceptual and physical aspects of the characters . . . when persons are parodying a copyrighted work, the constraints of the existing precedent do not permit them to take as much of a component part as they need to make the 'best parody'.")

31 For example, the Second Circuit found the third factor to tilt in favor of fair use because of: (i) the fragmentary and scattered nature of the snippets; (ii) the small size of the snippets (normally one-eighth of a page); (iii) the blacklisting of one snippet per page and of one page in every ten; (iv) the fact that no more than three snippets are shown – and no more than one per page – for each term searched; and (v) the fact that the same snippets are shown for a searched term no matter how many times, or from how many different computers, the term is searched. Authors Guild Inc. v. Google Inc., 804 F. 3d 202, 222–3 (2nd Cir. 2015).

The transformation doctrine in the first factor of fair use is a difficult one to elucidate. The phrase "the purpose and character of the use, including whether such use is of a commercial nature or is for nonprofit educational purposes" suggests that (a) a change in the purpose of the secondary infringing work vis-à-vis the original work (e.g. from entertaining to educational) *or* a change in character (e.g. change in content, context or style) is transformative; (b) such changes should be considered in the light of the commerciality of the secondary infringing work, although this examination overlaps with the fourth factor on market impact; (c) whether the secondary infringing work serves a commercial or nonprofit purpose is a separate consideration from "purpose and character of the use." Courts do not usually observe a strict distinction between "purpose" and "character," preferring to assess whether the secondary work was sufficiently transformative according to the guidelines laid down by the Supreme Court in *Campbell*.[32] Thomas Cotter takes issue with the "slipperiness" of the word "purpose," and contends that "if the word 'purpose' is defined at a sufficiently abstract level, both novel and movie [that is a derivative of the novel] do indeed serve the same purpose of enabling audiences to consume the work."[33] Cotter points out that "derivative merchandise such as toys and costumes based on a fictional character . . . transform the original from one medium to another and represent the original in the sense of symbolizing it. At the same time, however, they also transform the purpose of the original from passive consumption to active play. Describing both original and derivative as broadly fulfilling a common purpose of, say, entertainment renders the word 'purpose' virtually meaningless."[34] Anthony Reese, in his review of all the U.S. appellate court decisions from *Campbell* up to 2007, concludes that a finding of transformative purpose correlates reasonably well with a finding of fair use, regardless of whether there has been a transformation of content.[35] However, a transformation

[32] I have undertaken a comprehensive analysis of the possible meanings of 'transformative use' in another article. *See* David Tan, *The Transformative Use Doctrine and Fair Dealing in Singapore: Understanding the "Purpose and Character" of Appropriation Art*, 24 S. Ac. L.J. 832 (2012). *See also* Matthew D. Bunker & Clay Calvert, *The Jurisprudence of Transformation: Intellectual Incoherence and Doctrinal Murkiness Twenty Years after Campbell v. Acuff-Rose Music*, 12 Duke L.J. 72 (2014).

[33] Thomas F. Cotter, *Transformative Use and Cognizable Harm*, 12 Vand. J. Ent. & Tech. L. 701, 718 (2010).

[34] *Id.*

[35] R. Anthony Reese, *Transformativeness and the Derivative Work Right*, 31 Colum. J.L. & Arts 467, 485–94 (2008). *See also* Neil Netanel, *Making Sense of Fair Use*, 15 Lewis &

of content without a transformative purpose correlates with a finding of liability.[36] As Reese notes, the case law still leaves open many perplexing questions, among them how the courts should determine the defendant's purpose; whether the inquiry should focus on objective or subjective purpose; how to proceed when the user has multiple purposes; and whether a transformative purpose is merely a purpose different from the purpose of the original author, or something more.[37]

In the last decade, a number of decisions involving fair use of thumbnail images and book snippets published on the internet have introduced even greater confusion to the transformative use doctrine. Landmark decisions from the Ninth Circuit like *Kelly v. Arriba Soft Corp.*[38] and *Perfect 10 v. Amazon.com,*[39] and from the Second Circuit in *Authors Guild v. Google,*[40] have relied on the fact that such services have immense public benefits and would permit others to utilize these protected works to advance the progress of the useful arts and sciences. The judicial classification of such infringing uses in the Google Books case as "transformative" even though there is no change in content – in fact an identical reproduction of the original work – signifies a growing willingness on the part of U.S. courts to evaluate the public benefit of a secondary use, and then perhaps *ex post facto* rationalize that such uses are highly transformative in nature. In such cases, the invocation of the fair use doctrine may be justified on the premise that the positive externalities to the public flowing from the infringing use are likely to outweigh the economic harm to the copyright owner with a resulting significant enhancement of social welfare. It is, however, beyond the scope of this chapter to analyze how these decisions involving the application of the transformative doctrine in the context of digital technology may be reconciled with the parody and appropriation art cases. It suffices to note that the lack of cognizable market harm to the copyright owners in the Google cases appears to be a relevant consideration for the courts even after a finding of

CLARK L. REV. 715, 770 (2011) ("transformative purpose is almost universally a sufficient condition for fair use").

[36] Reese, *supra* note 35. [37] *Id.* at 494–5. *See also* Cotter, *supra* note 33, at 719–20.

[38] Kelly v. Arriba Soft Corp., 336 F. 3d 811 (9th Cir. 2003).

[39] Perfect 10 Inc. v. Amazon.com Inc., 508 F. 3d 1146 (9th Cir. 2007).

[40] Authors Guild Inc. v. Google Inc., 804 F. 3d 202 (2nd Cir. 2015) affirming 954 F. Supp. 2d 282 (S.D.N.Y., 2013) ("Google Books case") (it was held that Google engaged in fair use in digitally reproducing millions of copyrighted books, making them available for its library project partners to download, and displaying "snippets" from the books to the public).

transformativeness.[41] The notion of cognizable harm was also highlighted in *Campbell*,[42] where Souter J., delivering the opinion of the unanimous Supreme Court, noted:

> We do not, of course, suggest that a parody may not harm the market at all, but when a lethal parody, like a scathing theater review, kills demand for the original, it does not produce a harm cognizable under the Copyright Act. Because parody may quite legitimately aim at garroting the original, destroying it commercially as well as artistically, the role of the courts is to distinguish between biting criticism that merely suppresses demand and copyright infringement which usurps it.[43]

Nevertheless, the concept remains largely underappreciated in U.S. copyright jurisprudence,[44] as courts presume that there is usually no cognizable harm to the copyright owner if the infringing work was transformative in nature as a transformative work would appeal to a different market from that of an original work or its derivative works.[45]

Both Barton Beebe's pioneering empirical study of fair use decisions in the United States which covered judicial opinions from 1978 to 2005[46]

[41] *E.g.* Authors Guild Inc. v. Google Inc., 954 F. Supp. 2d 282, 292–3 (S.D.N.Y. 2013). Chin J. was of the view that "a reasonable factfinder could only find that Google Books enhances the sales of books to the benefit of copyright holders . . . In this day and age of on-line shopping, there can be no doubt but that Google Books improves books sales." *Id.* at 293. The Second Circuit also noted: "we see no reason in this case why Google's overall profit motivation should prevail as a reason for denying fair use over its highly convincing transformative purpose, together with the absence of significant substitutive competition, as reasons for granting fair use." Authors Guild Inc. v. Google Inc., 804 F. 3d 202, 221 (2nd Cir. 2015).

[42] *Campbell*, 510 U.S. at 593 ("Evidence of substantial harm to it would weigh against a finding of fair use").

[43] *Campbell*, 510 U.S. at 591–2 (internal citations and quotations omitted). Jane Ginsburg notes that a more cynical observation could say that "having determined that a use should not be ruled infringing, courts may announce that its 'transformativeness' precludes cognizable potential market harm." Jane C. Ginsburg, *Copyright 1992–2012: The Most Significant Development?*, 23 Fordham Intell. Prop. Media & Ent. L.J. 465, 491 (2013).

[44] Cotter, *supra* note 33, at 725–6.

[45] The Second Circuit has even coined the phrase "transformative market" to signify an exploitation that falls outside the copyright owner's zone of exclusivity. *See* Bill Graham Archives v. *Dorling Kindersley Ltd*, 448 F. 3d 605, 614–15 (2nd Cir. 2006) ('*Bill Graham Archives*'). On the contrary, Cotter argues that "the question of whether the use at issue threatens cognizable harm should be the most important aspect of the fair use analysis, and that transformative use should play only a subsidiary role." Cotter, *supra* note 33, at 736.

[46] Beebe, *supra* note 18.

and Matthew Sag's statistical analysis, which focused on the ex ante predictability of fair use based on 280 fair use cases decided between 1978 and 2011,[47] affirm the important role that transformative use – a judicial inquiry in the first statutory factor of the fair use inquiry when examining the 'the purpose and character of the use' – plays in the evaluation of fair use. Beebe observes that "in those opinions in which transformativeness did play a role, it exerted nearly dispositive force not simply on the outcome of factor one but on the overall outcome of the fair use test. More specifically, the data suggest that while a finding of transformativeness is not necessary to trigger an overall finding of fair use, it is sufficient to do so."[48] While courts have not demonstrated an overriding desire to find transformativeness in the cases before them, Beebe concludes that based on the regression analysis, if a use were found to be transformative, the defendant's chance of winning the fair use defense would be 94.9 percent.[49] Sag more confidently asserts that the evidence "confirms the centrality of transformative use" and when "[m] easured in terms of the variable Creativity Shift, it appears that transformative use by the defendant is a robust predictor of a finding of fair use."[50] Last but not least, Jane Ginsburg, in her review of the most significant developments in copyright law in the period 1992–2012, concludes that the last twenty years have marked the "extraordinary expansion" of the fair use doctrine, and, in particular, the concept of transformative use, with recent cases demonstrating a shift from focusing on finding a "transformative work" to discovering a "transformative purpose."[51]

The transformation use doctrine as articulated by the influential Second Circuit Court of Appeals in *Blanch v. Koons* is succinctly stated as: If "the secondary use adds value to the original – if [copyrightable expression in the original work] is used as raw material, transformed in the creation of new information, new aesthetics, new insights and understandings – this is the very type of activity that the fair use doctrine intends to protect for the enrichment of society."[52] The Second Circuit did not require the secondary work to comment on the original work or on the original author/

[47] Sag, *supra* note 17. [48] Beebe, *supra* note 18, at 605. [49] *Id.* at 606.
[50] Sag, *supra* note 17, at 84. [51] Ginsburg, *supra* note 43, at 487–9.
[52] *Koons*, 467 F. 3d (2nd Cir. 2006), at 251–2 (quoting *Castle Rock Entertainment Inc. v. Carol Publishing Group Inc.*, 150 F. 3d 132, 142 (2nd Cir. 1998)) (quoting Pierre N. Leval, *Toward a Fair Use Standard*, 103 HARV. L. REV. 1105, 1111 (1990)) (internal quotations omitted).

artist. Given the "distinct creative or communicative objectives"[53] of Jeff Koons and Andreas Blanch, the court held that Koons' use was transformative regardless of whether *Niagara* commented critically in any substantive way on Blanch's original photograph. Similarly, in *Cariou v. Prince*, the Second Circuit in 2013 reaffirmed *Koons* and held that the law "imposes no requirement that a work comment on the original or its author in order to be considered transformative, and a secondary work may constitute a fair use even if it serves some purpose other than those (criticism, comment, news reporting, teaching, scholarship, and research) identified in the preamble to the [Copyright Act]."[54] The notion of transformative recoding as ultimately perceived by the audience prominently figures in Parker J.'s holding:[55]

> What is critical is how the work in question appears to the reasonable observer, not simply what an artist might say about a particular piece or body of work. Prince's work could be transformative even without commenting on Cariou's work or on culture, and even without Prince's stated intention to do so. Rather than confining our inquiry to Prince's explanations of his artworks, we instead examine how the artworks may "reasonably be perceived" in order to assess their transformative nature.

In summary, Second Circuit courts have considered a broader examination of transformation that does not require the presence of comment so long as the purpose in using the original work is "plainly different from the original purpose for which it was created"[56] and have "given weight to an artist's own explanation of their creative

[53] *Koons*, 467 F. 3d at 253 (2nd Cir. 2006).

[54] Cariou v. Prince, 714 F. 3d 694, 706 (2nd Cir. 2013) ('*Prince*'). Note, however, a recent decision of the Seventh Circuit was less enamored of this approach. *See* Kienitz v. Sconnie Nation LLC, 766 F. 3d 756, 758 (7th Cir. 2014) ("We're skeptical of *Cariou*'s approach, because asking exclusively whether something is "transformative" not only replaces the list in § 107 but also could override 17 U.S.C. § 106(2), which protects derivative works.").

[55] *Prince*, 714 F. 3d at 707 (2nd Cir. 2013). The Ninth Circuit has also applied this new standard: Seltzer v. Green Day Inc., 729 F. 3d 1170, 1176–8 (9th Cir. 2013) ('*Seltzer*').

[56] *Bill Graham Archives*, 448 F. 3d at 609 (2nd Cir. 2006); *Koons*, 467 F. 3d at 252–3 (2nd Cir. 2006). In a decision handed down in October 2016 concerning the use of the famous Abbott and Costello comedic routine *Who's On First?* in the Broadway play *Hand To God*, the Second Circuit was of the view that the play "may convey a dark critique of society, but it does not transform Abbott and Costello's Routine so that *it* conveys that message." Essentially, there was nothing transformative in using the original work in the same humorous manner in which it was created to be used. TCA Television Corp. v. McCollum, 839 F. 3d 168, 181 (2nd Cir. 2016) (emphasis in original).

rationale when conducting the fair use analysis."[57] The Ninth Circuit has also rejected a narrow requirement of commenting or criticizing the original work in order to qualify as transformative use.[58] One should note that not all fair use claims based on transformativeness are exposed to a dichotomous choice; courts have recognized degrees of transformativeness – some uses are highly transformative, others are less so.[59] As the Supreme Court has exhorted in *Campbell*, "the more transformative the new work, the less will be the significance of other factors, like commercialism, that may weigh against a finding of fair use."[60] Since *Campbell*, the "transformativeness reasoning gradually rose to become the most important principle in interpreting fair use among judges . . . [and] became a central principle by which ordinary people could interpret fair use".[61] Michael Murray's empirical study concluded that even if original works were not changed in form, function or genre, the fair use works were transformed through an alteration of the contents, recontextualization of the copied material or addition of significant creative expression so that the predominant purpose of the new work was significantly different from the original work.[62] If one accepts that the infringing work is capable of repurposing or recharacterizing the original work to create "new information, new aesthetics, new insights and understandings,"[63] then the application of the transformative use doctrine becomes a more useful evaluative concept to

[57] *Koons*, 467 F. 3d at 255 (2nd Cir. 2006).

[58] Perfect 10 Inc. v. Amazon.com Inc., 508 F. 3d 1146, 1165 (9th Cir. 2007) ("*Perfect 10*") (a search engine puts images "in a different context" so that they are "transformed into a new creation"); Kelly v. Arriba Soft Corp., 336 F. 3d 811, 819 (9th Cir. 2003) ("*Kelly*") (Arriba's use of thumbnails was transformative because "Arriba's use of the images serve[d] a different function than Kelly's use – improving access to information on the internet versus artistic expression").

[59] Note the fair use analysis of the Ninth Circuit of the different uses of a video clip, each use being of a different degree of transformativeness. The court noted that: "[T]he opening montage was the more 'transformative' of the allegedly infringing uses, which in turn reduced the importance of the commerciality of the use. By contrast, the use of the clip in the coverage teasers was less transformative, meaning that a commercial purpose would take on greater weight." Los Angeles News Services v. CBS Broadcasting Inc., 305 F. 3d 924, 940 (9th Cir. 2002).

[60] *Campbell*, 510 U.S. at 579.

[61] Patricia Aufderheide & Peter Jaszi, Reclaiming Fair Use: How to Put Balance Back in Copyright 85 (2011) (internal citations omitted).

[62] Michael D. Murray, *What is Transformative? An Explanatory Synthesis of the Convergence of Transformation and Predominant Purpose in Copyright Fair Use Law*, 11 Chi.-Kent. J. Intell. Prop. 260, 291 (2012).

[63] *Koons*, 467 F. 3d at 252; *Seltzer*, 729 F. 3d at 1177.

determine how transformation may legitimately occur through a change of meaning as reasonably perceived by the audience to which the infringing work is directed.[64]

III Recoding of Signs and Fair Use

Contemporary cultural studies are concerned with the practices of popular culture, the relationships between audiences and producers, the formation of identity, and the nature of consumption. Scholars often adopt a multi-perspectival approach that blends together ideas from different theoretical disciplines including semiotics, gender and race studies, literary theory, sociology, consumer studies, and postmodernism. Cultural perspectives on law are a growing part of contemporary legal scholarship, paralleling the emergence of cultural studies as an academic discipline. For example, Barton Beebe, in his seminal works on a semiotic account of trademark doctrine,[65] has persuasively demonstrated that "semiotic concepts can be applied to clarify and ameliorate fundamental areas of trademark doctrine and policy."[66] His analysis of "sign value" as a "Saussurean structural value" that involves a "conspicuous display of distinctions, of 'marginal differences'"[67] has a parallel relevance to well-known literary, dramatic, musical and artistic works. I have previously also interrogated the potential influence of semiotics on a First Amendment approach to copyright fair use.[68]

Umberto Eco describes semiotics as a social science discipline that studies "everything that can be taken as a sign."[69] A sign is simply a thing that stands for something else. Although it has its origins in the study of language, semiotic analysis is a trans-linguistic activity[70] that can be applied to the inquiry of "[a system] of structural codes . . .

64 *See also* Tan, *supra* note 32, at 851. *See also* Peter Jaszi, *Fair Use and Education: The Way Forward*, 25 LAW & LIT. 33, 42 (2013) ("the recontextualization and repurposing of the quoted material made all the difference").

65 *E.g.* Barton Beebe, *The Semiotic Account of Trademark Doctrine and Trademark Culture*, in TRADEMARK LAW AND THEORY: A HANDBOOK OF CONTEMPORARY RESEARCH 42 (Graeme B. Dinwoodie & Mark D. Janis eds., 2008) ('*Semiotic Account*'); Barton Beebe, *The Semiotic Analysis of Trademark Law*, 51 UCLA L. REV. 621 (2004).

66 Beebe, *Semiotic Account*, *supra* note 65, at 42. 67 *Id.* at 62.

68 David Tan, *The Lost Language of the First Amendment in Copyright Fair Use: A Semiotic Perspective of the "Transformative Use" Doctrine Twenty-Five Years On*, 26 FORDHAM INTELL. PROP. MEDIA & ENT. L.J. 311 (2016).

69 UMBERTO ECO, THE THEORY OF SIGNS 7 (1979).

70 ROLAND BARTHES, ELEMENTS OF SEMIOLOGY 11 (Annette Lavers & Colin Smith trans., 2000) (1964).

that engages with culture, consumption, and communication in the marketplace."[71] The Swiss linguist Ferdinand de Saussure, widely credited as the most influential scholar in the field of semiotics, emphasized the nature of the sign as the coded association of a material *signifier*, such as the sound of a word, with a *signified* or preconceived meaning.[72] In his oft-cited work on the semiotic analyses of consumer cultures, *Mythologies*, Roland Barthes explains that "any semiology postulates a relation between two terms, a signifier and a signified"[73] and that a sign "is the associative total of the first two terms."[74] A well-known literary or artistic work does much more than simply educate, inform or entertain, but it also functions as a *signifier* of a set of *signified* meanings. The representative fictional characters from the works – for example, Mickey Mouse, Snow White and Sleeping Beauty from the canonical universe of Disney's works – may function as signifiers of both individualized and a shared set of meanings. A "myth" is thereby created when meaning within a semiological system is transformed into form as represented by a sign;[75] each sign becomes naturally associated with a set of meanings or "historical intention"[76] which is ultimately consumed. Like famous trademarks, the copyrighted character signifier/signified relationship would have become universally codified for the audience; the audience will automatically and consistently think of the coded meanings and values (the signified) when they are exposed to the character signifiers. In other words, the fictional character becomes a sign for a predetermined set of cultural codes and audience experiences associated with the work or the author of the work.[77]

Referring to Barthes' work on modern myths,[78] Stuart Hall discusses the politics of signification[79] and how ideological discourses of

[71] LAURA R. OSWALD, MARKETING SEMIOTICS: SIGNS, STRATEGIES, AND BRAND VALUES 47 (2012).

[72] *See generally* FERDINAND DE SAUSURRE, THE COURSE IN GENERAL LINGUISTICS (COURS DE LINIGUISTIQUE GÉNÉRALE) (Roy Harris trans., 1983) (1916).

[73] ROLAND BARTHES, MYTHOLOGIES 111 (Annette Lavers trans., 1972) (1957). [74] *Id.*

[75] *Id.* at 131. [76] *Id.* at 142.

[77] *See generally* David Tan, *The Semiotics of Alpha Brands: Encoding/Decoding/Recoding/Transcoding of Louis Vuitton and Implications for Trademark Laws*, 32 CARDOZO ARTS & ENT. L.J. 221, 227 (2013).

[78] ROLAND BARTHES, MYTHOLOGIES, *supra* note 73.

[79] Stuart Hall, *The Rediscovery of "Ideology": Return of the Repressed in Media Studies*, in CULTURE, SOCIETY AND THE MEDIA 56, 70–4 (Michael Gurevitch, Tony Bennett, James Curran, & Janet Woollacott eds., 1982).

a particular society are classified and framed through semiotic signs.[80] Like Barthesian myths, cartoon characters such as Mickey Mouse and Snow White, well-known superhero characters such as Superman, Captain America and Wonder Woman, as well as fictional characters from popular television series like Star Trek, contain subject positions and models for identification that are heavily coded ideologically.[81] In particular, Eleanor Byrne and Martin McQuillan argue that the "Disney [text] has become synonymous with a certain conservative, patriarchal, heterosexual ideology which is loosely associated with American cultural imperialism";[82] the canon of Disney films has been said to "open themselves onto the entire history of the West and act as a symptomatic concentration of all the ideological contests which are currently being fought in our world today."[83] Indeed many of Disney's texts present fertile opportunities for opposite or subversive readings that disrupt the hegemony of a hyperrealist utopian escapism. In terms of recoding, scholars like John Fiske have emphasized the potential of audience reconstruction of dominant symbols of a culture. Fiske coined the term "semiotic democracy" to describe a world where empowered audiences freely and widely engage in the use of cultural symbols to express meanings that are different from the ones intended by their creators.[84]

The writings of Rosemary Coombe[85] and Michael Warner[86] on subaltern groups and counterpublics have approached the constitution and politics of social and individual identity as being predicated on a power struggle between dominant and subordinate groups. The term

[80] *Id.* at 74. *See also* David Tan, *Harry Potter and the Transformation Wand: Fair Use, Canonicity and Fan Activity*, in AMATEUR MEDIA: SOCIAL, CULTURAL AND LEGAL PERSPECTIVES 94 (Dan Hunter, Ramon Lobato, Megan Richardson, & Julian Thomas eds., 2012).

[81] *See generally* David Tan, *The Transformative Potential of Countercultural Recoding in Copyright Law: A Study of Superheroes and Fair Use*, in DIVERSITY IN INTELLECTUAL PROPERTY: IDENTITIES, INTERESTS AND INTERSECTIONS 403 (Irene Calboli & Srividhya Ragavan eds., 2015).

[82] ELEANOR BYRNE & MARTIN MCQUILLAN, DECONSTRUCTING DISNEY 1–2 (1999). *See also* GIROUX, *supra* note 14, at 30–2.

[83] BYRNE & MCQUILLAN, *supra* note 82, at 168.

[84] JOHN FISKE, TELEVISION CULTURE 239 (1987). *See also* Sonia K. Katyal, *Semiotic Disobedience*, 84 WASH. U. L. REV. 489, 489–90 (2006); Michael Madow, *Private Ownership of Public Image: Popular Culture and Publicity Rights*, 81 CAL. L. REV. 127, 139 (1993).

[85] ROSEMARY J. COOMBE, THE CULTURAL LIFE OF INTELLECTUAL PROPERTIES: AUTHORSHIP, APPROPRIATION, AND THE LAW (1998).

[86] MICHAEL WARNER, PUBLICS AND COUNTERPUBLICS (2002).

"subaltern" or "subculture" is frequently used in cultural studies to denote the subordination of particular identities by a dominant ideological hegemony; the "subaltern's place [in society] is subsumed within . . . an experience of oppression which privileges particular exemplars as the 'proper' figures of identity."[87] Warner's analysis of the struggles that bring individuals together as a public postulates that "subaltern counterpublics" usually articulate alternative power relations with the dominant public defined by race, gender, sexual orientation, and other subordinated status.[88] According to Warner, a counterpublic maintains "an awareness of its subordinate status . . . [with respect] not just to ideas or policy questions but to the speech genres and mode of address that constitute the public".[89]

Hall has also defined the taking of an existing meaning and reappropriating it for new meanings as "trans-coding,"[90] and explained that repressed groups may use trans-coding strategies to reverse stereotypes, substitute negative portrayals with positive ones or contest subordinate representations from within.[91] This notion of recoding is arguably applicable to the transformation doctrine in the fair use defense of copyright law. In copyright fair use, the pertinent inquiry is whether the secondary work "adds something new, with a further purpose or different character, altering the first with new expression, meaning, or message";[92] many trans-coding practices, especially in appropriation art, can be said to be "transformative" under the fair use doctrine.[93] A countercultural or counterpublic agenda may be best communicated to mainstream society through the use of widely recognized semiotic signs to which members of the public have ascribed particular representative values or characteristics. In the area of copyright, parodies, satires, fan fiction, and appropriation art are the best examples of trans-coding practices where an irreverent portrayal of an iconic literary, dramatic, musical, or artistic

[87] *Id.* at 92. [88] *Id.* at 44–63, 117–20. [89] *Id.* at 119.

[90] Stuart Hall, *The Spectacle of the "Other"*, in REPRESENTATION: CULTURAL REPRESENTATIONS AND SIGNIFYING PRACTICES 223, 270 (Stuart Hall ed., 1997). The term 'transfunctionalize' has also been used to describe how subcultures assign new and often contradictory meanings to signs as understood by mainstream society. PAUL NATHANSON, OVER THE RAINBOW: THE WIZARD OF OZ AS A SECULAR MYTH OF AMERICA 241 (1991).

[91] Hall, *supra* note 90, at 270–5. [92] *Campbell*, 510 U.S. at 579.

[93] *See generally* David Tan, *What Do Judges Know About Contemporary Art?: Richard Prince and Reimagining the Fair Use Test in Copyright Law*, 16 MEDIA & ARTS L. REV. 381 (2011); William M. Landes & Richard A. Posner, *The Legal Protection of Postmodern Art*, in THE ECONOMIC STRUCTURE OF INTELLECTUAL PROPERTY LAW 254 (2003).

work has recoded its semiotic meanings to express a different or counter-viewpoint that creates new insights and understandings, thus rendering the secondary use "transformative" in nature. Rebecca Tushnet explains that "[t]ransformativeness in fanworks takes many forms, from critique to celebration to reworking a text so that it better addresses the concerns of a specific audience.[94] I have previously maintained that "in their interpretive activities, fans may arguably, as fair use, comment or criticize the canonical universe of the original author, create parodies of the original works or to express their own creative teleologies that draw on the primacy of the canon."[95] As Tushnet contends, if a work was used as a building block for an argument, it should be understood as possessing a *transformative purpose*, in contrast to a work that was created purely for its entertainment value.[96]

IV The Semiotic Signs of Disney

In order to understand the cultural impact of the Disney phenomenon, Janet Wasko contends that it is crucial to study Disney the corporation and how its brand of fantasy is manufactured and marketed, and by whom.[97] In tracing the history of Disney, Wasko notes that Walter Elias Disney, the founder of Walt Disney Studio, who was born in Chicago in 1901, "idealized and romanticized" his memories of his early rural experiences, "which provided the basis for his attachment to small-town America and its values."[98] Following the debut of Mickey Mouse in *Plane Crazy* in May 1928, the first Mickey Mouse animated sound cartoon, *Steamboat Willie*, was released in November 1928, and was an instant success with the distributors, theater owners and the American public. Merchandising contracts were inked, and the company was reorganized in the late 1929 into four divisions: production, film recording, real estate, and licensing and merchandising. In particular, the expansion of the stable of Disney characters to include Minnie Mouse, Pluto, Goofy and Donald Duck in the *Silly Symphonies* series was synchronized with a proliferation of merchandising products and Mickey Mouse Clubs for children in the United States and the world.[99]

[94] Rebecca Tushnet, *User-Generated Discontent: Transformation in Practice*, 31 CCLUM. J.L. & ARTS 497, 503 (2008).
[95] Tan, *supra* note 80, at 96. [96] Tushnet, *supra* note 94, at 506.
[97] JANET WASKO, UNDERSTANDING DISNEY 108 (2001). [98] *Id.* at 8. [99] *Id.* at 9–11.

The ubiquitous products of the Walt Disney Company have a distinctive aura about them since their inception in the 1930s, and have steadily gained a cultural cachet through shrewdly constructed cartoon personalities and storylines, fantasy theme parks and merchandising. Disney today is not just about cartoons and family entertainment but "has become synonymous with the notion of childhood innocence" and a semiotic sign for "a pristine never-never land in which children's fantasies come true, happiness reigns, and innocence is kept safe through the magic of pixie dust."[100]

The television program *The Mickey Mouse Club* was a cultural tour de force, and it cemented the Disney values in the public consciousness of audiences worldwide. It debuted on 3 October 1956, and it combined songs, dances, comic skits, Disney cartoons with instructions on safety, hygiene, and good citizenship. Viewers were taught to be well-mannered and respectful of parents and other representatives of authority. At its peak, *The Mickey Mouse Club* commanded an audience of 12 million children and 7 million adults, selling 25 million Mickey Mouse-eared Mouseketeer caps.[101] The Mouseketeer caps emblematic of the iconic Mickey Mouse – also a ubiquitous merchandise at Disneyland theme parks around the world – have become the quintessential embodiment of Disney and its mythic cultural values.

Furthermore, the Walt Disney Company can be said to be the archetypal American-based transnational corporation that is driven by an enduring underlying profit motive, and expertly exploits international opportunities to expand its global franchise.[102] From its inception, the Walt Disney Company has created strong brands and trademarked characters that were marketed in various forms throughout the world. Indeed Disney has dedicated significant investments in promoting its encoded brand values, but it has at the same time become a cultural icon imbued with important social meanings and hence presenting itself as a target for myriad recoding opportunities.[103] For example, it has been said that:

> Disney uses its trademark techniques . . . and forms . . . to tell stories with popular yet enduring themes vital to the contemporary capitalist culture of the United States . . . Indeed, Disney narratives are unsurpassed in their

[100] GIROUX, *supra* note 14, at 17. [101] *Id.* at 75.

[102] *E.g.* WASKO, *supra* note 97, at 63–9.

[103] *See, e.g.*, RETHINKING DISNEY: PRIVATE CONTROL, PUBLIC DIMENSION (Mike Budd & Max H. Kirsch eds., 2005); BYRNE & MCQUILLAN, *supra* note 82; GIROUX, *supra* note 14.

> narrative fidelity to dominant ideology and cultural values, consistently asking audiences to enter believable fantasy worlds.[104]

There are those who resist such fantasy worlds. In as early as the 1940s, there was already a body of anti-Disney thought that attacked Walt Disney's "corruption of the American folk legacy" and that "his fairy tales presented a falsely neat, dishonestly orderly, over-sentimentalized view of life."[105] By placing a Mouseketeer hat on every child – or adult – Disney is making him or her share in these values. A countercultural movement in the 1960s had accused Disney's oeuvre as "illustrative of the barriers that impeded the wholesale reform of American values – unquestioning patriotism, bourgeois moral nostrums, gauche middle-class taste, racist elitism, corporate profit-mongering, bland standards of social conformity."[106] After Walt Disney's death in 1966, Paul Krassner and Wally Wood delivered a countercultural strike by publishing *Walt Disney Memorial Orgy* that showed "Mickey shooting up, Goofy screwing Minnie and the Seven Dwarfs having their way with Snow White," and released *Orgy* in poster form.[107]

It is generally assumed that "there is universal recognition of what Disney represents."[108] Undoubtedly as Amy Davis observes, "Disney has become an inseparable aspect of American popular culture, as well as an integral part of the American social fabric."[109] Walt Disney himself was quoted to have said:

> Disney is a thing, an image in the public mind . . . It stands for something, and you don't have to explain what it is to the public. They know what Disney is when they hear about our films or go to Disneyland.[110]

Indeed Michael Real's study revealed that the audience's identification of the values represented by Disney was clear and unequivocal – such as happiness, friendliness, honesty, innocence and

[104] Lee Artz, *Monarchs, Monsters, and Multiculturalism: Disney's Menu for Global Hierarchy*, in RETHINKING DISNEY: PRIVATE CONTROL, PUBLIC DIMENSION, *supra* note 103, at 75, 79.

[105] BOB LEVIN, THE PIRATES AND THE MOUSE: DISNEY'S WAR AGAINST THE COUNTERCULTURE 78 (2003).

[106] *Id.* at 79.

[107] *Id.* Disney sued its publisher, Sam Ridge, and forced him out of business.

[108] WASKO, *supra* note 97, at 221 (internal quotations omitted).

[109] AMY M. DAVIS, GOOD GIRLS & WICKED WITCHES: WOMEN IN DISNEY'S FEATURE ANIMATION 222 (2006).

[110] WASKO, *supra* note 97, at 221–2 (citing KATHY MERLOCK JACKSON, WALT DISNEY: A BIO-BIBLIOGRAPHY 68 (1993)).

industriousness – concluding that "Disney attracts participants into mass-mediated utopian typifications and that Disney instructs through morality plays that structure personal values and ideology."[111] Meanwhile, the Global Disney Audiences Project, which involved researchers in eighteen countries, attempted to examine the global proliferation of Disney products.[112] Unsurprisingly, the results showed that "certain core values represented by Disney have been consistently received and understood across cultures" and that "despite cultural and language differences and certain individualized product offerings, Disney has been amazingly successful in consistently communicating specific values."[113]

The term "Classic Disney" has been commonly used to identify a corpus of cartoon characters and narratives in cartoons and films that exhibit a consistent set of common themes and values that generally represent "Disney" to the general public and for the purpose of critical analysis.[114] While the first Disney cartoons tend to be playful and open-ended, after 1932, the cartoons had more distinctive beginnings and usually happy endings.[115] The Classic Disney style came to be "typified by light entertainment, punctuated with a good deal of music and humor which revolved around mainly physical gags and slapstick, relying heavily on anthropomorphized (human-like), neotenized (childlike) animal

[111] Michael Real, Mass-Mediated Culture 84 (1973).

[112] Janet Wasko, Mark Phillips, & Eileen Meehan, Dazzled by Disney?: The Global Disney Audience Project (2001).

[113] Wasko, *supra* note 97, at 192. On the significant role of Disney as a moral educator with immense cultural authority and legitimacy, *see generally*, Henry A. Giroux, *Animating Youth: The Disneyfication of Children's Culture*, 24(3) *Socialist Rev.* 23, 24–5 (1994); Annalee R. Ward, Mouse Morality: The Rhetoric of Disney Animated Film 2–5 (2002); John Taylor, Storming the Magic Kingdom: Wall Street, the Raiders, and the Battle for Disney viii (1987). The Disney characters and their adventures are inextricably intertwined with the beliefs and values of Walt Disney himself. Walt Disney has "loudly proclaimed a commitment to wholesome, family-oriented entertainment . . . [he] possessed the gentleman's quota of anti-Semitic, homophobic, racist views common to WASP males of his era . . . [and he] was also an ardent patriot." Levin, *supra* note 8, at 73. Walt Disney geared his company's output to support America's war efforts during World War II. He had shown the stable of iconic Disney characters like Donald, Goofy and Pluto at war with the Axis and his characters adorned war planes and over 1,200 pieces of military insignia. It is therefore unsurprising that *Air Pirates Funnies* recoded the Disney characters perhaps as a critical comment on Disney. *See infra* Section V.A.

[114] Wasko, *supra* note 97, at 110.

[115] Robert Sklar, *The Making of Cultural Myths – Walt Disney*, in The American Animated Cartoon: A Critical Anthology 58–65 (Danny Peary & Gerald Peary eds., 1980).

characters."[116] Steven Watts calls the Disney style one of "sentimental modernism" and describes the well-defined ideology and characteristics of Classic Disney as follows:

> First, it blended the real and unreal, naturalism and fantasy, and manipulated each in an attempt to illuminate the other.
>
> Second, it secured nonlinear, irrational, quasi-abstract modernist explorations comfortably on the cultural map by utilizing certain tropes from the Victorian past – an exaggerated sentimentality, clearly defined moralism, disarming cuteness – as familiar artistic signposts.
>
> Third, it willingly dug down through layers of consciousness to engage in the fluidity of experience and action, but always returned to embrace rationality.
>
> Fourth, it animated the world – literally – by ascribing intention, consciousness, and emotion to living and inanimate objects alike, but did so in such a way as to downplay the presence of evil and tragedy.
>
> Fifth and finally, it good-naturedly satirized the pretensions of high culture and sought to invigorate it with the vitality of popular cultural expression.[117]

The Classic Disney characters follow a predictable formula: the hero/heroine is strikingly handsome/beautiful (sometimes known as the Prince Charming/Princess tropes); the villain, who is the exact opposite of the hero/heroine, often ugly, extremely fat or extremely thin, with exaggerated facial features; and the sidekick who is comical in appearance and demeanor. Even as Disney draws from ancient tales, legends and history,[118] "[i]t 'Disneyfies' each plot to fit its formula for commercial success … [choosing] certain moral lessons over others according to Disney's value structure."[119] It was noted that "Disney heroines are *always* beautiful, shapely, and often sexually attractive, while female

[116] WASKO, *supra* note 97, at 111.

[117] STEVEN WATTS, THE MAGIC KINGDOM: WALT DISNEY AND THE AMERICAN WAY OF LIFE 104–5 (1997).

[118] It has been observed that Disney's narratives draw heavily from Shakespeare's plays and Hans Christian Andersen's tales: for example, *The Lion King* from *Hamlet*, *The Little Mermaid* from *The Tempest*, and *Hercules* from *Macbeth*. *See* Richard Finkelstein, *Disney's Tempest: Colonizing Desire in The Little Mermaid*, in THE EMPEROR'S OLD GROOVE: DECOLONIZING DISNEY'S MAGIC KINGDOM 131 (Brenda Ayres ed., 2003).

[119] ANNALEE R. WARD, MOUSE MORALITY: THE RHETORIC OF DISNEY ANIMATED FILM 113 (2002). This "Disneyfication" portrays the acceptable majoritarian culture as "the white, middle-class, American, Protestant, conservative nuclear family, with clearly defined and separate gender roles performed by a heterosexual couple, committed to raising their children in the same mold." Brenda Ayres, *The Wonderful World of Disney: The World That Made the Man and the Man That Made the World*, in THE EMPEROR'S OLD GROOVE: DECOLONIZING DISNEY'S MAGIC KINGDOM, *supra* note 118, at 15, 18.

villains are typically ugly and either extremely thin (Cruella) or grossly fat (Ursula), thus perpetuating norms of physical beauty prevalent in mainstream American culture."[120] The Classic Disney Princess-characters like Snow White, Cinderella and Sleeping Beauty are invariably portrayed as innocent, naïve, passive and beautiful, and while the more modern incarnations like Ariel in *The Little Mermaid*, Jasmine in *Aladdin* and Belle in *Beauty and the Beast* may display more independence and intelligence, they nonetheless ultimately find fulfillment in a happy ending with their Prince Charmings.[121] Although the New Disney characters like Pocahontas (1995), Mulan (1998), Rapunzel in *Tangled* (2010) and Elsa in *Frozen* (2013) may be infused with a feminist empowerment ethos and occasionally propelled by a conscious attempt to avoid racial stereotyping, these Princesses still conformed to the beautiful physique of the Disney Princess-trope and the stories persisted with the tried-and-tested romantic themes. Lee Artz concludes from a textual analysis of Disney animated features that this Disney dreamworld "rests on cultural privilege, social inequality, and human alienation – the same ingredients obtained and produced by the socioeconomic practices of Disney and other capitalist enterprises – validating the observations . . . that Disney's representations promote capitalist hegemony and political quiescence."[122] This subordination of particular values and identities by Disney's dominant worldview as constituted by its semiotic signs undoubtedly present fertile opportunities for counter public challenges.

V Recoding Disney Signs – An Assault on Innocence, Idealized Values, and Consumerism?

These Barthesian modern myths or semiotic connotations of Mickey Mouse and other Disney characters as an idealized America with its moralistic overtones are well recognized by consumers of Disney products around the world. Here, the Disney myths refer not simply to a falsehood, but to narrative tales which 'function to express social values,

[120] Wasko, *supra* note 97, at 116.

[121] *Id. See also* Ward, *supra* note 119, at 116–20; Brenda Ayres, *The Poisonous Apple in Snow White: Disney's Kingdom of Gender*, in The Emperor's Old Groove: Decolonizing Disneys Magic Kingdom, *supra* note 118, at 39; Kellie Bean, *Stripping Beauty: Disney's "Feminist" Seduction*, in The Emperor's Old Groove: Decolonizing Disney's Magic Kingdom, *supra* note 118, at 53. *See generally* Davis, *supra* note 109; Amy M. Davis, Handsome Heroes & Vile Villains: Men in Disney's Feature Animation (2013).

[122] Artz, *supra* note 104, at 81–2.

norms of behavior, and/or the consequences of deviating from them.'[123] A challenge to these myths should qualify as a transformative use of the original myths – be they embodied in literary or artistic works – under the copyright fair use doctrine. Sonia Katyal has argued that in cyberspace, the original works have become performative cultural texts that are "ripe for commentary, recoding, transgression, and appropriation."[124] Focusing on the genre of slash fiction, which "involves fictional, homoerotic pairings between male characters in mainstream television programs and films,"[125] Katyal demonstrates how slash fiction "empowers the virtual community to actively rework traditional narratives between men, demonstrating how queering mainstream characters can actually deconstruct and then transcend traditional gender norms and stereotypes."[126] Under copyright fair use doctrine, such reimaginations clearly add "something new, with a further purpose or different character, altering the [original author's work] with new expression, meaning, or message"[127] and are transformative. However, Rebecca Tushnet cautions that "it is difficult to draw clear lines between parody and other types of transformative use, including political protest"[128] but nonetheless fan fiction:

> involves original input, taking the borrowed characters into new situations and exploring their thoughts and feelings in ways not present in the official texts. This type of elaboration, involving the addition of much time and effort, should fall into the category of transformative use.[129]

There are ample and highly persuasive arguments marshaled by commentators like Katyal and Tushnet that fan fiction – regardless of whether they are classified as parody, satire, homage or commentary – is transformative and that this transformative nature inherent in such secondary works precludes market substitution for the original canonical works.

[123] Stephen L Harris & Gloria Platzner, Classical Mythology: Images and Insights 13 (4th ed., 2004).

[124] Sonia Katyal, *Performance, Property, and the Slashing of Gender in Fan Fiction* 14 Am. U. J. Gender & Soc. Pol'y & L. 461, 467 (2006). For a thorough examination of fan fiction, *see, e.g.*, Henry Jenkins, Textual Poachers: Television Fans and Participatory Culture (1992); Fan Fiction and Fan Communities In The Age Of The Internet: New Essays (Karen Hellekon & Kristina Busse eds., 2006).

[125] Katyal, *supra* note 124, at 468. *See also* Anne Kustritz, *Slashing the Romance Narrative*, 26 J. Am. Cult. 371, 372 (2003).

[126] Katyal, *supra* note 124, at 469. [127] *Campbell*, 510 U.S. at 579.

[128] Rebecca Tushnet, *Legal Fictions: Copyright, Fan Fiction, and a New Common Law*, 17 Loy. L.A. Ent. L. Rev. 651, 668 (1997).

[129] *Id.* at 665.

Indeed fan fiction "often imagines rather earthshaking changes for the characters . . . that the 'canon' cannot accept . . . So long as such stories are not official, they retain their appeal because the characters return unscathed in the next episode or official form."[130] The rest of this section will analyze whether three countercultural or counterpublic subversive uses of Disney iconography may qualify as fair use.

A *The Air Pirates Comics*

In 1978, the Ninth Circuit Court of Appeals held that Ted Richards, Dan O'Neill and Bobby London had infringed Disney copyrights by copying the graphic depiction of over seventeen characters in the *Air Pirates Funnies* comics and rejected a claim of fair use on the grounds that "[b] y copying the images in their entirety, defendants took more than was necessary to place firmly in the reader's mind the parodied work and those specific attributes that are to be satirized."[131] The *Air Pirates* decision is unlikely to be good law today as it applied a different test from that articulated by the Supreme Court in *Campbell*, and did not evaluate how the presence of a high degree of transformativeness may render less significant the other fair use factors that weigh against a finding of fair use.[132]

The individual defendants had published two issues of cartoon comics entitled *Air Pirates Funnies* which portrayed a number of well-recognized Disney characters in unflattering scenarios; the themes of defendants' publications differed markedly from those of Disney. The Ninth Circuit advanced the observation that:

> the Air Pirates was an underground comic book which had placed several well-known Disney cartoon characters in incongruous settings where they engaged in activities clearly antithetical to the accepted Mickey Mouse world of scrubbed faces, bright smiles and happy endings. It centered around a rather bawdy depiction of the Disney characters as active members of a free thinking, promiscuous, drug ingesting counterculture.[133]

Each issue of the Pirates' books was marked "Adults Only." The cover of the first issue showed Mickey Mouse piloting an open-cockpitted,

[130] *Id.* at 671.

[131] Walt Disney Productions v. The Air Pirates, 581 F. 2d 751, 758 (9th Cir. 1978) ('*Air Pirates*').

[132] *Campbell*, 510 U.S. at 579.

[133] *Air Pirates* at 753 (internal citations and quotations omitted).

propeller-powered plane with two sacks labelled "Dope" tied to its fuselage. The image had been lifted from the cover of a Disney comic *Mickey the Mail Pilot* with the word "Dope" having replaced the original "Mail." The cover of the second issue depicted Mickey Mouse and Minnie Mouse on horseback, hands raised, confronted by a bat-winged, cloaked figure with a revolver in one hand and the "Dope" sacks in the other.

The Ninth Circuit Court of Appeals accepted that the *Air Pirates Comics* had targeted the original Disney characters, and had "parodied their personalities, their wholesomeness and their innocence."[134] This is therefore unequivocally a target parody[135] and like 2 Live Crew's song *Pretty Woman* in *Campbell*, it "reasonably could be perceived as commenting on the original or criticizing it, to some degree."[136] In fact, the defense attorneys for the Air Pirates argued that the creators of *Air Pirates Funnies* were respected parodists following in the footsteps of Cervantes, Swift, Whitman, Hemingway, and Faulkner, that the countercultural comics were aimed at adult hippies not children, these comics were not competing with any past, current or future Disney creations, and the Disney-buying public was unlikely to have its cravings for Mickey Mouse satisfied by an issue of *Air Pirates Funnies*.[137] In Dan O'Neill's affidavit, he said:

> [W]e approach Mickey Mouse as our major American mythology ... I chose to parody *exactly* the style of drawing and the characters to evoke the response created by Disney. My purpose in using the Mouse as a character is not to destroy the Disney product, but to deal with the image in the American consciousness that the Disney image *implanted*.[138]

Unfortunately it was this close copying of the original Disney characters in *Air Pirates* that precluded the defendants from relying on the fair use defense, despite the high degree of transformativeness in terms of

134 *Id.* at 758. It was also noted that there were satirical elements present as well. *Id.* at 758 fn 15 ("the 'Air Pirates' were parodying life and society in addition to parodying the Disney characters. Such an effect is almost an inherent aspect of any parody.").

135 *Campbell*, 510 U.S. at 580 ("For the purposes of copyright law, the nub of the definitions, and the heart of any parodist's claim to quote from existing material, is the use of some elements of a prior author's composition to create a new one that, at least in part, comments on that author's works.") On the difference between target and weapon parodies, see Richard A. Posner, *When is Parody Fair Use?*, 21 J. LEGAL STUD. 67, 70–1 (1992).

136 *Campbell*, 510 U.S. at 583.

137 LEVIN, *supra* note 8, at 98.

138 *Id.* at 100 (emphases in the original). O'Neill was also reported to have said: "The closer you draw the parody, the greater the shock, the greater the criticism." *See id.* at 101.

the parodic purpose of *Air Pirates Funnies*. In 1978, the standards for applying the fair use defense in parody cases, like the standards for applying fair use in other contexts, had been a source of considerable attention and dispute, with a number of Second Circuit and Ninth Circuit Court decisions consistently focused on the substantiality of the taking.[139] In particular, the *Air Pirates* court was persuaded to rely on the Second Circuit's holding in *Berlin v. E C Publications*,[140] which asked whether the parodist has appropriated a greater amount of the original work than is necessary to "recall or conjure up" the object of his parody. The Court held that:

> it is our view that defendants took more than is allowed even under the *Berlin* test as applied to both the conceptual and physical aspects of the characters. In evaluating how much of a taking was necessary to recall or conjure up the original, it is first important to recognize that given the widespread public recognition of the major characters involved here, such as Mickey Mouse and Donald Duck, in comparison with other characters very little would have been necessary to place Mickey Mouse and his image in the minds of the readers ... here the copying of the graphic image appears to have no other purpose than to track Disney's work as a whole as closely as possible.[141]

This archaic reasoning that the factor of substantiality of the taking can trump a high degree of transformativeness is highly unlikely to be supportable in light of precedents post-*Campbell*. As scholars like Beebe and Sag have concluded in their review of cases, a finding of transformativeness exerts nearly dispositive force on the overall outcome of the fair use test.[142] The Second Circuit Court had also commented that "courts have concluded that such copying does not necessarily weigh against fair use because copying the entirety of a work is sometimes necessary to make a fair use of the image."[143]

More specifically, Justice Souter in *Campbell* characterized the transformation as follows:

> 2 Live Crew juxtaposes the romantic musings of a man whose fantasy comes true, with degrading taunts, a bawdy demand for sex, and a sigh of relief from paternal responsibility. The later words can be taken as a comment on the naiveté of the original of an earlier day, as a rejection

[139] *E.g.* Rosemont Enterprises Inc. v. Random House Inc., 366 F. 2d 303 (2nd Cir. 1966); Benny v. Loew's Inc., 239 F. 2d 532 (9th Cir. 1956).

[140] Berlin v. E C Publications Inc., 329 F. 2d 541 (2nd Cir. 1964).

[141] *Air Pirates*, 581 F. 2d at 757–8.

[142] Beebe, *supra* note 18; Sag, *supra* note 17.

[143] *Bill Graham Archives*, 448 F. 3d at 613; *Prince*, 714 F. 3d at 710.

of its sentiment that ignores the ugliness of street life and the debasement that it signifies.[144]

In *Air Pirates Funnies*, the defendants similarly presented a contrasting countercultural critical work that attacked the Disney myth. They argued that Mickey Mouse had become "part of the national collective unconscious" and an internationally known symbol of American culture and power; while Mickey is usually perceived as innocent and delightful, he has now been recoded in *Air Pirates Funnies* as a reactionary force devoted to Establishment values and an enthusiastic promoter of capitalism and unrestrained violence,[145] a representation which challenged the morality espoused by Disney. But perhaps they went too far in the 1970s, an era when the public, and more importantly the judiciary, would regard an overly sexualized parody as crossing the boundaries of permissible fair use. In *MCA v. Wilson*, the transformation of the wholesome 1940 Andrews Sisters hit *The Boogie-Woogie Bugle Boy of Company B* to the raunchy song titled *The Cunnilingus Champion of Company C* in a cabaret musical was not fair use;[146] in *Walt Disney Productions v. Mature Pictures Corp.*, the makers of the film *The Life and Times of the Happy Hooker* were denied the fair use defense when they used the Mickey Mouse Club's theme song to accompany the defining cinematic moment where the female protagonist sexually serviced – orally, anally and vaginally – three teenagers wearing Mouseketeer hats upon a billiards table.[147] The defendants in the latter case claimed "the music is used to 'highlight and emphasize the transition of such teenagers from childhood to manhood . . . in a highly comical setting', and as such is merely a 'humorous take-off' on the music."[148] However, Judge Duffy noted that the "original song lasts for only two minutes, yet defendants used the work over and over again for substantially more time than is

144 *Campbell*, 510 U.S. at 583. 145 Levin, *supra* note 8, at 98–9.

146 677 F. 2d 180 (2nd Cir. 1981). The defendant argued that, "because Cunnilingus Champion deals with the humorous practice of cunnilingus and [he] was trying to portray that practice as joyous, he was entitled to use a competing copyright owner's music that was immediately identifiable as something happy and joyous and it brought back a certain period in our history when we felt that way." *Id.* at 184 (internal quotations omitted). However, it should be noted that unlike the *Air Pirates Funnies* comics, the "plaintiffs and defendants were competitors in the entertainment field. Both Bugle Boy and Cunnilingus Champion were performed on the stage. Both were sold as recordings. Both were sold in printed copies. Testimony, accepted as credible by the trial court, indicated that Cunnilingus Champion was made to sound like Bugle Boy to create publicity." *Id.* at 185.

147 389 F. Supp. 1397 (S.D.N.Y. 1975). 148 *Id.* at 1398.

required to 'conjure up the original.' While defendants may have been seeking in their display of bestiality to parody life, they did not parody the Mickey Mouse March but sought only to improperly use the copyrighted material."[149] Unlike *Air Pirates Funnies* which arguably endeavored to provide a highly transformative counter-narrative or engage in trans-coding of the Disney characters, the teenage sex scene in *The Life and Times of the Happy Hooker* only serves to reinforce the values embodied in the Disney emblems of the Mouseketeer hats, and the Mickey Mouse March provided neither significant critical commentary nor introduced "new information, new aesthetics, new insights and understandings"[150] sufficient to satisfy the relative low threshold for transformativeness in the post-*Campbell* era. If the *Air Pirates* case were decided today, its use of the iconic cultural symbols of Mickey, Minnie and other Disney characters to express meanings that are opposite to the ones intended by their creators, and to disparage the original portrayal of innocence and familial values, would no doubt be considered highly transformative. Indeed as the Supreme Court in *Campbell* cautioned: the "threshold question when fair use is raised in defense of parody is whether a parodic character may reasonably be perceived. Whether, going beyond that, parody is in good taste or bad does not and should not matter to fair use."[151]

B Hero, Leader, God *by Alexander Kosolapov*

Alexander Kosolapov is a Russian artist who moved to New York in 1975, and is famous for drawing ironic parallels between Soviet communism and American materialism. He has been identified with the "Sots Art" or Socialist Art movement, a form of Soviet pop art that combined socialist realism with some dadaist and humorous elements.[152] He has also exhibited at the Saatchi Gallery in London, appropriating cultural icons like Coca Cola, Marlboro and the Virgin Mary/Baby Christ in his works, and his works have been collected by the Museum of Modern Art (MoMA) and the Guggenheim Museum in New York. In 2007, Kosolapov exhibited *Hero, Leader, God*, a bronze sculpture depicting Lenin, Mickey Mouse and

[149] *Id.* [150] *Koons*, 467 F. 3d at 251–2; *Prince*, 714 F. 3d at 706.
[151] *Campbell*, 510 U.S. at 582.
[152] The Moscow Times, *A Clash of Cultures in Alexander Kosolapov's Art, The Moscow Times* (Jul. 19, 2013), www.sotsart.com/2013/10/28/a-clash-of-cultures-in-alexander-kosolapov-s-art/.

Jesus Christ holding hands and walking together. The sculpture was estimated then to be worth between £50,000 and £70,000.[153]

Traditionally, the Russian Orthodoxy reveres the icon, and this very reverence was transposed by Russian art onto the painting. Kosolapov engages in "the profanation of the sacred"[154] by appropriating the icons of commercial mass culture – a practice of renowned American Pop artists such as Andy Warhol. Where Warhol used a Campbell's Soup Can in his critique of mass consumption, Kosolapov invoked the ubiquitous Mickey Mouse as a symbol of the purchasing power of contemporary masses. Throughout the 1970s to the 1990s, Kosolapov created numerous works in which he combined symbols of the Soviet space with symbols of Western commercial civilization; for instance, Lenin was associated with Mickey Mouse to convey the message of the sanctification of the masses and mass culture that was very characteristic of Soviet political ideology.[155] Kosolapov also saw in Christianity the initial form and archetype of our current consumer society. The figure of Christ often appears in Kosolapov's work as a symbol of the contemporary masses' purchasing power.

Boris Groys commented that Kosolapov's works present an insight into how the sanctification of the masses is as much a phenomenon of Western capitalist civilization as it was of the Soviet regime:

> During the years of Soviet power, the masses were sanctified for their capacity to work, and due to the monotony and reproducability of their social and productive practices. A key symbol of this monotonous reproduction are the portraits of Lenin that marked every corner of Soviet space, and were carried aloft by the workers during demonstrations. In contrast, the source of the masses' sanctification in capitalist society is the monotony and reproducability of their ability to consume. A symbol of this monotony of consumption is Mickey Mouse . . .[156]

The sculpture *Hero, Leader, God* may reasonably be perceived to be drawing a comparison between politics (Lenin), mass production (Mickey Mouse) and religion (Jesus Christ) as interconnected and perhaps interchangeable forms of mass consumption, that "[t]he sacred potential of the contemporary masses consists in their collective power of purchase."[157]

153 Phillips, *Lot #221 Alexander Kosolapov* (Oct. 10, 2008), www.phillips.com/detail/ALEXANDER-KOSOLAPOV/UK010708/221.

154 Boris Groys, *The artist in the age of commodity fetishism* (2012) (translated by Elena Sorokina and Emily Speers Mears), www.sotsart.com/2012/06/20/the-artist-in-the-age-of-commodity-fetishism/.

155 *Id.* 156 *Id.* 157 *Id.*

Unlike the *Air Pirates Funnies* comics which were targeting the original Disney characters for parody – arguably a type of trans-coding – *Hero, Leader, God* is more analogous to the type of recoding uses in *Koons* and *Prince* where the original works were "transformed" by the appropriation artists when the artworks would "reasonably be perceived" by the audience to offer "new information, new aesthetics, new insights and understandings."[158] Disney is known for its "narrative fidelity to dominant ideology and cultural values"[159] and the Mickey Mouse character, which is universally recognized as embodying Disney the corporation, connotes this ideological representation; in the same vein, the semiotic signs of Lenin and Christ connote political and religious ideologies embraced by the masses. Annalee Ward also refers to Disney as being a competitor of religion in its creation of narratives (like parables) and acting as a moral educator.[160] This representation of the triumvirate suggests that buying into a political ideology or religion is no different from buying a product – Lenin, Mickey and Christ are united as icons of mass consumption in contemporary society attempting to convince the populace of their honesty and authenticity. According to Groys, Kosolapov's artistic message is that:

> any commodity can be interpreted as the manifestation of an invisible, symbolic monetary value . . . [T]he secularization and profanation of the mechanisms of sanctification themselves . . . [constitute] private appropriation of the symbols of this purchasing power [and] occurs as a frivolous and even mocking act of irreverence towards the sacrament.[161]

It should be noted that the law "imposes no requirement that a work comment on the original or its author in order to be considered transformative."[162] Like Richard Prince's recoding of Patrick Cariou's photographs, Kosolapov's purpose in using the Mickey Mouse character is "plainly different from the original purpose for which it was created."[163] While such a portrayal does not offer an oppositional or subversive coding of Mickey Mouse – like in typical parodic works – it nonetheless offers a new insight and understanding to the audience who is familiar with Disney and its products. As the Second Circuit Court pointed out in *Prince*, "[w]hat is critical is how the work in question appears to the reasonable observer, not simply what an artist might say

[158] *Koons*, 467 F. 3d at 252; *Prince*, 714 F. 3d at 707.
[159] *See* Artz, *supra* note 104 and accompanying text.
[160] WARD, *supra* note 119, at 128–31. Ward observes that "Disney sells a worldview, and that worldview has the force of religion for many people." *Id.* at 131.
[161] Groys, *supra* note 154. [162] *Prince*, 714 F. 3d at 706.
[163] *Bill Graham Archives*, 448 F. 3d at 609; *Koons*, 467 F. 3d at 252–3.

about a particular piece or body of work. Prince's work could be transformative even without commenting on Cariou's work or on culture, and even without Prince's stated intention to do so."[164]

Last but not least, regarding the substantiality of the taking, the Second Circuit Court held in *Blanch v. Koons* that despite Koons taking almost the entire photograph – the legs, feet and sandals sans the background – the copying was "indeed reasonable when measured in light of his purpose, to convey the 'fact' of the photograph to viewers of the painting."[165] The Supreme Court has also cautioned that a use does not necessarily become infringing the moment it does more than simply conjure up another work. Rather, "[o]nce enough has been taken to assure identification, how much more is reasonable will depend, say, [1] on the extent to which the [work's] overriding purpose and character is to parody the original or, in contrast, [2] the likelihood that the parody may serve as a market substitute for the original."[166] In *Suntrust Bank v. Houghton Mifflin Co.,* the Eleventh Circuit Court found it difficult to conclude, on an analysis of the third fair use factor, whether the amount and substantiality of Alice Randall's copying of *Gone With The Wind* characters and famous lines wholesale (albeit with a twist to their original meanings) was reasonable in relation to the purpose of the copying;[167] but the court nonetheless found fair use in light of the high degree of transformativeness[168] and that the subversive version is unlikely to displace sales of the original work or supplant demand for the licensed derivatives.[169] In this instance, analogous to the reasoning in *Suntrust Bank*, and also in the same vein that Prince's work appeals to an entirely different sort of collector than Cariou's as highlighted by the Second Circuit,[170] it is highly unlikely

164 *Prince*, 714 F. 3d at 707. 165 *Koons*, 467 F. 3d at 258.

166 *Campbell*, 510 U.S. at 588.

167 Suntrust Bank v. Houghton Mifflin Co., 268 F. 3d 1257, 1273 (11th Cir. 2001) ('*Suntrust Bank*'). Notwithstanding, the court commented that it is "hard to imagine how Randall could have specifically criticized *GWTW* without depending heavily upon copyrighted elements of that book." *Id.* at 1271.

168 *Id.* at 1270 ("It is principally and purposefully a critical statement that seeks to rebut and destroy the perspective, judgments, and mythology" of *Gone with the Wind*).

169 *Id.* at 1275–6.

170 *Prince*, 714 F. 3d at 707 (Prince's artworks "have sold for two million or more dollars. The invitation list for a dinner that Gagosian hosted in conjunction with the opening of the *Canal Zone* show included a number of the wealthy and famous such as the musicians Jay-Z and Beyonce Knowles, artists Damien Hirst and Jeff Koons, professional football player Tom Brady, model Gisele Bundchen, . . . and actors Robert DeNiro, Angelina Jolie, and Brad Pitt . . . Cariou on the other hand has not actively marketed his work or sold work for significant sums").

that anyone will not now purchase Disney's works, or derivative non-transformative works (whether Disney's own or licensed by Disney) as a result of the market space that Kosolapov's work has taken up.[171]

C *Mickey Mao and Mickey Obama*

Political leaders like Mao Zedong (former Chairman of the Chinese Communist Party) and Barack Obama (former President of the United States of America) are often the subject of parody, satire and caricatures. In the United States, the First Amendment invariably provides a constitutional shield to political speech which targets political figures. However, in actions for copyright infringement, the Supreme Court in both *Golan v. Holder* and *Eldred v. Ashcroft* has held "the 'traditional contours' of copyright protection, *i.e.,* the 'idea/expression dichotomy' and the 'fair use' defense . . . are recognized in our jurisprudence as 'built-in First Amendment accommodations.'"[172] In particular, the fair use defense as codified in 17 U.S.C. §107 "allows the public to use not only facts and ideas contained in a copyrighted work, but also [the author's] expression itself in certain circumstances."[173] It is unsurprising that in the context of a robust free speech culture emboldened by the First Amendment, U.S. courts have interpreted the notion of transformative use liberally – and consequentially the fair use defense – when freedom of speech would be unduly constrained by the enforcement of the rights of copyright or trademark owners.

Political discourse enjoys a special status at the top of the free speech hierarchy and this is reinforced by U.S. Supreme Court decisions that consistently accord to political speech the highest constitutional value in the system of American democracy.[174] Generally, political speech covers all discussion on public issues, especially if intended by the speaker to influence governmental action.[175] Political speech has been defined by commentators as speech that has "a reasoned, cognitive connection to some identifiable political issue that has the potential of entering the legislative

171 *Id.* at 709.

172 Golan v. Holder, 565 U.S. 302, 329 (2012); Eldred v. Ashcroft, 537 U.S. 186, 219 (2003).

173 *Golan*, 565 U.S. at 329; *Eldred*, 537 U.S. at 219.

174 Dun & Bradstreet v. Greenmoss Builders, 472 U.S. 749, 759 (1985). *See also* Morse v. Frederick, 551 U.S. 393, 403–4 (2007); Virginia v. Black, 538 U.S. 343, 365 (2003).

175 NAACP v. Claiborne Hardware Co., 458 U.S. 886, 913–14 (1982); Garrison v. Louisiana, 379 U.S. 64, 74–5 (1964); New York Times v Sullivan, 376 U.S. 254, 270 (1964).

arena";[176] or "which bears, directly or indirectly, upon issues with which voters have to deal";[177] or "when it is both intended and received as a contribution to public deliberation about some issue."[178] In examining the constitutionality of governmental action, the Ninth Circuit has developed a test which protects merchandise that conveys "a religious, political, philosophical or ideological message";[179] while the Second Circuit uses a weighing methodology to determine whether the defendant's work was "predominantly expressive" in order to separate expressive art from commercial merchandise.[180] The right of publicity, which allows an individual to control the commercial exploitation of his or her identity, is widely accepted as a form of intellectual property right in the United States.[181] When evaluating liability, courts have used the "transformative elements" test in the First Amendment defense derived from the first factor of the fair use doctrine in copyright law: an unauthorized use of celebrity identity would be permitted if it was "transformative."[182] The California Supreme Court held that "the transformative elements or creative contributions . . . are not confined to parody and can take many forms, from factual reporting to fictionalized portrayal, from heavy-handed lampooning to subtle social criticism."[183] The court commented that literal depictions, such as Andy Warhol's silkscreens of celebrities, may also be transformative if they carry a particular social message.[184] From a right of publicity perspective,

[176] Patrick M. Garry, *The First Amendment and Non-Political Speech: Exploring a Constitutional Model that Focuses on the Existence of Alternative Channels of Communication*, 72 Mo. L. Rev. 477, 516 (2007).

[177] Alexander Meiklejohn, Free Speech and its Relation to Self-Government 79 (1948).

[178] Cass R. Sunstein, Democracy and the Problem of Free Speech 130 (1993).

[179] *E.g.* ACLU v. Nevada, 333 F. 3d 1092, 1107 (9th Cir. 2003).

[180] *E.g.* Mastrovincenzo v. City of New York, 435 F. 3d 78, 96 (2nd Cir. 2006); Bery v. City of New York, 97 F. 3d 689, 696–7 (2nd Cir. 1996).

[181] *Restatement (Third) of Unfair Competition* § 46 (1995); Acme Circus Operating Co. Inc. v. Kuperstock, 711 F. 2d 1538, 1541 (11th Cir. 1983). *See also* William Fisher, Theories of Intellectual Property, in New Essays in the Legal and Political Theory of Property 168, 194–9 (Stephen Munzer ed., 2001); J. Thomas McCarthy, *The Human Persona as Commercial Property: The Right of Publicity*, 7 Aust. Intellect. Prop. J. 20, 22–3 (1996); Fred Weiler, *The Right of Publicity Gone Wrong: A Case for Privileged Appropriation of Identity*, 13 Cardozo Arts & Ent. L.J. 223, 223 (1994).

[182] Comedy III Productions Inc. v. Saderup Inc., 25 Cal. 4th 387, 406 (2001) ('*Comedy III*'); Winter v. DC Comics, 30 Cal. 4th 881, 891 (2003).

[183] *Comedy III*, 25 Cal. 4th at 406.

[184] *Id.* at 408–9 ("Through distortion and the careful manipulation of context, Warhol was able to convey a message that went beyond the commercial exploitation of celebrity images and became a form of ironic social comment on the dehumanization of celebrity itself").

the use of Barack Obama's likeness with the Mouseketeer cap[185] would be conveying myriad possible comments or criticisms of Obama's effectiveness as a political leader invoking an association with Disney's semiotic meanings; this work would undoubtedly be found to have satisfied the transformative elements test under the First Amendment defense in right of publicity jurisprudence. Similarly, the Mickey Mao merchandise with the likeness of Mao Zedong with a Mouseketeer cap[186] would also satisfy the transformative elements test.

As explained in Section IV, Disney can connote "unquestioning patriotism, bourgeois moral nostrums, gauche middle-class taste, racist elitism, corporate profit-mongering, bland standards of social conformity."[187] The placement of a Mouseketeer cap on the President of the United States or the former Chairman of the Chinese Communist Party is a perfect shorthand to express one's criticism of the incumbent political ideology. Such expressions also may, borrowing a phrase from the Supreme Court in *Campbell*, "reasonably be perceived as commenting on the original or criticizing it, to some degree,"[188] through the introduction of new insights and understandings into the Disney corporation's close connection with governments[189] and Disney's highly successful "mass-mediated utopian typifications . . . that structure personal values and ideology"[190] much like how these two political leaders strove to advance democratic and communist dogmas respectively in their own countries. While Disney executives may be concerned with the potential negative impact of comparisons of its brand to communism, Mickey Mao is nonetheless highly transformative, and it would appear that these political parodies would not be in competition with official Disney memorabilia.

In advocating a judicious focus on *both* the expert and consumer in copyright infringement cases, Jeanne Fromer and Mark Lemley also argue that:

> A use that does not interfere with the IP owner's market generally does not interfere with the incentives to innovate that IP rights create. In fact,

185 T-shirts bearing the likeness of Barack Obama with Mouseketeer ears are easily available for purchase on the internet. *See, e.g.*, Mickey Mouse Barack Obama T-shirt, www.thoseshirts.com/mic.html.

186 *See, e.g.*, Mickey Mao T-shirt, www.tshirtbordello.com/mickey-mao-t-shirt.

187 Levin, *supra* note 8, at 79. *See also* Artz, *supra* note 104, at 82 (Disney's representations promote capitalist hegemony and political quiescence).

188 *Campbell*, 510 U.S. at 583. 189 *E.g.* Levin, *supra* note 8, at 73.

190 Real, *supra* note 111.

> IP owners' efforts to take control over the use of their works in completely different markets create the biggest problems for the IP system.[191]

Referring to the Obama Hope poster case, they observe that "using the photograph [of Barack Obama] in a completely different context may be copying the photograph as a technical matter, but if the photograph is used for a transformative purpose in a different market, we generally don't want the copyright owner to control that use."[192]

VI Conclusions – Fairly Taking the Mickey out of Disney

Although Disney as the copyright owner of the artistic works of Mickey Mouse and the other iconic characters is unlikely to be pleased with the blatant copyright infringement in many instances, the recontextualizations of these cartoon characters outside of their hegemonic narratives give these characters "a new expression, and employ new aesthetics with creative and communicative results distinct from [the original canon]."[193] Although there is no question that some of these infringing works are commercial, the courts do not place much significance on that fact due to the transformative nature of the works. The courts' concern is "not whether the secondary use suppresses or even destroys the market for the original work or its potential derivatives, but whether the secondary use *usurps* the market of the original work."[194] Moreover, in the same manner that Richard Prince's works appeal to an entirely different sort of collector than Patrick Cariou's photographs, or that 2 Live Crew's irreverent rap song targets a different audience from Roy Orbison's *Pretty Woman*, the consumers of these countercultural recodings of Disney characters are fundamentally different from those who want to buy the wholesome family-oriented Disney products. Granted that one may concede that there will be consumers who have grown up on Disney fare and may now also want to buy subversive Disney merchandise – because they appreciate the parodic or satirical content of these products – there is arguably no economic threat to Disney's markets for both

191 Jeanne C. Fromer & Mark A. Lemley, *The Audience in Intellectual Property Infringement*, 112 MICH. L. REV. 1251, 1291–2 (2014).

192 *Id.* at 1291. *See also* H. Brian Holland, *Social Semiotics in the Fair Use Analysis* 24 HARV. J.L. & TECH. 335, 367–90 (2011).

193 *Prince*, 714 F. 3d at 707. *See also* Leibovitz v. Paramount Pictures Corp., 137 F. 3d 109, 113–14 (2nd Cir. 1998).

194 *Prince*, 714 F. 3d at 708; *Koons*, 467 F. 3d at 258; NXIVM Corp. v. Ross Institute, 364 F. 3d 471, 481–2 (2nd Cir. 2004).

the original copyrighted works or their derivatives since Disney would not even contemplate entering the countercultural markets that poke fun at or are critical of its original works.

Fromer and Lemley have urged that the fair use analysis "would also benefit from an explicit appreciation of both consumer and expert views", and that "[c]opyright's hybrid audience … is intimately related not only to its infringement analysis but also to the fair use doctrine."[195] If "new information, new aesthetics, new insights and understandings"[196] may be reasonably perceived by both the expert and the consumer in the infringing work, following from Fromer and Lemley's analysis,[197] then such a work would be transformative and would have a strong likelihood of qualifying for fair use protection. Such an approach would permit "a variety of transformative reuses of both creative and inventive works, which not only increases dissemination of creative works but also allows for the sorts of remix and user creativity that may themselves be essential to human flourishing. And it does so without imposing any significant cost on the IP owner, who does not face market substitution."[198]

As I pointed out in another article, courts may find that "a legitimate transformation exists when the new work makes overt that which was present in the original text covertly … transformative fair uses make subtext text."[199] This different way of framing works of copyright that have mass appeal to a global audience is consonant with the current trajectory of a majority of the U.S. fair use decisions. The Air Pirates' new creative works in using copyrighted works of the Disney cartoon characters in a different context to serve a different function than the original falls squarely within the transformative use doctrine today. Likewise, Kosolapov's sculpture could not take less than the entire Mickey Mouse figure in order to effectively convey his powerful critique of ideological

[195] Fromer & Lemley, *supra* note 191, at 1300–1.

[196] *Koons*, 467 F. 3d at 251–2. *See also Prince*, 714 F. 3d at 706.

[197] Fromer & Lemley, *supra* note 191, at 1292–3. Such an approach arguably is consistent with how the infringement analysis is conducted by the U.S. Circuit Courts, in particular the Ninth Circuit, which assess infringement using a "hybrid of technical similarity and market substitution from the vantage point of both the consumer and the expert." *Id.* at 1299. Furthermore, "given copyright law's underlying goals, multiple vantage points matter." *Id.*

[198] *Id.* at 1293.

[199] Tan, *Transformative Potential, supra* note 81, at 403, 424 (citing Rebecca Tushnet, *Copyright Law, Fan Practices, and the Rights of the Author*, in FANDOM: IDENTITIES AND COMMUNITIES IN A MEDIATED WORLD 60, 68 (Jonathan Gray, Cornel Sandvoss, & C. Lee Harrington eds., 2007).

consumption of the masses. Putting Mouseketeer caps on political leaders is clearly contextually transformative in both copyright and right of publicity laws. Like famous trademarks, well-known copyrighted works of Disney function like Barthesian myths with universal ideological codings that are recognized globally.[200] The intrinsic strength and stability of the Disney semiotic signs is quintessential to the success of the Disney brand, but, at the same time, it renders the brand far more susceptible to countercultural recodings, parodies, and satires that lampoon the hyperreality of modernist consumerism, deconstruct the simulacra of childhood innocence and familial values, and challenge the icons of capitalist hegemony. Perhaps all this is but a small price to pay for global success.

[200] Tan, *supra* note 77, at 255.

8

Authors' Human Rights in the Intellectual Property Framework

GRAEME W. AUSTIN*

I Introduction

What happens when we acknowledge the common ground between intellectual property and human rights, and we bring them together within the same conceptual "framework"? One response might be to ask why this matters. The pursuit of coherence in intellectual property concepts and values[1] perhaps has only limited utility. Intellectual property rights might be more usefully regarded as policy levers that, ideally, facilitate the realization of broader social policy ends: that people are "fed, enjoy the benefits of literacy, are healthy, have viable agricultural bases, and can participate in technological and cultural development."[2] As the

* Some passages in this chapter are also included in Graeme W. Austin, *Authors' Human Rights and Copyright Policy*, 40 COLUM. J. OF L. & ARTS 405 (2017). These passages are reproduced with permission of the editors. For helpful commentary on an earlier draft, thanks to Professors Rochelle Cooper Dreyfuss, Graeme Dinwoodie, and Elizabeth Siew-Kuan Ng, together with the participants in the National University of Singapore Centre for Law and Business Symposium on "Framing Intellectual Property." Thanks also to Carlos Smith Diaz, LL.B. candidate, Victoria University of Wellington for excellent research assistance.

[1] For an illuminating discussion of intellectual property values, *see* GRAEME B. DINWOODIE & ROCHELLE COOPER DREYFUSS, A NEOFEDERALIST VISION OF TRIPS: THE RESILIENCE OF THE INTERNATIONAL INTELLECTUAL PROPERTY REGIME 81 (2012) [hereinafter DINWOODIE & DREYFUSS]. *See also*, Graeme B. Dinwoodie & Rochelle Cooper Dreyfuss, *Designing a Global Intellectual Property System Responsive to Change: the WTO, WIPO, and Beyond*, 46 HOUSTON L. REV. 1187, 1198 (2009).

[2] Graeme W. Austin, *Valuing Domestic Self-Determination in International Intellectual Property Jurisprudence*, 77 CHI.-KENT L. REV. 1155, 1191 (2002). *See also* Ruth L. Okediji, *Public Welfare and the Role of the WTO; Reconsidering the TRIPS Agreement*, 17 EMORY INT'L L. REV. 819 (2003) (emphasizing national goals served by intellectual property laws). *See also* Commission on Intellectual Property Rights, U.K. Sec'y of State for Int'l Dev., *Integrating Intellectual Property Rights and Development Policy* (2002) (reasoning that "an intellectual property right is best viewed as one of the means by which nations and societies can help promote the fulfilment of human, economic and social rights.").

U.N. Committee on Economic, Social and Cultural Rights said in 2005, "[u]ltimately, intellectual property is a social product and has a social function."[3] Solicitude for the internal logic of any area of law, including intellectual property, hardly passes muster as a "social function." The practical and empirical question of how to ensure that all members of the human family have what they need to realize their capabilities[4] is surely more important than preserving any legal subject area's internal logic or structural integrity.[5] As Professor Ruth Okediji reminds us, intellectual property is no more, and no less, than an instrument of social policy.[6]

That said, it would be naïve not to be concerned with the organization of a legal subject area[7] even if we might question the normative importance accorded to it. Consider domestic intellectual property policy development. It is surely likely that the way a subject is presented – in treatises and textbooks, for example – has some "gravitational pull"[8] on the way legal and policy actors apprehend the available policy options. In the U.S. context, the "constitutional turn" in intellectual property litigation in recent decades provoked intense interest in identifying grounding norms.[9] The internationalization of intellectual property law adds further impetus to the task of "clarify[ing] [its] normative underpinnings."[10] And recent scholarship examining the workings of international organizations has identified ways that conceptual frameworks and forms of

[3] Comm. on Econ., Soc., & Cultural Rights, *General Comment No. 17: The Right of Everyone to Benefit from the Protection of Moral and Material Interests Resulting from Any Scientific, Literary or Artistic Production of Which He is the Author*, art. 15(1)(c), U.N. Doc. E/GC.17/2005 (Jan. 12, 2006), para. 35 [hereinafter *General Comment No. 17*].

[4] For a useful summary of "capabilities" approaches to social and legal policy, *see* MARTHA C. NUSSBAUM, CREATING CAPABILITIES: THE HUMAN DEVELOPMENT APPROACH (2011). On the connections between these capabilities-focused approaches to policy development and intellectual property law, *see* Margaret Chon, *Intellectual Property and the Development Divide*, 27 CARDOZO L. REV. 2821 (2006). *See also*, MADHAVI SUNDER, FROM GOODS TO A GOOD LIFE (2012).

[5] The tensions between intellectual property and human rights was recently highlighted in the 2016 report of United Nations Secretary General's High-Level Panel on Access to Medicines. *See* www.unsgaccessmeds.org/final-report/.

[6] *See, e.g.*, Okediji, *supra* note 2.

[7] *See, e.g.*, Alan Watson, *The Structure of Blackstone's Commentaries*, 97 YALE L.J. 795 (1988) (discussing the external influences on the structure of Blackstone's Commentaries on the Laws of England).

[8] Amy Kapczynski, *The Access to Knowledge Mobilization and the New Politics of Intellectual Property*, 117 YALE L.J. 804, 808 (2008).

[9] Elizabeth Townsend-Gard & Ron Gard, *Marked by Modernism: Reconfiguring the Traditional Contours of Copyright Law*, in MODERNISM AND COPYRIGHT 155 (Paul Saint-Amour ed., 2012).

[10] *See* DINWOODIE & DREYFUSS, *supra* note 1, at 176.

argument portray particular policy orientations as more tenable than others.[11] In the public international context, the Vienna Convention on the Law of Treaties requires treaties to be interpreted *inter alia* "in the light of its objects and its purpose;"[12] confronted with textual ambiguities, legal actors are required to consider grounding norms, as appropriate to the relevant instrumental context. This is also true at the domestic level: in an area that is principally regulated by statute, recourse to some perceived statutory purpose is a familiar judicial maneuver. Taking a wider lens, the conceptual understanding of a subject area helps construct "frames" through which problems are apprehended and solutions developed.[13]

Given all of this, it might be useful to ask whether, in the terms suggested by the theme of this book, human rights and intellectual property can be brought together in the same "frame." This chapter first makes a descriptive claim: that human rights are not typically understood as being part of the international intellectual property framework that provides part of the conceptual structure of domestic intellectual property laws. In the discussion that follows, the label "international intellectual property law" will be used for the cluster of international instruments typically considered to be part of international intellectual property law architecture, beginning with the great nineteenth-century treaties, the Paris Convention for the Protection of Industrial Property (1883)[14] and the Berne Convention for the Protection of Literary and Artistic Works of (1886),[15] and progressing through to the WIPO

[11] Andrew T. F. Lang, *Re-Thinking Trade and Human Rights*, 15 TULANE J. OF INT'L & COMP. L. 335, 355 (2007). David Kennedy, for example, has analyzed ways that international trade institutions organize their thinking around notions of the "ordinary" and the "deviant" trading nation. David Kennedy, *Turning to Market Democracy: A Tale of Two Architectures*, 32 HARV. INT'L L.J. 373 (1991). *See also*, Guy Fiti Sinclair, *To Reform The World: The Legal Powers of International Organizations and the Making of Modern States* (2013) (unpublished J.S.D. dissertation, N.Y.U. School of Law).

[12] Vienna Convention on the Law of Treaties, art. 31, May 23, 1969, 8 I.L.M. 679 (1969). *See* Susy Frankel, *WTO Application of "The Customary Rules of Interpretation of Public International Law" to Intellectual Property*, 46 VA. J. INT'L L. 365, 389–400 (2006).

[13] John Harrington & Alasdair O'Hare, *Framing the National Interest: Debating Intellectual Property and Access to Essential Medicines in Kenya*, 17 J. WORLD INT'L PROP. 16 (2014); Kapczynski, *supra* note 8 at 810.

[14] Paris Convention for the Protection of Industrial Property, as last revised at the Stockholm Revision Conference, July 14, 1967, 21 U.S.T. 1583; 828 U.N.T.S. 303 [hereinafter "Paris Convention"].

[15] Berne Convention for the Protection of Literary and Artistic Works, art. 6*bis*(1), Sept. 9, 1886, as revised at Paris on July 24, 1971 and amended in 1979, S. Treaty Doc. No. 99–27 (1986) [hereinafter "Berne Convention"]. Prior to the completion of the Paris and Berne

Marrakesh Treaty to Facilitate Access to Published Works for Persons Who Are Blind, Visually Impaired, or Otherwise Print Disabled (2016),[16] and now taking account of the amendment to the TRIPS Agreement that came into force in 2017,[17] facilitating the cross-border distribution of medications produced under the TRIPS Agreement's compulsory license provisions.

The chapter then turns to the relationship between human rights and international intellectual property. To focus the discussion, the chapter considers human rights that specifically concern the rights of authors. Article 15(1)(c) of the International Covenant on Economic Social and Cultural Rights (ICESCR)[18] recognizes the rights of authors to the moral and material interests in their work. Its language echoes a similarly worded statement on authors' rights in the Universal Declaration of Human Rights.[19] The discussion draws on the 2005 *General Comment* on Article 15(1)(c) that was issued by the Committee on Economic, Social and Cultural Rights in 2005,[20] as well as the December 2014 Report to the Human Rights Council entitled *Copyright Policy and the Right to Science and Culture,* by the Special Rapporteur in the field of cultural rights, Farida Shaheed.[21] The interpretive jurisprudence on author-focused human rights indicates that a human rights approach to intellectual property is not a pretext for expanding or strengthening the intellectual property rights owned and exploited by corporate actors. To the contrary, the *General Comment*'s emphasis on the constraints on author-focused human rights underscores the narrow compass of these rights. Most

Conventions, various nations entered into a complex web of bilateral treaties relating to intellectual property. *See* STANIFORTH RICKETSON, THE BERNE CONVENTION FOR THE PROTECTION OF LITERARY AND ARTISTIC WORKS (1987).

16 Completed at Marrakesh on June 27, 2013, www.wipo.int/treaties/en/text.jsp?file_id=301016#preamble.

17 *See* WTO, *Amendment of the TRIPS Agreement* (Decision of Dec. 6, 2005), WT/L/641, www.wto.org/english/tratop_e/trips_e/wtl641_e.htm; and WTO, *TRIPS – WTO IP rules amended to ease poor countries' access to affordable medicines* (Jan. 23, 2017), www.wto.org/english/news_e/news17_e/trip_23jan17_e.htm.

18 International Covenant on Economic, Social and Cultural Rights, Dec. 16, 1966, S. Exec. Doc. D, 95–2, 993 U.N.T.S. 3 (entered into force Jan. 3, 1976) [hereinafter ICESCR].

19 Universal Declaration of Human Rights, G.A. Res. 217A, art. 27(2), U.N. GAOR, 3d. Sess., 1st plen. Mtg. U.N. Doc. A/810 (Dec. 12, 1948) [hereinafter UDHR].

20 *General Comment No. 17, supra* note 3.

21 Farida Shaheed, *Copyright Policy and the Right to Science and Culture: Report of the Special Rapporteur in the Field of Cultural Rights,* Human Rights Council, Twenty-Eighth Session, Agenda Item 3, A/HRC/28/47 (2014) [hereinafter 2014 *Special Rapporteur Report*].

importantly, however, its approach provides a human rights justification for both limiting intellectual property and protecting authors' moral and material interests in a way that remains sharply focused on the dignity of the human creator. The final section offers some preliminary observations on possible "spheres of influence" for author-focused human rights.

II Intellectual Property and Human Rights

In intellectual property law, human rights typically occupy an "outsider" position. Human rights law is of course relevant to intellectual property, as many NGOs, civil society groups, international organizations,[22] activists, and scholars have urged when invoking human rights as a platform for challenging the expansion of intellectual property rights. In the conventional way these claims are advanced, some aspect of intellectual property law is identified as breaching one or more human rights obligations.[23] Taking human rights seriously demands that intellectual property should yield.[24] According

[22] Sub-Commission on Human Rights Res. 2000/7, *Intellectual property rights and human rights*, ESCOR, Commission on Human Rights, Sub-Commission on the Promotion and Protection of Human Rights, 52nd Sess., 25th Mtg., U.N. Doc. E/CN.4/Sub.2/Res/2000/7 (2000) [hereinafter Resolution 2000/7], noting the "apparent conflicts" between the international human rights regime and intellectual property. In 2001, the Sub-Commission adopted a further resolution on the relationship between human rights and intellectual property, in which it called for the "integration" of human rights and intellectual property, and further called "upon Governments to integrate into their national and local legislation and policies provisions that, in accordance with international human rights obligations and principles, protect the social function of intellectual property" and urged "all Governments to ensure that the implementation of the TRIPS Agreement does not negatively impact on the enjoyment of human rights as provided for in international human rights instruments by which they are bound." Sub-Commission on the Promotion and Protection of Human Rights, Sub-comm. Res. 2001/21, U.N. Doc. E/CN.4/SUB.2/RES/2001/21 (2001).

[23] *See, e.g.*, Andrew T. F. Lang, *Re-Thinking Trade and Human Rights*, 15 TULANE J. INT'L COMP. L. 335, 348 (2007), describing, in the context of the relationship between international trade law generally and human rights: "first, commentators scrutinize WTO agreements carefully to determine the kinds of policy choices these agreements may require or proscribe; and second, these policy choices are themselves carefully analyzed to determine whether and in what ways they may respectively undermine or enhance the enjoyment of human rights in particular circumstances."

[24] "Human rights are a principal source for delimiting intellectual property, not simply expanding it." SUNDER, *supra* note 4, at 101–2. *See also*, Resolution 2000/7, *supra* note 22, para. 12, noting that any intellectual property regime that makes it more difficult for a State party to comply with its core obligations in relation to health, food, [or] education . . . is inconsistent with the legally binding obligations of the State party."

to this logic, human rights are not a "part of" or "internal" to intellectual property.[25]

But what if we saw human rights, not as being situated beyond the boundaries of intellectual property – not outside its borderlines, but as part of the same policy and legal framework? Perhaps this shift is already occurring, as is suggested by the WIPO Marrakesh Treaty,[26] the Preamble of which begins: "Recalling the principles of non-discrimination, equal opportunity, accessibility and full and effective participation and inclusion in society, proclaimed in the Universal Declaration of Human Rights and the United Nations Convention on the Rights of Persons with Disabilities."[27] While this placement of international human rights obligations front-and-center provides a welcome framing statement, this does not, however, represent any radical repositioning of human rights in the international intellectual property law architecture.[28] The new Marrakesh Treaty certainly represents a new kind of initiative: an international agreement mandating provision in domestic laws of a *sustained* set of exceptions to intellectual property rights.[29] But, to the extent that the Marrakesh Treaty reflects the influence of human rights on intellectual property, it seems to entrench human rights' typical role: a catalyst and justification for crafting exceptions. The Marrakesh Treaty standardizes exceptions in domestic laws to accommodate the needs of visually impaired people, and promises to enhance opportunities for cross-border distribution of copies made in reliance on these exceptions. It is possible that the Marrakesh Treaty will come to be recognized as a new kind of initiative, situated at the intersection between human rights and intellectual property – one that invites an understanding of international intellectual property instruments as themselves *serving* human rights ends.[30] But structurally, at least, the Treaty does not represent any commitment to the radical integration of human rights into the international intellectual property regime.

[25] *See* LAURENCE R. HELFER & GRAEME W. AUSTIN, HUMAN RIGHTS AND INTELLECTUAL PROPERTY 504 (2011).

[26] Completed at Marrakesh on June 27, 2013, *supra* note 16. [27] *Id.*

[28] Graeme B. Dinwoodie, *The Architecture of the International Intellectual Property System*, 77 CHI-KENT L. REV. 993 (2002).

[29] Other exceptions to intellectual property rights that are subject to international commitments tend to be more piecemeal. For example, article 9(2) of the TRIPS Agreement requires that members exempt from copyright protection, "ideas, procedures, methods of operation or mathematical concepts as such."

[30] LAURENCE HELFER ET AL., THE WORLD BLIND UNION GUIDE TO THE MARRAKESH TREATY FACILITATING ACCESS TO BOOKS FOR PRINT-DISABLED INDIVIDUALS (2017).

A key indicator of the outsider status of human rights is the typical approach of treatise and textbook writers to international law sources of intellectual property. Today, these texts reflect a widespread acknowledgement that international law (and, in the case of the European Union, regional law) is part of the international intellectual property "complex."[31] But for most commentators, human rights law is not included in recitations of the international sources of intellectual property law – even though the international human rights guarantees directed at authors share significant common ground with at least one branch of intellectual property law: copyright.[32] Article 27 of the 1948 Universal Declaration on Human Rights stipulates that: "Everyone has the right to the protection of the moral and material interests resulting from any scientific, literary or artistic production of which he is the author."[33] This statement was broadly contemporaneous with the adoption of a similar recognition in the 1948 American Declaration on the Rights and Duties of Man,[34] and it was reaffirmed as Article 15(1)(c) of the ICESCR.[35] Other parts of article 15 concern the right of everyone to take part in cultural life and to enjoy the benefits of scientific progress, concepts that are also enshrined in the Universal Declaration,[36] and, in terms of international intellectual property, are consistent with the growing emphasis on "balance" in the intellectual property system.[37] The European Convention on Human Rights and Fundamental Freedoms[38] is another relevant source of human rights guarantees that is relevant to intellectual property. The European Convention makes no specific mention of authors' moral and material interests. Nevertheless, the protection

[31] Peter K. Yu, *International Enclosure, the Regime Complex, and Intellectual Property Schizophrenia*, MICH. ST. L. REV. 1 (2007).

[32] *See generally* Graeme W. Austin, *Authors' Human Rights and Copyright Policy*, 40 COLUM. J. OF L. & ARTS 405 (2017).

[33] UDHR, *supra* note 19, art. 27(2).

[34] American Declaration of the Rights and Duties of Man, O.A.S. Res. XXX, art. 13(2), *reprinted in* Basic Documents Pertaining to Human Rights in the Inter-American System, OEA/Ser.L.V/II.82 doc.6 rev.1 at 17 (1992).

[35] ICESCR, *supra* note 18.

[36] UDHR, *supra* note 19, art. 27(1). The right to participate in cultural life is found in other human rights instruments, including the Convention on the Elimination of All Forms of Discrimination against Women, art. 3(c), Sept. 30, 1981, 1249 U.N.T.S. 13.

[37] *See, e.g.*, Agreement on Trade-Related Aspects of Intellectual Property Rights, art. 7, Apr. 15, 1994, Marrakesh Agreement Establishing the World Trade Organization, Annex 1C, Legal Instruments – Results of the Uruguay Round, vol. 31, 33 I.L.M. 81 (1994) (referring to "a balance of rights and obligations") [hereinafter TRIPS Agreement].

[38] Convention for the Protection of Human Rights and Fundamental Freedoms, art. 53, Nov. 4, 1950, 213 U.N.T.S. 221.

of the right of property under the optional protocol has been applied to intellectual property.[39] The status of intellectual property under the Charter of Fundamental Rights of the European Union, article 17(2) of which provides that "[i]ntellectual property shall be protected,"[40] is less clear. According to the Court of Justice of the European Union, this "right" to intellectual property is fundamental, but not "inviolable,"[41] and therefore is to be balanced against other fundamental rights.[42] Nowadays, most treatise and textbook writers readily acknowledge international law as a source for domestic intellectual property law – that is, as a body of law that increasingly accounts for the shape of domestic law and policy. However, they do not typically acknowledge human rights law in this context.

What might account for the separation of intellectual property and authors' human rights? For textbook writers, the principal task is to describe and organize sources of law that are relevant to any subject. The jurisprudence on author-focused human rights is thin, and there is not much "law" with which textbook and treatise writers can engage.[43] The status of international intellectual property law is very different. To be sure, until the Berne and Paris Conventions were brought under the aegis of the WTO, there were few, if any, dispositive interpretations of their principles in decisional law. There were, however, important scholarly exegeses, most notably Professor Sam Ricketson's path-breaking analysis of the Berne Convention.[44] Today, with the integration of

[39] *See, e.g.*, Anheuser-Busch v. Portugal, No. 73049/01 (Eur. Ct. H.R. Grand Chamber, Jan. 11, 2007) (right to the "peaceful enjoyment of . . . possessions" in Article 1 of Protocol No. 1 to the European Convention on Human Rights includes trademarks and trademark applications). The UN Committee on Economic, Social and Cultural Rights characterized the protocol as recognizing "albeit not explicitly" authors' human rights to benefit from the protection of their moral and material interests in their works. *See General Comment No. 17, supra* note 3.

[40] Charter of Fundamental Rights of the European Union, art. 17(2), 2000 O.J. C 364/1 [hereinafter European Charter].

[41] UPC Telekabel Wien GmbH v. Constantin Film Verleih GmbH, Case C-312/12 (Mar. 27, 2014).

[42] This point is made especially clearly in the Opinion of Advocate-General Cruz Villalón in *UPC Telekabel Wien GmbH v. Constantin Film Verleih GmbH*, Case C-312/12 (Nov. 26, 2013), para. 81.

[43] Mary W. S. Wong, *Toward an Alternative Normative Framework for Copyright: From Private Property to Human Rights*, 26 CARDOZO ARTS & ENT. L.J. 775, 808 (2009) (noting, with respect to art. 27 of the UDHR and art. 15 of the ICESCR, the "lack of specific guidance within these general provisions, case law, and other authoritative normative pronouncements").

[44] RICKETSON, *supra* note 15.

major international intellectual property instruments in the WTO system, there are international bodies, including the TRIPS Council, that are specifically charged with the task of interpreting the substantive provisions of the TRIPS Agreement.[45] And as a result of decisions made under the Dispute Settlement Understanding, there is now an emerging body of intellectual property decisions under the WTO dispute settlement agreement that elaborate on the meaning of the TRIPS Articles and the other intellectual property conventions that are incorporated within the WTO framework. To be sure, the body of law is not large,[46] but it is growing and the understanding of TRIPS norms continues to evolve.[47]

Domestic analysts (and those to whom they report) also know that it is failure to comply with the disciplines of TRIPS that will attract trade sanctions or fines, not human rights law. The situation is quite different for human rights instruments that recognize the human right of authors. The jurisprudence on these obligations has, at least until fairly recently, been quite thin. Moreover, it is likely that the prospect of international embarrassment for failing to respect, protect, and fulfill[48] author-focused human rights guarantees seems far more remote than the prospect of trade sanctions or fines under the WTO system.

The fullest elaboration of the substantive content of these rights has been a 2005 *General Comment* by the Committee on Economic, Social and Cultural Rights on Article 15(1)(c) of the ICESCR,[49] and the 2014 *Special Rapporteur Report.* In its first paragraph, the former document draws a sharp distinction between author-focused human rights and intellectual property:

> human rights are fundamental as they are inherent to the human person as such, whereas intellectual property rights are first and foremost means by which States seek to provide incentives for inventiveness and creativity, encourage the dissemination of creative and innovative protections as well as the development of cultural identities, and preserve the integrity of

[45] The TRIPS Council is tasked under TRIPS with monitoring the operation of the agreement (TRIPS, art. 68).

[46] This work includes the important early interpretive studies of TRIPS by Professors Dreyfuss and Lowenfeld: Rochelle Cooper Dreyfuss & Andreas Lowenfeld, *Two Achievements of the Uruguay Round: Putting TRIPS and Dispute Settlement Together*, 37 VA. J. OF INT'L L. 275 (1997).

[47] *See, e.g.*, Patricia Judd, *Toward a TRIPS Truce*, 32 MICH. J. INT'L LAW 613 (2011).

[48] *See generally* Maastricht Guidelines on Violations of Econ., Soc. & Cultural Rts., Jan. 22–26, 1997, para. 6 *reprinted in* 20 HUM. RTS. Q. 691–705 (1998).

[49] *General Comment No. 17, supra* note 3.

> scientific, literary and artistic productions for the benefit of society as a whole.[50]

In contrast, the guarantee of rights under Article 15(1)(c) "derives from the inherent dignity and worth of all persons"[51] – not something that, at least according to the *General Comment*, can be said of intellectual property rights. Similar points are advanced in the 2014 *Special Rapporteur Report*.[52] Thus, even those *tasked* with developing the normative content of this article consider author-focused human rights to be distinct from intellectual property. If intellectual property and human rights are ontologically distinct, there is no need to consider the latter when describing the former.

III The Scope of Authors' Human Rights

A *Normative Content*

We now have two prominent analyses of the normative content of authors' human rights: the 2005 *General Comment* and the 2014 *Special Rapporteur Report*. Both documents will help in the evolution of standards by which individual states' compliance with the Covenant can be scrutinized.[53] The *General Comment* characterized the core obligations imposed by Article 15(1)(c) in the following terms – terms that will be very familiar in the context of economic, social and cultural rights:

> The obligation to respect requires States parties to refrain from interfering directly or indirectly with the enjoyment of the right to benefit from the protection of the moral and material interests of the author. The obligation to protect requires States parties to take measures that prevent third parties from interfering with the moral and material interests of authors. Finally, the obligation to fulfil requires States to adopt appropriate legislative, administrative, budgetary, judicial, promotional and other measures towards the full realization of article 15(1)(c).[54]

Noting the distinction drawn in the *General Comment* between "intellectual property" and "human rights", particularly the characterization of human rights as "fundamental, inalienable and universal entitlements,"

[50] *Id.*, at para. 1. [51] *Id.*, at para. 1.1.

[52] 2014 *Special Rapporteur Report, supra* note 21, at para. 26.

[53] As to the General Comment, see Laurence Helfer, *Toward a Human Rights Framework for Intellectual Property*, 40 U.C. Davis L. Rev. 971 (2007) [hereinafter Helfer, *Human Rights Framework*].

[54] *General Comment No. 17, supra* note 3, at para. 28.

Professor Laurence Helfer reasons that the analysis advanced in the *General Comment* reflects "a vision of authors' rights as human rights that exist independently of the vagaries of state approval, recognition, or regulation."[55] This is a very different conception from that typically advanced in the intellectual property context, especially in common law jurisdictions. Of course, the international law of intellectual property imposes obligations on domestic nations, and, in the majority of cases, it will be politically and economically untenable to flout or withdraw from them.[56] But these obligations do not have the same sense of universality as human rights. Moreover, the grounds for permissible limitations on author-focused human rights appear to be more constrained. According to the *General Comment*, such limitations must "be determined by law in manner compatible with the nature of these rights, must pursue a legitimate aim, and must be strictly necessary for the promotion of the general welfare in a democratic society . . .,"[57] language that is facially far stricter even than the three-step test, against which limitations on intellectual property rights must be tested.[58]

All of this foregrounds the importance of the substantive content of the author-focused human rights guaranteed by the ICESCR. Here, the *General Comment* is quite circumspect. Contrary to the fears of some who oppose the integration of human rights and intellectual property, the *General Comment* makes it perfectly clear that a measure that in some respect furthers authors' moral or material interests does not, for that reason alone, advance authors' human rights guarantees. The vision of author-focused human rights advanced by the *General Comment* and the 2014 *Special Rapporteur Report* is much more constrained.

Consistent with a commitment to the indivisibility of rights, key parts of the analysis in the General *Comment* approach authors' rights through the lens of other human rights,[59] including those articulated in the ICESCR, such as the right to culture and the right to benefit from scientific progress[60] – also the right to be given the opportunity to gain

[55] Helfer, *Human Rights Framework, supra* note 53, at 993.

[56] *See generally,* Susan K. Sell, *TRIPS was Never Enough: Vertical Forum Shifting, FTAs ACTA, and TPP,* 18 J. Intell. Prop. L. 447 (2011). As Professor Sell notes, these costs are not merely borne by states: individuals too have much to lose. *Id.*, at 468–74 (describing attacks against individuals who have resisted the expansion of intellectual property).

[57] *General Comment No. 17, supra* note 3, at para. 22.

[58] Helfer, *Human Rights Framework, supra* note 53, at 994–5.

[59] This analysis draws from *General Comment No. 17, supra* note 3, para. 4.

[60] ICESCR, art. 15(1)(a).

one's living by which one freely chooses,[61] to adequate remuneration,[62] to an adequate standard of living,[63] and those set forth elsewhere in the international Bill of Rights, including the right of property that is recognized in the UDHR.[64] According to the *General Comment*, the protection of authors' human rights is also a "material safeguard for the freedom of scientific research and creativity activity."[65] As for moral interests, the *General Comment* recognizes the "protection of the personal link between the author and his/her creation."[66] A leading commentator has distilled from the *General Comment*'s analysis of the substantive "content" of the right, a commitment to the protection of "a zone of personal autonomy in which authors can achieve their creative potential, control their productive output, and lead independent intellectual lives that are essential requisites for any free society."[67] Author "autonomy" is also mentioned in the 2014 *Special Rapporteur Report*.[68]

The 2014 *Special Rapporteur Report* accords further attention to the relationship between copyright and authors' human rights. As to moral rights, the Report suggests that in some contexts, a human rights approach might afford stronger protections than are currently provided under some regimes, again emphasizing the importance of the personal autonomy interests of creative workers, noting that in the domestic policy context those who exploit works of authorship in the marketplace – producers, publishers, and distributors – often wield greater influence than individual authors.[69] Even so, moral rights protections should not intolerably limit other users of protected works for such purposes as parody and pastiche.[70] As to authors' material interests, the 2014 *Special Rapporteur Report* recognizes the imbalance of bargaining power under which individual authors labor when entering into publication contracts, and suggests that copyright policies can be directed at protecting authors from unfair bargains.[71] The Report usefully explores a variety of policy

[61] ICESCR, art. 6(1). [62] ICESCR, art. 7. [63] ICESCR, art. 11(1).

[64] *See* Mary W.S. Wong, *Toward an Alternative Normative Framework for Copyright: From Private Property to Human Rights*, 26 CARDOZO ARTS & ENT. L.J. 775, 810 (2009).

[65] *General Comment No. 17, supra* note 3, at para.4. [66] *Id.*, at para. 1.23.

[67] Laurence R. Helfer, *Collective Management of Copyright and Human Rights: An Uneasy Alliance*, in COLLECTIVE MANAGEMENT OF COPYRIGHT AND RELATED RIGHTS 85, 97 (Daniel J. Gervais ed., 2006).

[68] *2014 Special Rapporteur Report, supra* note 21, at para 39. [69] *Id.*, at para. 38.

[70] *Id.*, at paras. 36–7. The Special Rapporteur cites the recent decision of the Court of Justice of the European Union, *Deckmyn v. Vendersteen*, Case C-201/13 (Sept. 3, 2014) as an illustration of how the various interests and rights could be balanced.

[71] *2014 Special Rapporteur Report, supra* note 21, at para. 43.

vehicles directed at helping with the realization of authors' rights to material interests, including reversion rights, *droit de suite*, and statutory licenses.[72] Like the General Comment, however, the 2014 *Special Rapporteur Report* emphasizes that the human rights guarantee directed at securing authors' material interests does not always equate with "stronger" copyright protections.[73]

Even so, the Report also notes that the exposure of authors to large-scale piracy of their works on digital networks implicates human rights issues, but deferred fully engaging with these issues in the light of countervailing concerns relating to remedial steps such as website blocking, internet access, and content filtering which the Special Rapporteur also considered to raise human rights concerns.[74]

In both documents, a connection is drawn between the protection of moral and material interests and cultural survival and self-determination.[75] Both, for example, eschew the idea that corporations could be beneficiaries of author-focused human rights,[76] focusing for the most part on the individual rights holder, but they also recognize that indigenous groups might be the *collective* objects of these rights. So doing, the documents tap into rich multi-forum debates as to the "confluence of indigenous knowledge and intellectual property."[77] Here, the *General Comment* anticipated by two years the completion of the 2007 Declaration on the Rights of Indigenous Peoples, which makes specific reference to indigenous peoples' intellectual property rights.[78] As is explained by Professor James Anaya, then Special Rapporteur on the situation of human rights and fundamental freedoms of indigenous peoples, the Declaration affirms both individual rights, and "rights of a collective character in relation to self-government and autonomous political, legal, social and cultural institutions; cultural integrity,

[72] *Id.*, at paras. 44–51. [73] *Id.*, at para. 48. [74] *Id.*, at para. 51.

[75] HELFER & AUSTIN, *supra* note 25, at 447–57.

[76] In this context, the 2014 *Special Rapporteur Report* gives more emphasis to the size of the corporate entity, noting that large corporations have greater leverage in domestic policy circles (at para. 42). To the extent that this distinction is drawn (the Report is ambiguous on the point), it is appropriate. Individual authors might use closely held companies (in some jurisdictions requiring only one member) as the economic vehicle through which the exploitation of their rights occurs. This should not impede recognition of authors' human right to the moral and material interests in their works.

[77] Peter Drahos & Susy Frankel, *Indigenous Peoples' Innovation and Intellectual Property: The Issues*, in INDIGENOUS PEOPLES' INNOVATION: INTELLECTUAL PROPERTY PATHWAYS TO DEVELOPMENT 1 (Peter Drahos & Susy Frankel eds., 2012).

[78] Declaration on the Rights of Indigenous Peoples, G.A. Res. 61/295, art. 32(2), U.N. GAOR, 61st Sess., 107th Plen. Mtg., U.N. Doc. A/RES/61/295 (Sept. 13, 2007).

including cultural and spiritual objects, languages and other cultural expressions."[79] Understood in this light, the *General Comment*'s extension of author-focused human rights to indigenous groups is entirely consistent with a concern for the humanity and dignity of the creative person – but tailored to a context in which these are enlivened in a collective way.

B Limitations

Author-focused human rights are limited in a number of key respects. The *General Comment*'s principal statement on limitations warrants quoting in full:

> The right of authors to benefit from the protection of the moral and material interests resulting from their scientific, literary and artistic productions cannot be isolated from the other rights recognized in the Covenant. States parties are therefore obliged to strike an adequate balance between their obligations under article 15, paragraph 1(c), on one hand, and under the other provisions of the Covenant, on the other hand, with a view to promoting and protecting the full range of rights guaranteed in the Covenant. In striking this balance, the private interests of authors should not be unduly favoured and the public interest in enjoying broad access to their productions should be given due consideration. States parties should therefore ensure that their legal or other regimes for the protection of the moral and material interests resulting from one's scientific, literary or artistic productions constitute no impediment to their ability to comply with their core obligations in relation to the rights to food, health and education, as well as to take part in cultural life and to enjoy the benefits of scientific progress and its applications, or any other right enshrined in the Covenant. Ultimately, intellectual property is a social product and has a social function. States parties thus have a duty to prevent unreasonably high costs for access to essential medicines, plant seeds or other means of food production, or for schoolbooks and learning materials, from undermining the rights of large segments of the population to health, food and education. Moreover, States parties should prevent the use of scientific and technical progress for purposes contrary to human rights and dignity, including the rights to life, health and privacy, e.g. by excluding inventions from patentability whenever their commercialization would jeopardize the full realization of these rights. States parties should, in particular, consider to what extent the patenting of the human body and its parts would affect their obligations under the

[79] S. James Anaya, *Report of the Special Rapporteur on the Situation of Human Rights and Fundamental Freedoms of Indigenous People*, Human Rights Council, Ninth Session, Agenda Item 3, A/HRC/9/9/ (2008).

> Covenant or under other relevant international human rights instruments. States parties should also consider undertaking human rights impact assessments prior to the adoption and after a period of implementation of legislation for the protection of the moral and material interests resulting from one's scientific, literary or artistic productions.[80]

Presumably, the kinds of limitations that are envisaged here would also satisfy the *General Comment*'s overarching, and, as we have seen, quite strict test for permissible limitations on authors' human rights. "Limitations must be compatible with the very nature of the rights protected in article 15, paragraph 1(c), which lies in the protection of the personal link between the author and his/her creation and of the means which are necessary to enable authors to enjoy an adequate standard of living." The 2014 *Special Rapporteur Report* also emphasized the importance of limitations, and the possibility of international cooperation on the topic, noting that the Marrakesh Treaty offers an example. Additionally, the Report explores the possibility of extending the Marrakesh initiative to develop internationally mandated exceptions for libraries and archives, as well as exceptions in the context of education. In the light of the connection between copyright exceptions and the rights to science and culture, the Special Rapporteur recommended further exploration of the topic.[81]

In the context of Article 15(1)(c), there is probably a much richer discussion of limitations yet to be had. For author-focused human rights, there are at least three sources of limitations. First, the ICESCR has its own "justified limitations" clause. Article 4 provides:

> The States Parties to the present Covenant recognize that, in the enjoyment of those rights provided by the State in conformity with the present Covenant, the State may subject such rights only to such limitations as are determined by law only in so far as this may be compatible with the nature of these rights and solely for the purpose of promoting the general welfare in a democratic society.

While not as capacious as equivalent clauses that exist in some domestic constitutional contexts – limitations are still required to be "compatible with the nature of these rights" – the clause does provide an important basis for constraining author-focused rights so as to avoid tension with other rights and values. For the most part, the limitations sought to be imposed on authors' rights can plausibly be tied to one or

[80] *General Comment No. 17, supra* note 3, at para. 35.
[81] *2014 Special Rapporteur Report, supra* note 21, at para. 76.

other human rights guarantee and to the promotion of the general welfare in a democratic society.

Typically invoked in this context are human rights commitments concerning health, free expression and information, food, participation in culture, development, sharing the benefits of scientific advancement, education, and the rights of indigenous peoples. These have received the most attention from NGOs, human rights-focused international agencies, civil society groups, and scholars. Another source of limitations on intellectual property rights is the Convention on Biodiversity (CBD), which, in the context of sustainable use of biological diversity, requires member states to: "respect, preserve and maintain knowledge, innovations and practices of indigenous and local communities."[82] In a variety of ways, these sources of international law have been invoked in the context of arguments that intellectual property rights should be limited, so that they do not trespass on human rights guarantees. In the European Human Rights context, an especially fertile source of argument along these lines has invoked Article 10 of the European Convention on Human Rights, which guarantees the right to freedom of expression and the right to seek, receive and impart information and ideas of all kinds.[83] Some European courts have recognized that this is at least a

[82] Convention on Biodiversity, art. 8(j), which is concerned with *in situ* conservation, requires every state party:

> subject to its national legislation, to respect, preserve and maintain knowledge, innovations and practices of indigenous and local communities embodying traditional lifestyles relevant for the conservation and sustainable use of biological diversity and promote their wider application with the approval and involvement of the holders of such knowledge, innovations and practices and encourage the equitable sharing of the benefits arising from the utilization of such knowledge, innovations and practices.

Convention on Biological Diversity, art. 8(j), U.N. Doc. UNEP/BIO.Div/N7-INC.5/4, 31 I.L.M. 818 (June 5, 1992). These articles in the CBD can be understood as precluding the use of intellectual property rights in ways that trespass on certain indigenous rights. To this extent, they can be understood as setting forth a right to be protected "from" intellectual property. Some care is needed in associating this broad agenda with indigenous rights. Some international instruments and initiatives at the domestic law level recognize a right of indigenous peoples "to" intellectual property. For example, recognition of the rights of indigenous peoples to intellectual property form part of the 2007 United Nations Declaration on the Rights of Indigenous Peoples, G.A. Res. 61/295, Annex, art. 2., U.N. GAOR, 61st Sess., U.N. Doc. A/RES/61/295 (Sept. 13, 2007). *See generally*, HELFER & AUSTIN, *supra* note 25, at 432–502.

[83] Convention for the Protection of Human Rights and Fundamental Freedoms, art. 10, Sept. 3, 1953, 213 U.N.T.S. 221.

potential limitation on the scope of copyright protections.[84] The *General Comment* makes it quite clear that the recognition and protection of author-focused human rights does not marginalize other rights.[85]

With its approach to limitations and to the balancing of rights, the Committee's approach shares much common ground with the approach of the Court of Justice of the European Union in recent case law in which the "fundamental" protections of intellectual property under Article 17 (2) of the European Charter of Fundamental Rights[86] have been invoked. In a recent case involving the power to issue injunctions against intermediaries,[87] requiring internet service providers to block access to third party websites that infringe and facilitate the infringement of copyright-protected works,[88] the Court of Justice has held that, in the application of this power, intellectual property rights must be balanced against other fundamental rights. These include the right to conduct a business,[89] and the freedom of information of internet users.[90] The Court's reasoning also underscores that, even in this highly commercial context, the principle of proportionality[91] has work to do.

Second, there are important definitional limitations reflected in the idea, reiterated in both the General Comment and the 2014 *Special Rapporteur Report*, that "material interests" do not equate with maximizing the potential income to be derived from any intellectual product. Author-focused human rights can plausibly be limited to rights that provide authors with the opportunity to derive an adequate livelihood from their creativity. Less clear is whether definitional limitations may be imposed on the scope of the right by the other rights with which, according to the *General Comment*, author-focused human rights must be "balanced." The reference to balancing suggests that the right remains intact, but there is no violation of the right where limitations are imposed

[84] *See, e.g.*, Ashdown v. Telegraph Group Ltd. [2001] EWCA (Civ.) 1142 (Eng.).

[85] *Cf.* Eric A. Posner, *Martii Koskenniemi on Human Rights: An Empirical Perspective* n 4 (U. of Chicago, Public Law Working Paper No. 467, 2014), http://ssrn.com/abstract=2414699 (examining the argument that "rights become oppressive when they are institutionalized because they marginalize certain interests that are not embodied in these rights").

[86] European Charter, *supra* note 40.

[87] Directive 2001/29/EC of the European Parliament and of the Council of 22 May 2001 on the Harmonization of Certain Aspects of Copyright and Related Rights in the Information Society, 2001 O.J. (L 167) 10, art. 8(3).

[88] UPC Telekabel Wien GmbH v. Constantin Film Verleih GmbH, Case C-312/12 (Mar. 27, 2014).

[89] European Charter, *supra* note 39, art. 16. [90] *Id.*, art. 11.

[91] Explicitly recognized in art. 52(1) of the European Charter, *supra* note 40.

in order to further other human rights, especially rights to food, health, and education. From a policy perspective, this distinction probably seems like an unimportant quibble: certainly, an approach that limits author-focused human rights transparently, with explicit reference to other human rights, seems preferable to one that hides the bases for limitations by defining the right itself in a limited way. Whatever the approach, it is clear enough that author-focused human rights will be protected only insofar as they are consistent with, and do not intolerably trespass upon, other human rights guarantees.[92]

A third source of limitations comes from the character of the rights recognized in the ICESCR. Some aspects of these rights – such as the accompanying prohibitions against discrimination as to the objects of protection – must be realized immediately. Much of the substantive content of the right, however, is to be progressively realized, taking account of the material circumstances of the state party. As is frequently true of economic, social, or cultural rights, what can be achieved in one setting will not necessarily set the floor or a ceiling in other contexts.

Distilling all of this, author-focused human rights seem to be quite limited in scope, but normatively powerful in their (limited) sphere of operation. They are, at least in the international law context,[93] tightly tethered to the moral and material interests in works of authorship. They recognize as a human rights issue the need for creative people to have the opportunity to earn an adequate standard of living; they also recognize the close connection between the creative person and his or her work – or, in the indigenous peoples' context, between the group and their

[92] *Cf. Ashby Donald and Others v. France* (European Court of Human Rights, Fifth Section, Application No. 36769/08, Jan. 10, 2013). English translation available at 45 INT. REV. INTELLECT. PROP. COMPET. LAW 354 (2014) (holding that rights of authors are "rights of others" for the purposes of limitations on the right to freedom of expression in article 10 of the European Convention on Human Rights). *See also The Football Association Premier League Ltd v. British Telecommunications Plc* [2017] EWHC 480 (Ch.), where Arnold, J. observed in a case involving a blocking order against a number of ISPs: "As for freedom of internet users to impart or receive information, this plainly does not extend to a right to engage in copyright infringement." *Id.* at [47].

[93] A question that is beyond the scope of this chapter is whether the scope of rights is constrained in quite the same way in the context of the European Charter of Fundamental Rights. As is noted above, the Court of Justice of the European Union has reasoned that the protection of intellectual property under article 17(2) of the Charter is not "inviolable," and must be balanced against other fundamental rights. However, the Court has *not* stated that the right recognized in article 17(2) is definitionally limited in quite the same way as article 15(1)(c) of the ICESCR – that is, by reference to the moral and material interests of creative people, as that concept is elaborated in *General Comment No. 17, supra* note 3.

creative expression. Author-focused human rights are constrained in meaningful ways: by the connection with authors' moral and material interests itself (a definitional constraint); by reference to other human rights; and through the concept of progressive realization of rights.

IV Spheres of Potential Influence

While the WTO regime is concerned with national provenance, authors' human rights are concerned with the human provenance of the creative endeavor. The limitations on the scope of author-focused human rights put the rights bearer – the creative individual (or group) – into a much sharper focus than a regime concerned with items of trade circulating in streams of domestic and international commerce.

There are, however, other spheres in which a focus on author-focused human rights might be influential. One sphere of influence should be at the domestic policy level. In nations in which serious intellectual property policy analysis occurs, it is possible that something very different would occur if policy analysts tasked with developing domestic intellectual property law not only pulled from their shelves their copies of the TRIPS Agreement, but also referred to the relevant parts of the UDHR and the ICESCR. When, for example, policy analysis of topics such as protections against unfair bargain, reversion rights, or *droit de suite* are raised, it should be recognized that these issues trigger both economic issues and human rights guarantees. Ideally, this approach would engender, and be informed by, a commitment to the idea that "when we are doing intellectual property policy" we are engaged with human rights issues. That is, the sources of international law that must be consulted include both international intellectual property *and* author-focused human rights, together with limitations that might temper or limit these rights.[94]

[94] Recent legislative initiatives in Australia are suggestive of this possibility. On March 22, 2017 a Bill was introduced into the Australian Federal Parliament to give effect *inter alia* to the Marrakesh Treaty. Parliament of the Commonwealth of Australia, House of Representatives, *Copyright Amendment (Disability Access and Other Measures) Bill 2017*. The accompanying Explanatory Memorandum included an assessment under Human Rights (Parliamentary Scrutiny) Act 2011 (Cth.). That assessment addressed a variety of different human rights, including the rights of authors that are guaranteed under the ICESCR. *See* www.aph.gov.au/Parliamentary_Business/Bills_Legislation. Though the discussion was fairly brief, the approach is suggestive of ways that legislators and their advisers might take account of international human rights norms when engaging in law reform initiatives in the intellectual property context.

What this might mean in practice will depend on a variety of factors, including the policy problem under scrutiny, and, of course, the strength of the policy directives received from above. In some contexts, this may involve foregrounding the rights of the human creators involved – and asking whether, for instance, the particular policy measure is sufficiently solicitous of the opportunity of authors to derive an adequate standard of living from their works. These kinds of concerns might also bring important rule of law issues to the surface, particularly those involving access to justice questions, such as whether costs of enforcement of rights preclude individual authors from securing meaningful protection of their rights.

Of course, all intellectual property policy development should engage with these issues. The distinguishing characteristic of intellectual property law is the persistent calibration of rights so as to encourage, not stifle, innovation, especially so-called downstream innovation. But bringing human rights into the intellectual policy mix does something a little different, and introduces a measure of friction into the "innovation for innovation's sake" narrative. Lurking close to the surface of the innovation narrative is a commitment to economic trickle-down; there is typically far less concern with the distributive consequences of achieving some optimal calibration of incentives.

From a human rights perspective, an unmediated "incentives for creativity approach" to intellectual property protections is difficult to tolerate. Consider the right to education.[95] Copyright has from the beginning protected educational materials. The first copyright statute, the English Statute of Anne of 1709 was, after all, entitled "An Act for the Encouragement of Learning."[96] From the outset, copyright law has been premised on the idea that the flourishing of private markets in copyright-protected works will promote learning and the progress of knowledge. In contrast, the human right to education imposes public law obligations on governments, which include, in some contexts, the provision of free educational materials.[97] Accordingly, the human right to education cannot be delimited by the ability to participate as a consumer in the private markets that copyright laws create and sustain, even if, as an empirical fact, these markets "encourage" the production of marketable educational materials. Even less can it be satisfied by the hope that the

[95] This section draws from the analysis in HELFER & AUSTIN, *supra* note 25, at p. 316.

[96] Copyright Act, 1709, 1710, 8 Ann., c. 19 (Eng.)

[97] *See* Comm. on Econ., Soc. & Cultural Rights, *General Comment No. 13: The Right to Education*, para. 6, U.N. Doc. E/C.12/1999/10 (Dec. 8, 1999).

enrichment of copyright owners will redound to the benefit of us all, thereby enhancing aggregate welfare. Not all members of the human family can wait that long. Familiar debates over how much should be left in the public domain so as to facilitate downstream creativity miss part of the point.

There is no easy route to resolution of issues such as these. By invoking author-focused human rights – together with their limitations – we may enhance the chances that these issues will be considered in intellectual property contexts. The tools used to achieve distributive ends may be the familiar intellectual property levers – defenses, creativity thresholds, and the like. But the *reasons* for using these tools might be different. In turn, invoking human rights in this context might shape expectations as to the reasonableness of expectations accompanying the ownership of intellectual property.

A second sphere of influence connects to the important work by Professors Graeme Dinwoodie and Rochelle Cooper Dreyfuss,[98] in developing a "neo-federalist" approach to the TRIPS Agreement. Through a detailed scholarly analysis of the text of the WTO instruments and the jurisprudence they have generated, as well as the institutional and political context, Professors Dinwoodie and Dreyfuss advance a compelling case for valuing domestic self-determination in the intellectual property context by rendering international intellectual property law more "porous," and more accommodating of domestic values – and, most importantly, the legal basis for achieving this end.

One especially powerful strand of their argument emphasizes the salience of contextualized understandings of specific intellectual property measures adopted within different domestic legal systems. Recent developments in TRIPS jurisprudence have increased the possibilities for doing so.[99] Augmenting in domestic policy contexts author-focused human rights discourse, and rendering it a serious contribution to the shaping of intellectual property policy, may enhance the possibilities for taking more seriously the domestic policy reasons for particular intellectual property measures. Such an approach would also require taking seriously the moral and material interests of authors and other creative workers. At the same time, the interpretive material on author-focused human rights gives its imprimatur to constraining those rights in certain circumstances. "Values" in the intellectual

[98] DINWOODIE & DREYFUSS, *supra* note 1. [99] *See generally,* Judd, *supra* note 46.

property context are divergent and changing.[100] If the international intellectual property jurisprudence is making greater space for domestic policy choices – and, persuaded by the compelling neo-federalist perspective advanced by Professors Dinwoodie and Dreyfuss, might make more – it would be a welcome development for human rights to occupy more of it.

A third sphere of influence for author-focused human rights may be to enrich and deepen policy critiques of intellectual property advanced by civil society groups, and lend to these critiques some deeper moral purchase. It is very difficult to find examples of sustained NGO critiques directed at intellectual property that are grounded in human rights that also take seriously the human rights of authors. Occasionally, some parsimonious recognition of the rights of authors is offered, such as this statement in "Right to Share: Principles on Freedom of Expression and Copyright in the Digital Age", which was promulgated by NGO "Article 19" in 2013:

> Copyright enjoys limited protection under international human rights law as part of the right to property; like the right to property itself, it is not an absolute right. In particular, States may enforce such laws as they deem necessary to control the use of property, including copyright, in accordance with the general interest or to secure the payment of taxes or other contributions or penalties.[101]

As the foregoing discussion suggests, this is a cabined depiction of author-focused human rights. The statement manifests very little appreciation of the human rights status of authors' material and moral interests in their work beyond the human right of property. Rhetorically, the emphasis on property serves to banish authors from the picture – those whose material and moral interests are put on the line.

In many respects, this lack of engagement with author-focused human rights is understandable: activism and nuance are seldom close companions. Even so, human rights advocacy such as this risks atomizing human rights, and betraying important commitment to their indivisibility. Such critiques might be more enduring and salient if those advancing

[100] J. Janewa OseiTutu, *Value Divergence in Global Intellectual Property Laws*, 87 Indiana L.J., 1639, 1658 (2012).

[101] Article 19, *Right to Share: Principles on Freedom of Expression and Copyright in the Digital Age* (Apr. 25, 2013), www.article19.org/data/files/medialibrary/3716/13-04-23-right-to-share-EN.pdf.

them could also demonstrate that the policy positions they endorse also acknowledge and accommodate the human rights of authors – accompanied by more compelling moral bases for recognizing limitations that may legitimately be imposed upon them.

V Conclusion

When intellectual property policy development occurs, human rights are also engaged. Human rights law has not, however, played much of a role in the evolution of the subject area of intellectual property. For the most part, they are not recognized as a relevant source of law. They occupy an uneasy position on the margins, largely ignored, and only invoked, for the most part, when the exercise of intellectual property rights is considered intolerable from a human rights perspective. Attending to author-focused human rights provides an opportunity for a modest shift in thinking about intellectual property, one that acknowledges the humanity and dignity of authors and other creative workers while, at the same time, also acknowledging limitations on those rights and engaging with other human rights concerns. It enables a focus on the distributive consequences of intellectual property policy – and opens up intellectual property policymaking to a set of concerns that is broader than the more cabined desideratum of "encouraging innovation."

As Professor Claudia Geiringer points out, the relationship between human rights and intellectual property has not been helped by over-inflated claims on both sides.[102] The overreaching claims in the intellectual property context are well known – it is these that provoke recourse to human rights in many contexts. But, as Geiringer notes, when human rights law tries to cozy up to other areas of law, including intellectual property, that cozying "may sometimes bear a close relationship to strangulation."[103] This is especially the case when human rights advocacy overlooks authors' human rights – which, of all the reasons for protecting intellectual property, seems to be the most morally salient. The case for enhancing freedom of expression, for example, is not made stronger by squeezing the life from human rights guarantees focused on protecting authors.

[102] Claudia Geiringer, Book Review, 34 HUMAN RIGHTS Q. 652, 653 (2012) (reviewing HELFER & AUSTIN, *supra* note 25).

[103] *Id.*, at 655.

Much work has yet to be done to recognize that authors' human rights – *and* the limitations that necessarily accompany them – are part of the intellectual property framework. This has not been helped by the insistence on the separation between these areas, or the neglect of the connections between them. Both should be at the policy table.

9

Intellectual Property in the Image of Human Rights: A Critical Review

RUTH L. OKEDIJI[1]

The relationship between intellectual property protection and international human rights law has historically been a thorny topic in global economic relations.[2] Since the conclusion of the 1995 Agreement on Trade-Related Aspects of Intellectual Property (TRIPS or TRIPS

[1] William L. Prosser Professor of Law and McKnight Presidential Endowed Professor, University of Minnesota Law School. I am grateful to Rochelle Cooper Dreyfuss, Margo Bagley, Olufunmilayo Arewa, and Molly Land for reading earlier drafts and providing helpful comments; Carla Baumel, University of Minnesota J.D., 2015, for excellent research assistance, and to Loren Turner and Scott Dewey of the University of Minnesota Law Library for outstanding research support. Final edits to the chapter were made with the assistance of library staff at Harvard Law School, especially Heather Pierce, Rachel Parker, and Candice Boos. I am also grateful to participants at the Harvard Law School conference on Law and Development held on July 16–18, 2017 for questions and feedback.

[2] Negotiations leading to the Paris Convention for the Protection of Industrial Property, Mar. 20, 1883, as last revised at Stockholm, July 14, 1967, 21 U.S.T. 1583, 828 U.N.T.S. 305 [hereinafter Paris Convention], and the Berne Convention for the Protection of Literary and Artistic Works, Sept. 9, 1886, 1161 U.N.T.S. 31 [hereinafter Berne Convention], were marked by serious differences in viewpoints about the economic, moral, and philosophical bases for granting exclusive rights to intellectual creations. *See* Heinrich Kronstein & Irene Till, *A Reevaluation of the International Patent Convention*, 12 LAW & CONTEMP. PROBS. 765, 766–76 (1947). Certainly, with regard to patents, the competing views in the late nineteenth century roughly paralleled what exists today, with countries divided over whether patents should be treated as private property or merely as instruments of public policy. *Id.* The majority proposal for the Paris Convention, based on a view of patents as property, described the right of "inventors and industrial creators in their own works" as one based on natural law. *Id.* at 775. This was countered by a Swiss proposal stating that rights of inventors and creative workers are a creation of "equitable and useful principles of the law of each nation which should reconcile this right . . . with the rights of society." *Id.* For similar themes in the debates leading up to the Berne Convention, *see* SAM RICKETSON, THE BERNE CONVENTION FOR THE PROTECTION OF LITERARY AND ARTISTIC WORKS: 1886–1986 46–47 (1987); *see also* P. J. Pointet, *The Role of Industrial Property in the Economic Development of States*, 6 INDUS. PROP. 61, 64–5 (1967) (describing public resentment to patents in some European countries).

Agreement),[3] most scholars agree this relationship has only grown more difficult.[4] Rival claims about the role that intellectual property plays in economic development – and the human welfare costs associated with strong intellectual property rights – compete for dominance in domestic strategies for implementing TRIPS and other international intellectual property obligations. The same rival claims vie for influence in the international agenda-setting processes of leading multilateral organizations such as the World Intellectual Property Organization (WIPO) and the World Trade Organization (WTO). The impassioned contest over the nature, scope, and implications of the intellectual property/human rights interface has important consequences for the way nations understand and comply with their obligations in each field. It also significantly affects the methods and substance of intellectual property technical assistance offered to developing countries.[5] Intellectual property law and policy thus exist in a persistent state of normative conflict that weighs heavily on the already complex relations among domestic and international actors involved with intellectual property policymaking, cementing a highly politicized environment at all levels of global, regional, and national governance.

In this chapter, I advance an argument and encourage caution about the contemporary construction of the intellectual property/human rights interface. On the whole, I view the human rights frame as problematic for the development interests and aspirations of most people living in the global South. My skepticism arises initially from the strongly individualistic focus of human rights – both in its ideological orientation towards western liberal tradition and in the reliance of human rights norm-setting

[3] Agreement on Trade-Related Aspects of Intellectual Property Rights, Apr. 15, 1994, Marrakesh Agreement Establishing the World Trade Organization, Annex 1C Legal Instruments – Results of the Uruguay Round, vol. 31, 33 I.L.M. 81 (1994) [hereinafter TRIPS].

[4] *See* Laurence R. Helfer, *Toward a Human Rights Framework for Intellectual Property*, 40 U.C. Davis L. Rev. 971, 982–7 (2007); *see also* Peter K. Yu, *Reconceptualizing Intellectual Property Interests in a Human Rights Framework*, 40 U.C. Davis L. Rev. 1039, 1041–7 (2007).

[5] Concerns of leading developing countries that WIPO's technical assistance did not address development considerations were central to efforts to establish the WIPO Development Agenda. Of the forty-five Recommendations that constitute the Development Agenda, the first relates to technical assistance. *See* WIPO, *The 45 Adopted Recommendations Under the WIPO Development Agenda* (2007), www.wipo.int/ipdevelopment/en/agenda/recommendations.html ("WIPO technical assistance shall be, *inter alia*, development-oriented, demand-driven and transparent, taking into account the priorities and the special needs of developing countries, especially LDCs, as well as the different levels of development of Member States").

institutions on external constituencies for expertise and guidance. At least in the field of intellectual property, those constituencies usually comprise international non-governmental organizations that, while well meaning, can stymie the necessary domestic debate that is a precursor for the growth of local actors who can more ably challenge the structural challenges imposed by international intellectual property regimes. The human rights discourse certainly has provided important grist for the international debate over global intellectual property norms; but it has accomplished remarkably little on the domestic front. Ultimately, my skepticism matured into a full-blown critique after consideration of how heavily influenced by intellectual property the human rights norm-setting process is. This feature of the relevant U.N. institutions creates significant challenges for the promise of a redemptive effect of human rights arguments on local intellectual property reform initiatives.

I present a series of related claims: First, a human rights frame for intellectual property does not, ineluctably, facilitate socially desirable outcomes for all countries; slapping human rights ideals on intellectual property regimes can, instead, actually strengthen intellectual property rights in non-socially helpful ways. Second, human rights-driven responses to the serious global challenges exacerbated or caused by an outsized global intellectual property system are not neutral. To the extent human rights objectives have imposed important limits on the domestic exercise of intellectual property rights, that progress has occurred principally in the developed countries. In multilateral arenas where norm-setting agendas are set, the most successful intellectual property-related human rights arguments are those that resonate predominantly in the western liberal tradition,[6] or that build on the intellectual property jurisprudence of U.S. and European courts.[7] Indeed, other than where

[6] I first sketched out this claim in the context of international copyright law in Ruth L. Okediji, *Reframing International Copyright Limitations and Exceptions as Development Policy*, in COPYRIGHT LAW IN AN AGE OF LIMITATIONS AND EXCEPTIONS 429 (Ruth L. Okediji ed., 2017) [hereinafter Okediji, *Reframing International Copyright Limitations and Exceptions as Development Policy*]. Makau Mutua has made a similar claim in his work regarding human rights scholarship more broadly. *See generally* Makau W. Mutua, *The Ideology of Human Rights*, 36 VA. J. INT'L L. 499 (1996) [hereinafter Mutua, *Ideology*]. *See also* Makau W. Mutua, *Savages, Victims, and Saviors: The Metaphor of Human Rights*, 42 HARV. INT'L L.J. 201, 204 (2001) ("The human rights corpus, though well-meaning, is fundamentally Eurocentric.").

[7] *See generally* Okediji, *Reframing International Copyright Limitations and Exceptions as Development Policy*, *supra* note 6; Ruth L. Okediji, *Securing Intellectual Property Objectives: New Approaches to Human Rights Considerations*, in CASTING THE NET WIDER: HUMAN RIGHTS, DEVELOPMENT AND NEW DUTY-BEARERS 211 (Margot

the right to health is concerned, human rights advocacy for intellectual property reform is frequently driven by concerns that implicate the values and institutions of leading developed countries. Third, and most significant, the limited effect of the human rights frame on the intellectual property/human rights interface can be attributed to the narrow vision of human rights that has long dominated the discourse – one that excludes economic, social, and cultural rights.

To be clear, human rights arguments (and related recommendations for intellectual property reform) can be beneficial. But they are limited insofar as they do not offer a meaningful pathway to improve the welfare of people whose conditions of life consistently fall beneath the ideals articulated in international human rights instruments. Reasons for this have to do partly with weak or non-existent intellectual property institutions – and institutions more broadly – in many developing and least-developed countries.[8] Human rights arguments that have garnered salience proceed on the flawed assumption that solutions to the adverse welfare effects of strong intellectual property rights look and function the same way regardless of the institutional, social, or cultural environments in which those human rights must take root and be realized. Even more troubling, those same arguments assume that intellectual property's human rights problems are principally the result of the unbridled power of private actors engulfed in rent-seeking behavior. However, they are not. Global intellectual property rules had a human rights problem long before the TRIPS Agreement triggered an intellectual property rights race.[9]

E. Salomon, Arne Tostensen, & Wouter Vandenhole eds., 2007) [hereinafter Okediji, *Securing Intellectual Property Objectives*].

[8] *See* Okediji, *Reframing International Copyright Limitations and Exceptions as Development Policy, supra* note 6, at 450–1.

[9] Certainly, the adverse effects of international IP rules on the material well-being of developing countries has been well recognized since the integration of those countries in the international legal order following independence. *See generally* Ruth L. Gana, *The Myth of Development, The Progress of Rights: Human Rights to Intellectual Property and Development*, 18 LAW & POLICY 315 (1996) [hereinafter Gana, *The Myth of Development*] (arguing that any human right to IP must be understood in the context of the right to development and the right to self-determination in order to protect the right of developing countries to establish IP regimes consistent with their unique socioeconomic and cultural norms and with development objectives). Technical assistance efforts in the field have largely revolved around ways to accommodate the interests of developing and least-developed countries. *Id.* Largely framed in the discourse of "development," these efforts fundamentally are about human rights goals. *Id. See also* Ruth L. Gana, *Has Creativity Died in the Third World? Some Implications of The Internationalization of Intellectual Property*, 24 DENV. J. INT'L L. & POL'Y 109 (1995).

The prevalent view that politics is the problem with intellectual property has impoverished the discourse about the appropriate design of the intellectual property/human rights interface. Given the significant power imbalance in global intellectual property relations, this politics-centric view animates the conclusion that a countervailing force to politics is needed, and that the higher moral power of a human rights frame provides the required counterweight. Moreover, depending on the specific issue in intellectual property, the politics-centric view invariably links past and future successes in intellectual property norm-setting with the efficacy of human rights advocacy, leaving developing and least-developed countries largely dependent on the agendas of international human rights actors. Certainly, in the context of the right to health, this linkage has considerable merit when considering how important these actors have been to securing outcomes such as the Doha Declaration[10] and other gains in the area of access to essential medicines.[11]

There is, however, reason to be skeptical about claims regarding a unique value associated with a human rights frame for intellectual property. On close reflection, most of the successes that could be attributable to the human rights/intellectual property interface are anchored in norms and values that are *already* quite authoritative in the intellectual property or constitutional frameworks of developed countries. Intellectual property law is directed at human welfare;[12] when properly designed and implemented it can accomplish human rights goals without any resort to human rights norms and obligations.[13] In my view, then, a key importance of articulating

[10] Declaration on the TRIPS Agreement and Public Health, WT/MIN(01)/DEC/2 ¶ 4 (Nov. 14, 2001), www.wto.org/english/thewto_e/minist_e/min01_e/mindecl_trips_e.htm [hereinafter Doha Declaration].

[11] *See* Kelly Morris, *Global Initiatives to Promote Wider Access to Medicines*, 8(9) THE LANCET: INFECTIOUS DISEASES 535, 535 (2008), www.who.int/medicines/areas/human_rights/Lancet_Infect_Dis_2008_8_535.pdf?ua=1. *See also* UNITED NATIONS SECRETARY-GENERAL'S HIGH-LEVEL PANEL ON ACCESS TO MEDICINES, PROMOTING INNOVATION AND ACCESS TO HEALTH TECHNOLOGIES 3 (Sept. 14, 2016), www.unsgaccessmeds.org/final-report/ [hereinafter High-Level Panel Report].

[12] The TRIPS Agreement recognizes the public interest in Article 7, which sets forth its objectives: "[t]he protection and enforcement of intellectual property rights should contribute to the promotion of technological innovation and to the transfer and dissemination of technology, to the mutual advantage of producers and users of technological knowledge and in a manner conducive to social and economic welfare, and to a balance of rights and obligations." *See* TRIPS, *supra* note 3, at art. 7.

[13] *See* Okediji, *Securing Intellectual Property Objectives, supra* note 7, at 213–14 (arguing that intellectual property's own tools, when properly deployed, can achieve human rights ends).

a distinct human rights frame for intellectual property is the possibility that doing so might provide a welfare surplus beyond what intellectual property doctrines can accomplish. In other words, are there claims that human rights law can make, or outcomes it could facilitate, that would not otherwise be possible within intellectual property law's own normative frame?

To be clear, advances based on human rights arguments that redound principally to the developed countries, or that improve norm coherence across regimes, are significant feats in their own right. Developing countries enjoy collateral benefits from efforts to enhance dissemination of knowledge, secure privacy, and promote liberty – all of which are guaranteed by human rights instruments.[14] Access to knowledge is especially crucial in a global economy increasingly reliant on transnational innovation networks to support technology flows in aid of productivity and trade. Nonetheless, for the ideals enshrined in human rights law to meaningfully benefit all peoples – for the genuinely transformative vision of international human rights to be more equally realized – the deployment of human rights frames for intellectual property must be done with greater attention to the specific needs and constraints of developing countries *as countries*. There must be a willingness to reorient the discourse to address the appropriate design of the intellectual property/human rights interface, and to accept solutions that look nothing like the legal framework that TRIPS and other multilateral intellectual property arrangements might characteristically dictate.[15] Human rights frames should constrain states to make choices along a continuum of possible models that incentivize innovation, facilitate access to and dissemination of technologies, and they should do so without mandating the dislocation of cultural values around which each society most ably functions. To this end, consideration of the intellectual property/human rights interface must extend beyond discussion of the intellectual property rights currently recognized in international human rights instruments, and embrace possibilities for intellectual property reform that could emerge from a serious engagement with the panoply of economic, social, cultural, and group rights. It is these rights, I argue, that can most deeply and

[14] *See, e.g.*, International Covenant on Economic, Social, and Cultural Rights, art. 5, Dec. 16, 1966, 993 U.N.T.S. 3 [hereinafter ICESCR]; Universal Declaration of Human Rights, art. 27, Dec. 12, 1948, GA Res. 217A, U.N. Doc. A/810 [hereinafter UDHR].

[15] *See generally* Copyright Law in an Age of Limitations and Exceptions (Ruth L. Okediji ed., 2017).

genuinely inform meaningful prospects for human and economic development.[16]

The chapter proceeds in three sections. First, I review the historical context of the relationship between intellectual property and human rights. I highlight the inattention of the intellectual property/human rights interface to economic, social, and cultural rights and suggest how that inattention has constrained the impact of the human rights frame on global intellectual property norm-setting. Next, I briefly highlight some recent national case law and other global legal developments at the intellectual property/human rights interface, showing how some economic, social, and cultural rights have been upheld in specific national contexts. I also point to limits of the human rights frame in the areas of health and education; those limits underscore the need for scholars, advocates, and policymakers to more critically question the human rights frame for intellectual property.

Finally, instead of accommodating human rights concerns principally in the form of limitations and exceptions to the various intellectual property subjects, policymakers have the ability and, arguably, the obligation to leverage the array of available legal and political tools in international and domestic law to ensure that all citizens have equal opportunities to flourish. To this end, I suggest policy initiatives that may facilitate a more complete vision and realization by all people of the material conditions envisaged and guaranteed by economic, social, and cultural rights. Those conditions, I argue, are necessary for the exercise of freedoms that make possible the creation, use, and enjoyment of knowledge assets in pursuit of development.

I The Incomplete Evolution of the Intellectual Property and Human Rights Interface

Historically, there was very little formal interaction between intellectual property and human rights law, though this has changed dramatically as

[16] Ruth L. Okediji, *Legal Innovation in International Intellectual Property Relations: Revisiting Twenty-One Years of the TRIPS Agreement*, 36 U. Pa. J. Int'l L. 191, 204 (2014) (noting that "access to technology and cultural goods materially affects individual exercises of social and political rights vital to innovation and creativity . . . [T]he relationship between the production and use of knowledge cannot be sensibly divorced from the equality-related aspirations that define most of the societies in which IP rights have been an important part of economic and political flourishing") (internal citations omitted) [hereinafter Okediji, *Legal Innovation*].

both fields have expanded in scope.[17] The international legal framework for intellectual property emerged in the early nineteenth century, a period in which the grant of a limited term monopoly for innovative creations was not evenly accepted among the leading industrialized countries.[18] Over time, however, the idea of recognizing proprietary rights for inventions and works of authorship continued to develop through a series of intellectual property-specific, bilateral, regional, and, eventually, multilateral conventions. The early foundational agreements in this respect were the Paris Convention for Industrial Property[19] and the Berne Convention for Literary and Artistic Works.[20] The conclusion of these Great Conventions initiated a progressive era of expansion of protectable subject matter and the delineation of a robust system of exclusive rights. However, the early, formative years of the multilateral intellectual property system contained few substantive rules and no effective enforcement tools,[21] permitting countries to shape their national regimes in a way that cohered with domestic development goals and strategies.

Over time, the passionate, moral justifications for intellectual property in the nineteenth century – championed in the field of copyright by prominent authors such as Victor Hugo[22] – yielded to the

[17] Professor Laurence Helfer has produced a leading body of work exploring the historical development of the two regimes. *See, e.g.*, LAURENCE R. HELFER & GRAEME W. AUSTIN, HUMAN RIGHTS AND INTELLECTUAL PROPERTY: MAPPING THE GLOBAL INTERFACE (2011); Laurence R. Helfer, *Pharmaceutical Patents and the Human Right to Health: The Contested Evolution of the Transnational Legal Order on Access to Medicines*, in TRANSNATIONAL LEGAL ORDERS 311 (Terence C. Halliday & Gregory Shaffer eds., 2015) [hereinafter Helfer, *Pharmaceutical Patents*]; Laurence R. Helfer, *Human Rights and Intellectual Property: Conflict or Coexistence?*, 5 MINN. INTELL. PROP. REV. 47, 49–51 (2003) ("Human rights and intellectual property, two bodies of law that were once strangers, are now becoming increasingly intimate bedfellows. For decades, the two subjects developed in virtual isolation from each other. But in the last few years, international standard setting activities have begun to map previously uncharted intersections between intellectual property law on the one hand and human rights law on the other.").

[18] *See, e.g.*, Kronstein & Till, *supra* note 2; Helfer, *Pharmaceutical Patents, supra* note 17, at 314.

[19] *See* Paris Convention, *supra* note 2. [20] *See* Berne Convention, *supra* note 2.

[21] *See* DANIEL GERVAIS, THE TRIPS AGREEMENT: DRAFTING HISTORY AND ANALYSIS 10 (2d ed. 2003) ("The two fundamental perceived flaws of the Paris and Berne Conventions were (a) the absence of detailed rules on the enforcement of rights before national judicial administrative authorities; and (b) the absence of a binding and effective dispute settlement mechanism (for disputes between states).").

[22] *See* Tim Wu, *On Copyright's Authorship Policy*, 1 UNIV. OF CHICAGO LEGAL FORUM 355, 340 (Article 8, 2008) (quoting Victor Hugo) ("Think of a man like Dante, Moliere,

incentive theory of the twentieth century, which justifies intellectual property almost exclusively in terms of national technical advancement and economic progress.[23] The rapid expansion of trade and technological innovation played a pivotal role in producing a robust, private technology sector with powerful political capital.[24] As global competitiveness intensified and the terms of competitive trade demanded greater access to overseas markets, leading technology sectors in the United States, Japan, and the European Union leveraged their political power in an extraordinary undertaking to introduce new rules for intellectual property protection in the

Shakespeare. Imagine him at the time when he has just finished a great work. His manuscript is there, in front of him; suppose that he gets the idea to throw it into the fire; nobody can stop him. Shakespeare can destroy Hamlet, Molière Tartufe, Dante the Hell"); *cf. Victor Hugo Still Rules EU Copyright*, SCIENCE GUIDE (Oct. 16, 2013), www.scienceguide.nl/201310/victor-hugo-still-rules-eu-copyright.aspx ("Continental European copyright is based on the idea that there is a strong link between the maker and his work. You might say a part of the author's identity is contained in the book. The central figure of this thinking is Victor Hugo who in 19th century France fought for authors rights. Today, we are still very much at that stage of thought."). *But see* James Boyle, *Victor Hugo: Champion of the Public Domain*, THE PUBLIC DOMAIN (Jul. 18, 2014), www.thepublicdomain.org/2014/07/18/victor-hugo-guardian-of-the-public-domain/ (noting that Hugo spoke "about the need to create a system that respected not just the rights of authors but the public's rights, the public's *ownership* of the public domain ... Victor Hugo, guardian of the public domain and a proponent of the exact kind of right of the public to the public domain ... ").

23 *See* TRIPS, *supra* note 3, at preamble (stating that part of the motivation for TRIPS was the desire "to reduce distortions and impediments to international trade, and taking into account the need to promote effective and adequate protection of intellectual property rights, and to ensure that measures and procedures to enforce intellectual property rights do not themselves become barriers to legitimate trade"); *see also* Pointet, *supra* note 2, at 63 ("Technical progress is the essential condition of all economic development"); Alois Troller, *Intellectual Property and Justice*, 6 INDUS. PROP. 119, 122 (1964) (observing that the debate at that time over the usefulness of patent law was grounded "in the assumed or disputed increase of production, and in the development of techniques ... In its eyes, the increase in national wealth and income becomes identified with the public good"); Kronstein & Till, *supra* note 2.

24 *See* SUSAN L. SELL, PRIVATE POWER, PUBLIC LAW: THE GLOBALIZATION OF INTELLECTUAL PROPERTY RIGHTS (2003); Ruth L. Okediji, *Public Welfare and the Role of the WTO: Reconsidering the TRIPS Agreement*, 17 EMORY INT'L L. REV. 819, 845–6 (2003) (discussing cooperation of U.S., Japanese and E.U. firms in getting their governments to push the TRIPS Agreement through) [hereinafter Okediji, *Public Welfare*]; *see also*, Helfer, *Pharmaceutical Patents, supra* note 17, at 314 (noting how the pharmaceutical industry launched a campaign for stronger IP rights and "framed its objection [for the lack of IP rights in medicines] in economic and moral terms. The unfettered copying of patented medicines was, the industry complained, a competitive disadvantage for industrialized economies and a deplorable form of modern-day 'piracy'").

international trade system.[25] The singular success of this effort brought nations together at the Uruguay Round multilateral trade negotiations where the TRIPS Agreement was concluded. The package deal clinched at the Uruguay Round established an unprecedented baseline for modern intellectual property relations.[26] In addition, the Uruguay Round established a complex institutional framework that implicates the realization of a wide range of human rights.[27]

A The TRIPS Agreement: Human Rights in the International Intellectual Property System

The TRIPS Agreement dramatically altered the normative contours of international intellectual property law by obligating all WTO members to adhere to certain minimum standards of intellectual property protection, including the requirement that nations recognize patents in all fields of technology.[28] In addition, the TRIPS Agreement broadened the infamous three-step test against which domestic law exceptions to the mandatory minimum international rules for patent and copyright protection are to be assessed.[29] Importantly, unlike the Paris and Berne Conventions, the TRIPS Agreement came with legal teeth. Under the Agreement, allegedly non-compliant WTO members are subject to the WTO's dispute

[25] *See* Okediji, *Public Welfare, supra* note 24, at 845–8; *see also*, Sell, *supra* note 24.

[26] *See generally* J. H. Reichman, *Universal Minimum Standards of Intellectual Property Protection Under the TRIPS Component of the WTO Agreement*, 29 Int'l Lawyer 345 (1995).

[27] There is a vast body of literature on trade and human rights expressing a wide range of opinions about the impact of the WTO on human rights. For a particularly trenchant critique, see J. Oloka-Onyango & Deepika Udagama, The Realization of Economic, Social and Cultural Rights: Globalization and its Impact on the Full Enjoyment of Human Rights, Preliminary Report Prepared for the UN Commission on Human Rights, Sub-Commission on the Promotion and Protection of Human Rights, United Nations, Economic and Social Council (2000) (arguing that the WTO is a vexatious instrument where human rights are concerned). For another view, see Alan O. Sykes, *International Trade and Human Rights: An Economic Perspective* (John M. Olin Center for Law & Economics, Working Paper No. 188, 2003) (concluding that "economists will find little merit in most of the human rights critique ... the evidence suggests that the growth of the trading system generally tends to promote rather than undermine human rights"). For a seminal comprehensive mapping of the intersections between IP and human rights, see Helfer & Austin, *supra* note 17.

[28] *See* TRIPS, *supra* note 3, at art. 27.1. *See generally*, Reichman, *supra* note 26.

[29] *See* TRIPS, *supra* note 3, at arts. 13, 30.

settlement system with the prospect of meaningful trade sanctions.[30] Finally, to accommodate the significant changes that would be required to become TRIPS compliant, certain flexibilities were built into the agreement – many that offer specific and important benefits for developing and least-developed nations.[31] For reasons that have been well developed in the intellectual property literature, and others that I elaborate on here, these flexibilities have not been successful in promoting the interests of developing countries.[32]

Since the conclusion of the Uruguay Round, human rights frames have had far less impact on global intellectual property norms than might have been anticipated given the intense global mobilization against the TRIPS Agreement. To the contrary, progressive harmonization of international

[30] *See* TRIPS *supra* note 3, at arts. 63–64; *see also* Rochelle Cooper Dreyfuss & Andreas F. Lowenfeld, *Two Achievements of the Uruguay Round: Putting TRIPS and Dispute Settlement Together*, 37 VA. J. INT'L L. 275 (1997).

[31] *See* J. H. Reichman, *The TRIPS Agreement Comes of Age: Conflict or Cooperation with the Developing Countries?*, 32 CASE W. RES. J. INT'L L. 441, 456–64 (2000); Peter K. Yu, *Six Secret (and Now Open) Fears of ACTA*, 64 SMU L. REV. 975, 1040 (2011) ("Second, even if countries are aware of the flexibilities that have been built into the agreement, policymakers may be strongly discouraged from introducing limitations and exceptions. For example, they may face external pressure from their powerful trading partners . . ."); Amy Kapczynski, *The Access to Knowledge Mobilization and the New Politics of Intellectual Property*, 117 YALE L.J. 804, 876 (2008) ("Organizing around law has helped not only to galvanize the A2K mobilization, but also to shape its language and self-construction. This is evident in the architecture of the mobilization, in the investment of A2K actors in arguments and strategies that operate internal to the logic of the law and legal discourse of IP, and in the tendency of movement actors strategically to modulate their claims by, for example, embracing TRIPS flexibilities rather than opposing TRIPS. These are effects of what I call the gravitational pull that law exerts on framing processes"); *see also* WIPO, ADVICE ON FLEXIBILITIES UNDER THE TRIPS AGREEMENT (last visited Aug. 11, 2017), www.wipo.int/ip-development/en/legislative_assistance/advice_trips.html (identifying four clusters of flexibilities: (i) flexibilities as to the method of implementing TRIPS obligations; (ii) flexibilities as to substantive standards of protection; (iii) flexibilities as to mechanisms of enforcement; (iv) flexibilities as to areas not covered by the TRIPS Agreement).

[32] For a leading account of the pathologies of TRIPS implementation in developing and least-developed countries, see CAROLYN DEERE, THE IMPLEMENTATION GAME: THE TRIPS AGREEMENT AND THE GLOBAL POLITICS OF INTELLECTUAL PROPERTY REFORM IN DEVELOPING COUNTRIES chs. 3, 6 (2009); *see also* James Gathii & Cynthia Ho, *Regime Shifting of IP Lawmaking and Enforcement from the WTO to the International Investment Regime*, 18 MINN. J.L. SCI. & TECH. 427, 429 (2017) (suggesting that investor-state disputes have the potential to systematically undermine built-in TRIPS flexibilities); *cf.* Henning Grosse Ruse-Khan, *The International Law Relation Between Trips and Subsequent Trips-Plus Free Trade Agreements: Towards Safeguarding Trips Flexibilities?*, 18 J. INTELL. PROP. L. 325, 332 (2011) (exploring the relationship between TRIPS flexibility provisions and TRIPS-plus free trade agreements).

intellectual property law has continued in various fora, exacerbating historical and continuing burdens on the development prospects of developing and least-developed countries. In particular, multilateral, regional, and bilateral trade agreements have assumed a crucial role in the creation of new international intellectual property norms[33] with even stronger requirements and less safeguards for public welfare interests. Many of these trade agreements, coined "TRIPS-plus"[34] agreements, oblige the contracting parties to heighten intellectual property protections beyond that which is required by the TRIPS Agreement and to compromise, or abandon altogether, built-in TRIPS flexibilities. And, of course, norm-setting activities continue in WIPO where proposals for new intellectual property agreements are on the agenda,[35] while long-standing proposals for establishing new limitations and exceptions for libraries, museums, and archives are languishing despite years of discussion.[36] Beyond these manifestations of the ongoing expansion of intellectual property[37] is an elaborate network of technical assistance that

[33] *See* Okediji, *Legal Innovation, supra* note 16, at 194 (noting that "new sites of resistance to the built-in normative flexibility recognized by the TRIPS Agreement have become entrenched in a viral web of bilateral, regional and plurilateral agreements"); *see also id.* at 251–9 (briefly reviewing some of the post-TRIPS multilateral initiatives); *see generally* Henning Grosse Ruse-Khan, *Protecting Intellectual Property under BITs, FTAs, and TRIPS: Conflicting Regimes or Mutual Coherence?*, in Evolution in Investment Treaty Law and Arbitration 485 (K. Miles & C. Brown eds., 2011).

[34] *See* Helfer, *supra* note 4, at 982 n. 28 ("These treaties are referred to as 'TRIPS Plus' because they (1) contain IP standards more stringent than those found in TRIPS; (2) oblige developing countries to implement TRIPS fully before the end of their transition periods; or (3) require such countries to accede to or comply with other multilateral IP agreements"); *see also* Genetic Resources Action International (GRAIN), *'TRIPS-Plus' Through The Back Door: How Bilateral Treaties Impose Much Stronger Rules for IPRs on Life than the WTO* (July 2001), www.grain.org/system/old/docs/trips-plus-en.pdf.

[35] Jeremy Malcolm, *The WIPO Broadcasting Treaty Would be a Body Blow for Online Video*, Electronic Frontier Foundation (May 2, 2017), www.eff.org/deeplinks/2017/05/wipo-broadcasting-treaty-would-be-body-blow-online-video; Catherine Saez, *Potential Treaty to Protect Broadcasters' IP Rights: Technicalities Explained*, Intellectual Prop. Watch (Feb. 8, 2017), www.ip-watch.org/2017/02/08/potential-treaty-protect-broadcasters-ip-rights-technicalities-explained/; Catherine Saez, *Geographical Indications, Design Law Treaty Up Next At WIPO*, Intellectual Prop. Watch (Nov. 14, 2015), www.ip-watch.org/2015/11/14/geographical-indications-design-law-treaty-up-next-at-wipo/.

[36] *See* WIPO, Standing Committee on Copyright and Related Rights (SCCR) www.wipo.int/policy/en/sccr/ (last visited Aug. 11, 2017) (listing items under discussion); *see also* Okediji, *Reframing International Copyright Limitations and Exceptions as Development Policy, supra* note 6.

[37] *See, e.g.*, WIPO, *Geneva Act of the Lisbon Agreement on Appellations of Origin and Geographical Indications and Regulations Under the Geneva Act of the Lisbon*

profoundly drives the extent to which intellectual property norms are applied to advance or retard states' capacity to integrate human rights obligations, much less its aspirations, as key considerations of intellectual property treaty implementation.[38] For example, a recent review of WIPO's technical assistance programs notes a variety of concerns related to how activities directed at developing and least-developed countries fall short of enabling development interests.[39] I will not review these well-known criticisms of WIPO and the international intellectual property system here.[40] Suffice it to say, technical assistance should become a far more significant focus of concern in securing the vision of human well-being and progress enshrined in international human rights instruments – a vision that has been placed under tremendous pressure by the global intellectual property system. This ongoing confluence of new trade agreements with TRIPS-plus provisions, continuing intellectual property harmonization, and new tools such as investor-state provisions in investment agreements, questions the notion that human rights frames are having a significant or distinct impact on international intellectual property norms. As I discuss further below, the limited effect of the human rights frame on intellectual property reform may be attributed to the narrow vision of human rights – one that excludes economic, social, and cultural rights – that has dominated the intellectual property/human rights interface.

B Assimilating Intellectual Property in the International Human Rights Framework

The international human rights regime is of a more recent vintage than international intellectual property law. Scholars generally credit the

Agreement on Appellations of Origin and Geographical Indications, LI/DC/19 (May 20, 2015), www.wipo.int/edocs/lexdocs/treaties/en/lisbon/trt_lisbon_009en.pdf.

[38] *See* Ruth L. Okediji, *Africa at WIPO and Other Myths of Intellectual Property Law-Making* (forthcoming).

[39] Carolyn D. Birkbeck & Santiago Roca, *Independent External Review of WIPO Technical Assistance in the Area of Cooperation for Development*, SSRN (2011), https://ssrn.com/abstract=2195872.

[40] Criticism of WIPO has been an enduring feature of scholarly and other commentary on the international IP system. For some important reviews, see SISULE F. MUSUNGU & GRAHAM DUTFIELD, MULTILATERAL AGREEMENTS AND A TRIPS-PLUS WORLD: THE WORLD INTELLECTUAL PROPERTY ORGANIZATION (2003); James Boyle, *A Manifesto on WIPO and the Future of Intellectual Property*, 9 DUKE L. & TECH. REV. 1 (2004); *see also* CHRISTOPHER MAY, THE WORLD INTELLECTUAL PROPERTY ORGANIZATION: RESURGENCE AND THE WIPO DEVELOPMENT AGENDA ch. 6 (2007).

beginning of the modern human rights legal framework to the establishment of the United Nations and the adoption of the Universal Declaration of Human Rights (UDHR) in 1948.[41] Participating nations agreed that individuals should be guaranteed certain rights including, among other things, freedom of expression, the right to a standard of living adequate for health and well-being, the right to education, the right to freely participate in cultural life, and the right to the protection of the moral and material interests resulting from any scientific, literary or artistic creations.[42]

The international community eventually concluded work on other treaties designed to make concrete legal obligations out of the general principles of the UDHR. One such treaty is the International Covenant on Economic, Social, and Cultural Rights (ICESCR).[43] Adopted by the U.N. General Assembly in 1966, the ICESCR recognizes the importance of securing certain material, social, and cultural conditions to facilitate human progress and national development. Article 15 of the ICESCR mirrors the provision of Article 27 of the UDHR, which provides for the right of individuals "to freely participate in the cultural life of the community, to enjoy the arts and to share in scientific advancement and its benefits" and "the right to the protection of the moral and material interests resulting from any scientific, literary or artistic production of which he is the author."[44] These provisions clearly recognize a right to engage with, own, and earn rent or reward from one's created works. It should be no surprise, then, that to the extent other provisions in international human rights instruments purport to place limits on the scope and exercise of intellectual property rights, those limits certainly have not displaced the political, moral, or legal premium associated with the unequivocal recognition of authorial interests in Article 27 of the UDHR and Article 15 of the ICESCR.

[41] *See* UDHR, *supra* note 14. [42] *Id.*

[43] *See* ICESCR, *supra* note 14. With respect to intellectual property, human rights scholars have paid increasing attention to the moral and material interests of creators. Closely tracking article 27(2) of the UDHR, article 15(1)(c) of the ICESCR requires each state party to the Covenant to "recognize the right of everyone … [t]o benefit from the protection of the moral and material interests resulting from any scientific, literary or artistic production of which he [or she] is the author." *Id.* The third treaty referenced above, the International Covenant on Civil and Political Rights (ICCPR), Dec. 16, 1966, 999 U.N.T.S. 171, focuses on the civil and political dimensions of human rights and figures less prominently in the issues presented in this chapter.

[44] *See* UDHR, *supra* note 14, at art. 27(1)–(2).

The historical record fails to offer much insight into what the drafters intended by the chosen text contained in the UDHR and ICESCR.[45] Nonetheless, these instruments serve as the basis for claims that intellectual property rights are human rights and they have long been the formal 'hook' on which human rights arguments in support of strong national and international intellectual property rights have hung.[46] Reinforcing this perspective is the fact that the Committee charged with monitoring state compliance with the ICESCR has provided interpretive guidance to governments through its General Comment 17.[47] This General Comment affirms Article 15 as an obligation to protect author's rights, even though neither the UDHR nor the ICESCR uses the phrase "intellectual property." Strong versions of this view claim that intellectual property is a human right per se,[48] emphasizing the dependence of

[45] Paul Torremans, *Copyright as a Human Right*, in Copyright and Human Rights: Freedom of Expression, Intellectual Property, Privacy (2004).

[46] Victor Hugo's speech in 1878 to the Congress of Literary, Industrial and Artistic Property, Paris, certainly reflects this view. *See* Victor Hugo, *Address of Victor Hugo to the International Literary Congress*, in Copyright Perspectives 1, 1–6 (B. Fitzgerald & J. Gilchrist eds., Benedict Atkinson, trans., Springer International Publishing, 2015). Indeed, the Congress adopted the resolutions among which was a resolution that "[t] the right of the author in his work constitutes, not a concession by the law but one of the forms of property which the legislature must protect." *See* Ricketson, *supra* note 2, at 46; *see also* G. Béguin, *The Universal Declaration of Human Rights (of the 10th December, 1948) and the Protection of Intellectual Property*, 12 Indus. Prop. 267 (1963); Stojan Pretnar, *Contemporary Problems of the Rights of the Authors of Scientific Discoveries*, 11 Indus. Prop. 264, 265 (1962) (noting that the UDHR helped keep alive the idea of a right of authors/creators in the period following World War II. "By introducing paragraph 2 of Article 27 into the Universal Declaration of Human Rights, proclaiming the right of the material and moral interests to protection in favour of the authors of every industrial production ... and of literary and artistic works, the United Nations have, without doubt, renewed and accentuated the movement which, in the second half of the nineteenth century, enabled the foundation of the Berne and Paris Conventions to take place.").

[47] U.N. Econ. & Soc. Council [ECOSOC], Comm. on Econ., Soc. & Cultural Rights [CESCR], General Comment No. 17: The Right of Everyone to Benefit from the Protection of the Moral and Material Interests Resulting from Any Scientific, Literary or Artistic Production of Which He or She Is the Author (Article 15, Paragraph 1(c), of the Covenant), U.N. Doc. E/C.12/GC/17 (Jan. 12, 2006) [hereinafter General Comment No. 17].

[48] *See Foreword*, WIPO, UNHCR, *Intellectual Property and Human Rights* (stating that "[i] ntellectual property rights are enshrined as human rights in the [Universal Declaration of Human Rights]") [hereinafter *Intellectual Property and Human Rights*]. More recently, however, the U.N. Special Rapporteur in the field of cultural rights has adopted a more nuanced approach to the relationship between IP and human rights. Among other things, two reports on copyright and patent law note that considerations of human rights must prevail over IP rights. *See* Report of the Special Rapporteur in the field of cultural rights,

human progress on the technologies and cultural goods incentivized by intellectual property regimes.[49] The result is that the human rights/intellectual property framework has largely operated as a justification for the core architecture of the international intellectual property system, with human rights considerations channeled through doctrines already hard-wired in contemporary intellectual property jurisprudence.

Although General Comment 17 on ICESCR Article 15(1)(c) appears to subordinate intellectual property to human rights, it does so by attempting to distinguish intellectual property principally as an instrumentalist tool used by states to achieve broader public aims. According to the Comment, "[h]uman rights are fundamental, inalienable and universal entitlements belonging to individuals" while intellectual property rights are "first and foremost means by which States seek to provide incentives for inventiveness and creativity . . . for the benefit of society as a whole."[50] This utilitarian justification for intellectual property, however, hardly tells the full story – other theories of intellectual property (and some historical accounts of debates leading to the Great Conventions) unequivocally assimilate intellectual property into human rights frames reinforced by ideals of freedom and justice.[51] While it is true, as the ICESCR Committee notes, that a state's chosen justification for intellectual property may produce differences in scope between intellectual property rights and human rights law,[52] the foundational premise that creators have fundamental rights that can be curtailed by states only in extraordinary circumstances is an idea with a strong historical pedigree in the intellectual property field.

Farida Shaheed, U.N. Doc. A/70/279 (Aug. 4, 2015) [hereinafter "2015 Shaheed Report"]; Report of the Special Rapporteur in the field of cultural rights, Farida Shaheed, U.N. Doc. A/HRC/28/57 (Dec. 24, 2014) [hereinafter "2014 Shaheed Report"]. The Special Rapporteur notes explicitly, for example, the human right to the protection of moral and material interests arising from authorship or inventorship. "In her thematic report on the right to science, the Special Rapporteur stressed that innovations essential for a life with dignity should be accessible to everyone, in particular marginalized populations. From a human rights perspective, mechanisms are needed to protect to the public interest wherever a particular technology is critical to human welfare, as might be the case in areas of health, agriculture or housing." *See* 2015 Shaheed Report at ¶ 49.

49 *Id.* ("The role of intellectual Property law in the progress of societies cannot be overemphasized.")

50 *See* General Comment No. 17, *supra* note 47, at ¶ 1.

51 Troller, *supra* note 23 (arguing that the protection of IP is a moral necessity and important for developing human identity, social relations and ensuring freedom to develop as a person). These themes are, of course, central to Hegel's view of real property. *See* Margaret Jane Radin, *Property and Personhood*, 34 Stan. L. Rev. 957, 1004 (1982).

52 *See* General Comment No. 17, *supra* note 47, at ¶ 2.

The ICESCR Committee urges that "it is . . . important not to equate intellectual property rights with the human right recognized in article 15," but it nevertheless adopts a strong position limiting the extent to which states may interfere with the rights of creators[53] – a position that fully coincides with the basic thrust of the strongest international intellectual property instruments.

More recently, however, the U.N. Special Rapporteur in the field of cultural rights has adopted a more nuanced approach to the relationship between intellectual property and human rights. In the field of patent law, the Special Rapporteur's Report explicitly states that the human right to the protection of moral and material interests arising from authorship or inventorship "cannot be used to defend patent laws that inadequately respect the right to participate in cultural life, to enjoy the benefits of scientific progress and its applications, to scientific freedoms . . . The human rights perspective demands that patents do not extend so far as to interfere with individuals' dignity and well-being. Where patent rights and human rights are in conflict, human rights must prevail."[54] Similarly, the Special Rapporteur's Report on Cultural Rights takes a firm position that an author's right to remuneration does not entitle an author to every possible revenue stream associated with the copyrighted work.[55] It remains to be seen whether and how these reports will influence national intellectual property lawmaking, particularly in the developing countries where the power of human rights rhetoric is, ironically, usually a less persuasive platform for domestic

[53] For example, the Committee recognizes that the right to the protection of the moral and material interests resulting from one's scientific, literary and artistic productions is "subject to limitations" and "must be balanced with the other rights recognized in the Covenant", it states that "limitations on the rights protected under article 15(1)(c), must be determined by law in a manner compatible with the nature of these rights, must pursue a legitimate aim, and must be strictly necessary for the promotion of the general welfare in a democratic society . . . " *Id.* at ¶ 22; *see also* Laurence R. Helfer, *Collective Management of Copyrights and Human Rights: An Uneasy Alliance Revisited*, in COLLECTIVE MANAGEMENT OF COPYRIGHT AND RELATED RIGHTS 75 (Daniel J. Gervais ed., 2d ed. 2010) (noting "the stringent standard" for assessing the legality of state limitations of the rights in the ICESCR).

[54] 2015 Shaheed Report, *supra* note 48, at 2.

[55] "In contrast to the perpetual moral interests of authors, the Committee on Economic, Social and Cultural Rights has emphasized that the material interests of authors need not necessarily be protected forever, or even for an author's entire life (general comment No. 17, para 16). The human right to protection of authorship is fully compatible with an approach to copyright that limits the terms of protection in order to ensure a vibrant public domain of shared cultural heritage, from which all creators are free to draw." *See* 2014 Shaheed Report, *supra* note 48, ¶ 50.

legal reform.[56] Moreover, the international NGOs that have been crucial for ensuring positive domestic action following a Special Rapporteur's report[57] largely do not exist in areas of intellectual property other than in the area of access to medicines and, more limitedly, access to knowledge. Ultimately, to the extent the soft weight of a Report is countered by the more formal "hard" view institutionalized in General Comment 17, the latter is likely to hold more sway. Despite important caveats, admonitions to states to adopt a balanced approach to intellectual property rights, and highlighting the need to protect the rights of indigenous peoples, General Comment 17, in the end, appears mainly to establish the point that intellectual property rights are an imperfect, but legitimate, expression of the obligations contained in the international human rights framework. In doing so, it adopts not only the instrumentalist vision of intellectual property, but also the set of values that underlie it – values that inform ideas about human dignity, freedom, culture, and society in liberal developed countries.

Many commentators and leading actors have also viewed the protections required in the UDHR and ICESCR as synonymous with, or, at the very least, expressed by the rights recognized in international intellectual property instruments.[58] An official publication by WIPO and the Office of the United Nations High Commission for Human Rights asserts that "[i]intellectual property rights are enshrined as human rights" in the UDHR and ICESCR,[59] and that "[h]uman rights and the equitable treatment of authors and inventors ... remain the underpinnings of

[56] In addition, as Molly Land observes, S.R. reports on intellectual property rights are likely to be less impactful in developing and less-developed countries due to the lack of domestic interest groups interested and equipped to engage in advocacy efforts. This is especially true in the context of sub-Saharan Africa. *See* Molly K. Land, *The Marrakesh Treaty as "Bottom Up" Lawmaking: Empowering Local Human Rights Action on IP Policies*, U.C. Irvine L.R. (forthcoming 2018).

[57] *See* Jo Becker, Campaigning For Human Rights: Human Rights Advocacy In Practice 77–94 (2013); Sally E. Merry, Human Rights and Gender Violence: Translating International Law into Local Justice 61–5 (2006).

[58] *Cf.* ECOSOC, Comm. on Econ., Soc. & Cultural Rights, *Background Paper: Drafting History of the Article 15(1)(c) of the International Covenant on Economic, Social and Cultural Rights* 45, 24th Sess., U.N. Doc. E/C.12/2000/15 (Nov. 27, 2000) (prepared by Maria Green) ("By raising both [access and protection] to the level of human rights, the drafters set up a tension that must be resolved if Article 15 is to be made effective. It is fascinating to note, however, that the distinguished men and women who gave us the ICESCR did not seem to deeply consider the difficult balance between public needs and private rights when it comes to intellectual property.").

[59] *See Intellectual Property and Human Rights*, *supra* note 48.

intellectual property systems."[60] This *de facto* equality of intellectual property and human rights means that the interaction of the two regimes requires or warrants reconciliation between their competing means. Reconciliation *itself* – not fulfillment of human rights ends or development goals – thus becomes an added obligation of states, and a central preoccupation of government efforts to implement intellectual property rights even when those rights clearly inhibit human rights aspirations. Reconciliation requires acceptance of, and adherence with, established premises of the global intellectual property system thus restricting the extent to which states might challenge or redesign the interface of human rights obligations and intellectual property laws. As I conclude elsewhere:

> At its core, the human rights [frame] does not encounter intellectual property as much as it complements it; it does not resist it as much as it attempts to contain its effects. The ... [intellectual property/human rights interface] frames human rights as a redemptive discipline important to the mission of recognizing and protecting the ability of people to participate in the public interest goals animating the intellectual property

[60] Intellectual Property Rights and Human Rights: Report of the Secretary General, ESCOR, Commission on Human Rights, Sub-Commission on the Promotion and Protection of Human Rights, 52nd Sess., Provisional Agenda item 4, § II.B.2, U.N. Doc E/CN.4/Sub.2/2001/12 at 7 (2001). In general, scholars and international organizations have not always been clear when describing the relationship between IP and human rights, at times referencing IP rights "as" human rights, and, at other times, distinguishing between the "moral and material interests of authors" and IP rights. For the latter approach, see Report of the Special Rapporteur, *supra* note 48. Consistently defining these terms will improve the discourse on this burgeoning legal intersection. *Cf.* Helfer, *supra* note 4, at 975–6:

> Both the ... UDHR ... and the ... ICESCR ... recognize the moral and material interests of authors and inventors and the right "to enjoy the arts and to share in scientific advancement and its benefits" ... Without elaboration, however, these textual provisions provide only a faint outline of how to develop human rights-compliant mechanisms to promote creativity and innovation. They also invite governments and activists on both sides of the [IP] divide to use the rhetoric of human rights to bolster arguments for or against revising [IP] protection standards in treaties and in national laws. Without greater normative clarity, however, such 'rights talk' risks creating a legal environment in which every claim (and therefore no claim) enjoys the distinctive protections that attach to human rights. The skeletal and under-theorized [IP] provisions of human rights law also leave critical questions unanswered. What, for example, is the relationship between the [IP] clauses of the UDHR and ICESCR and the remaining civil, political, social, and economic rights enshrined in human rights pantheon? And how do human rights law's [IP] rules interface with the rules set out in multilateral agreements emanating from WIPO, the WTO, and regional and bilateral trade and investment treaties?

> system. The point of the human rights [frame] is not to transform intellectual property rights . . . [i]ndeed, the human rights [frame] sees the intellectual property system as a constitutive part of the universal values it seeks to affirm in and among states . . .[61]

The project of reconciling intellectual property and human rights has been foremost in the international human rights agenda. It is evident in the bulk of scholarly commentary on the intellectual property/human rights interface, in official documents of the U.N. Sub-Committee on Human Rights,[62] and in the ICESCR Committee. It has also been dominant in advocacy initiatives by many international non-governmental organizations (INGOs). The effort by human rights actors and institutions charged with providing guidance to states about the obligations in the UDHR and the ICESCR has fixated on a search to "balance" the interests of the two regimes, rather than to (re)conceive a vision of intellectual property rights informed by a more fulsome analysis that includes the full range of human rights. The practical activities of leading INGOs, such as Médecins sans Frontières and Oxfam, have certainly focused on prioritizing human rights ends. Nonetheless, the thick jurisprudence of the international intellectual property framework, reinforced by the international human rights discourse, continues to bedevil prospects for the kind of wide-scale transformative redirection of norms necessary to ensure that policymakers can reflect the enabling power of group, economic, cultural, and social human rights in enacting legislation or when ratifying treaties. As a result of this dense international intellectual property jurisprudence, the intellectual property/human rights interface has flourished most around issues implicating individual rights that are quasi-political or within a creator's "zone of autonomy."[63]

Finally, the intellectual property/human rights interface has relied almost solely on limitations and exceptions to intellectual property as the dominant technique for rationalizing or reconciling intellectual

[61] Ruth L. Okediji, *The Limits of Development Strategies at the Intersection of Intellectual Property and Human Rights*, in INTELLECTUAL PROPERTY, TRADE AND DEVELOPMENT 355, 361 (Daniel Gervais ed., 2d ed. 2014) [hereinafter Okediji, *The Limits of Development Strategies*].

[62] *See, e.g.*, Sub-Commission on Human Rights Res. 2000/7, *Intellectual Property Rights and Human Rights*, ESCOR, Commission on Human Rights, Sub-Commission on the Promotion and Protection of Human Rights, 52nd Sess., 25th Mtg., U.N. Doc. E/CN.4/Sub.2/Res/2000/7 (2000).

[63] *See* Okediji, *The Limits of Development Strategies, supra* note 61, at 353; *see also* Helfer, *supra* note 53.

property rights and human rights. Freedom of speech, freedom to compete, and privacy rights are well-established limits to intellectual property rights; these limitations and exceptions have served as important, public-minded carve-outs to the otherwise robust endowment of private control over knowledge assets. However, a realistic and meaningful human rights frame requires consideration of all human rights – including economic, cultural, and social rights – to advance the vision of a "common standard of achievement for all peoples and all nations."[64] For example, I have argued that "[r]arely is the right to development raised as part of the [human rights] discourse; instead . . . human rights analyses are predicated on the articulation of [a limited set of individual] rights."[65] Even with the relatively more ambitious work of the United Nations Sub-Commission on the Promotion and Protection of Human Rights (now the Human Rights Council) in regards to the right to health, the focus has been to decry the absence of a human rights approach to TRIPS implementation, "rather than [deal] with state obligations to create substantive legal regimes to address innovation needs relevant to the specific national context."[66] Given this focus on individual civil and political rights, the intellectual property/human rights interface is underdeveloped and incomplete; its evolution must remain a work in progress for scholars, advocates, and international institutions.

C *The Limits of Framing Intellectual Property Rights as Expressions of Human Rights Obligations*

So-called group rights and economic, social, and cultural rights have historically faced resistance in the industrialized countries, including among human rights scholars and activists.[67] They have also been largely

[64] *See* UDHR, *supra* note 14, at preamble.

[65] *See* Okediji, *The Limits of Development Strategies*, *supra* note 61, at 353. Indigenous rights are a notable exception to this tendency.

[66] *Id.* at 359.

[67] *See* Mutua, *Ideology*, *supra* note 6; *see also* Okediji, *Securing Intellectual Property Objectives*, *supra* note 7, at 217–18, n. 25. *But see* Katharine G. Young, *The New Economic and Social Rights*, 107; *Proceedings of the ASIL Annual Meeting* 486, 486 (2013) (stating that "in the last two decades, economic and social rights have experienced a notable repositioning in international law. No longer a proxy for the ideological stand-offs of the Cold War, such rights are now embraced as a fundamental part of the international human rights agenda").

ignored in human rights frames of the global intellectual property regime.[68] Yet, it is precisely the pressures of ongoing national health, education, environmental, or other development challenges that have evoked the most intense interactions between human rights and intellectual property laws. The TRIPS Agreement and other intellectual property instruments provide legal and normative space for countries to address these challenges in an ad hoc, case-by-case resolution of specific claims through limitations and exceptions to intellectual property rights recognized in intellectual property treaties and in national laws. This approach, though imperfect, works to address some of the interests and concerns of consumers in developed countries. However, it ignores entirely the structural conditions that exist in most least-developed and developing countries, and it belies what development economists counsel is required for development progress.[69]

Further, the unpredictability of ad hoc determinations regarding the applicability, scope, and meaning of any of the limitations and exceptions available in intellectual property law is at odds with the direction provided by the ICESCR Committee which, in General Comment No. 17, emphasizes the need for security for creators in the realization of the rights granted in the ICESCR.[70] The quest for "balance" or "reconciliation" that permeates the intellectual property/human rights literature reflects an implicit assumption – or acceptance of the assumption – that intellectual property rights are an optimal means to advance human development in a globalized world. With the premise (discussed earlier in Section I) that the two regimes are formal equals, the discourse of reconciliation reinforces the legitimacy of the current version of intellectual property rights, and fosters acceptance of the idea that intellectual property and human rights are justifiably in a competitive jostle over which should prevail as the dominant paradigm for promoting human welfare.

Below, I highlight two problematic aspects of the current human rights frame which are reflected somewhat in the ICESCR Committee's General Comment: (1) the importance of the collective for the realization of rights enshrined in the ICESCR; and (2) the unsuitability of intellectual

[68] *But see* Gana, *The Myth of Development*, *supra* note 9 (arguing that the human right to intellectual property must be understood in context with the right to development and self-determination); Lea Shaver & Caterina Sganga, *The Right to Take Part in Cultural Life: On Copyright and Human Rights*, 27 Wis. Int'l L.J. 637 (2010).

[69] Okediji, *Reframing International Copyright Limitations and Exceptions as Development Policy*, *supra* note 6 (developing this claim in the context of international copyright law).

[70] *See* General Comment No. 17, *supra* note 47, at ¶¶ 39–40 ("Core Obligations").

property limitations and exceptions designed for individuals to satisfy the obligations required of states under the ICESCR.

1 The Importance of the Collective

The aspiration of individual liberty at the core of the UDHR is grounded in the physical and intellectual well-being of individuals. However, aspirations about the socio-material conditions of life find their source and significance in the shared experience of a collective; indeed, under Article 22 of the UDHR, individuals hold their rights as members of society and not just as atomistic individuals:

> Everyone, *as a member of society*, has the right to social security and is entitled to realization, through national effort and international co-operation and in accordance with the organization and resources of each State, of the economic, social and cultural rights indispensable for his dignity and the free development of his personality.[71]

As Amartya Sen and Martha Nussbaum[72] argue, the freedom to participate in the development process, to pursue and experience justice, to exercise liberty, and to engage on equal terms in the public policy arena are all central aspects of human development. The capabilities approach to development highlights the necessity of the collective not in binary opposition to the individual, but precisely because the collective provides the space and defines the context for individual expression. Individuals hold the rights codified in Article 22 as part of a set of cultural values upon which the state is constituted. Those values define an individual's sense of self, of society, of freedom, and guides her aspirations. In short, cultural values provide the parameters within which human dignity is understood, preserved, and respected.

The ICESCR Committee seems to appreciate the importance of the collective in the realization of human progress. With regard to Article 15 of the ICESCR, which recognizes the right of everyone to take part in cultural life,[73] the Committee's General Comment

[71] UDHR, *supra* note 14, at art. 22.

[72] *See* AMARTYA SEN, DEVELOPMENT AS FREEDOM 3 (1999) ; MARTHA C. NUSSBAUM, WOMEN AND HUMAN DEVELOPMENT: THE CAPABILITIES APPROACH 144 (2000) (discussing her version of Sen's capabilities approach and noting need for "a theory of human capability that includes accounts of equality and liberty – to provide the normative basis that desire fails reliably to provide us").

See also OLUFUNMILAYO AREWA, FREEDOM TO COPY: COPYRIGHT, CREATION AND CONTEXT, 41 U.C. DAVIS L. REV., 477 (2007) (discussing how a capabilities approach would challenge – and possibly transform – copyright law's conception of creativity as something that occurs without copying).

[73] ICESCR, *supra* note 14, at art. 15(1)(a).

No. 21 provides that the content or scope of the terms "to participate" or "to take part" requires "three interrelated components (a) participation in, (b) access to, and (c) contribution to cultural life."[74] The Comment goes on to describe "access" as something which "covers in particular the right of everyone – alone, in association with others or as a community – . . . to learn about forms of expression and dissemination through any technical medium of information or communication, to follow a way of life associated with the use of cultural goods . . . and to benefit from the cultural heritage and the creation of other individuals and communities."[75]

With regard to "contribution to cultural life," General Comment No. 21 states that this "refers to the right of everyone to be involved in creating the spiritual, material, intellectual and emotional expressions of the community. This is supported by the right to take part in the development of the community to which a person belongs, and in the definition, elaboration and implementation of policies and decisions that have an impact on the exercise of a person's cultural rights."[76]

Commentators rightly view General Comment No. 21 as an important source of adjustments for the intellectual property system[77] – requiring doctrines that permit participation and secure the freedom to engage in the individual and collective creation of culture.[78] The recommendations flowing therefrom still, nonetheless, largely focus on limitations and exceptions to balance the intellectual property system.[79] A human rights frame can and should mean more. The right to participate in cultural life, together with the right to education, the right to health, the right to social security – the bundle of economic, social, and cultural rights – create an expectation and place a demand on the governance structures of society to invest in the material conditions that enable human flourishing and thus human capacity

[74] *See, e.g.*, General Comment No. 17, *supra* note 47, at ¶4.

[75] CESCR, General Comment No. 21: The Right of Everyone to Take Part in Cultural Life (article 15, para. 1(a), of the Covenant), U.N. Doc. E/C.12/GC/21 (Dec. 21, 2009) [hereinafter General Comment No. 21].

[76] *Id.* at para. 1(c). [77] Shaver & Sganga, *supra* note 68. [78] *Id.*

[79] *Id.* at 654 ("One essential means to strike the appropriate balance between cultural participation and protection of authorship is through exceptions and limitations to copyright. Common examples include exceptions to permit the free use of copyrighted materials for: classroom use, scholarship, personal copies, format conversion, library lending, archiving, criticism and comment, translation into lesser-used languages, reverse-engineering for interoperability, research purposes, disabled accessibility, distance education, time-shifting, sampling, etc.").

to participate in cultural life.[80] As a legal framework, the ICESCR makes clear that governments bear responsibility for the exercise of political power in designing economic rules and institutions, and that those rules should be intentional in promoting access to goods, enabling development, and fostering equality in societies.

Human rights law imposes an obligation on states to attend to the rights in the ICESCR and to consider legal means to operationalize the loftier principles of the UDHR. Some states are doing so by constitutionalizing certain economic, social, and cultural rights.[81] As I have just suggested, the right to education, the right to health, and the right to participate in culture are rights that facilitate demands on the exercise of political power and market processes. Since the ICESCR is directed to states, individuals must be able to make claims for rules and norms that offer a pathway to the conditions that economic, social, and cultural rights seek to secure. In India with respect to the right to education (or the right to participate in cultural life), and in Kenya with respect to the right to health, such claims have already been made and affirmed by courts.[82] In general, economic, social, and cultural rights are increasingly justiciable in some developing countries, and they represent a rising sophistication in the ability of those countries to innovate around and within the rules imposed by TRIPS and other multilateral intellectual property arrangements.[83] This "legal innovation" is an important exercise of the right to self-determination, and represents significant steps in addressing development goals burdened by intellectual property rights, but the realization of which are compelled by the ICESCR.

Group, economic, social, and cultural rights must assume a far greater role in human rights frames directed at international intellectual property law and policymaking. More than ever today, the exercise of intellectual property rights is essential to the capacity of individuals to flourish. In the digital environment, personal and national advancement

[80] Young, *supra* note 67. [81] *Id.*

[82] *See Chancellor, Masters & Scholars of the University of Oxford v. Rameshwari Photocopy Services*, CS(OS) 2439/2012, I.As. No. 14632/2012, 2016 SCC OnLine Del. 5128 (Sept. 16, 2016), http://lobis.nic.in/ddir/dhc/RSE/judgement/16-09-2016/RSE16092016S24392012.pdf (allowing a broad educational use exception); *Asero Ochieng v. Attorney-General* (2010) Petition No. 409 of 2009, (H.C.K.) (Kenya), www.escr-net.org/sites/default/files/Judgment-Petition-No-409-of-2009%20Anti%20counterfeit%20case.pdf (holding that the Anti-Counterfeit Act violated the Kenyan Constitution because it precluded access to essential medicines and therefore infringed the fundamental right of life, human dignity, and health).

[83] *See* Okediji, *Legal Innovation, supra* note 16.

requires access to technologies and access to knowledge.[84] Intellectual property policies are the tools that governments utilize for redistributing knowledge across society; thus, the design of intellectual property policy is central to the realization of human rights at the individual level. On the other hand, economic, social, and cultural human rights impose affirmative duties on states for the way intellectual property law is formulated and implemented in a systemic, institutional, and collective context. These rights, at a minimum, require justification for choices made by states in the exercise of sovereign power to shape legislation that reaches beyond the protection of individual rights but that also consider the well-being of the collective. Economic, social, and cultural rights require vigilance by human rights activists and intellectual property scholars in evaluating the structure of intellectual property laws and the scope of rights that states guarantee in domestic policy instruments. This should include whether states are using existing normative tools to address issues such as access to knowledge and access to medicines. A greater appreciation for the importance of the collective could also materially strengthen arguments for new intellectual property norms in other areas such as the environment and access to green technologies.[85] The privatization (through intellectual property rights) of tools that are essential for mitigating climate change, addressing pollution, or generating energy has profound consequences for the development and security of the poorest regions and peoples in the world.

2 Limitations and Exceptions

Despite recognition of the many challenges imposed by intellectual property rules, with dogged persistence, scholars along with national and international policymakers continue to defer to the notion of "balance": balance within the intellectual property system – and between intellectual property and human rights – as the best response to the human welfare costs of global intellectual property rules. The leading

[84] Julie Cohen, Configuring the Networked Self: Law, Code, and the Play of Everyday Practice (2012); Okediji, *Reframing International Copyright Limitations and Exceptions as Development Policy, supra* note 6; Ruth L. Okediji, *Sustainable Access to Copyrighted Digital Information Works in Developing Countries*, in International Public Goods & Transfer of Technology Under a Globalized Intellectual Property Regime 148 (Jerome Reichman & Keith Maskus eds., 2005) [hereinafter Okediji, *Sustainable Access*]; Shaver & Sganga, *supra* note 68.

[85] *See* Abbe E. L. Brown, *Lessons from Technology and Intellectual Property in the Oil and Gas Industry in Scotland: A Scholarly Journey and an Empirical Review*, 11 SCRIPTed 9, 18–19 (2014).

human rights institutions do the same. As an example, the ICESCR Committee in General Comment No. 17[86] states that:

> [t]he right to the protection of the moral and material interests resulting from one's scientific, literary and artistic productions is subject to limitations and must be balanced with the other rights recognized in the Covenant. ... However, limitations on the rights protected under article 15, paragraph 1 (c), must be determined by law in a manner compatible with the nature of these rights, must pursue a legitimate aim, and must be strictly necessary for the promotion of the general welfare in a democratic society ...[87]

The Committee further stated that:

> [l]imitations must therefore be proportionate, meaning that the least restrictive measures must be adopted when several types of limitations may be imposed. Limitations must be compatible with the very nature of the rights protected in article 15, paragraph 1(c), which lies in the protection of the personal link between the author and his/her creation and of the means which are necessary to enable authors to enjoy an adequate standard of living.[88]

Intellectual property scholars will easily note the close parallels between these provisions in General Comment No. 17 and the leading multifactor tests such as fair use and the three-step test. The language of balance, proportionality, and compensation are standard features of the judicial application of limitations and exceptions in intellectual property law. Limitations and exceptions to intellectual property rights certainly can address specific challenges, but rarely are they sufficient to meet the development-related challenges – such as bulk access to educational works – facing many least-developed and developing countries.[89] When dealing with individual cases involving an author and user, the most well-known doctrines regarding limitations and exceptions wield important influence in ensuring that specific applications of law consider multiple competing interests – such as those between the author and the state, the user and the state, and between authors and users at large – consistent with broader national policies. The application of the first sale doctrine, freedom of speech, and other limitations reflect a "balance" required by intellectual property law, but typically only with respect to

[86] *See* General Comment No. 17, *supra* note 47. [87] *Id.* at ¶ 22.

[88] *Id.* at ¶ 23. Extrapolating from the Special Rapporteur's arguments, the right to an adequate standard of living does not mean that authors and inventors can control all uses of their creative works. *See* 2015 Shaheed Report, *supra* note 48.

[89] *See* Okediji, *Sustainable Access, supra* note 84.

the specific individual and the specific knowledge asset at issue. Existing limitations and exceptions available in international copyright law, and in many domestic copyright laws, do not extend to institutional, community or group needs.[90] To the contrary, national exceptions to copyright are *required* to be limited to "special" cases – a requirement that, in itself, has peculiar implications.[91] Simply put, the broader the exception the less likely countries and users can be confident that it is compliant with international intellectual property and human rights obligations.[92]

Even where they exist, broad, open-ended doctrines such as the U.S. fair use doctrine,[93] do not guarantee users the dignity, security, and freedom to participate in culture as envisioned by the UDHR and ICESCR. Fair use and the three-step test are famously ambiguous with little certainty about whether a particular user can engage in activities and under what terms or conditions she may do so.[94] Moreover, books are needed in bulk to educate entire populations not just individuals.[95] Similarly, medicines need to be available for all and not only for those who can afford them.[96] The right to education and the right to health, in particular, are elemental to the discourse of emancipation that is core to the human rights project and they are fundamental to development. The state has an obligation to adopt policies that can achieve the realization of these rights because a necessitous people cannot be free.[97]

Intellectual property doctrines that are primarily intended to "balance" the interests of individual authors and users are ill suited to address the

[90] Okediji, *Reframing International Copyright Limitations and Exceptions as Development Policy, supra* note 6.

[91] Even under the exceptional Marrakesh Treaty for Visually Impaired Persons, the question whether the treaty – whose benefits are limited to persons who are visually impaired – satisfies the three-step test was left unanswered. *See* LAURENCE R. HELFER, MOLLY K. LAND, RUTH L. OKEDIJI, & JEROME H. REICHMAN, THE WORLD BLIND UNION GUIDE TO THE MARRAKESH TREATY: FACILITATING ACCESS TO BOOKS FOR PRINT-DISABLED INDIVIDUALS (2017) [hereinafter Marrakesh Treaty Guide].

[92] *See* Ruth L. Okediji, *Toward an International Fair Use Doctrine*, 39 COLUM. J. TRANSNAT'L L. 75 (2000).

[93] 17 U.S.C. § 107 (2012).

[94] *See* Niva Elkin-Koren & Orit Fischman-Afori, *Rulifying Fair Use*, 59 ARIZ. L. REV. 161, 186 (2017).

[95] *See* Okediji, *Sustainable Access, supra* note 84 (addressing the need for bulk access to copyrighted works).

[96] *See* High-Level Panel Report, *supra* note 11.

[97] Here, I am paraphrasing Franklin D. Roosevelt's 1944 State of the Union Address in which he declared that "necessitous men are not free men." Franklin D. Roosevelt, *State of the Union Message to Congress*, THE AMERICAN PRESIDENCY PROJECT (Jan. 11, 1944), www.presidency.ucsb.edu/ws/?pid=16518.

collective interest in, and need for, consistent and effective access to knowledge goods. At a minimum, different kinds of limitations and exceptions to intellectual property rights are needed.[98] An appropriately conceived intellectual property/human rights interface requires international legal recognition not just of an obligation to have the right kind of national intellectual property policy, but the freedom and obligation to implement such a policy for the collective. In sum, the call for balance reflected in General Comment No. 17 (and in the intellectual property/ human rights literature) unhelpfully substitutes the internally required balance of intellectual property rights with what human rights law requires of states in pursuit of the highest ideals of human flourishing.

General Comment No. 21 emphasizes both a descriptive view of the right to participate in culture, as well as a set of prescriptions that make the realization of that right feasible. Read in conjunction with the other economic, social, and cultural rights, the Comment arguably recognizes that intellectual property policy should, in some sense, be an expression of the cultural distinctiveness of each society, enabling learning, facilitating access to cultural goods, and ensuring the exercise of freedoms of expression and association.[99] The Comment could also extend to an obligation to ensure policies that facilitate access to technologies that are indispensable to civic and economic engagement, such as the internet.[100] The point is that as viewed from Article 27 of the UDHR and Article 15 of the ICESCR, the intellectual property/human rights interface extends beyond intellectual property per se. The General Comment paints a picture of a human rights regime that reflects values and accomplishes goals in a broad cultural context, and that promotes human flourishing in ways that are deeply meaningful to the society and the individuals that constitute it.[101] This task

[98] With regard to copyright, I have suggested that certain limitations and exceptions should be mandatory. I have also suggested the need for limitations and exceptions for libraries, archives and educational institutions – actors that are vital to assuring access to works on a large scale. *See* Okediji, *Reframing International Copyright Limitations and Exceptions as Development Policy, supra* note 6.

[99] *See, e.g.*, General Comment No. 21, *supra* note 75, at ¶35 (requiring balance).

[100] *See* Molly K. Land, *Toward an International Law of the Internet*, 54. HARV. INT'L L.J. 393, 394 (2013).

[101] As the General Comment states, "[t]he right of everyone to take part in cultural life is closely related to the other cultural rights contained in article 15: the right to enjoy the benefits of scientific progress and its applications (art. 15, para. 1(b)); the right of everyone to benefit from the protection of moral and material interests resulting from any scientific, literary or artistic production of which they are the author (art. 15, para. 1 (c)); and the right to freedom indispensable for scientific research and creative activity (art. 15, para. 3). The right of everyone to take part in cultural life is also intrinsically

is far greater than what limitations and exceptions to intellectual property, alone, can accomplish.

II Developing the 'New' Intellectual Property and Human Rights Interface

A properly constructed human rights frame for intellectual property should bring more to bear on the conditions that destabilize expectations for material well-being for a substantial majority of the world's population. The project of designing the most balanced intellectual property policy and delineating appropriate limitations and exceptions is valuable; but without more, the best intellectual property policies cannot meaningfully advance, much less achieve, change in the rules that reinforce deep disparities between those who have access to knowledge goods that are essential to human flourishing and those who do not.

There are at least three ways that a broadened vision of the intellectual property/human rights interface might produce a richer discourse for intellectual property reform: (1) economic, social, and cultural rights offer room to argue for doctrines that allow for use of knowledge goods at a greater *scale* than intellectual property law currently allows, thus impacting a greater number of users; (2) economic, social, and cultural rights could facilitate rules that require recognition of "users rights" and requires states to *ensure justiciability* of these rights in domestic law; (3) economic, social, and cultural rights could be used to require state accountability for its choices with respect to the *implementation* of international intellectual property obligations. Indeed, the ideals expressed in economic, social, and cultural rights may require states to consider more seriously new models of innovation, including new business models, that can ensure returns to creators and access to users.

In sum, the vision of human dignity reflected in the economic, social, and cultural rights guaranteed in the UDHR, and made more concrete in the ICESCR, requires precisely such a change in the core rules and assumptions that pervade the intellectual property system. What economic, cultural, and social rights offer is a framework to challenge these rules, to question settled assumptions about the content of specific

linked to the right to education (arts. 13 and 14) . . . " General Comment No. 21, *supra* note 75, at ¶¶2–3.

intellectual property norms, and to create additional space to assert state responsibility for promoting structures that more easily align with human welfare. As one scholar puts it, "economic and social rights offer a rich set of tools to analyze the distributive impact of the background laws – the rights, immunities, and privileges – that undergird market arrangements."[102] These collective human rights strip away any pretense of neutrality and permit scrutiny of, or legal challenges to, private laws with distributive implications that undercut the ideals of human progress and development. As such, economic, social, and cultural rights hold particular importance for the future of human rights as a frame for intellectual property reform – both national and global.

To be clear, the point is not simply that intellectual property rules are skewed against the public interest unless they are tempered by appropriate limits; it is that intellectual property law cannot – regardless of how carefully it is designed – effectively meet the most critical needs of human development. Economic, social, and cultural rights require the state to be responsive to the material environment in which her citizens live; framing intellectual property rights as private, individual rights does not free the state from this responsibility.

Below, I point to two well-known examples to highlight just how difficult it is to overcome structural rules that systemically make it unlikely that "balanced" intellectual property policies, without more, can effectuate the material goals and aspirations embedded in the ICESCR. The examples are the failure of the Doha Declaration's paragraph 6 solution with respect to access to medicines, and the demand for an international treaty mandating a copyright exception to address the needs of visually impaired persons.

[102] *See* Katharine G. Young, *Freedom, Want, and Economic and Social Rights: Frame and Law*, 24 MD. J. INT'L L. 182, 203–4 (2009). One aspect of such market arrangements that must be reexamined if economic, social, and cultural rights are to become a more prominent moral guide in the systemic design of IP policies are the types of business models that leverage and rely on IP protection. In opening the IP discourse to these values, lawmakers must dislodge themselves from the rigidity of a property-rule-only construct and consider an array of regulatory, policy, and fiscal tools with which to accommodate human rights and development-oriented considerations. *Cf.* Niva Elkin-Koren, *Copyright in a Digital Ecosystem: A User Rights Approach*, in COPYRIGHT IN AN AGE OF LIMITATIONS AND EXCEPTIONS 132 (Ruth Okediji ed., 2017); Michael Geist, *The Canadian Copyright Story: How Canada Improbably Became the World Leader on Users' Rights in Copyright Law*, in COPYRIGHT IN AN AGE OF LIMITATIONS AND EXCEPTIONS 169 (Ruth Okediji ed., 2017).

A *Intellectual Property, Access to Medicines, and Access to Literary Works*

Since the TRIPS Agreement, considerable attention has been paid to how human rights can reshape and reframe intellectual property to address human welfare needs[103] and, by extension, to pursue development goals. No issue has attracted as much attention – and dominated the intellectual property/human rights interface – like the right to health. Indeed, the challenge of access to medicines has become *the* central policy concern of the human right to health.[104] Galvanized by the HIV/AIDS crisis of the late 1990s,[105] the use of patent protection to secure export markets for drugs, with resulting monopoly prices, led to a global outcry on behalf of consumers in developing and least-developed countries.[106] Since then, public health concerns and the impact of patents on access to drugs and adequate healthcare have remained among the most vexing problems of the global intellectual property system[107] and of the intellectual property/human rights interface.

The right to health is guaranteed by various international instruments. It was first defined in the constitution of the World Health Organization (WHO) which describes the right to health as "one of the fundamental rights of every human being without distinction of race, religion, political belief, economic or social conditions."[108] In addition, Article 25 of the UDHR states that "[e]veryone has the right to a standard of living

[103] UCOSOC, Sub-Comm'n on the Promotion & Prot. of Human Rights, *The Impact of the Agreement on Trade-Related Aspects of Intellectual Property Rights on Human Rights: Report of the High Commissioner*, ¶ 60, U.N. Doc. E/CN.4/Sub.2/2001/13 (June 27, 2001) ("Members should therefore implement the minimum standards of the TRIPS Agreement bearing in mind both their human rights obligations as well as the flexibility inherent in the TRIPS Agreement, and recognizing that 'human rights are the first responsibility of Governments.'").

[104] *See* Helfer & Austin, *supra* note 17, at 90–171.

[105] *See, e.g.*, Helfer, *Pharmaceutical Patents, supra* note 17, at 311 ("Disputes over the regulation of [access to medicine] are occurring in multiple transnational, national, and local venues, including the World Trade Organization (WTO), the World Intellectual Property Organization (WIPO), the UN Human Rights Council (UNHRC), the World Health Organization (WHO), bilateral treaty negotiations, national parliaments, constitutional courts, and domestic administrative agencies. Competing groups of states and non-state actors shift horizontally and vertically among these forums in an effort to develop competing legal rules over the propriety of granting intellectual property (IP) protection to newly developed life-saving drugs.").

[106] *See* Helfer, *Pharmaceutical Patents, supra* note 17, at 327-32.

[107] *Id.* at 332–3.

[108] World Health Org., *Constitution* (Apr. 7, 1948), http://apps.who.int/gb/gov/assets/constitution-en.pdf (last visited June 26, 2017).

adequate for the health and well-being of himself and of his family, including food, clothing, housing and medical care and necessary social service . . . "[109] The ICESCR similarly provides that states "recognize the right of everyone to the enjoyment of the highest attainable standard of physical and mental health."[110]

As explained by the U.N. Secretary-General's High-Level Panel on Intellectual Property and Access to Medicines (High-Level Panel), these considerations have come into tension with intellectual property in part because:

> [p]olicies and agreements related to human rights, trade, [IP] rights and public health were developed with different objectives at different times. State obligations include duties not only to respect, but to protect and fulfil, the right to health. This requires taking proactive measures to promote public health . . . [E]nsuring access to medicines, and particularly to essential medicines, is a fundamental element of these obligations. Trade rules and [IP] laws were developed to promote economic growth and incentive innovation. On the one hand, governments seek the economic benefits of increased trade. On the other, the imperative to respect patents on health technologies could, in certain instances, create obstacles to the public health objectives of [WTO] members.[111]

Prior to the TRIPS Agreement, many nations (including some developed ones) resisted the expansion of patent law to pharmaceutical medications as a matter of policy.[112] These states argued that excluding pharmaceuticals from the limited term monopoly system of intellectual property would contribute to society by ensuring the free-flow of generic medicines.[113] The TRIPS Agreement's requirement that patents be available to "all fields of technology," including pharmaceutical products and processes, represented a major victory for the pharmaceutical industry.[114] The backlash that resulted from this attempt to standardize and expand intellectual property protection was swift and strategic. It ultimately resulted in high-profile litigation that sought to enforce patent rights over antiretroviral medications for HIV/AIDS in Brazil and South Africa.[115]

109 UDHR, *supra* note 14, at art. 25. 110 ICESCR, *supra* note 14, at art. 12.

111 *See* High-Level Panel Report, *supra* note 11.

112 *See* Helfer, *Pharmaceutical Patents, supra* note 17, at 314; *see also* Okediji, *Legal Innovation, supra* note 16.

113 *See* Helfer, *Pharmaceutical Patents, supra* note 17, at 314. 114 *Id.* at 322.

115 *See* Ellen 't Hoen, Jonathan Berger, Alexandra Calmy, & Suerie Moon, *Driving A Decade of Change: HIV/AIDS, Patents and Access to Medicines For All*, 14:15 J. of Int'l Aids Soc'y (2011), www.ncbi.nlm.nih.gov/pmc/articles/PMC3078828/pdf/1758-2652-14-15.pdf.

Following a series of events, including the publication of a General Comment on the right to health, and a resolution on intellectual property and human rights by the U.N. Sub-Commission on the Promotion and Protection of Human Rights,[116] the international community emerged with the consensus that the human right to health includes the right to access life-saving medicines.[117] Policymakers argued in both domestic and international fora that the human right to health takes moral and legal precedence over intellectual property rights.[118] This position and subsequent advocacy campaign – the access to medicine movement – resulted in a number victories for developing nations, NGOs, and human rights activists.[119] The most visible of these triumphs occurred in 2001 with the signing of the Declaration on TRIPS and Public Health, adopted at the November 2001 Ministerial Conference that launched the Doha Round of WTO trade negotiations.[120] The Doha Declaration "balanced" the TRIPS Agreement by explicitly recognizing the freedom of countries to tailor their domestic intellectual property regimes to address public health concerns.[121] Further, in paragraph 6, it explicitly adopted

[116] *See* Helfer, *Pharmaceutical Patents, supra* note 17, at 325–8.

[117] *Id.* at 328 (outlining various statements endorsing one or both of these principles including "declarations by the UN General Assembly in 2001 and 2006; resolutions of the Commission on Human Rights in 2001, 2002, 2003, and 2005; a 2001 study by the UN High Commissioner for Human Rights; several reports of Special Rapporteurs on the right to health; Human Rights Guidelines for Pharmaceutical Companies in Relation to Access to Medicines adopted in 2008; a 2001 Statement on Human Rights and Intellectual Property by the ICESCR Committee; a 2003 general comment by the UN Committee on the Rights of the Child; and a 2008 resolution of the African Commission on Human and Peoples' Rights . . . ").

[118] *Id.* at 327 ("The UN Sub-Commission's attention to access to medicines originated in a statement by a consortium of NGOs that forcefully asserted 'the primacy of human rights obligations over the commercial and profit-driven motives upon which agreements such as TRIPS are based'") (internal citations omitted).

[119] A corollary movement, reacting to international copyright obligations, the access to knowledge movement, also emerged. *See, e.g.*, Kapczynski, *supra* note 31.

[120] The declaration accomplished many goals, including: (1) the affirmation of WTO members to protect the right to health and to use TRIPS flexibilities to support that right; and (2) the grant of an additional ten years for least-developed countries to defer IP protection of pharmaceutical products. *See* Helfer, *Pharmaceutical Patents, supra* note 17, at 329–30. In addition, the declaration resolved to find a mechanism for more efficient generic drug importation for those countries who needed it, a goal that was later realized in 2003 when the TRIPS Council waived the domestic use requirement for compulsory licenses. *Id.* at 330. In 2005, that waiver was made permanent by way of an amendment to TRIPS, which, to date, marks the only formal revision of that treaty. *Id.*

[121] *See* Doha Declaration, *supra* note 10 ("We agree that the TRIPS Agreement does not and should not prevent members from taking measures to protect public health. Accordingly, while reiterating our commitment to the TRIPS Agreement, we affirm

a practical solution to the problem of access to medicines by recognizing the right of qualifying countries to import/export drugs manufactured under a compulsory license. Laudable and important as these developments are, access to medicines remains a key and growing challenge in virtually all countries.[122]

Realization of the right to health is a key source of political pressure on the intellectual property system. Moreover, addressing the cost of essential medicines in developed and developing countries is a central aspect of, on the one hand, managing global intellectual property relations and, on the other hand, managing international public health and human rights obligations. While the advocacy campaign was successful – at least in terms of maintaining political pressure on the issue – meaningful and sustainable access to essential medicines still eludes a substantial percentage of the world's population.[123] For a number of reasons, the paragraph 6 solution has not been successful in ensuring that those who need medicines actually receive them.[124] In the meantime, costs for drugs continue to rise and the world faces new global health challenges for which incentives in the form of intellectual property rights are simply ineffective.[125] As explained by the High-Level Panel:

> [m]arket-driven R&D has been credited by some for producing a number of important health technologies that have improved health outcomes significantly worldwide. However, significant gaps in health technology innovation and access persist . . . Rare diseases that affect comparatively small proportions of the population have not traditionally attracted investments although this is changing. Various efforts are being undertaken by governments, philanthropic organizations, international entities, civil society groups and the private sector to resolve the incoherence between market-driven approaches and public health needs. However, such efforts tend to be fragmented, disparate and insufficient to deal with

that the Agreement can and should be interpreted and implemented in a manner supportive of WTO members' right to protect public health and, in particular, to promote access to medicines for all.").

[122] *See* High-Level Panel Report, *supra* note 11, at 3. [123] *Id.*

[124] *See, e.g.*, Alan O. Sykes, *TRIPS, Pharmaceuticals, Developing Countries, and the Doha "Solution"* 10–22 (John M. Olin Program in Law and Econ. Working Paper No. 140, 2002) (offering an economic perspective on how the declaration undermines patent rights in developing nations). *See generally* Brook K. Baker, *Arthritic Flexibilities for Accessing Medicines: Analysis of WTO Action Regarding Paragraph 6 of the Doha Declaration on the Trips Agreement and Public Health*, 14 IND. INT'L & COMP. L. REV. 613 (2004) (offering a historical account and critique of the paragraph 6 solution).

[125] *See* High-Level Panel Report, *supra* note 11, at 8.

> priority health needs on a sustainable, long-term basis. A much greater effort must be directed to supplementing the existing market-driven system by investing in new mechanisms that delink the costs of R&D from the end prices of health technologies.[126]

In short, despite significant political pressure regarding the right to health, and other notable legal and extralegal efforts, the formal balance achieved with respect to the intellectual property regime and access to medicines has been relatively unsuccessful in meaningfully advancing realization of the right to health.

Another significant development at the intellectual property/human rights interface emerged with respect to the rights of visually impaired persons to access copyrighted works. Shortly after the Doha Declaration, INGOs, and particularly Knowledge Ecology International,[127] began to give increasing attention to the "book famine" that existed with respect to print materials available in accessible formats for visually impaired persons (VIPs).[128] At the time these efforts began, over 300 million people in the global South lacked access to books and other print materials. The consequences of insufficient access to books for visually impaired persons are profound, even in the most developed countries.[129]

In 2006, the U.N. Convention on the Rights of Persons with Disabilities affirmed states' obligations to "take all appropriate steps to

[126] *Id.*

[127] Knowledge Ecology International, https://keionline.org/ (last visited Aug. 11, 2017).

[128] *See* Marrakesh Treaty Guide, *supra* note 91, at 12 ("This global famine is alarming in its scope and impact. Many of the estimated 300 million print-disabled persons around the world, especially those living in developing countries, lack adequate access to printed materials in accessible formats, even though the technology to create such works has long existed and continues to evolve rapidly.").

[129] According to a 2016 WIPO report, 285 million people worldwide are blind or visually impaired, 90% of which live on low incomes in developing and least-developed nations. WIPO, The Marrakesh Treaty – Helping to End the Global Book Famine (2016), www.wipo.int/edocs/pubdocs/en/wipo_pub_marrakesh_overview.pdf. Only 1–7% of books are published in accessible formats for VIPs. *Id.* As many scholars highlight, part of the challenging nature of addressing the global book famine stems from the multifaceted nature of improving text "accessibility," a broad and encompassing concept that includes access to the physical environment, transportation, information and communication technology, education, and other facilities necessary to enjoy printed materials in the same or similar manner as sighted individuals. *See* Kartik Sawhney, *Perspective: End The "Book Famine" With Better Technology, Attitudes, and Copyright Law*, in The State of the World's Children 2013: UNICEF (2013), www.unicef.org/sowc2013/perspective_sawhney.html (concluding, based on an informal survey of nearly sixty VIP Indian children, that less than 20% had access to material in their preferred format, and less than 35% to material in any format).

ensure that laws protecting [IP] do not consider an unreasonable or discriminatory barrier to access by [VIPs] to cultural materials."[130] Only a third of Berne Convention members had copyright exceptions for the visually impaired, and a critical problem of cross-border sharing of accessible copyright works persisted.[131] The Berne Convention, although lacking in many respects in the arena of limitations and exceptions, did not foreclose exceptions in national copyright laws for visually impaired persons. However, many states simply did not enact such exceptions. Where such an exception existed, cross-border exchanges of works typically were deemed illegal.[132]

In 2013, fifty-one states gathered in Marrakesh, Morocco to sign The Marrakesh Treaty to Facilitate Access to Published Works for Persons Who Are Blind, Visually Impaired, or Otherwise Print Disabled ("VIP Treaty").[133] The treaty was a significant breakthrough with respect to "[ensuring] that visually impaired persons have sustainable access to published works on the same terms as sighted persons" and "realizing the vision of a world in which all persons can participate fully and equally in the political, economic and cultural life of society."[134] The treaty's milestone achievements are many, but chief among them are its requirements that signatories: (1) establish mandatory exceptions to the exclusive rights of copyright owners; and (2) permit the import and export of accessible formats of works without the permission of the copyright holder.[135]

As with the right to health and its reinforcement in the WTO system via the Doha Declaration, the VIP Treaty's power to meet human rights obligations lies not in what the treaty says but in what the treaty does. A human rights approach to implementation of the treaty requires methods of compliance by state actors that are intentional about achieving the treaty's human rights ends.[136] An intellectual property-centric

[130] *See* Marrakesh Treaty Guide, *supra* note 91, at 19 (internal citations omitted).

[131] *Id.* at 12.

[132] *Id.* ("[T]he scarcity of copyrighted works in accessible formats is a global problem that requires a global solution. All national laws limit copyright protection to achieve important public policy goals, and exceptions for the blind are among the most long-standing of these limitations. Nonetheless, more than two thirds of countries have not adopted such exceptions, and many of the exceptions that exist do not fully satisfy the needs of print print-disabled persons, especially in developing nations and with respect to new technologies such as e-books and audiobooks.")

[133] *Id.* at 9. [134] *Id.* at 8. [135] *Id.* at 20–54.

[136] *Id.* at 10 (explaining that the WBU Guide "views the MT as an international agreement that employs the legal doctrines and policy tools of copyright law to advance human

approach could require something entirely different.[137] Which approach a state adopts, and the options for redress available for the treaty's beneficiaries, will depend significantly on the way the state views the intellectual property/human rights interface. If the primary factors are grounded in the "human right" to protect the interest of authors,[138] realization of the aspirations of the UDHR, the ICESCR, and the Convention of the Rights of Persons with Disabilities are undoubtedly at some risk.

Take, for example, the so-called "commercial availability" provision in Article 4(4) which states that a "Contracting Party may confine limitations or exceptions under this Article to works which, in the particular accessible format, cannot be obtained commercially under reasonable terms for beneficiary persons in that market." Article 4(5) further provides, "[i]t shall be a matter for national law to determine whether limitations or exceptions under this Article are subject to remuneration." This provision is one of the most contentious aspects of the Treaty. It allows a state to choose to implement the treaty by conditioning access to the accessible format copies on whether or not the copyrighted work is "commercially available." The meaning of commercial availability is unsettled and the treaty offers no guidance to states. Moreover, commercial availability could mean that rights holders can charge more than most beneficiaries under the treaty can afford – a problem that also exists under the compulsory license provisions in relation to the paragraph 6 solution in regards to public health. Meaningful access to knowledge goods requires terms, especially price, that ensure that those who need such goods can afford them. The World Blind Union Guide identifies a number of unresolved questions about the meaning of commercial

rights ends. This approach is inspired by several features of the Treaty, including its express references to widely-adopted international human rights instruments in the first paragraph of the Preamble, its status as the first multilateral agreement to establish mandatory exceptions to the exclusive rights of copyright owners, and its designation of print-disabled individuals as the Treaty's beneficiaries.").

137 *See* Mihály J. Ficsor, *Commentary to the Marrakesh Treaty on Accessible Format Copies for the Visually Impaired*, Copyright See-Saw (Oct. 11, 2013), www.copyrightseesaw.net/archive/?sw_10_%20item=50&sw_10_page=2&sw_10_item=50.

138 *See* Marrakesh Treaty Guide, *supra* note 91, at 13 ("The Marrakesh Access Treaty – which lies at the intersection of international human rights law and international intellectual property law – is the first international agreement to require exceptions to copyright in order to enhance the human rights of a specific population. In interpreting and implementing the MAT, therefore, public officials and private actors must strive to comply with both sets of legal obligations.").

availability,[139] and it counsels states to eschew this option. According to the Guide:

> [s]uch a restriction would be fundamentally inconsistent with the MT's overarching goal of ensuring that individuals with print disabilities have an equal opportunity to enjoy covered works on the same terms as sighted persons. The restriction also risks restricting the rights that print-disabled individuals have under other copyright E&Ls, such as exceptions for private copying. The lack of clarity about what constitutes commercial availability would also create significant legal risks for authorized entities and beneficiaries that could deter the effective exercise of their rights under the Treaty.[140]

However, given the limitations in General Comment No. 17 imposed on states attempting to limit authorial rights, and the requirements for proportionality, compensation, etc., in the same Comment, a country could impose the commercial availability requirement as part of its domestic implementation of the Treaty and still claim compliance with the UDHR and ICESCR.[141] Indeed, a number of countries, including least-developed countries, have done just that.[142] The commercial

[139] The Guide asks:

> What does commercial *availability* entail? Does it require availability in bookstores? Online? Do bookstores carrying the accessible format copy need to be accessible to beneficiaries in terms of geographic location and physical accessibility? Should the notion of availability include affordability?
>
> What does *commercial* availability entail? Does it need to be offered by a for-profit entity? Or does "commercial" refer to how widespread the accessible copy is offered?
>
> *When* should availability be assessed – at the time of publication of the work, at the time a print disabled person seeks to purchase the work, or at some other time?
>
> *Where* should commercial availability be assessed – Globally? Regionally? In the relevant national market of a print disabled person?

Id. at 49–50.

[140] *Id.* at 50.

[141] *See* General Comment No. 17, *supra* note 47, at ¶ 24 (The imposition of limitations may, under certain circumstances, require compensatory measures, such as payment of adequate compensation for the use of scientific, literary, or artistic productions in the public interest).

[142] *See, e.g.*, Elec. Info. for Libraries, African Library and Info. Ass'ns and Insts., & Int'l Fed'n of Library Ass'ns and Insts., *Malawi: Embrace The Spirit Of The Marrakesh Treaty – No Commercial Availability Test* (Aug. 4, 2017), www.ifla.org/files/assets/clm/statements/malawi_marrakesh_statement.pdf (explaining the organizations' "call for the removal of a commercial availability test on the making of accessible format copies in Malawi. Inclusion of this test in the Malawi law undermines the objective of the

availability option allows states to tilt towards strong intellectual property rights and this arguably would be acceptable under the traditional intellectual property/human rights frame.

In short, as noted earlier, the contemporary intellectual property/ human rights frame tends to devolve very quickly to a defense of intellectual property interests – rather than promote human rights ends as envisioned in economic, cultural, and social rights. However, invoking these rights in evaluating compliance methods by states opens up a realm in which states have to defend the chosen implementation method in view of its effect on the goals animating the VIP Treaty. Given how many VIPs live below the poverty line, how few are able to attend institutions of higher learning, and the overwhelming gap in the number of books available to sighted persons, there can be no question that adopting provisions that burden access to works by VIPs can give rise to a claim of a violation of rights guaranteed by the ICESCR. Moreover, a state that chooses to implement the VIP Treaty using the safe-harbor provisions[143] (such as in Articles 4, 5 and 6) should be utterly immune from claims of violations of intellectual property rights,[144] regardless of whether the claims of violation arise under TRIPS or under the UDHR and ICESCR.

B Civil and Political Rights as the Prototype of Intellectual Property/Human Rights Interface

Beyond the multilateral treaty platform, national and regional courts in developed countries have relied heavily on human rights ideals when addressing intellectual property disputes,[145] particularly rights that implicate political freedoms and liberty considerations. In the United States, for example, the First Amendment has always played a major role in copyright jurisprudence, with leading scholars suggesting that an uncensored marketplace of ideas is a fundamental justification for the

Marrakesh Treaty which is to end the global 'book famine' for persons with print disabilities").

143 *See* Marrakesh Treaty Guide, *supra* note 91, at 45–57 (discussing the safe-harbor options under arts. 4, 5, and 6).

144 *Id.*

145 *See* Laurence R. Helfer, *Mapping the Interface Between Human Rights and Intellectual Property*, in Research Handbook on Human Rights and Intellectual Property 6, 7–8 (Christopher Geiger ed., 2015) (describing recent case law in Europe and Latin America implicating the rights to expression and health in the context of copyright and patent disputes, respectively).

copyright system.[146] In case after case, the First Amendment has been heralded as a robust limit on intellectual property rights.[147] As explained by the Supreme Court:

> [t]he Copyright Clause and First Amendment were adopted close in time. This proximity indicates that, in the Framers' view, copyright's limited monopolies are compatible with free speech principles. Indeed, copyright's purpose is to promote the creation and publication of free expression ... "[T]he Framers intended copyright itself to be the engine of free expression. By establishing a marketable right to the use of one's expression, copyright supplies the economic incentive to create and disseminate ideas." In addition to spurring the creation and publication of new expression, copyright law contains built-in First Amendment accommodations. First, it distinguishes between ideas and expression and makes only the latter eligible for copyright protection ... Second, the "fair use" defense allows the public to use not only facts and ideas contained in a copyrighted work, but also expression itself in certain circumstances.[148]

Since the TRIPS Agreement, human rights arguments have also increasingly imposed limits on intellectual property rights in Europe.[149] Recently, the European Court of Human Rights (ECtHR) discussed the role of the right to freedom of expression when ruling on a pair of high-profile digital copyright cases.[150] In *Ashby Donald and Others v. France*, the ECtHR was presented with three petitioners, photographers who had violated French copyright law by publishing pictures online that were taken at various Paris fashion shows without the permission of five fashion houses.[151] For the first time, the ECtHR clarified that Article 10 of the European Convention on Human Rights serves as an independent, external limit on copyright.[152]

[146] *See* Neil W. Netanel, *Copyright and a Democratic Civil Society*, 106 YALE L.J. 283 (1996).

[147] For a compelling argument about the absolute limit of the First Amendment on copyright protection, *see* DAVID LANGE & H. JEFFERSON POWELL, NO LAW: INTELLECTUAL PROPERTY IN THE IMAGE OF AN ABSOLUTE FIRST AMENDMENT (2008).

[148] *Eldred v. Ashcroft*, 537 U.S. 186, 219 (2003) (internal citations omitted); *see also Harper & Row Publishers, Inc. v. Nation Enters.*, 471 U.S. 539, 556 (1985) ("[C]opyright's idea/expression dichotomy 'strike[s] a definitional balance between the First Amendment and the Copyright Act by permitting free communication of facts while still protecting an author's expression'") (internal citations omitted).

[149] Laurence R. Helfer, *The New Innovation Frontier? Intellectual Property and the European Court of Human Rights*, 49 HARV. INT'L L.J. 1 (2008).

[150] *Neij and Kolmisoppi v. Sweden*, App. No. 40397/12, ECtHR (Feb. 19, 2013); *Ashby Donald and Others v. France*, App. No. 36769/08, ECtHR (Jan. 10, 2013).

[151] *See* Marrakesh Treaty Guide, *supra* note 91.

[152] *Id.* ("The outcomes of these cases is less significant than the [ECtHR's] reasoning, which for the first time affirmed that the enforcement of IP laws interfere with the right to

In other words, the act of copyright infringement may, under certain circumstances, interfere with the human right to expression if prohibited and, therefore, be a valid defense to infringement.[153]

Similarly, in *Neij and Sunde Kolmisoppi v. Sweden*, the cofounders of "The Pirate Bay" were convicted by a Swedish court of illegally allowing users to share and distribute copyrighted works through one of the largest file-sharing services on the internet.[154] The ECtHR held that sharing, or allowing others to share, copyrighted works on the internet, even for commercial gain, was covered by the right to "receive and impart information" under Article 10.[155] Nonetheless, in both the French and Swedish cases, the ECtHR gave a wide margin of appreciation to the ways national courts balanced conflicts between the fundamental rights at issue and thus upheld their decisions.[156]

These 'human rights' cases in the United States and in Europe reflect strong democratic commitments to liberal values of human liberty. Freedoms of speech, competition, and privacy interests certainly are part of the UDHR and its vision of human emancipation. However, at the national level in developed countries, a human rights frame doesn't appear to add much to what national intellectual property law or national constitutions already guarantee. In these cases, "human rights" is simply another way of saying "intellectual property."

receive and impart information and ideas and must therefore be prescribed by law and necessary in a democratic society for the achievement of certain societal aims, such as the rights and freedoms of others. The decisions suggest that Strasbourg judges may one day conclude that national IP laws transgress these principles and thus violate the right to freedom of expression protected by the European Convention on Human Rights (ECHR).").

153 *Id.* 154 *Id.*

155 *See* Dirk Voorhoof & Inger Høedt-Rasmussen, *ECHR: Copyright vs. Freedom of Expression II (The Pirate Bay)*, Kluwer Copyright Blog (Mar. 20, 2013), http://copyrightblog.kluweriplaw.com/2013/03/20/echr-copyright-vs-freedom-of-expression-ii-the-pirate-bay/?print=pdf ("In the present case, the Court was called upon to weigh, on the one hand, the interest of the applicants to facilitate the sharing of the information in question and, on the other, the interest in protecting the rights of the copyright-holders. Thus, the Swedish authorities had to balance two competing interests which were both protected by the Convention.").

156 *Id.; see also* Dirk Voorhoof and Inger Høedt-Rasmussen, *ECHR: Copyright vs. Freedom of Expression*, Kluwer Copyright Blog (Jan. 25, 2013), http://copyrightblog.kluweriplaw.com/2013/01/25/echr-copyright-vs-freedom-of-expression/.

C *Economic, Social, and Cultural Rights at the Intellectual Property/Human Rights Interface*

Some developing countries have approached the intellectual property/human rights interface somewhat differently. As observed earlier, economic and social rights are increasingly embedded in national constitutions, providing a legality and principles not normally associated with these rights in international human rights law.[157] The constitutionalization of economic and social rights offer an independent premise to transform the ideals of the UDHR and ICESCR into concrete rights for citizens. In the case of *Asero Ochieng v. Attorney-General*, the Kenyan High Court overturned a TRIPS-driven anti-counterfeiting statute,[158] in order to preserve access to generic medicines.[159] The Court reasoned that the statute did not effectively distinguish between counterfeit drugs and generic medicines, and so undermined the fundamental human right to health guaranteed by the Kenyan Constitution[160] and by the ICESCR. According to the Court:

> [U]ntil the passage of the Industrial Property Act in 2001 (Act No. 3 of 2001), it was not possible for poor people infected with HIV/AIDS to access anti-retroviral medication as the only ones available were expensive branded medicine. Generic anti-retroviral drugs were not available in Kenya as the existing legislation did not allow parallel importation of generic drugs and medicines ... [The new law] allowed the parallel importation of generic drugs. It is on the basis of this legislation that availability and access to anti-retroviral drugs has increased and greatly enhanced the life and health of persons such as the petitioners who have been living with HIV/AIDS. It is against this context that any legislative measure that would affect accessibility and availability of anti-retroviral medicines must be viewed. If such measure would have the effect of limiting access, then such measure would ipso facto threaten the lives and health of the petitioners and others infected with HIV and AIDS, and would be in violation of their rights under the Constitution.

Notably, the Court referred to the ICESCR and General Comment No. 14 on the right to health, as well as General Comment No. 17 on the right of everyone to benefit from the protection of the moral and material

[157] Young, *supra* note 102.
[158] Anti-Counterfeit Act, No. 13 (2008), KENYA GAZETTE SUPPLEMENT No. 97, 261.
[159] *Asero Ochieng v. Attorney-General* (2010) Petition No. 409 of 2009, (H.C.K.) (Kenya), www.escr-net.org/sites/default/files/Judgment-Petition-No-409-of-2009%20Anti%20counterfeit%20case.pdf.
[160] *Id.* at ¶¶ 75–8.

interests resulting from any scientific, literary or artistic production of which he or she is the author. The Court concluded:

> [T]he right to health, life and human dignity are inextricably bound.[161] . . . The "socio-economic factors that promote conditions in which people can lead a healthy life" [set forth in the ICESCR Committee General Comment No. 14] imply. . . a situation in which people have access to the medication they require to remain healthy. If the state fails to put in place such conditions, then it has violated or is likely to violate the right to health of its citizens[162] . . . The state's obligation with regard to the right to health therefore encompasses not only the positive duty to ensure that its citizens have access to health care services and medication but must also encompass the negative duty not to do anything that would in any way affect access to such health care services and essential medicines. Any legislation that would render the cost of essential drugs unaffordable to citizens would thus be in violation of the state's obligations.[163]

Kenya's codification of economic, social, and cultural rights in the national constitution afforded a level of justiciability for claims by individuals who rarely have the political capital to influence legislative change. Certainly, in the African context, these cases on the right to health offer new possibilities for the intellectual property/human rights interface by illustrating legal avenues to hold states accountable for human rights obligations. Deploying claims for access to knowledge goods within a constitutionally guaranteed framework, while leveraging norms from international human rights instruments, helped guide the Court in delineating the substantive contours of the rights at issue, without sacrificing cultural values. Cases on the right to health[164] are few in number and represent activity in only two countries in sub-Saharan Africa – Kenya and South Africa. It is unclear how widely these developments will spread or if they will be sustainable. Nonetheless, they illuminate the power of economic, social, and cultural rights to transform a general principle into clear legal entitlement for citizens, thus limiting the State's power to simply effectuate laws without regard for its welfare effect.

A recent copyright case in India confirms the importance of the national legal framework in securing significant human rights gains that advance development goals. Though not framed explicitly in human rights language, an Indian Court interpreted the Indian Copyright Act in a manner that arguably implements the right to

[161] *Id.* at ¶ 56. [162] *Id.* at ¶ 63. [163] *Id.* at ¶ 66.
[164] *See Minister of Health v. Treatment Action Campaign*, 2002 (5) SA 721 (CC) (S. Afr.).

education and the right to participate in cultural life.[165] In 2012, three, large international publishers – Oxford University Press, Cambridge University Press, and Francis & Taylor – sued Delhi University for the sale of photocopied books and pages of copyrighted texts (course packs) to students. The University argued that the use of photocopied copyrighted books by students was a "reasonable educational need" and that this form of reproduction of copyrighted books for educational purposes qualified under India's fair dealing exception and under its separate educational use exception.[166]

Agreeing with the University, the Delhi High Court interpreted India's educational use exception in the Copyright Act broadly to include not only the:

> process of imparting instruction by the teacher, but also the entire academic session for which the pupil is under the tutelage of the teacher … a process commencing from the teacher readying herself/himself for imparting instruction setting syllabus, prescribed text books, readings and ensuring … that the pupil stands instructed in what he/she has approached the teacher to learn.[167]

This appears to be the first definition by a developing country of the inchoate education exception recognized by most countries, and it clearly goes against the grain of established jurisprudence and practice in the developed countries.[168] According to the Indian Court:

> Copyright, specially in literary works, is … not an inevitable, divine, or natural right that confers on authors the absolute ownership of their creations. It is designed rather to stimulate activity and progress in the

[165] *University of Oxford v. Rameshwari Photocopy Services* (2016) 2016 SCC OnLine Del 5128 (India), http://lobis.nic.in/ddir/dhc/RSE/judgement/16-09-2016/RSE16092016S24392012.pdf.

[166] *See* Rocky Soibam Singh, *Publishers Lose Copyright Case Against DU's Photocopy Shop*, HINDUSTAN TIMES (Sept. 16, 2016), www.hindustantimes.com/delhi-news/publishers-lose-copyright-case-against-du-s-photocopy-shop/story-Yly8FJ1mNjf71snIL8tpvO.html.

[167] Anubha Sinha, *Delhi High Court's Ruling Against Publishers is a Triumph for Knowledge*, THE WIRE (Sept. 23, 2016), https://thewire.in/68151/delhi-hc-ruling-photocopying-du// (citing the High Court).

[168] *Basic Books, Inc. v. Kinko's Graphics Corp.*, 758 F. Supp. 1522, 1526 (S.D.N.Y.1991) (rejecting a fair use defense for a copy shop that copied excerpts from the publishers' books and sold the copies for profit in course packs to students for use in colleges); *see also Cambridge University Press v. Patton*, 769 F.3d 1232 (11th Cir. 2014); *Princeton University Press v. Michigan Document Services, Inc.*, 99 F.3d 1381, 1383 (6th Cir. 1996) (*en banc*) (same).

arts for the intellectual enrichment of the public. Copyright is intended to increase and not to impede the harvest of knowledge.[169]

Certainly, Articles 9 and 10 of the Berne Convention and Article 13 of TRIPS could be read to bar an exception of such breadth; indeed, the plaintiffs made this argument. However, the Court held that India's legislators were deemed to be aware of the country's international copyright obligations and that the legislature was empowered to determine justified or reasonable exceptions to the legitimate interests of authors.[170] On these grounds, the court denied the publishers an interim injunction in September 2016 and dismissed the lawsuit.[171] Three months later, in December 2016, a Division Bench of the Delhi High Court also denied an interim injunction to the publishers, agreeing that Article 13 of TRIPS and Article 9 of the Berne Convention provided sufficient leeway for nations to design their domestic copyright laws with the aim of promoting dissemination of creative works.[172] Following these defeats, the publishers dismissed the suit.[173]

Neither the fair use doctrine nor any traditional limitation and exception to copyright could produce a result in which large numbers of students receive, on a regular basis, affordable access to copyrighted works for educational purposes. Indeed, similar cases involving course packs and applying the fair use standard have not been equivocally favorable for educational use defendants in other jurisdictions.[174] Moreover, if one takes seriously the requirements in General Comment No. 17 regarding domestic limits to authorial rights, India's Copyright Act eschews both the constraints of international copyright law and international human rights law. Yet, the Court's decision arguably advances access to knowledge and other human rights.

169 *University of Oxford v. Rameshwari Photocopy Services* (2016) 2016 SCC OnLine Del 5128 (India), http://lobis.nic.in/ddir/dhc/RSE/judgement/16-09-2016/RSE16092016S24392012.pdf.

170 Id. 171 Id.

172 *See* Krishna & Saurastri Associates LLP, *The Appeal Bench's decision Delhi university photocopying case: fair use re-visited*, LEXOLOGY (Jan. 9, 2017), www.lexology.com/library/detail.aspx?g=bb41f1ab-d0b8-4706-8b7b-87342c645351.

173 Id.

174 *See, e.g.*, *Cambridge University Press v. Patton*, 769 F.3d 1232 (11th Cir. 2014); *Princeton University Press v. Michigan Document Services, Inc.*, 99 F.3d 1381, 1383 (6th Cir. 1996) (*en banc*); *Basic Books, Inc. v. Kinko's Graphics Corp.*, 758 F. Supp. 1522, 1526 (S.D.N.Y. 1991).

III Limits of the Current Human Rights Frame of Intellectual Property

The manner in which the right to health, freedom of expression, access to knowledge, and the rights of disabled persons have been recently addressed in the intellectual property regime indeed suggests that human rights ends can be accomplished within flexible intellectual property frameworks. The intellectual property/human rights interface offers a platform for creating new places or appealing to alternative institutions where intellectual property rights can be challenged, modified, and otherwise "balanced."[175] Despite this, intellectual property rights have continued to grow and enhancing protection for intellectual creations is still a high priority for the developed countries. As the interaction between intellectual property and human rights continues to unfold, certain key limitations of placing intellectual property in a human rights frame have emerged.

A *Reconsidering the Limits of Intellectual Property for Innovation*

First, as highlighted by the ongoing challenge of access to medicines,[176] the utilitarian justification that drives the intellectual property system falls significantly short of ensuring the supply of medicines to address the disease burden in the developing world.[177] Despite the virtues of the incentive theory, dependence on private sources for research and development in health-related technologies simply cannot address the serious gap in technologies that exist to treat different categories of disease.[178] This is particularly true with respect to rare, orphan diseases, or drug-resistant viruses or bacteria, which require years of expensive research with little, if any, financial reward.[179] Likewise, diseases affecting people

[175] Laurence R. Helfer, *Regime Shifting: The TRIPs Agreement and New Dynamics of International Intellectual Property Lawmaking*, 29 Yale J. Int'l L. 1 (2004).

[176] *See generally* High-Level Panel Report, *supra* note 11. [177] *Id.* [178] *Id.* at 8.

[179] *Id.; see also* Orphan Drug Act of 1983, Pub. L. No. 97-414, 96 Stat. 2049, Sec. 1(b) (1982) ("The Congress finds that: (1) there are many diseases and conditions, such as Huntington's disease, myoclonus, ALS (Lou Gehrig's disease), Tourette syndrome, and muscular dystrophy which affect such small numbers of individuals residing in the United States that the diseases and conditions are considered rare in the United States; (2) adequate drugs for many of such diseases and conditions have not been developed; (3) drugs for these diseases and conditions are commonly referred to as "orphan drugs"; (4) because so few individuals are affected by any one rare disease or condition, a pharmaceutical company which develops an orphan drug may reasonably expect the drug to generate relatively small sales in comparison to the cost of developing the drug

in the developing world with relatively little purchasing power are systematically ignored, despite the potentially vast number of citizens affected.[180] These limits to intellectual property as a tool for innovation suggest that the current human rights frame is most useful to the extent the underlying legal regime delivers expected technologies through market incentives. When market incentives do not work, the moral utility of the current intellectual property/human rights interface is far more difficult to defend. New models for innovation and new rules to incentivize research for treatment of diseases in poor populations are important pieces of the puzzle. A broader conception of the intellectual property/human rights frame could facilitate claims that require states to take concrete action with respect to addressing the need for new innovation models. Indeed, the ICESCR offers a framework that obligates and urges states to undertake necessary regulatory and policy initiatives to address a series of serious global health challenges that affect human welfare in all countries, and especially the least-developed countries.

Second, and relatedly, concerns regarding the pricing of intellectual goods continue to hinder human rights agendas within the technology sector.[181] As demonstrated recently by a number of high-profile cases in the United States, public health technologies remain subject to the economic forces of market demand.[182] Despite the life-saving nature of

and consequently to incur a financial loss; (5) there is reason to believe that some promising orphan drugs will not be developed unless changes are made in the applicable Federal laws to reduce the costs of developing such drugs and to provide financial incentives to develop such drugs; and (6) it is in the public interest to provide such changes and incentives for the development of orphan drugs.").

180 High-Level Panel Report, *supra* note 11, at 16 ("Another key aspect of incoherence lies in the misalignment between market-based models that incentivize innovation and the need to obtain treatment for patients. State obligations include duties not only to respect, but to protect and fulfil the right to health; which requires States to take proactive measures to promote public health. As reaffirmed by a recent resolution of the Human Rights Council, ensuring access to medicines, and particularly to essential medicines, is a fundamental element of these obligations. Yet, insufficient investment is being made in R&D for diseases that predominantly affect the poor. Furthermore, the prices charged by some right holders place severe burdens on health systems and individual patients, in wealthy and resource-constrained countries alike.").

181 *Id.*

182 *See* Daniel Kozarich, *Mylan's EpiPen Pricing Crossed Ethical Boundaries*, FORTUNE (Sept. 27, 2016), http://fortune.com/2016/09/27/mylan-epipen-heather-bresch/ ("EpiPen has gone from $100 for a two-pack in 2009 to $608 today. Usually, companies would be applauded for the ability to create revenue through such pricing power. But when it comes to life-saving drugs, consumers interpret these significant increases as the producer profiteering off a person's life or death need.").

patented innovations or copyrighted knowledge goods, ultimately, the development cost of intellectual property products must be allocated somewhere. And, private or public financiers must have sufficient incentives to make their investment advantageous, while at the same time ensuring that products go to market at affordable prices that ensure large-scale availability.[183] The human rights frame simply has no clear answer to the question upon whom these financial burdens should fall.[184] The aspirations embedded in the UDHR and ICESCR require serious and unrelenting attention by states to seek effective solutions; reliance on market mechanisms is insufficient to fulfill the requirements of economic, social, and cultural rights.

B *The Persistence of Institutional Weakness*

Last, and quite important, the human rights frame fails to account for powerful, institutional constraints in the developing and least-developed countries. As I have already pointed out, the intellectual property/human rights interface has been preoccupied with establishing crucial flexibilities in the intellectual property system, such as the Bolar exception in patent law,[185] the legitimacy of compulsory licenses, or fair use and other limitations and exceptions in copyright law. Limitations and exceptions require institutions – relatively sophisticated institutions – to effectively apply and enforce the limits on intellectual property.[186] In least-developed countries in particular, such institutions are lacking or are insufficiently mature to deploy existing limitations and exceptions, much

[183] *See* High-Level Panel Report, *supra* note 11, at 9–10, 15–16. Indeed, such concerns about pricing with respect to essential medicines was expressly stated in the Doha Declaration. *Id.* at 18 ("We recognize that [IP] protection is important for the development of new medicines. We also recognize the concerns about its effect on prices.").

[184] *Id.* at 55 (commentary by Andrew Witty) ("The huge achievements of the current system of healthcare innovation are often ignored or taken for granted. Equally, although many different stakeholders (particularly academia and public and philanthropic funding institutions) contribute significantly, it is often forgotten that almost all of the world's medical technology has come directly from, or with the enormous contribution of, the research-based pharmaceutical, biotechnology and medtech industries. Those contributions have been largely stimulated by incentives underpinned by intellectual property The approaches and partnerships referenced above all operate within and alongside the IP system.").

[185] After *Roche Prods. v. Bolar Pharmaceuticals Co.*, 733 F.2d 858 (Fed. Cir. 2014), which led the U.S. Congress to allow generic drug companies to engage in pre-market clearance research during the patent term.

[186] Justin Hughes, *Fair Use and Its Politics*, in Copyright Law in an Age of Limitations and Exceptions 234 (Ruth Okediji ed., 2017).

less creatively assert new ones within the uncertain framework of international intellectual property laws. Moreover, if all that the intellectual property/human rights interface produces are outcomes that could be achieved without resort to human rights, it is hard to justify the need to resort to human rights frames in the first place. For developing and least-developed countries, the types of intellectual property limits that are necessary – such as exceptions for institutional users or an explicit right of translation – are difficult to reconcile with, if not completely absent from, the international intellectual property framework.[187]

Education, for example, commands no mandatory privilege in international intellectual property treaties such as the Berne Convention.[188] Thus, unsurprisingly, in countries where the copyright lobby is strong, the level of flexibility with respect to access to copyrighted works for educational purposes remains critically low.[189] As the post-TRIPS experience has shown, developing countries have rarely fully employed available flexibilities within their domestic intellectual property systems.[190]

[187] *Cf.* Okediji, *Reframing International Copyright Limitations and Exceptions as Development Policy, supra* note 6, at 429 ("There is very little that aligns the current design of international copyright law with the requirements for economic development. This chapter advances the proposition that copyright limitations and exceptions (L&Es) needed to promote economic development differ in important respects from the set of L&Es around which there is international consensus. Existing international copyright L&Es do not allow access to copyrighted works at a scale, or on terms, needed for economic development progress; they also insufficiently enable key stakeholders, such as educational institutions and libraries, to facilitate access to knowledge in support of human capital formation."). *See* 2014 Shaheed Report, *supra* note 48, at 14.

[188] Okediji, *supra* note 6, at 463–5. The human rights framework could certainly supply the external demand for change in this regard. To do so effectively, however, human rights law will require a distinct vision of IP – one that, perhaps, may need to be delinked from the extant provisions in the UDHR and its progeny. The idea of a conception of human rights not grounded in the UDHR may appear blasphemous. Or it could be liberating, at least in the IP space. But this is a claim to be tackled another day.

[189] *Cf. id.* at 468 ("A good example is L&Es in national copyright laws to support access to educational materials. The scenario is not complicated; in most countries, the cost of educational materials for primary education is borne by the government. In low-income countries, the cost of such materials can be prohibitive, contributing to low quality education. The situation usually worsens as children advance from primary school to tertiary education where the cost of textbooks makes them inaccessible to most families. An insufficiently educated workforce has implications for the labor market and for domestic productivity. Firms are unable to employ workers with suitable technical skills, and so are less likely to adopt technologies that require skilled labor.").

[190] *See* Gaëlle Krikorian, *The Politics of Patents: Conditions of Implementation of Public Health Policy in Thailand*, in Politics of Intellectual Property: Contestation over the Ownership, Use, and Control of Knowledge and Information 29, 49 (Sebastian Haunss & Kenneth C. Shadlen eds., 2009) ("So far, very few countries have

In fact, many countries have gone beyond the level of intellectual property protection required by the TRIPS Agreement.[191] Thus, while the human rights narrative can certainly promote the use of flexibilities and advance welfare benefits, whether or not countries that ultimately need those same flexibilities deploy them is another, complicated story.[192]

Ultimately, the current narrow construction of the intellectual property/human rights interface provides reprieve from the grander, more contested, distributive justice-oriented vision of human progress and flourishing embodied in the economic, social, and cultural rights. To be sure, a human rights frame offers new language and a "moral hegemony" that can be usefully leveraged to support important public welfare goals. Thus far, however, the practical outworking of these efforts has had limited effects on the real needs and interests of most of the world's population, while the agenda for stronger intellectual property rights continues unabated.

C *Reimagining the Human Rights Frame*

In a recent chapter considering use of the international copyright system for development, I suggest a mandatory obligation for developing and least-developed nations to employ copyright limitations and exceptions. The same principle could easily extend to patents. For example, Article 27 of the TRIPS Agreement provides crucial policy space to create definitions of patentability and invention that foster human health development goals, such as curtailing the "evergreening" of patents through successive applications for protection for similar compounds.[193] Few developing countries have capitalized on these or other policy tools.[194] In order to effectively utilize pro-development norms in the context of comprehensive sustainable intellectual property reform, institutions such as the WHO, WIPO, and WTO must cooperate and meaningfully

exercised their right to issue compulsory license. The experience of Thailand with CL points to the difficulties that may exist for developing countries to establish and maintain the political conditions in which they can make a concerted use of TRIPS flexibilities.").

191 *See* Helfer, *supra* note 4, at 982–7.

192 *See* Deere, *supra* note 32 (discussing factors that led to how TRIPS was implemented differently in different developing countries).

193 *See* High-Level Panel Report, *supra* note 11, at 9.

194 *Id.* And, to ensure compulsory licensing work to the benefit of human rights objectives, the license system should be designed in a manner that is maximally efficient, predictable, and transparent, so that both public and private actors can ensure essential technologies are available on reasonable terms. *Id.*

support countries that take on development challenges.[195] To do so under a human rights frame will require systematic support for local intellectual property and human rights agencies working, ideally, in cooperation to demand changes to laws that hinder meaningful access to the knowledge assets needed to foster human flourishing.[196]

Second, due to the increasing difficulty of implementing comprehensive intellectual property policies that promote meaningful domestic development agendas, I reinforce the call for a moratorium of intellectual property harmonization efforts at the regional and multilateral levels.[197] Skepticism of aggressive global intellectual property harmonization efforts is not new;[198] for more than two decades, intellectual property scholars have: (1) warned that the lack of consensus on how a global intellectual property system can effectively serve both developed and developing countries would cause disproportionate harm to the Global South; and (2) urged a "thin" harmonization, if at all.[199]

[195] Jerome H. Reichman, *Intellectual Property in the Twenty-First Century: Will the Developing Countries Lead or Follow?*, 46 Houston L. Rev. 1115 (2009).

[196] *See* High-Level Panel Report, *supra* note 11, at 9–10.

[197] *Cf.* Jerome H. Reichman & Rochelle Cooper Dreyfuss, *Harmonization Without Consensus: Critical Reflections on Drafting a Substantive Patent Law Treaty*, 57 Duke L.J. 85, 86 (2007) ("More controversially, we argue that a deep harmonization would boomerang against even its developed country promoters by creating more problems than it would solve. There is no vision of a properly functioning patent system for the developed world that commands even the appearance of a consensus. The evidence shows, instead, that the worldwide intellectual property system has entered a brave new scientific epoch, in which experts have only tentative, divergent ideas about how best to treat a daunting array of new technologies. The proposals for reconciling the needs of different sectors, such as information technology and biotechnology, pose hard, unresolved issues at a time when the costs of litigation are rising at the expense of profits from innovation. These difficulties are compounded by the tendency of universities to push patenting up stream, generating new rights to core methodologies and research tools. As new approaches to new technologies emerge in different jurisdictions, there is a need to gather empirical evidence to determine which, if any, of these still experimental solutions are preferable over time.").

[198] *Cf. id.* at 123 ("Nonetheless, modest harmonization of the standards of patentability could dramatically lower private costs and make work sharing among national patent offices feasible. It is not, however, necessary to rely on top-down negotiation at WIPO; beneficial moves toward a more unified approach could be made even in the face of a moratorium on new international lawmaking.").

[199] *See id.* at 93–102 ("Although TRIPS specifically leaves room for nations to tailor their laws to their internal needs and pace of intellectual advancement, experience shows that emerging economies are, in fact, greatly challenged by the costs and hardship associated with adjusting their development strategies to new legal realities and that successive rounds of negotiations tend to reduce the flexibilities available for nations to tailor intellectual property law to their own needs.").

A moratorium need not be permanent; it could be designed simply to offer more time for governments to better align policy initiatives with the complex dynamics of innovation policy in a global knowledge economy. Moreover, a moratorium is, arguably, a necessary feature of embracing economic, social, and cultural rights. The text of the ICESCR was purposefully drafted in an ambiguous manner, and designed to be implemented progressively depending on the state of social, political, and legal affairs of a given country.[200] Progressive implementation implies both time to adapt to the impact of global economic arrangements as well as the policy space to do so. One might argue that the extended period for implementation of certain TRIPS obligations, and other forms of special and differential treatment for developing countries, is consistent with the obligations of the ICESCR. A moratorium on stronger intellectual property rights, coupled with constructive, creative engagement with the obligations in the ICESCR, including the development of domestic institutions, may ultimately serve to create domestic intellectual property regimes in which these complicated global frameworks can more cohesively engage to the benefit and flexibility of all countries in their pursuit of sustainable development goals.

Third, there is a need for a built-in compliance and reporting infrastructure for TRIPS flexibilities similar to that which is in place for human rights.[201] In the human rights context, periodic reporting on issues related to compliance is a fundamental requirement for the effective protection of human rights guarantees.[202] For example, Article 17 of the ICESCR requires participating countries to conduct both an initial report within a period of time following ratification and periodic compliance updates thereafter.[203] Such reports must include "factors and difficulties affecting the degree of fulfillment of obligations" under the

[200] *See* Helfer, *supra* note 4, at 987–8 ("Its provisions are drafted in gradualist and ambiguous language that requires each ratifying state to take steps . . . to the maximum of its available resources, with a view to achieving progressively the full realization of the rights recognized in the present Covenant by all appropriate means"); *see also* David Weissbrodt et al., International Human Rights: Law, Policy, and Process 88–93 (3d ed. 2001) (same).

[201] *See* Marrakesh Treaty Guide, *supra* note 91, at 75–89 (highlighting how states can "achieve effective implementation by creating legal remedies that allow beneficiaries and authorized entities to assert their rights; by vesting authority in appropriate human rights and IP institutions, and by authorizing those institutions to engage in monitoring and enforcement activities").

[202] *See* U.S. Dep't of State, *Human Rights Reports*, www.state.gov/j/drl/rls/hrrpt/ (last visited June 26, 2017).

[203] *See* ICESCR, *supra* note 14, at art. 17.

Covenant.[204] Within the context of TRIPS, however, no such reporting requirement exists except for compliance with the obligation to protect intellectual property rights. This one-sided process shields states from accountability for the conditions that undermine human rights goals and subordinates compliance with flexibilities to compliance with authorial rights.

Fourth, I have argued elsewhere that various, development-oriented limitations and exceptions could be made mandatory across global copyright regimes. For instance, copyright law must: "(1) facilitate the production of knowledge consistent with a robust public domain; (2) facilitate access to information; (3) assist in the formation of human capital and absorptive capacity by; (4) supporting access to knowledge and education."[205] Mandatory limitations and exceptions for developing and least-developed countries play a crucial role in supporting the free flow of knowledge goods to support development.[206] To foster a society where knowledge is accessible and enables development, mandatory limitations and exceptions must be focused on building robust institutional intermediaries and distribution channels. Thus, for example, a comprehensive education exception, applicable not only to individuals, but also museums, archives, and libraries would serve to support the international copyright framework in promoting critical human rights objectives.[207] Moreover, an international fair-use, or similar doctrine, for those who do not already have such a construct in place would support a diffusion of knowledge that "ensure[s] the dynamic interplay between the public domain and production and introduction of new goods in society," consistent with the cultural values of different human societies.[208]

IV Conclusion

One reason we employ human rights frames is to challenge the rules that limit or deny opportunities for human flourishing. The intensity of the intellectual property/human rights interface has increased because the welfare considerations animating concerns over intellectual property are

[204] *Id.* Unfortunately, the ICESCR did not initially create a body to receive these reports, making this lever far weaker than was the case with other human rights treaties. The problem was remedied in 1985 with the creation of the ESCR Committee. *See* Economic and Social Council Res. 1985/17 (May 28, 1985).

[205] *See* Okediji, *Sustainable Access, supra* note 84, at 463. [206] *Id.* at 480–2.

[207] *Id.* at 487. [208] *Id.* at 489–94.

no longer limited to the developing or least-developed world. In addition to mounting concerns over access to medicines and healthcare in the developed countries, the pervasive reach of digital technologies has fundamentally altered the nature and range of individual choices and the exercise of individual freedoms in all societies.[209] Resort to arguments and methods steeped in the human rights framework have become important as a universal language uniting opposition to the excesses of the intellectual property system. It would appear, then, that the intellectual property/human rights interface could become even more influential given the shared interests of citizens across the globe as they relate to the power wielded by intellectual property owners over knowledge goods that are fundamental to living meaningful lives. But this influence tends to privilege values and concerns that resonate in the developed world; the current intellectual property/human rights interface simply cannot deliver sustained welfare outcomes for developing and least-developed countries.

Both the intellectual property and human rights regimes ostensibly seek to accomplish human welfare goals linked, ultimately, to human and economic development. In isolation, both fall short; in engagement both regimes protect the intellectual property status quo. The guarantees enshrined in the UDHR and ICESCR generate important momentum toward the goals of equality, security, human dignity, and freedom. Progress toward attaining the highest levels of human flourishing will require novel approaches in the intellectual property *and* in the human rights legal space. In this context, intellectual property flexibilities are certainly important. But, what is also crucial is the ability of nations to enact different kinds of rules, choose different models of innovation, and live under their own set of values, leveraging domestic norms to help shape cultural and technological conditions that strengthen their capacity to participate meaningfully in a globalized world.

As human rights frames continue to exert moral force on the direction and exercise of intellectual property rights, they also must exert similar force on the design of those rights and the means by which states become obliged to adopt them within local conditions. The human rights frame will not, inexorably, facilitate outcomes consistent with human flourishing in the way that resonates with communities laboring under distinct

[209] Cohen, *supra* note 84; *Cf. Neij and Kolmisoppi v. Sweden*, App. No. 40397/12, ECtHR (Feb. 19, 2013) (discussing the right to freedom of expression in the context of an online, file-sharing copyright case).

cultural, social, and institutional environments. Intellectual property scholars must remain attentive to the distributive justice elements and inherent biases of the human rights frame as much as they are alert to those in the intellectual property frame. The task ahead requires ongoing commitment to evaluating the interaction between the global human rights and intellectual property frameworks, and to do so with a critical lens so that each regime, acting independently and in concert, can be molded and applied in ways that meaningfully respond to the serious challenges that constitute barriers to human well-being.

10

Framing the International Intellectual Property System

GRAEME B. DINWOODIE* AND ANNETTE KUR

The TRIPS Agreement was concluded almost a quarter century ago.[1] This was clearly a watershed moment for the international intellectual property (IP) system. Five years earlier, in the lead up to that event, luminaries at the Max Planck Institute had published a book that asked which international institution would shape the system: "WIPO or GATT?".[2] It was a matter of serious debate whether the advent of the TRIPS Agreement, or the incorporation of intellectual property within the full embrace of the revised trade regime,[3] would pre-empt specialist international intellectual property institutions, such as the World Intellectual Property Organization (WIPO), which was responsible for the Berne and Paris Conventions,[4] in favour of the World Trade Organization (WTO), which administered the General Agreement on Tariffs and Trade (the GATT).[5]

* This chapter draws on material first published as Dinwoodie, Graeme B., Diversifying Perspectives of the International Intellectual Property System in a Time of Change? European and International Perspectives 222 (Christophe Geiger ed. 2016); Oxford Legal Studies Research Paper No. 49/2017. Available at SSRN: http://ssrn.com/abstract=2997918

1 *See* Agreement on Trade-Related Aspects of Intellectual Property Rights, Apr. 15, 1994, Marrakesh Agreement Establishing the World Trade Organization, Annex 1C, Legal Instruments – Results of the Uruguay Round, vol. 31, 33 I.L.M. 81 (1994) [hereinafter *TRIPS Agreement*].

2 *See* Friedrich Karl Beier & Gerhard Schricker (eds.), GATT or Wipo?: New Ways in the International Protection of Intellectual Property(1989).

3 *See* Marrakesh Agreement establishing the World Trade Organization, April 15, 1994 1867 U.N.T.S. 154, 33 I.L.M. 1144, reprinted in The Legal Texts: The Results of the Uruguay Round of Multilateral Trade Negotiations 3 (1999 pb. ed.).

4 *See* Berne Convention for the Protection of Literary and Artistic Works, September 9, 1886, as last revised at Paris, July 24, 1971, 1161 U.N.T.S. 3; Paris Convention for the Protection of Industrial Property, March 20, 1883, as last revised at Stockholm, July 14, 1967, 21 U.S.T. 1583, 828 U.N.T.S. 305.

5 *See* Convention Establishing the World Intellectual Property Organization, July 14, 1967, 21 U.S.T. 1749, 828 U.N.T.S. 3 (establishing WIPO).

While the question was an interesting one, it also presented a false choice. No choice was necessary. In fact, WIPO has reinvented itself and has continued to be a leading force in the normative work in the field, along with the WTO. To some extent, that reinvention has reflected and has been necessitated by the post-TRIPS political climate. That climate arguably is itself a by-product of the TRIPS Agreement. The global and substantive scope of the TRIPS Agreement might have been the catalyst to some of the more contested debates we have seen in the twenty years since that treaty was concluded.

But it is not just WIPO and the WTO that are making international intellectual property law. We have in fact seen a multiplication of institutions turning their attention to intellectual property. Examples include the United Nations Educational, Scientific and Cultural Organization (UNESCO), the Conference of the Parties to the Convention on Biological Diversity (CBD), the World Health Organization (WHO) and United Nations Conference on Trade and Development (UNCTAD).[6] And quite often, these institutions do not have the development of intellectual property policy as their main *raison d'être*. Rather, their interest in intellectual property stems from the impact that protection can have on their distinct objectives. As the sources of these intellectual property relevant norms have begun to arise from institutions with different concerns, the perspectives from which intellectual property is developed are growing increasingly diverse.

These varying approaches have attracted the attention of a large group of scholars, writing under a rubric that can be called the framing of intellectual property. The title is apt, as how one views the field depends on how intellectual property is framed. In particular, Susan Sell's work attributed the development and nature of the TRIPS Agreement to the framing of intellectual property as a matter of trade.[7] Others, unsatisfied

[6] *See, e.g.*, UNESCO, *Administered IP-related Treaties*, WIPO LEX, www.wipo.int/wipolex/en/profile.jsp?code=UNESCO (last visited Nov. 2015) (listing IP treaties); Food and Agricultural Organization, *Administered IP-related Treaties*, WIPO LEX, www.wipo.int/wipolex/en/profile.jsp?code=FAO (last visited Nov. 2015) (listing IP treaties); Convention on Biological Diversity, *Administered IP-related Treaties*, WIPO LEX, www.wipo.int/wipolex/en/news_treaties/2010/article_0002.html (last visited Nov. 2015) (listing IP treaties); Ministerial Declaration, *Packaging and Labelling of Tobacco Products: Opportunities and Challenges for Implementation of Articles 11 and 13 of the WHO FCTC* (May 24, 2016), at www.who.int/fctc/implementation/Ministerial-declaration-packaging-labelling-tobacco.pdf?ua=1; UNCTAD, *About the Intellectual Property Programme Division on Investment and Enterprise*, UNCTAD, http://unctad.org/en/Pages/DIAE/Intellectual%20Property/About-the-Programme.aspx (last visited Nov. 2015).

[7] *See* SUSAN K. SELL, PRIVATE POWER, PUBLIC LAW: THE GLOBALIZATION OF INTELLECTUAL PROPERTY RIGHTS 174(2003) (discussing the framing of IP as a trade issue).

with the TRIPS Agreement, have sought to view intellectual property through different frames, such as development or human rights.[8] The supposition clearly is that the policy that will emanate from the system will be substantially affected by whether we frame it as a matter of economics, or trade, or development, or culture or human rights, to name but a few of the frames that have been referenced.[9]

One can of course overstate the novelty of the premises of this literature. To be sure, the TRIPS Agreement brought IP within the trade apparatus. But developments in cross-border exchange were, in fact, part of the original impetus for the Paris and Berne Conventions in the late nineteenth century. The effect of IP on development had been raised and discussed in the 1960s both in the United Nations generally[10] and in WIPO-based unions, such as the Berne Union.[11] And cultural matters clearly informed some of WIPO's copyright agenda before the TRIPS Agreement.

So, viewing IP from different perspectives is not entirely new. The multiplication of sources and institutions playing in the intellectual property space since 1994 might simply be a difference of degree rather than a complete novelty. But it does seem at one with the general trend toward the so-called fragmentation of international law, a phenomenon that has prompted inquiry by international law scholars into the ways in which we can effect integration of these diverse norms and institutions.[12]

But what does it mean to "frame" intellectual property. What is the *relationship* or dynamic between these diverse values or frames, on the one hand, and intellectual property, on the other? In this essay, we focus

8 *See, e.g.*, DUNCAN MATTHEWS, INTELLECTUAL PROPERTY LAW, HUMAN RIGHTS AND DEVELOPMENT: THE ROLE OF NGOS AND SOCIAL MOVEMENTS 7–9 (2011) (framing strategies connected to human rights and development).

9 *See, e.g.*, Peter Drahos, *Does Dialogue Make a Difference? Structural Change and the Limits of Framing*, 117 YALE L.J. POCKET PART 268, 272 (2008) (discussing dangers of framing as a "master mechanism" for the development of international IP); SEBASTIAN HAUNSS & KENNETH C. SHADLEN (EDS.), POLITICS OF INTELLECTUAL PROPERTY: CONTESTATION OVER OWNERSHIP, USE AND CONTROL OF KNOWLEDGE AND INFORMATION (2009) (noting cultural frame); MATTHEWS, *supra* note 8; SELL, *supra* note 7.

10 *See* Pedro Roffe & Gina Vea, *The WIPO Development Agenda in a Historical and Political Context*, in THE DEVELOPMENT AGENDA: GLOBAL INTELLECTUAL PROPERTY AND DEVELOPING COUNTRIES 93 (Neil Weinstock Netanel ed., 2009).

11 *See* Barbara A. Ringer, *The Role of the United States in International Copyright – Past, Present, and Future*, 56 GEO L.J. 1050 (1968).

12 *See, e.g.*, International Law Commission, *Fragmentation of International Law: Difficultie Arising from the Diversification and Expansion of International Law: Report of the Stud Group on the Fragmentation of International Law*, finalized by Martti Koskenniemi, ¶ 24[illegible], U.N. Doc. A/CN.4/L.682 (Apr. 13, 2006).

on the role of economics, trade, development, culture, and human rights. But what we say about the relationship between competing norms emanating from these different institutions might be more broadly applicable to other norm-conflicts within intellectual property (and potentially even in other areas of international relations where fragmentation of norms is rife). We will not engage – as, for example, Amy Kapczynski[13] does – with the political science literature on the concept of framing to explain the lawmaking process and the development of particular agendas. Instead, we are simply going to use the vehicle of the normal meanings of the term "frame" to highlight the different approaches to the relationship between intellectual property and these different fields of knowledge.

We reach the conclusion that we must embrace pluralism in IP. By that, we mean that not only does intellectual property need to have regard to all of the frames of economics, trade, development, culture, and human rights, but also that it needs to do so in a number of different ways. We must be pluralistic about the ways in which these five frames or bodies of knowledge interact with intellectual property law. That is because these different frames possess varying characteristics, and will operate in different ways in different institutional settings. Indeed, we might not expect or want each frame to have equal weight in every setting. That is to say, these do seem like values all surely relevant to IP in some macro sense, but is it necessarily true that all law (or indeed any law or any legal analysis) must take them all into account simultaneously? When viewed institutionally, might it be inappropriate for some bodies to develop *certain* aspects of IP, or might it be inappropriate for other bodies to have regard to certain of the five frames we mentioned?

I What Does It Means to "Frame" IP?

A *Frame as Constraint*

One definition of "frame" found in the dictionary is this: "a rigid structure that surrounds or encloses something such as a door or window."[14] This definition, which suggests the frame as a constraint, resonates metaphorically with at least how we often debate the significance of the

[13] *See* Amy Kapczynski, *The Access to Knowledge Mobilization and the New Politics of Intellectual Property*, 117 YALE L.J. 804 (2008).

[14] *See* Oxford English Dictionary, *Frame*, OED, www.oxforddictionaries.com/us/definition/american_english/frame (last visited Nov. 2015).

classic multilateral IP treaties. A pervasive question in the literature asks: Does the TRIPS Agreement, or Berne or Paris Conventions for that matter, provide ceilings as well as floors, the implication being that floors and ceilings represent outer boundaries for acceptable national law?[15]

Of course, constraints can be tight or they can be loose. They can have varying degrees of "give," of "plasticity." So, even if we think of frames as constraints, they might vary in the extent to which they constrain intellectual property law. After all, while the TRIPS Agreement broadly *confines* national legislative autonomy, it does not *define* in a granular way what precise policy choice has to be implemented at the national level.[16] Moreover, even rigid structures can be porous. One of the themes that Rochelle Dreyfuss and one of us have developed in our work is the importance of allowing norms from other sources to inform the interpretation of the TRIPS Agreement.[17] A porous frame (permitting the influence of norms from other frames) might be a feature rather than a defect of IP law for any number of pragmatic or institutional reasons, including the competence or legitimacy of a single institution to be the uber-legislator developing law by reference to all possible values.

Of course, there might be reasons to have a very rigid, almost impervious frame within which to consider all these questions. For example, political economy might require that kind of frame in order to serve as a bulwark against power asymmetries – one can see this as at least some of the motivation behind mandatory exceptions.[18] Thus, no country should be pressured into not including a right to quote from copyright works; Article 10(1) of the Berne Convention *requires* countries to provide such a right to users.[19] Or the frame may be so fundamental,

[15] *See* Annette Kur & Henning Grosse Ruse-Khan, *Enough Is Enough: The Notion of Binding Ceilings in International Intellectual Property Protection*, in INTELLECTUAL PROPERTY IN A FAIR WORLD TRADE SYSTEM: PROPOSALS FOR REFORMING THE TRIPS AGREEMENT (Annette Kur ed., 2011); Graeme B. Dinwoodie & Rochelle Cooper Dreyfuss, *Designing a Global Intellectual Property System Responsive to Change: The WTO, WIPO, and Beyond*, 46 HOUS. L. REV. 1187 (2009).

[16] *See* TRIPS Agreement, *supra* note 1, art. 1(1).

[17] *See* GRAEME B. DINWOODIE & ROCHELLE COOPER DREYFUSS, A NEOFEDERALIST VISION OF TRIPS: THE RESILIENCE OF THE INTERNATIONAL INTELLECTUAL PROPERTY SYSTEM (2012).

[18] P. BERNT HUGENHOLTZ & RUTH L. OKEDIJI, CONCEIVING AN INTERNATIONAL INSTRUMENT ON LIMITATIONS AND EXCEPTIONS TO COPYRIGHT (2008), *available at* www.ivir.nl/publicaties/hugenholtz/finalreport2008.pdf.

[19] There might be some reasonable debate as to the *scope* of that right at the edges. *See* Lionel Bently & Tanya Aplin, *Whatever Became of Global, Mandatory, Fair Use? A Case Study in Dysfunctional Pluralism*, in IS INTELLECTUAL PROPERTY PLURALISM

so basic, that it cannot reasonably be breached. That type of frame is perhaps brought to mind most readily by the frame of human rights. Larry Helfer's definition of human rights as rights "that exist independently of the vagaries of state approval, recognition, or regulation" fits well with that understanding.[20] Copyright owners may not be concerned about relief that enjoins members of the public from exercising their right to free expression, but that is not a preference that governments can validate (or, in some human rights regimes, to sanction private parties to allow).[21]

B *Justify/Support*

A second definition of frame that one finds in the dictionary is: "basic structure that underlies or supports a system, concept, or text."[22] That is, a frame may offer the normative foundation that justifies the intellectual property system. Indeed, IP protection is often considered a mechanism for ensuring that authors and inventors benefit from their creativity and innovation. However, all of the frames we have mentioned might be thought to underlie intellectual property in some normative sense. Intellectual property can be a catalyst to trade, it can further development, it can contribute to a flourishing culture, or it can be conceived as a human right.

Of course, there are those who see at least some of these frames (especially development, human rights, and culture) as *challenges* to intellectual property, rather than supports. And certainly viewing intellectual property through these particular lenses can intensify the importance of limits to intellectual property protection. But each frame supports *some* level of intellectual property.

FUNCTIONAL? (S. Frankel ed., 2018) (forthcoming), *available at* https://papers.ssrn.com/sol3/papers.cfm?abstract_id=3119041; Tanya Apin & Lionel Bently, *Displacing the Dominance of the Three-Step Test: The Role of Global, Mandatory Fair Use*, in COMPARATIVE ASPECTS OF LIMITATIONS AND EXCEPTIONS IN COPYRIGHT LAW (Wee Loon Ng, Haochen Sun, & Shyam Balganesh eds., 2018) (forthcoming), *available at* https://papers.ssrn.com/sol3/papers.cfm?abstract_id=3119056.

20 *See* Laurence R. Helfer, *Toward a Human Rights Framework for Intellectual Property*, 40 U.C. DAVIS L. REV. 971 (2007).

21 *See* Case C-314/12, UPC Telekabel Wien GmbH v. Constantin Film Verleih GmbH, EU:C:2014:192 (CJEU 2014) (requiring private parties to accommodate the free expression rights of users under Article 11 of the EU Charter of Fundamental Rights).

22 *See* Oxford English Dictionary, *supra* note 14.

This notion of frame comports we believe most easily with scholarly work, in that it gives us a way of thinking about, assessing, and evaluating intellectual property law. But it should also lend itself to the way policymakers think about framing intellectual property law.

C *Skew?*

The third definition of frame that we considered is not one found in the dictionary, but we think is a popular connotation (perhaps not unrelated to how behavioral economists might think of framing): that is, to "fix or predetermine an outcome." In the vernacular of detective shows, to "frame" intellectual property might be to stitch it up.

Certainly, there are copyright holders who think that is precisely what is going on when scholars seek to frame intellectual property in terms of human rights. But that is not necessarily the case, as the decisions of the European Court of Human Rights or the text of the E.U. Charter of Fundamental Rights show. The European Court of Human Rights has recognised that trademark *applications* constitute protected parcels of property under Article 1, Protocol 1, of the European Convention on Human Rights.[23] And the Court of Justice of the European Union has justified web-blocking orders as the product of balancing fundamental rights, including the Article 17 right to the protection of intellectual property, notwithstanding that that remedy brought internet users onto the streets to protest when it was legislatively proposed in the United States.[24]

Likewise, there are many user groups who would view with great skepticism the suggestion that contemporary trade thinking frames intellectual property because they fear it will inevitably elevate protection of investment over competing social values.[25] But as a case on the practice of stopping infringing goods in transit demonstrates, it is not

[23] *See* Anheuser-Busch Inc. v. Portugal, App. No. 73049/01, 45 Eur. H.R. Rep. 36 [830] (Grand Chamber ECtHR 2007).

[24] *See* Case C-314/12, UPC Telekabel Wien GmbH v. Constantin Film Verleih GmbH, EU:C:2014:192 (CJEU 2014); *see also* Elaine Burke, *SOPA, PIPA, ACTA and the Battle for Freedom on the Internet*, SILICONREPUBLIC (Jan. 3, 2013), *available at* www.siliconrepublic.com/life/sopa-pipa-acta-and-the-battle-for-freedom-on-the-Internet

[25] Rochelle Cooper Dreyfuss & Susy Frankel, *From Incentive to Commodity to Asset: How International Law Is Reconceptualizing Intellectual Property*, 36 MICH. J. INT'L L. 557 (2015).

inconceivable that the trade regime, and the genuinely free flow of goods, might require something less than ever-expanding IP protection.[26]

II The Differing Characteristics of the Different Frames

We suggested above that we may have to adopt a pluralistic approach not only to incorporating the various values mentioned, but also to defining the role that each of those values has in framing intellectual property. Different frames evince diverse characteristics. As a result, these frames can play a role in different settings within the intellectual property system, and the settings inevitably inform the role that is appropriate for them to play.

A *Characteristics of Each Frame*

Economics provides a justification or perspective, a support for the grant or denial of legal rights. Trade and human rights also suggest a normative perspective, but those frames also bring with them (at least potentially) institutional and interpretative arrangements tied to legal regimes that are dedicated to elevating those particular frames. Aspects of the current trade *apparatus* in particular may greatly affect our willingness to elevate our regard for the trade frame in embracing a pluralist approach to intellectual property.

Development and culture have *some* legal resonance, but (without suggesting firm lines between law, politics, and society) speak perhaps more overtly and maybe more readily to political (or social) norms and institutions. This does not diminish their role in framing intellectual property. However, it does suggest that these frames may play a greater part in establishing the legitimacy of intellectual property policies and have a lesser role in shaping legal doctrine in many national settings.

Once could parse the frames to find other differences. For present purposes, the point simply is that if the frames we are discussing are different from one another, then perhaps they should be integrated differently or at different places in the broader system we call "IP law".

[26] Request for Consultations by Brazil, *European Union and a Member State – Seizure of Generic Drugs in Transit*, WT/DS409/1 (May 19, 2010).

B The Different Roles of Frames

This discussion requires us to consider the roles that these different frames play in the IP system: With an eye to our definitions, do they constrain, do they justify, or do they shape or skew? And where in the IP system do they do that: At the international level, shaping the IP laws of about 180 countries, or at the national policymaking level, affecting local legislation? In scholarly justification or explanation, or in doctrinal interpretation in the course of deciding particular disputes? Let us set out just a couple of variables.

1 International versus National

If the frame is deployed to develop IP law at the international level, whether in the negotiation of agreements or the resolution of disputes, the analysis must recognize the need for greater margins of appreciation to accommodate diverse social priorities and legal cultures. And it must take account of the fact that entrenched international norms are difficult to reverse. More finely grained analysis might be warranted in the domestic context, where a more homogeneous climate might prevail and where experimentation can more readily be tried and reversed.

2 Explanatory versus Doctrinal

Some frames may have a greater explanatory role than a direct doctrinal application. Thus, some scholars have argued that recent U.S. fair use doctrine has largely vindicated what cultural theorists would call countercultural recoding.[27] This is an important and helpful social assessment of what has been achieved. But cultural theory may be of less direct use to courts at a doctrinal level, as they are untrained in evaluations of this sort. And indeed, the U.S. courts have reached that point (if they have) without substantial engagement with cultural theory.

3 Institutional Competence/Legitimacy

This is a particular instance of a broader point. Different institutions – scholars, policymakers, national legislators, courts, varied international adjudicators – may each, by virtue of their composition or training, have different competences to handle and use different frames in their treatment of intellectual property. And with competence, to some

[27] *See* David Tan, *The Lost Language of the First Amendment in Copyright Fair Use: A Semiotic Perspective of the "Transformative Use" Doctrine Twenty-Five Years on*, 26 FORDHAM INTELL. PROP. MEDIA & ENT. L.J. 311 (2016).

extent, comes legitimacy. Do we want a trade body (or any other international body for that matter) to consider so many diverse intellectual frameworks in resolving discrete problems? To be sure, if WTO panels were to integrate the varied approaches, this might ease the problem of fragmentation. But designating a trade panel, which intentionally is composed only of trade experts, to referee any competing norms may bring order at the expense of legitimacy.

4 The False Allure of Conceptual Order?

Moreover, strategically, does one also wish to incorporate these different frames within the intellectual property system? As scholars, we have an attraction to the "internal logic" of intellectual property. But history suggests that there are pragmatic merits to being an outsider.[28] What we have seen with regime shifting suggests that reframing may be as important as framing, encouraging our use of varied institutional options in developing international IP law.

The lessons to be learned from international relations or political economy might furnish a useful illustration. Counternorms developed autonomously within an external frame may flourish more fully outside the mainstream setting, tended or enforced by experts or players in those other fields with a different set of expertise or normative commitments. Take competition law. Yes, intellectual property law must surely incorporate competition values, but there might be merit in competition authorities – not working with the intellectual property industries on a daily basis – having external capacity to regulate intellectual property. Much of the same might be said of expertise in health or agriculture. Decisions on what is essential to maintaining life and sustainable nutrition should not be overwhelmed by considerations about the interests of patent holders.

Lawmaking by expert international institutions could also be useful to countries new to intellectual property law, that lack the capacity to craft a legal regime for themselves. However, without transparency and participation, such legislation may be considered illegitimate. And as Rochelle Dreyfuss has stressed, even these procedural values may not be enough, for they rely on effective advocacy, including a clear understanding of the law's potential impact. When that is lacking, there is danger that local interests will be disregarded.[29]

[28] *See* generally GRAEME B. DINWOODIE, INTELLECTUAL PROPERTY AND GENERAL LEGAL PRINCIPLES: IS IP A LEX SPECIALIS? (2015).

[29] *See* Rochelle Cooper Dreyfuss, *The Max Planck Principles as an Aspect of Global Administrative Law*, 44 INT'L REV. INTELL. PROP. & COMP. L. 906 (2013).

5 A "Theory of Everything" in IP Law?

Having come to this point, the question can be posed whether it is possible to progress from deconstructing the frames and analysing their various elements to envisaging a new kind of structure that comprises them all, assigning to each one its proper place not only in IP, but within the larger legal, cultural, and economic space surrounding it. In other words: can the varied frames – that is, theories and observations brought together from many different angles in the legal, sociological, and economic scholarship – serve as building material for what could be termed a "Theory of Everything" in IP law? Would it help in that context to conceive of IP as a discrete living organism, confined in its contours, yet interacting with the outside world, on the one hand absorbing impulses and integrating them into its living matter, and on the other hand impacting the environment by its own emanations?

The previous analysis and, more prominently, the chapters in this book serve as the foundations for such an effort. On that basis one can discern different ingredients – or, staying within the metaphorical picture: different lines of stem cells – out of which that organism would be constructed. The first one concerns exigencies deriving from globalization and the impetus it creates for legal harmonization, while respecting the pluralism of norms where that reflects the pluralism of value and policy judgments that should not be sacrificed on the altar of convenience and efficiency.[30] Second, in close connection with the first, is trade policy, the need to readjust the IP justification narrative, and to develop a new dialogic culture among trading partners.[31] Third, one might proffer the implications of technology, the economic functions of IP,[32] and the "human factor" (the role and activity of those on whose anticipated conduct the law depends, and whose reactions it seeks to influence) in their theoretical and empirical dimensions. Finally, fourth (certainly not least) are the ethical and cultural parameters, in particular regarding

[30] *See* Chapter 5, Elizabeth Siew-Kuan Ng & Albert Guangzhou Hu, *Flexibilities in the Implementation of TRIPS: An Analysis of Their Impact on Technological Innovation and Public Health in Asia.*

[31] *See* Chapter 3, Jerome Reichman, *Reframing Intellectual Property Rights with Fewer Distortions of the Trade Paradigm*; and Chapter 4, Susy Frankel, *The Fusion of Intellectual Property and Trade.*

[32] Including the incentives deriving therefrom; see Chapter 1, Rochelle Cooper Dreyfuss, *In Praise of an Incentive-Based Theory of Intellectual Property Protection*, with comments by Mark Fung Chian Lim; and Chapter 2, Christopher Sprigman, *Copyright and Creative Incentives: What Do(n't) We Know?*

moral issues inherent in the topics addressed by the law,[33] but also regarding the manner in which the legal discourse is organized and conducted, and whose interests tend to be neglected therein.

If we purify those ingredients so as to approximate an optimal, evenly calibrated model sample in each category and then place them all together in an imaginary petri dish, will it bring forth the unifying theory that can be employed as a blueprint for developing a sound, resilient but also sensitive IP system on the international, regional or national level? The disillusioned answer must be: no, it is certainly not that easy. We are a long way from designing the lab conditions for bringing an optimal system to actual life, and the magic formula for achieving that all at once has not yet been found. On the other hand, we have come quite some part of the way if we can at least agree on the basic structure of what is to be achieved, and on the necessity of the elements to be included in the construction plan.

Staying within the picture of IP as a living organism, one can evoke the image of an "IP Tree." Built on the bioconstruction plan addressed above, the IP Tree illustrates the ways in which IP is shaped and impacted by the different kinds of frames that are addressed and discussed above and, more comprehensively, in the individual chapters of this book:

- human rights are the ground in which the roots of the tree are anchored and from which nourishment is derived;
- (economic) incentives are needed and must be monitored so as to determine the strength and structure of the trunk and its branches;
- culture (and other forms of interaction with society) stand for the climate and other environmental influences shaping the form and density of the foliage;
- trade corresponds to the forest management whose policy decides on mono-cropping, (over-)harvesting, or sustainable and organic growth.

If the image is accepted as – in principle – a useful metaphor, we can embark more confidently on studying the construction plan, its various elements, and the ways in which they can be combined to form a coherent pattern on which legislative and adjudicative decisions are based. Studying the building components addressed in this book can also assist in improving the transparency of reasoning and establishing a better dialogue culture: ideally, under conscious consideration of the various frames, it

[33] *See* Chapter 8, Graeme Austin, *Authors' Human Rights in the Intellectual Property Framework*; and Chapter 9, Ruth Okediji, *Intellectual Property in the Image of Human Rights.*

will be possible to arrive at a point in the legal discourse where inflated and phoney arguments are discarded, established doctrines are seriously tested, and the legal-political ratio of the ultimate decision becomes clearly visible.

III Conclusion

In conclusion, it is a common complaint that those urging a pluralist perspective offer insufficient structure: that legal order and certainty requires commitment to a particular set of metrics, or to some sort of rule of recognition that will identify the norms (or frames) by which to determine any particular issue. But each of the frames we have mentioned can advance our understanding of intellectual property and thus have a role to play in assessing intellectual property law, developing and reforming that law, and in deciding disputes about intellectual property law. But it may be that the "framing" performed by each of economics, trade, development, culture, and human rights will be different, suggesting that the concept of a frame itself has to be understood in a pluralist sense.

IV Post Scriptum

It has been some time since this chapter was first written, and it seems like long ago. The cautious spirit of optimism pervading our text as well as the book in general has given way in both of us to a more skeptical attitude, as we look at the world of today. For instance, while we, as most scholars, were wary about increasing tendencies to include intellectual property into bilateral and multilateral trade agreements, we are now faced with a world where trade wars may be imminent, and where existing treaties are jettisoned when they get in the way of growing nationalism. It has also become obvious that values previously taken for granted within scholarly circles, such as human rights and respect for diversity of cultures, are precarious (and maybe always were) in a world where the strongest openly claim a "natural right" to prevail. Moreover, there is a risk that recognition and appreciation of human and cultural values by the public at large are seriously undermined by exactly the same tools of unlimited global communication that we once greeted as a magic wand, capable of procuring access to information and knowledge for all.

How does all that affect the process of framing intellectual property in the future? Perhaps recent changes in the political and societal landscape reflect some degree of saturation on the scholarly level; have we reached too far in developing grand visions and unifying theories of what intellectual property is and should be? Maybe in today's more contentious political climate it is time to get back to basics and do the less glamorous, small-scale work of developing pragmatic solutions for the many urgent problems challenging us today? That does not mean that the intellectual stimulus of the conceptual debates in the decades immediately following the TRIPS Agreement is lost – it continues to inform and inspire the endeavor of those carrying on the good work.

This brings us to Elizabeth Siew-Kuan Ng, who, together with Rochelle Cooper Dreyfuss, was the organizer and good spirit of the conference out of which this book has grown, and who so sadly left us before it was published. Her outstanding human and professional qualities are accounted for in another part of this volume. However, as one of many personal reminiscences it shall be recalled here that in her last year she had developed, as one of her many plans and ideas, a project on how to turn utility model protection from its traditional, exclusivity-based concept into a liability regime, thus encouraging incremental innovation without excluding others from using the fruits it might bear. There is no doubt that devising and implementing such a system is fraught with many open issues and potential drawbacks. Nevertheless, it is exactly that kind of pragmatic effort that fits within the frames of intellectual property, now and in the future.

Commentary

Framing Intellectual Property Law in the 21st Century: A Policy Practitioner's Perspective

YIH-SAN TAN AND SANDRA YU*

I Introduction

Intellectual property protection is an instrument of public policy. It had historically based, and probably still bases, its relevance on the strengthening of economies that belonged to territorially sovereign states. Its origins can be traced to the enactment of the English Statute of Monopolies (1624) and the Statute of Anne (1710) for patents and copyright protection, respectively. These Acts provided for a form of economic protection for industries, in particular new ones, and were therefore intended to be tools through which England's economy could be strengthened towards self-sufficiency. The grant of such monopoly rights is territorial and codified in state legislation that is typically tuned to the domestic considerations of each state. The key policy consideration in the formulation of intellectual property regimes of the world, though, has remained unchanged over the past hundred years, and that is to help calibrate monopoly incentives given to current creators without stifling the creative space of future creators.[1]

* As recast by Yih-San Tan, CE IPOS and Sandra Yu from the speech prepared for 2014 Centre for Business and Law conference "Framing Intellectual Property Law in the 21st Century: Integrating Incentives, Trade, Development, Culture, and Human Rights."

[1] Statute of Monopolies (1624), § 6–9: " . . . shall not extend to any letters patents (b) and grants of privilege for the term of fourteen years or under, hereafter to be made, of the sole working or making of any manner of new manufactures within this realm (c) to the true and first inventor (d) and inventors of such manufactures, which others at the time of making such letters patents and grants shall not use (e), so as also they be not contrary to the law nor mischievous to the state by raising prices of commodities at home, or hurt of trade, or generally inconvenient."

In the twenty-first century, no country could contemplate operating on its own. While tending to their domestic economy, intellectual property policymakers across the world have found it increasingly important to utilize intellectual property policies to position their trade regimes positively so as to assist their domestic companies to internationalize. In fact, some of these calibrations for the purpose of cross-border transactions were made legitimate with the establishment of international agreements that had since formed the norm. Two principal organizations have shaped the intellectual property world for the past twenty years, and they are the World Trade Organization (WTO) and the World Intellectual Property Organization (WIPO). WTO administers the Agreement on Trade-Related Aspects of Intellectual Property Rights (TRIPS) whereas WIPO has numerous intellectual property related treaties under its management such as the Berne Convention for the Protection of Literary and Artistic Works and the Madrid Agreement Concerning the International Registration of Marks.

Tectonic shifts are starting to take place in the global intellectual property landscape. Intellectual property, which had started out as essentially an instrument to sharpen domestic industrial policies, has since become an interesting part of international trade conversations. Any calibrations of intellectual property policies to provide incentives for industries and businesses will have to take into account the incessant flow of ideas across the World Wide Web. With technological disruptions and globalization, the intellectual property landscape in the twenty-first century must find new ways to navigate these challenges and evolve so as to stay relevant to global development. Two principal trends have become increasingly clear and are worthwhile for all, in particular policymakers, across the world to ponder over.

II Emergence of a Multipolar Intellectual Property Architecture

For some years, the intellectual property world was nicely segregated into two spheres, namely, the United States of America (U.S.), and the Rest-of-the-World. The largest and most innovative economy for the past forty years was the U.S. The U.S. had the largest number of intellectual property filings, a well-established set of precedents, and probably the most sophisticated intellectual property management practice and marketplace. The Rest-of-the-World was amply represented by the European countries and Japan. These two related but distinct intellectual property spheres peacefully coexisted for the past forty years.

In the twenty-first century, we will see the emergence of China as another intellectual property powerhouse. In 2013, it was reported that the State Intellectual Property Office of China (SIPO) received the greatest number of patent applications in the world, widening the gap considerably between IP5 (namely SIPO, United States Patents and Trademark Office, European Patent Office, Japan Patent Office, and Korean Intellectual Property Office) and the rest of the world considerably since SIPO first took the world's leading position in 2011.[2] While it will take some time for China to rival the U.S. in both intellectual property quality and intellectual property regime sophistication, this time will come, surely.

Specifically, any prior art search will soon have to include a scan of the Chinese Journal. One other significant development in China is the establishment of intellectual property courts in three key Chinese cities, namely Beijing, Shanghai and Guangzhou, which should improve intellectual property enforcement. Further, China may contemplate amalgamating the Trademark, Patent and Copyright Offices into an integrated intellectual property Office that would then house no less than half a million staff. As China's share of world trade increases, it is not beyond imagination that China will have its own equivalent of the International Trade Commission, and that efficient and powerful intellectual property-based Import Investigations will be conducted through administrative hearings.

The question that should be asked is not whether there will be a difference in the judicial outcome of any intellectual property dispute. It is more relevant to ask what the rest of the world should do if there are repeated and persistent differences in outcomes from two different intellectual property courts systems. The question that neutral countries such as Singapore must contemplate is whether there could be a neutral forum for such disputes to be mediated and/or arbitrated.

This story could well be extended to other emerging economies, such as the other countries within the BRICS group (Brazil, Russia, India, and South Africa), as they embark on transforming and developing their economies. It would be interesting also to track how the other rapidly developing economies, including ASEAN countries, will grow in the coming decades.

[2] WIPO, *2014 World Intellectual Property Indicators*, www.wipo.int/edocs/pubdocs/en/wipo_pub_941_2014.pdf.

As such, the architecture of the world of intellectual property system would become multipolar, complex and probably deeply interconnected. The intellectual property world of tomorrow would not be the same again.

III Digital World

The second shift to consider is the rise of the digital world in the twenty-first century. Whether the world will arrive at a global village where territorial boundaries and barriers will be broken down is something that cannot quite be seen, at least, not as yet. But what can be safely concluded is that the virtual world is "flattening" the physical world.

In 2007, if MySpace were a country it would have been the 8th largest country in the world. In 2014, if Facebook were a country, it would be the world's 3rd largest. Kids are "born digital", unlike adults today who have had to learn to become digitally savvy. Therefore, intellectual property reform will have to deal with a new generation of global "digital-natives" and how they interact with information.

One of the primary trends that can be observed right now is the blurring of lines across different types of media. Following that is the trend that international boundaries are broken down over cyberspace. Specifically, culture, norms and behaviors in the 21st century will no longer be simply shaped within territorial confines. In this respect, should intellectual property laws be founded on norms that are shaped by the internet community? In some ways, the adoption of the Uniform Domain Name dispute resolution policy had effectively piloted this approach. The European Union's Community Trademark system also raised the question of whether the rest of the world should adopt a similar approach, which could add to the possibility of a global trademark. Further, should trademark examination be discussed in the context of a common internet user?

In addition, the inexhaustible nature of the digital world critically challenged the notion of national or regional versus global exhaustion. The dichotomy was manifest in respect of intellectual property in the digital domain across countries of the world. Copyright attribution is but one way to encourage respect for intellectual property, but more could be done in order to cultivate the right behavior. If ever there is to be a law for everything, it should begin in the digital world.

In short, the intellectual property world of the twenty-first century may be pulled by the two diverging shifts – division by multiple poles and yet harmonization by the rise of the digital world.

IV The Singapore Story

Against the above two shifts as backdrop, it is fitting to recount that intellectual property policy formulation is still an instrument of public policy, of which the outcome is to support a creative and innovative economy that will offer people greater job opportunities and a better life. Before one can talk about Singapore's policy responses, a brief mention of her history is necessary, as it will be evident that Singapore has always been a small country trying to make a living in the sea of change.

In the 1970s, we saw the beginning of the disaggregation of the manufacturing processes. For example, cars and shoes were assembled from parts made in a number of countries. This had led to the rise of container shipping or vice versa. Singapore's reaction to this development was to build connectivity. We started our trans-shipment hub in the 1970s. By the 1990s, Singapore became one of the largest trans-shipment hubs of the world. This is possible not only because of our physical location, but also because of the software, the thinking that went into streamlining the shipping practices,[3] the harmonization of shipping law as well as the creation of a common place for dispute resolution. Today, we pride ourselves as one of the few go-to places for international shipping disputes.

In the 1990s, we saw the disintermediation effect of telecommunications. Financial services were at the forefront. Banking was once the most territorial industry as it requires the highest amounts of public safeguards, but we have taken pains to create connectivity. Today, Singapore is one of the few financial hubs of the world, while actively playing a role in shaping international norms for financial services. With the rise of China, Singapore has become one of the largest RMB trading hubs outside of China.

In the twenty-first century, globalization will entail more than the movement of goods and services. We will begin to enjoy the great flow of ideas across borders, either physically or digitally. Inventions are no longer dominated by a single territory; now, more patents are being filed by inventors from different countries of origin. There is also greater collaboration by innovators across borders. While intellectual property rules and norms guide the flows of ideas across borders, these flows are still largely territorial. Territorial-based intellectual property regimes will

[3] One way that this was done was via PORTNET (accessible from www.portnet.com/home) which is a nationwide business to business (B2B) port community solution.

not be adequate to support these flows if they continue to develop as such. For example, should an intellectual property dispute arise between a China-based company and a U.S.-based company in the near future, where would the parties go?

Therefore, the pertinent question for Singapore is: where are the opportunities in this brave new world of intellectual property?

V Singapore's Intellectual Property Policy Anchors

In dealing with the evolving intellectual property landscape of the future, there have been some considerations that Singapore has had to keep in mind.

A Accessibility to Intellectual Property for Local Innovators

Our intellectual property regime ought to be accessible by the public and businesses. We are constantly reminded that our market is small and internationalization is the only viable growth path for Singapore companies. Initiatives from various government agencies, such as SPRING Singapore, International Enterprise (IE) Singapore, Economic Development Board (EDB), and Workforce Development Authority (WDA) are focused on helping Singapore-based companies and Singaporeans ease into the international arena and face up to global competition. We will do well to assist our companies to learn the rules of the game of international trade, of which intellectual property accounts for a large part of the learning curve.

Many have lamented that intellectual property is a game for those with deep pockets. It should not be the case. To stay relevant, intellectual property must be a tool that can legitimately help businesses of all sizes to grow and gain a competitive footing both locally and internationally. Intellectual property should also serve as a scaffold for future creators to innovate and generate better ideas.

B Interoperability and Not Simply Harmonization

The second policy anchor is interoperability. This arises from the fact that the intellectual property landscape will evolve as previously articulated, and also from Singapore's need to internationalize our industries. The most robust intellectual property strategy is to engage and evolve with changes. Interoperability does not necessarily mean harmonization, but rather points us towards the aim of building an intellectual property regime that creators will be able to use to access overseas markets.

Singapore has begun to build outward connectivity in order to ensure interoperability in the potentially divided world. Even while Europe and China are separately encouraging greater integration, ASEAN countries have begun the ASEAN Integration Plan so as to realize a common market for 600 million people. For the moment, the ASEAN's objectives are much more limited than the European Union's. It took forty years for Europe to reach an agreement on a Unitary Patent. For ASEAN to develop something similar, the timeframe is anyone's guess. However, opportunities abound to drive towards the establishment of a common market in order to achieve greater economic progress for member states.

C *Quality*

Quality is essential and probably most crucial to the stakeholders we are supporting. As we render our intellectual property regime more accessible and interoperable, the accompanying downside risk will be a lowering of the quality of intellectual property standards. This is because interoperability will naturally drive quality down to the lowest common denominator. However, to instill confidence in an intellectual property regime that is both accessible and interoperable, it is essential that we take steps to ensure that quality is not compromised. A business owner who has obtained a trademark registration quickly and cheaply should also take comfort in the fact that his trademark can hold up in courts when its distinctiveness is being assessed in the event of a dispute.

In this respect, Singapore has raised the bar for our Patent Regime by converting to a positive-grant regime in 2015. To further ensure quality, we have even invested in indigenous capability to conduct substantive patent examination. We are tracking patent thickets, and possibly trademark cluttering, and we will continue to be less than friendly to patent trolls.

To conclude, these three policy anchors are but a way for a small country to stay afloat in the sea of changes that will inevitably come our way.

Chapter 1, "In Praise of an Incentive-Based Theory of Intellectual Property Protection" by *Rochelle Cooper Dreyfuss*

MARK FUNG-CHIAN LIM*

I General Comments

Professor Dreyfuss provides a voice of reason at a time when a number of distinguished scholars are arguing that there can be "IP (intellectual production) without IP (intellectual property)." Accordingly, there are circumstances in which intellectual property rights are not necessary.

While agreeing that there are many fields where, for various reasons, progress occurs without strong intellectual property protection (e.g. fashion designers, chefs, comedians, athletes, academia and open innovation), these examples do not cover all instances of creative production. Exclusive rights remain important in the modern economy, especially in the pharmaceutical industry, which requires such incentives in order to justify the huge investments in research and development. Indeed, it is often a mirage that intellectual production takes place without intellectual property. For example, many of the works of the famous artist, Tracey Emin, are arguably not protected (or only have very "thin" protection) by copyright or any other form of intellectual property. However, one major reason why her works are popular and command such high prices[4] is likely to be the "brand" which she has built up in her name, which is protected under trademark law.

Advocating for a return to an incentive-based theory of intellectual property protection, Professor Dreyfuss notes that this is in fact the traditional justification for granting such protection. Indeed, global leaders continue to emphasize the need for intellectual property protection to stimulate innovation.[5] Interestingly, more than 200 years ago, some of

* The views expressed in this note are made in the author's personal capacity.

[4] For example, her installation entitled *My Bed*, consisting of her own unmade dirty bed with used condoms and blood-stained underwear, was reportedly sold for a princely sum of 2.5 million pounds sterling at an auction in 2014: *see* Katya Kazakina, *Emin's Record Messy Bed Boosts Christie's London Auction,* BLOOMBERG (July 2, 2014), www.bloomberg.com/news/articles/2014-07-01/emin-s-messy-bed-fetches-4-3-million-in-artist-s-record. It is most unlikely that anyone else would have been able to sell their unmade bed for anywhere close to this sum.

[5] Some examples of statements by global leaders include – U.S. President Barack Obama: "China and Europe aren't standing on the side lines. Neither should we.

the Presidents of the United States had also stressed the importance of a patent system to encourage innovation.[6]

Importantly, Professor Dreyfuss emphasizes that an incentive-based theory of intellectual property protection should not be equated with continually ratcheting up the level of intellectual property protection conferred on inventions, copyright works, etc. Instead, it is essential to balance the interests of rights holders with other stakeholders such as users and future creators. I agree with this viewpoint and have attempted to illustrate this in a simple diagram (see Figure C.1).

We know that the nation that goes all-in on innovation today will own the global economy tomorrow. This is an edge America cannot surrender." *See* Office of the Press Secretary, *President Barack Obama's State of the Union Address*, THE WHITE HOUSE (January 28, 2014, www.whitehouse.gov/the-press-office/2014/01/28/president-barack-obamas-state-union-address; U.K. Minister for IP Baroness Neville-Rolfe: " ... the Government's aim is to make the UK the best place to start and invest in innovative companies. Our ambition is to increase the value generated by all sectors with a stake in the UK's intellectual property regime." *See* Baroness Neville-Rolfe, *Guest Post by Baroness Neville-Rolfe: The Lure of Intellectual Property*, MANAGINGIP (August 6, 2014), www.managingip.com/Blog/3368823/Guest-post-by-Baroness-Neville-Rolfe-The-lure-of-intellectual-property.html; Former China State Intellectual Property Officer Commissioner Tian Lipu: China's booming patent numbers is evidence of a "burst of innovation developing here among the Chinese people" that taps into China's long history and identity as a country of inventors and creators. *See* Peter Leung, *Can Intellectual Property ever be Non-Political?*, MANAGINGIP (June 30, 2014). The Chairman of Singapore's IP Steering Committee Teo Ming Kian also expressed similar sentiments: "In this knowledge-based, innovation-driven globalised economy ... [t]here is a window of opportunity for Singapore to develop itself as a Global IP Hub in Asia – a trusted, neutral node that services the needs of local and international companies in IP, and supports the development and growth of the larger IP landscape in Asia." *See* IP STEERING COMMITTEE, INTELLECTUAL PROPERTY (IP) HUB MASTER PLAN: DEVELOPING SINGAPORE AS A GLOBAL IP HUB IN ASIA (2013), www.ipos.gov.sg/Portals/0/Press%20Release/IP%20HUB%20MASTER%20PLAN%20REPORT%202%20APR%202013.pdf.

[6] The following are selected quotes taken from Gene Quinn, *Celebrating Presidents Who Advocated for the U.S. Patent System*, IPWATCHDOG (2013), www.ipwatchdog.com/2013/02/18/celebrating-presidents-who-advocated-for-the-u-s-patent-system/id=34896/: George Washington in advocating the establishment of a patent system: "I cannot forbear intimating to you the expediency of giving effectual encouragement as well to the introduction of new and useful inventions from abroad as to the exertions of skill and genius in producing them at home ... " (first State of the Union address, 1790); Abraham Lincoln (in an 1859 speech) describing the patent system as one of three great inventions in the history of the world: "[I]n the world's history, certain inventions and discoveries occurred, of peculiar value, on account of their great efficiency in facilitating all other inventions and discoveries. Of these were the arts of writing and of printing, the discovery of America, and the introduction of Patent laws." And later in the same speech explaining that "[t]he patent system ... added the fuel of interest to the fire of genius, in the discovery and production of new and useful things."

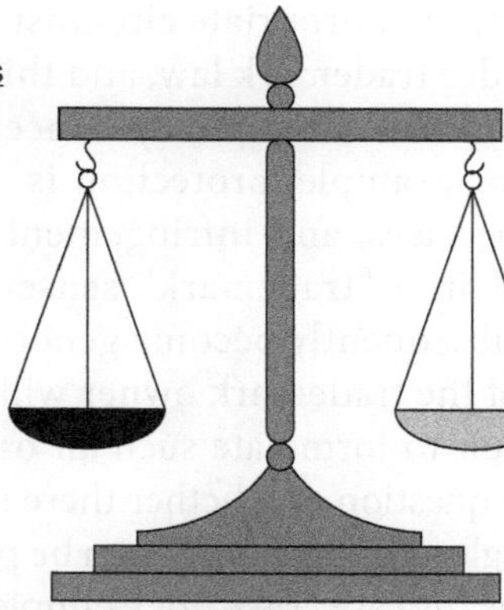

Figure C.1 Balancing the interests of rights holders with other stakeholders

II Implementation of Incentive-Based Theory? Discussion in the Context of Copyright in Words and Sentences

While I am of the view that the theoretical foundation of an incentive-based theory of intellectual property protection cannot be faulted, the practical implementation is not straightforward. In particular, it is likely that a policymaker or judge will be confronted with the perennial conflict that permeates most areas of law – between predictability and certainty on the one hand, and flexibility and fairness on the other. It is easy to reject tests which are extreme, but extremely difficult to formulate a test that is, in Goldilocks' words, "just right."[7]

Let us consider this in the context of copyright in single words and in sentences. It is clear that single words do not generally enjoy copyright protection.[8] This can be easily justified on policy reasons as conferring copyright protection on single words would impede the use and

[7] In the famous children's story of *Goldilocks and the Three Bears*, a girl named Goldilocks stumbles across a cottage owned by three bears, who were not in at the time. Goldilocks enters the house and sees three bowls of porridge laid out on a breakfast table and tastes each of them. Father Bear's porridge is too hot and Mother Bear's porridge is too cold, but Baby Bear's porridge is just right. In the living room, she sees three chairs and sits on each of them. Father Bear's and Mother Bear's chairs are both too big, but the size of Baby Bear's chair is just right. Finally, Goldilocks enters the bedroom and lies down on each bear's bed. Father Bear's bed is too hard and Mother Bear's bed is too soft, but again Baby Bear's bed is just right. It should be added that even Goldilocks did not get everything "just right"; when she sat on Baby Bear's chair it could not support her weight and broke into pieces.

[8] *See, e.g.*, Exxon Corp. v. Exxon Insurance Consultants International Ltd [1982] Ch. 119 (English Court of Appeal). The word in question (i.e. the invented word "Exxon") was "original" and was created after considerable research and labor. However, a single word is

development of language. In appropriate circumstances, single words can also be protected under trademark law, and this regime of protection does not give rise to the same policy concerns due to certain safeguards in the law: for example, protection is confined to certain categories of goods or services, and infringement only occurs if the word/trademark is used in a "trademark" sense to denote origin.[9] Further, marks which subsequently become generic may generally be revoked and the rights of the trademark owner will cease thereafter.[10]

It is much more difficult to formulate such an ostensibly bright-line test when it comes to the question of whether there should be copyright in a sentence.[11] While single sentences may often be pedestrian in nature, this may not necessarily be the case. Take, for example, a sentence such as "*For sale: Baby shoes, never worn*" described as a six-word novel, which suggests the tragic story of a woman who has lost her baby.[12] Or the well-known phrase, "The quick brown fox jumps over the lazy dog," which contains all twenty-six letters of the alphabet, and is therefore often used to test a student's handwriting, as a sample to permit viewing and selection of different font types, etc. A bright-line test denying protection to such sentences would appear to be unfair, and is also difficult to justify on legal grounds since these sentences are arguably "original" (created using "sufficient labor, skill and judgment") and also "literary works" (as they provide either information and instruction, or pleasure, in the form of literary enjoyment).

Furthermore, a bright-line test would in any event not eliminate uncertainty since the use of a sentence extracted from a story or article

not a literary work as it does not provide "either information and instruction, or pleasure, in the form of literary enjoyment."

9 This, at least, is the position in Singapore: *see* Nation Fittings (M) Sdn. Bhd. v. Oystertec Plc. [2006] 1 SLR 712.

10 For example, under section 22(1)(c) of the Singapore Trade Marks Act (Chapter 332, 2005 Revised Edition), "[t]he registration of a trade mark may be revoked on . . . the . . . ground that, in consequence of acts or inactivity of the proprietor, it has become the common name in the trade for the product or service for which it is registered."

11 In *The Newspaper Licensing Agency and Others v. Meltwater Holding BV and Others* [2011] EWCA Civ. 890, the English Court of Appeal held that copyright is capable of subsisting in newspaper headlines. In contrast, in Fairfax Media Publications Pty. Ltd. v. Reed International Books Australia Pty. Ltd. (2010) 189 FCR 109 at [44], the Australian Federal Court held that a headline is "simply too insubstantial and too short to qualify for copyright protection as literary works."

12 *See* (among many others) Josh Jones, *The (Urban) Legend of Ernest Hemingway's Six-Word Story: "For sale: Baby shoes, Never worn,"* OpenCulture (March 24, 2015), www.openculture.com/2015/03/the-urban-legend-of-ernest-hemingways-six-word-story.html.

may still infringe copyright in that story/article. Whether the copyright in a story or article has been infringed depends on the "quality" of what has been copied and not the "quantity." Thus, copying the first sentence in a novel or a poem may arguably infringe the copyright in the novel or poem as a whole.[13] This has occurred, for example, in the context of music copyright.[14]

Accordingly, in such cases, it will arguably be necessary to first determine if the sentence in question enjoys copyright protection. If so, it will be necessary to decide whether the use complained against is infringing. If the use is infringing, it will finally be necessary to establish whether the alleged infringer enjoys some sort of defense.

It may be helpful to tie the answers to the questions posed in the preceding paragraph to the incentive-based theory of intellectual property protection espoused by Professor Dreyfuss. Using the diagram I have put together (see Figure C.1), the parties whose interests need to be balanced in this case are primarily the author of the sentence in question (the "current creator") and "users" of the sentence. There is also a public interest in ensuring that the use and development of language is not impeded.

The answer to the first question (whether the sentence under consideration enjoys copyright protection), applying normal principles of copyright

[13] Take, for example, the famous introductions to novels such as *A Tale of Two Cities* (1859) by Charles Dickens ("It was the best of times, it was the worst of times, it was the age of wisdom, it was the age of foolishness ...") or *Pride and Prejudice* (1813) by Jane Austen ("It is a truth universally acknowledged, that a single man in possession of a good fortune, must be in want of a wife."). One could perhaps argue that, notwithstanding that the test of infringement depends on the quality and not the quantity of what is copied, in these examples, a single sentence forms such a small percentage of the novel as a whole that there should not be infringement in such cases even though many people might recognize the sentence copied. However, what about taking a single sentence from a short poem such as, for example, the well-known first line and a half ("Death be not proud, though some have called thee mighty and dreadful ... ") from John Donne's *Sonnet X* (published 1633), a forteen-line sonnet. As an aside, I note that there would of course be no copyright infringement in these specific examples since the copyrights in the novels and poem referred to have already expired.

[14] See *Larrikin Music Publishing Pty. Ltd. v. EMI Songs Australia Pty. Ltd.* [2010] FCA 29 (Federal Court of Australia) where the court held that the copyright in the song *Kookaburra Sits in the Old Gum Tree* ("*Kookaburra*") was infringed by the pop group *Men at Work's* iconic Australian song *Down Under*. In this case, part of a short flute riff in *Down Under* included music copied from the first line of *Kookaburra*, and this was held to be a substantial part of the song *Kookaburra* as a whole.

law, would depend on whether the sentence was created using "sufficient labor, skill and judgment" and whether it provides either information and instruction, or pleasure, in the form of literary enjoyment.[15]

To decide whether the use complained against is infringing, again applying normal principles of copyright law, the sentence in question must have been copied by user in the first place. If the user had independently come up with the identical sentence, there would be no infringement. This principle would greatly assuage concerns that the use and development of language would be impeded.

Further, certain uses of a sentence would arguably not amount to an infringement, for example, reproduction of a newspaper headline as a reference in an academic article. Alternatively, such a use may be accorded a defense against infringement.[16] How else can the news report be referred to? Conversely, the use of an identical headline by a competing publication for its own report on the same subject would arguably infringe and would not enjoy any sort of defense. In between, there would be less clear situations such as reproducing all the headlines (in a web publication operated by a competitor) as links to the full articles which were already freely accessible online.[17]

This approach would of course give rise to some uncertainty on the part of both prospective users as well as aggrieved content owners. Where

[15] For example, the descriptive headlines "Plane crashes after take-off in Medan" and "Only one cab operator meets taxi availability standards" would arguably not enjoy copyright protection. On the other hand, the headlines "No brass ceiling for women officers" (a report on the first-ever promotion of a female officer to the rank of Brigadier-General in the Singapore Armed Forces; the headline is a play on the phrases "glass ceiling" and "top brass") or "Taking baby steps to defend Singapore" (a report on an excursion of pre-schoolers to learn about the training which Singapore Armed Forces national servicemen undergo) could possibly enjoy copyright protection. (Both headlines were taken from the July 1, 2015 (i.e. the date when I wrote this portion of the note) issue of *The Straits Times*, which is the major English-language newspaper in Singapore.

[16] For example, under section 35 of the Singapore Copyright Act (Chapter 63, 2006 Revised Edition), "a fair dealing with a literary . . . work . . . for any purpose . . . shall not constitute an infringement of the copyright in the work." Under Section 36 of the same Act, "[a] fair dealing with a literary . . . work . . . shall not constitute an infringement of the copyright in the work if it is for the purpose of criticism or review . . . and a sufficient acknowledgment of the work is made."

[17] See, for example, *Shetland Times, Ltd. v. Jonathan Wills and Another* [1997] F.S.R. 604, which involved deep-linking by the defendant (bypassing the advertisements on the claimant's front page) to the claimant's news articles; the claimant's headlines were reproduced and used as hypertext links by the defendant.

possible, it could perhaps also be helpful to have mechanisms which reduce uncertainty or which mitigate the consequences of inadvertent infringement.[18] It could perhaps also be useful to have a cost-effective mechanism to determine the rights and liabilities of the relevant parties in the event of a dispute.[19]

III Conclusion

In summary, the incentive-based theory of intellectual property protection put forward by Professor Dreyfuss provides a sound theoretical framework for designing a system which provides sufficient incentives for innovation, while balancing the interests of other parties such as future creators, users and investors, as well as other public interests.

Nevertheless, its implementation is not straightforward. In some cases, it may be possible to adopt a bright-line test (e.g. no copyright protection in general for single words). This would have the advantage of certainty.

More often, it will not be possible (or unfair to some stakeholders) to adopt a bright-line test (e.g. whether there should be copyright protection in a sentence). In such cases, the theoretical framework advocated by Professor Dreyfuss will still be helpful to identify the relevant stakeholders and their respective interests, and to consider what levers can be used to balance these interests.

Of course, it will often still be difficult to get things "just right." This could be mitigated by designing mechanisms to reduce uncertainty, attenuate the consequences of inadvertent infringement, and resolve disputes in a cost-effective manner.

18 This could be achieved, for example, through the use of formal opinions published by a government agency in order to clarify the application of copyright law. These opinions would not be binding but the courts should have a duty to take account of them in considering cases to which they are relevant. This was (controversially) proposed in the report by Professor Ian Hargreaves. *See* IAN HARGREAVES, DIGITAL OPPORTUNITY: A REVIEW OF INTELLECTUAL PROPERTY AND GROWTH 10.21–10.24 (2011).

19 For example, through a court such as the U.K.'s Intellectual Property Enterprise Court, whose *raison d'être* is to provide access to justice for smaller players in the event of a dispute involving intellectual property: for details of this court and its practices and procedures, see generally ANGELA FOX, INTELLECTUAL PROPERTY ENTERPRISE COURT: PRACTICE AND PROCEDURE (2014).

Chapter 6, "Image Rights and Other Unorthodox Forms of Intellectual Property" by *Megan Richardson and Julian Thomas*

WEE LOON NG-LOY

I Introduction

The terms "image rights" and "personality rights" are familiar to lawyers from the civil law tradition. In Asia, for example, Article 100 of China's General Principles of Civil Code provides that:[20]

> Citizens shall enjoy the right of portrait (肖像权). The use of a citizen's portrait for profits without his consent shall be prohibited.

Within the common law world, many would have heard of the U.S. "right of publicity." In fact, the first jurisdiction to establish a "register of personality and images" is the State of Guernsey,[21] where the legal system is deeply entrenched in the English common law. This registration system, enabled by the Image Rights Ordinance 2012, is organized along the same lines as the trademark registration system: for example, there are provisions setting out the grounds for refusal of registration, the duration of protection and the possibility to renew the registration, the nature of the exclusive rights (confusion-based and dilution-based rights) of the registered proprietor, and provisions governing the assignment and licensing of the registered personality as personal or movable property. The personage whose personality is registered is even conferred moral rights (the right to be identified and the right against derogatory treatment). There is no doubt that image rights have been brought squarely within the intellectual property system of Guernsey.

Yet, as Professors Megan Richardson and Julian Thomas have observed in their chapter "Image Rights and Other Unorthodox Forms

[20] *See also* Article 18 of Taiwan's Civil Code which provides protection of "one's personality" (人格權). For Japan's position, *see* Dougherty, Foreword: The Right of Publicity – Towards a Comparative and International Perspective,18 LOY. L.A. ENT. L. REV. 421, 438–9 (1998) (reporting on, *inter alia*, the "*Oniyanki Club*" case (1991) in which the High Court of Tokyo held that the Japanese Civil Code granted rights akin to "property rights," which allowed a group of popular television actors to control the commercial exploitation of their image).

[21] Guernsey is not part of the United Kingdom. Rather, it is a possession of the British Crown.

of Intellectual Property," there is no protection for image rights as such in the mother of all common law countries and in some of her former colonies such as Australia. (The same can be said for the common law countries in Asia such as Singapore and Malaysia.) Their thesis is that nevertheless there is *de facto* protection for image rights within the English and Australian cases on passing off, as seen most recently in *Fenty v. Arcadia Group Brands Ltd.* where judgment was given in favor of the pop singer Rihanna even though there was very little evidence to support the claim of misrepresentation.[22]

II Passing Off: Misrepresentation and Not Mere Misappropriation?

This critique on the English court's finding of misrepresentation reminded me of a comment made by late Justice Hugh Laddie in the context of trademark infringement. He unapologetically said that the question whether there was a likelihood of confusion was "more a matter of feel than science."[23] The subjective nature of this factual inquiry means that judges in passing off cases have a fair bit of room for maneuver, to reach what in their assessment is a fair outcome. Where, for example, there is evidence that the defendant harbored an intention to deceive or confuse the relevant public, judges' disapproval for this mala fide is exhibited in their readiness to reach the conclusion that there was confusion in the marketplace.

Justice Laddie himself applied this principle in a passing-off case which, one might argue, also concerns image rights. The case is *Irvine v. Talksport Ltd.* where the plaintiff was Eddie Irvine, a well-known Formula One racing driver.[24] The defendants operated a radio station called "Talk Radio" which had acquired rights to cover the Formula One Championship. Their promotional materials included a brochure bearing an image of Eddie Irvine holding a portable radio with the words "Talk Radio." This image had been created by manipulating a photograph of Eddie Irvine, in particular by substituting the portable radio for the mobile phone he was holding in the photograph.[25] Justice

[22] [2013] EWHC 2310 (Ch.); [2015] 1 WLR 3291 (CA).

[23] *Wagamama Ltd. v. City Centre Restaurants Plc* [1995] FSR 713 at 732. This view was endorsed by the Singapore Court of Appeal in *The Polo/Lauren Co, LP v. Shop In Department Store Pte. Ltd.* [2006] 2 SLR(R) 690 at [35].

[24] [2002] FSR 60 (High Court).

[25] There was no question of infringement of the copyright in the photograph because this copyright belonged to a photo agency and the defendant had purchased the right to use this photograph from this photo agency.

Laddie found that the relevant public, the recipients of the brochure, would be confused into thinking that Eddie Irvine had endorsed the defendant's radio station. In reaching this conclusion, the learned judge took into account the fact that the defendant had the intention to convey the endorsement message to the public. With this finding, the burden of proof borne by the plaintiff to show confusion was lessened because "what the defendant intended to achieve by the promotion [could] give an indication of what it was likely to achieve."[26] On appeal, the Court of Appeal saw no reason to disturb Justice Laddie's conclusion on the issue of confusion.[27]

This principle applied by Justice Laddie – that a defendant who has the intention to deceive should be taken to have achieved this end – is a well-established one.[28] Its existence in the law of passing off has been explained by Lord Devlin in *Parker-Knoll v. Knoll International* in this way:[29]

> It is not easy to see why the defendant's estimate of the effect of his representation should be worth more than anyone else's. It seems probable that the rule is steeped in history rather than in logic and that it is the attenuated remains of the original doctrine, which prevailed until the intervention of equity, that fraud was an essential element in the tort [of passing off]. It is a wholesome rule which I for one have no wish to disturb.

Lord Devlin did not elaborate on why this principle, which he recognized as lacking in logic, was "wholesome." In my view, English judges are happy to abide by this principle because they see conduct driven by an intention to deceive as an act of unfair competition,[30] and because in a land where there is no general tort of unfair competition, passing off is often the only available legal means to stop such unfair conduct. The Singapore High Court has put it this way:[31]

> [T]he courts are more ready to find passing off where there is clear evidence of deliberate copying . . . because the issue becomes one of unfair competition and the defendant seeking to reap where he has not sown.

26 *Supra* note 24, at [68]. 27 [2003] FSR 35.

28 *See* the authorities listed in *Kerly's Law of Trade Marks and Trade Names* (15th ed.) at para. 18-230. In Singapore, this principle has been accepted by its courts including the Court of Appeal in *The Singapore Professional Golfers' Association v. Chen Eng Waye* [2013] 2 SLR 495 at [41].

29 [1962] RPC 265 at 290.

30 That is how Lord Diplock viewed such dishonest intention in *Erven Warnink Besloten Vennootschap v. Townend & Sons (Hull) Ltd* [1979] AC 731 at 740: "[The facts in this case] seem to me to disclose a case of unfair, not to say dishonest, trading of a kind for which a rational system of law ought to provide a remedy to other traders whose business or goodwill is injured by it."

31 *Pernod Ricard SA v. Allswell Trading Pte. Ltd.* [1993] 3 SLR(R) 817 at [52].

When celebrities bring actions to enforce their image rights or right of publicity in countries which recognize these rights, underlying their complaint is misappropriation – which is just a shorter formula for "reaping where one has not sown."

III Limits to Image Rights

Professors Richardson and Thomas also argued in their chapter that there is justification to protect the image rights of celebrities. The real debate, they urged, should lie in defining the socially desirable limits to this protection so that it will not be overly expansive.

It may be worth noting that in countries which have an anti-dilution right in their trademark law, this right can be very useful to celebrities seeking redress for unauthorized use of their image or likeness. In some cases, there are express statutory limits imposed on the exercise of the anti-dilution right. For example, the anti-dilution right in Singapore is subject to defenses including the following:[32]

(1) fair use in comparative commercial advertising or promotion;
(2) use for a noncommercial purpose; and
(3) use for the purpose of news reporting and news commentary

In particular, the defense to allow use for a "noncommercial purpose" would allow use of a celebrity's image or likeness in parody or satire etc.[33] Perhaps these defenses can serve as a starting point in the debate on where the boundaries of image rights should be drawn.

[32] *See* Trade Marks Act 1998, § 55A(3) (inserted in 2004). This provision is modeled on the former §1125(4) of the U.S. Lanham Act.

[33] No Singapore courts have interpreted the ambit of this defense. *See*, however, U.S. cases such as *Mattel Inc. v. MCA Records Inc.*, 296 F. 3d 894 (9th Cir. 2002) where this defense was interpreted in a way which fully preserved the First Amendment right.

INDEX